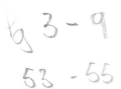

Contents

CONTENTS

Comple r Market
of the un

1992
Handbook

Second Edition

Mark Brealey, LL.B., LL.M., D.E.A.
of the Middle Temple, Barrister
Conor Quigley, LL.B., DIP.E.I.
of Gray's Inn, Barrister

Graham & Trotman
A member of Wolters Kluwer Academic Publishers
LONDON/DORDRECHT/BOSTON

Graham & Trotman Limited
Sterling House
66 Wilton Road
London SW1V 1DE
UK

Kluwer Academic Publishers Group
101 Philip Drive
Assinippi Park
Norwell, MA 02061
USA

British Library Cataloguing in Publication Data
Completing the internal market of the European
    Communities. 1992 Handbook
    1. European Community countries. Economic
    integration. European Economic Community law
    I. Commission of the European Communities   II.
    Brealey, Mark   III. Quigley, Conor
    341.7'5

ISBN 1-85333-474-X
       1-85333-475-8 (pbk)

1680840

Library of Congress Cataloging-in-Publication data
Completing the internal market of the European Communities : 1992
    handbook / Mark Brealey, Conor Quigley.
        p.   cm.
      ISBN 1-85333-474-X —— ISBN 1-85333-475-8 (pbk.)
      1. Tariff——Law and legislation——European Economic Community
    2. Tariff——Law and legislation——European Economic Community
    countries.   I. Brealey, Mark.   II. Quigley, Conor.
    KJE6415.C66   1989
    343.4'08——dc19
    [344.038]

Computer typeset by Graham & Trotman
Printed and bound in Great Britain by Hartnolls Ltd, Bodmin, Cornwall

CONTENTS

CONTENTS

CONTENTS

Preface

In 1985 the European Commission produced its White Paper to the European Council setting out its programme for the completion of the internal market in the European Community by the end of 1992. This programme consisted of some 300 legislative measures needed to guarantee the free movement of goods, persons, services and capital within the Community.

In this Handbook, we set out the legislative changes which the Commission's programme entails and put them in the context of the law of the single European market as a whole. After an introduction which briefly describes the functions and effects of the community, its institutions and legislation, the rest of the Handbook follows exactly the structure of the White Paper. This is divided into three parts: the removal of physical barriers, the removal of technical barriers and the removal of fiscal barriers. Each part is divided into a number of chapters covering separate sectors. These chapters begin with a brief analysis of the developments affecting the particular sector up to the date of the publication of the White Paper and then include detailed examination of the new provisions, including both the adopted and the proposed legislation.

Depending on the nature of the subject matter, as much information as possible regarding the content and effect of the new measures has been given. In certain cases, such as technical standards or plant and animal health, the analysis given describes the framework of the new measures but refers the reader to the full text of the legislation for a complete picture. In other cases, especially in those areas relating to business law, the fullest possible explanation of all the important provisions is given.

The purpose of the Handbook is that the businessman and his professional advisers will be given a detailed understanding of the legislative measures for the completion of the internal market. No previous knowledge of Community law and procedures is required but it is hoped that a fuller picture is obtained of the framework within which commercial, industrial and business law in the internal market is affected. The new measures are described as they are produced, amended and adopted by the Commission, the Parliament and the Council. In this Handbook, we have sought merely to describe the current situation with regard to the intended and adopted legislation and no attempt is made to criticise these measures.

By its very nature, the programme is fast moving and changes from month to month if not from week to week. Every effort has been made to state the law and the proposed measures as published in the *Official Journal of the European Communities* up to June 1991. Inevitably, since completing the manuscript, some new proposals have been published and some of the proposed measures which we describe have now been adopted.

This Handbook acts as a companion guide to the encyclopaedia entitled *Completing the Internal Market of the European Community: 1992 Legislation* which we have compiled and edited and which is co-published by Graham & Trotman and the Office for Official Publications of the European Communities.

Mark Brealey
Conor Quigley

Gray's Inn
London WC1

1 September 1991

Introduction

The European Community

The European Economic Community, which now has twelve Member States, was founded by the Treaty of Rome which was signed on 25 March 1957, and came into being on 1 January 1958. It was originally composed of Belgium, France, the Federal Republic of Germany, Italy, Luxembourg and the Netherlands. Denmark, Ireland and the United Kingdom joined the Community in 1973 and were followed by Greece in 1981 and Portugal and Spain in 1986. Following German unification in 1990, the former territory of East Germany was absorbed into the Community. All the Member States are also signatories to two other Treaties which established a European Coal and Steel Community (ECSC) and a European Atomic Energy Community (Euratom). It is now commonplace to refer to this organisation as the European Community. European Community law derives mainly from these treaties and also from a large body of secondary legislation, such as regulations and directives, adopted under the treaties.

By 31 December 1992 it is intended that the European Community, with a population in excess of 335 million, will be a single integrated market without internal frontiers in which the free movement of goods, services, persons and capital is ensured. In order to achieve this, a legislative programme has been adopted within the Community with the aim of removing the remaining physical, technical and fiscal barriers to free movement. The completion of the internal market constitutes the most important plan since the foundation of the Community over thirty years ago.

The common market

The aim of the Community is to establish a common market among its Member States and progressively to approximate their economic policies. Under the Treaty, a substantial body of legal rules were laid down to achieve this end, with the activities of the Community to include the following:

- the elimination, as between Member States, of customs duties and of quantitative restrictions on the import and export of goods, and of all measures having equivalent effect;
- the establishment of a common customs tariff and of a common commercial policy towards third countries;
- the abolition, as between Member States, of obstacles to freedom of movement for persons, services and capital;
- the adoption of a common policy in the sphere of agriculture;
- the adoption of a common policy in the sphere of transport;
- the institution of a system ensuring that competition in the common market is not distorted;
- the application of procedures by which the economic policies of Member States can be coordinated and disequilibria in their balance of payments remedied;
- the approximation of the laws of the Member States to the extent required for the proper functioning of the common market..

It is clear, therefore, that the Community, with its emphasis on all aspects of economic integration, is much more than a free trade area.

Separate Community institutions were established under the Treaty with the aim of adopting and enforcing legislation and ensuring the proper functioning of the common market. The main legislative body, the EC Council, is composed of representatives of the national Governments. The EC Commission, which has a broadly executive role, is appointed by agreement of the Member States, but is wholly independent of any national authority. Finally, the European Parliament is a body directly elected by the nationals of the Community. Legislative power is shared between these three bodies: the Commission proposes legislation which the Parliament and Council then examine, although the final decision lies with the Council. European Community law, which derives from the Treaty and also from legislation adopted in accordance with it, such as regulations, directives and decisions, constitutes a major force which affects not only the Member States but also the rights and obligations of individuals and companies. In order to interpret and enforce this, the Community also has its own Court of Justice.

By the mid-1980s much progress had been made in establishing the common market and many of the policies of economic integration which the Treaty envisaged were adopted. The common customs tariff was fully established in 1968. A common agricultural policy was established. Structural funds concerned with social, regional and industrial affairs had been established at Community level. However, not all the developments which might have taken place did happen. The 1970s was a time of economic recession, during which ideas of economic integration were not given as much support as might have been expected. Many national measures of short-term interest were taken, often having effects not only as against third countries but also in relation to the other Member States. These measures were often aimed at protecting the national markets and industries through, for example, the use of public funds to aid and maintain non-viable companies. Quite apart from recession, a further reason why economic integration was not given such primary importance was that so much effort was concentrated on the enlargement of the Community. Once the accession of Portugal and Spain was fully agreed, the mood in the Community changed and economic integration became once again a matter of prime importance. Attention was switched to the internal market of the Community and the measures which needed to be taken to remove the remaining barriers to the free movement of goods, services, persons and capital within the Community.

The Single European Act

The Heads of State and of Government of the European Community, meeting as the European Council in Copenhagen in 1982, pledged themselves to the completion of the internal market as a high priority. At subsequent meetings in Fontainebleau and Dublin in 1984 and in Brussels the following year, this pledge was repeated. It was then that the Commission seized the opportunity in a White Paper of June 1985 addressed to the European Council entitled 'Completing the Internal Market' in which a programme of legislative measures which were needed to be adopted was put forward.

The Commission stressed that the White Paper was not intended to cover every possible issue which might affect the integration of the economies of the Member States. Of primary importance was the internal market and the measures which were directly necessary to achieve a single integrated market. Many other matters which bear upon economic integration and indirectly affect the achievement of the internal market, while being of substantial importance, nevertheless do not form part of the programme to complete the internal market. These are contained in other Community policies, such as the competition, environment and social policies, industrial research and development and the European Monetary System. The White Paper, however, listed a host of measures which the Commission had been urging the Council to adopt for many years as well as new proposals which were deemed necessary.

It was recognised that the legislative powers which the Treaty had given to the Council had resulted in many of the measures which the Commission had proposed over the years remaining unadopted. One reason for this was that unanimity in the Council was required for much of the legislation. Accordingly, at the same time as the White Paper was produced, the Member States agreed to alter parts of the Treaty so as to enable the legislative programme to be more easily implemented. This resulted in the Single European Act (SEA) which came into force on 1 July 1987. As well as making certain alterations to the institutional structure of the Community, the SEA gave a proper legal basis to some of the economic activities, such as those relating to the environment and research and technological development, which the Community had in fact pursued over the years but which had not been specifically provided for in the original Treaty. A new development in European Union was made with the introduction of provisions on European cooperation in the sphere of foreign policy. But, as far as the programme for the completion of the internal market is concerned, the important provisions were those which declared the need to complete the internal market and which altered the voting procedure in certain cases. According to the new provisions, legislative measures were to be adopted with the aim of establishing throughout the Community by 31 December 1992, an area without internal frontiers in which the free movement of goods, services, persons and capital is ensured. This is the internal market.

The internal market and freedom of movement

Separate provisions of the Treaty govern the free movement of goods, services, persons and capital. Some of these rules are wholly self-sufficient and impose an outright prohibition on certain restrictions to free movement. In other cases, the rules allow for further legislation to be adopted by the Council. Where there are no specific provisions in the Treaty dealing with further legislative measures, the Council may issue directives for the approximation of national laws which directly affect the operation of the common market. In general, the Council, in issuing such directives, must act unanimously, on a proposal from the Commission. However, in many cases involving the completion of the internal market, the Council is to act by a qualified majority.

Goods

Fundamental to the common market is the elimination, as between Member States, of customs duties and of quantitative restrictions on the import and export of goods, and of all measures having equivalent effect. In addition, internal taxation of a Member State may not be used in a discriminatory manner so as to discourage trade within the Community.

With the adoption of the common customs tariff in trade with third countries, the customs union of the Community guarantees that all goods originating in the Community, or in respect of which import formalities into the Community have been complied with, may not be subject to any customs duties by reason of crossing an internal Community frontier. Measures of equivalent effect which are also prohibited cover any charge which is imposed unilaterally on goods by reason of the fact that they cross an internal frontier. Charges levied, for example, in respect of health inspections on imported goods will be contrary to these rules unless they are part of a general system applied to domestic and imported products alike or are payment for a service which is actually rendered to the importer.

It would clearly be contrary to the operation of the common market if imported goods could be taxed at a higher level than similar domestic goods. Accordingly, no Member State may impose directly or indirectly on the products of other Member States any internal taxation of any kind in excess of that imposed directly or indirectly on similar domestic products. Nor may it impose on the products of other Member States any internal taxation of such a nature as to afford indirect protection to other products.

Restrictions on imports and exports of goods between Member States are prohibited: (Articles 30-34 EEC). All trading rules enacted by Member States which are capable of hindering, directly or indirectly, actually or potentially, intra-Community trade are to be considered as measures having an effect equivalent to such restrictions and are also prohibited.

However, while the prohibition on customs duties on imports or exports in intra-Community trade is absolute, there are exceptions to the prohibition on quantitative restrictions. The Treaty provides that the prohibition does not apply if the restriction is on grounds of:
- public morality, public policy or public security;
- the protection of health and life of humans, animals or plants;
- the protection of national treasures possessing artistic, historic or archaeological value;
- the protection of intellectual property rights.

Such a restriction will not be permitted, however, if it constitutes a means of arbitrary discrimination against imported goods or is a disguised restriction on trade between Member States. These derogations from the basic prohibition, which are largely non-economic in nature, are construed very strictly and any measures taken pursuant to them must be proportionate to their purpose.

The European Court of Justice, in the Cassis de Dijon case, stated that in general a product, once lawfully manufactured in one Member State, must be allowed to be marketed throughout the Community. However, the Court also recognised that some other restrictions on trade might be permitted pending the harmonisation of national laws which seek to protect certain interests or values. This included restrictions justified on grounds of consumer protection, prevention of unfair commercial practices, protection of public health, protection of the environment, improvement of working conditions and the effectiveness of fiscal supervision.

Services

Restrictions on freedom to provide services within the Community are prohibited (Article 59 EEC) in respect of nationals of Member States who are established in a State of the Community other than that of the person for whom the services are intended. The Council may extend this right to nationals of third countries who are established within the Community. While a distinction is drawn between the freedom to provide services and freedom of establishment, a person providing a service is entitled temporarily to pursue his activity in the State where the service is provided, under the same conditions as are imposed by that State on its own nationals. Some exceptions apply in the special cases of transport services and financial services. Thus, freedom to provide services in the field of transport are governed by the special rules relating to the common transport policy and the liberalisation of banking and insurance services connected with movements of capital are to be effected in step with the progressive liberalisation of the movement of capital.

A practical restriction on the exercise of the right of freedom to provide services arises where the Member State insists on certain mandatory requirements, such as professional qualifications. Accordingly, the Council is empowered to issue directives for the mutual recognition of diplomas, certificates and other evidence of formal qualifications.

Persons

Provisions in the Treaty relating to the free movement of persons include rules on the rights of Community nationals to move from one Member State to another in order to exercise their vocation or profession or in order to look for and obtain work. Different rules apply depending on whether the person seeking to exercise his rights is employed (Article 48 EEC) or self-employed (Article 52 EEC). In certain cases, the person is entitled to remain in the host country after he has ceased working. Companies or firms formed in accordance with the law of a Member State and having their registered office, central administration or principal place of business within the Community are, for these purposes, to be treated in the same way as natural persons who are nationals of Member States. This includes companies or firms which are constituted under civil or commercial law, including cooperative societies, and other legal persons governed by public or private law, save for those which are non-profit making.

Employed persons

Employed persons are entitled to freedom of movement within the Community, a right which entails the abolition of any discrimination based on nationality between workers of the Member States as regards employment, remuneration and other conditions of work and employment. This also entails the right, subject to limitations justified on grounds of public policy, public security or public health:

- to accept offers of employment actually made;
- to move freely within the territory of Member States for this purpose;
- to stay in a Member State for the purpose of employment in accordance with the provisions governing the employment of nationals of that State laid down by law, regulation or administrative action;
- to remain in the territory of a Member State after having been employed in that State.

These rights do not apply to employment in the public service.

Community legislation has been adopted in order to strengthen the application of these rules. Any national of a Member State, irrespective of his place of residence, has the right to take up an activity as an employed person, and to pursue such activity, within another Member State in accordance with the laws governing the employment of nationals of that State. He has, in particular, the right to take up available employment in another Member State with the same priority as nationals of that State. National rules may not be applied where they limit application for, and offers of, employment, or the right of Community nationals to take up and pursue employment, or where they subject these to conditions not applicable in respect of their own nationals. Nor may they apply where, even though they apply irrespective of nationality, their exclusive or principal aim or effect is to keep nationals of other Member States away from the employment offered. An exception to this is where the conditions relate to linguistic knowledge required by reason of the nature of the job to be filled.

A Community worker may not be treated differently from national workers by reason of his nationality in respect of any conditions of employment and work, in particular as regards remuneration, dismissal, reinstatement or re-employment. He should enjoy the same social and tax advantages as national workers and have access to training in vocational schools and retraining centres. Any clause of a collective or individual agreement or of any other collective regulation concerning employment, eligibility for employment, remuneration and other conditions of work and dismissal is null and void in so far as it lays down or authorises discriminatory conditions in respect of workers who are nationals of the other Member States. Certain rights of residence attach also to members of the worker's family.

Member States must grant Community nationals, on production of a valid identity card or passport, the right to enter and leave their territory in order to take up activities as employed persons and to pursue such activities in another Member State. As proof of the right of residence, a document entitled 'Residence Permit for a National of a Member State of the EEC' must be issued. For the issue of such a permit, the authorities in the Member State may only require that the worker produce the document with which he entered the country and a confirmation of engagement from the employer or a certificate of employment. The residence permit must be valid throughout the Member State for at least five years and be automatically renewable. It may not be withdrawn from a worker solely on the grounds that he is no longer in employment, either because he is temporarily incapable of work as a result of illness or accident or because he is involuntarily unemployed.

Self-employed persons and companies

Restrictions on the freedom of establishment of Community nationals in another Member State are prohibited. This also applies to restrictions on the setting up of agencies, branches or subsidiaries in another Member State. Freedom of establishment includes the right to pursue activities as self-employed persons and to set up and manage companies and firms. While in the case of freedom to provide services, the supplier of the service is present in the Member State only temporarily, establishment implies a more substantial connection with the State in which the activity is carried on, although the dividing line between the two is not clear. A person will be established in a Member State where he has a permanent or long-term presence there or where he has a permanent place from which an economic activity is carried on. However, establishment may also be assumed where the presence is not permanent. Often, it is a matter to be decided on the facts of the particular case.

Generally, the right of establishment applies to all economic activities, with the exception of activities which involve the exercise of official authority. Certain restrictions on the right of establishment may be allowed on grounds of public policy, public security or public health. As with services, the directives on the mutual recognition of diplomas, certificates and other evidence of formal qualifications also make easier the exercise of the freedom of establishment.

Capital

Article 67 EEC states that, to the extent necessary to ensure the proper functioning of the common market, Member States are to abolish between themselves all restrictions on the movement of capital belonging to residents in Member States and any discrimination based on the nationality or on the place of residence of the parties or on the place where such capital is invested. Current payments connected with the movement of capital between Member States must be free from all restrictions. Unlike the provisions on the free movement of goods, services and persons, the rules in the Treaty on free movement of capital, while being independent in themselves, must be developed in the light of other Treaty provisions, including those relating to balance of payments and economic policy. Each Member State must pursue the economic policy needed to ensure the equilibrium of its overall balance of payments and to maintain confidence in its currency. In order to facilitate this, the Member States must coordinate their economic policies and provide for cooperation between their appropriate administrative departments and between their central banks.

There is an obvious connection between the free movement of capital and the free movement of goods, services and persons. Accordingly, each Member State must authorise, in the currency of the Member State in which the creditor or the beneficiary resides, any payments connected with the movement of goods, services or capital and any transfers of capital and earnings, to the extent that the movement of goods, services, persons and capital have been liberalised.

In 1960, Community legislation, based on the OECD Code of Liberalisation of Capital Movements, provided for the liberalisation of exchange control restrictions on capital movements. Four categories of capital movements were established. For three of these categories, to varying degrees, the Member States were required to liberalise foreign exchange authorisations for the conclusion or performance of the transactions in question. Member States were not obliged to abolish the restrictions which applied in respect of the fourth category. Other provisions required the adoption of rules governing investment on the money market and payment of interest on deposits by non-residents and the regulation of loans and credits which were not related to commercial transactions or to the provision of services by non-residents to residents. In order to neutralise those effects produced by international capital flow on domestic liquidity which are considered undesirable, certain rules govern the regulation of the net external position of credit institutions and the fixing of minimum reserve ratios in particular for the holdings of non-residents.

In order to promote the coordination of monetary policy in the Community, a Monetary Committee was established with the task of keeping under review the monetary and financial situation of the Member States and of the Community and the general payments system of the

Member States. If movements of capital lead to disturbances in the functioning of the capital market in any Member State, the Commission must, after consulting the Monetary Committee, authorise that State to take protective measures in the field of capital movements. A Member State which is in difficulties may, on grounds of secrecy or urgency, take these measures on its own initiative, although, if it does so, it must inform the Commission which might order that the measures be amended or abolished.

The White Paper: completing the internal market

By the time of the publication of the White Paper in 1985, substantial progress had been made by the Community in giving effect to these legal rules on freedom of movement. However, the Commission insisted that much needed to be done to complete the internal market. It listed some three hundred measures which were required to be adopted by the Council. The proposals were divided into three parts: the removal of physical barriers; the removal of technical barriers; and the removal of fiscal barriers.

Physical barriers

The most obvious example of physical barriers are customs posts at frontiers which continue to exist largely because of the technical and fiscal divisions between Member States. However, they also serve as useful points at which other State controls can be exercised, such as immigration and drugs controls. It would not, therefore, be sufficient merely to abolish the technical and fiscal barriers without also providing for alternative methods whereby these other controls may continue without the need for customs barriers. To this end, the White Paper envisages measures covering arms legislation, drugs control, immigration, right of asylum and the status of refugees, national visa policies and extradition.

Technical barriers

Technical barriers to free movement provide the greatest number of problems facing the Community. These barriers present themselves in a variety of different ways. The most obvious examples are those technical requirements which goods must satisfy under national rules relating to health and safety or for environmental or consumer protection. Government procurement policies which favour national suppliers are a serious impediment to inter-State trade in goods and services. It was proposed to strengthen and extend the current Community laws in these area. Other proposed measures tackle the remaining obstacles to the free movement of persons, services and capital. National company laws, intellectual property rights and taxation rules contain many provisions which operate as a disincentive in inter-State business. The White Paper makes a number of proposals in these areas which are designed to create suitable conditions for industrial cooperation between companies in different Member States and to open up the market to companies wishing to expand throughout the Community.

Fiscal barriers

The measures relating to the removal of fiscal barriers are concerned with further harmonisation of the structures of indirect taxation within the common market and deal with value added tax and excise duties. A uniform system of VAT was established in 1977, but some derogations were permitted to the Member States. Furthermore, the Member States retained the right to set tax rates within their territory and a system of taxation on importation and remission of tax on exportation was continued, even in intra-Community trade. With the removal of fiscal barriers, the intention is that VAT rates should be within set bands and that tax would no longer be charged on importation from another Member State so that in general goods and services would be subject to taxation in the country where supply takes place. As regards excise duties, the plan is that these would be applied to alcoholic products, tobacco and mineral oils with a harmonised structure and rate for each of these throughout the Community.

European Community policies and the internal market

As has been stated above, the European Community pursues a number of activities, not all of which are solely economic. However, many of the policies have a direct bearing on the internal market and it is appropriate to have a knowledge of their main characteristics. These include agriculture, competition, social policy, environment and international trade.

Common agricultural policy

The common market extends to agriculture and trade in agricultural products and the rules laid down for the establishment of the common market apply also to agricultural products. This is, however, subject to certain qualifications and a special agricultural policy is also established in the Treaty. The objectives of this policy are increased agricultural productivity, a fair standard of living for the agricultural community, stabilised markets, the availability of supplies and reasonable prices for consumers. These objectives were to be attained by the establishment of a common organisation of agricultural markets which would include measures such as regulation of prices, aids for the production and marketing of various products, storage and carryover arrangements and common machinery for stabilising imports or exports. As part of this organisation, a major part of the Community's budget is allocated to an agricultural guidance and guarantee fund which supplements prices for agricultural products and seeks to encourage developments in productivity and use of the land.

Common organisations have been set up to cover cereals, milk, beef and veal, sheepmeat, pigmeat, poultry and eggs and sugar. In addition, a special regime applies to fisheries.

Competition policy in the internal market

The Treaty provides for the institution of a system ensuring that competition policy in the common market is not distorted. European Community competition law deals with restrictive practices, abuse of a dominant position, mergers and acquisitions and state aids.

Anti-competitive agreements, decisions and concerted practices

All agreements between undertakings, decisions by associations of undertakings and concerted practices which may affect trade between Member States and which have as their object or effect the prevention, restriction or distortion of competition within the common market are prohibited. Any agreements or decisions which are prohibited under these rules are automatically void, at least to the extent that the anti-competitive provisions are not severable from the rest of the agreement or decision. However, an agreement, decision or concerted practice may be exempted from this prohibition if it contributes to improving the production or distribution of goods or to promoting technical or economic progress, while allowing consumers a fair share of the resulting benefit. This exemption may apply as long as the anti-competitive provisions are strictly necessary and do not eliminate competition in respect of a substantial part of the products in question.

Only the Commission may declare the prohibition to be inapplicable. With certain minor exceptions, all agreements, decisions and concerted practices which are to be exempted must be notified to the Commission. However, the Commission has granted block exemptions, without the need for individual notification, to a number of classes of agreements. As long as the agreements are in accordance with the rules set out in these block exemptions, they should generally comply with the anti-trust rules of the Treaty. To date, block exemptions have been adopted dealing with, inter alia, exclusive distribution, exclusive purchasing, research and development, patent licensing, know-how licensing and franchise agreements. In each of these cases, the Commission has established a list of restrictions which will be allowed together with a list of those restrictions which will not be allowed and which deprive the agreement of the benefit of the block exemption.

The Commission has extensive powers of investigation. In addition to declaring agreements, decisions and concerted practices to be unlawful, it may also fine the undertakings concerned, in some cases up to a maximum of 10% of annual worldwide turnover. Decisions of the Commission are subject to review by the European Court.

Abuse of a dominant position

Any abuse by one or more undertakings of a dominant position within the common market or in a substantial part of it is prohibited in so far as it may affect trade between Member States. The use of this provision as a means of combating abusive behaviour has been strengthened by the Commission and the Court applying a wide definition to the concept of a dominant position. This has been achieved, inter alia, by means of tightly defining the relevant product market of the undertaking in question, so that an undertaking may be dominant in a particular market sector where it is not dominant in a wider context. There are no exemptions available to this type of anti-competitive behaviour. Indeed, an agreement which is drafted in terms of a block exemption as discussed above will still be unlawful if it constitutes an abuse of a dominant position. The Commission's powers of investigation and fines also apply to this type of behaviour.

Mergers and acquisitions

Mergers and acquisitions are in general subject to a separate regime. Where the aggregate worldwide turnover of the undertakings concerned exceeds ECU 5,000 million and the aggregate Community-wide turnover of each of at least two of the undertakings concerned exceeds ECU 250 million, the Commission has the power to prohibit a proposed merger if it would create or strengthen a dominant position as a result of which effective competition would be significantly impeded in the common market or in a substantial part of it. Where these turnover thresholds are not reached, the Commission will not normally intervene and it is then for the national competition authorities to determine the validity of a merger. This is also the case where the thresholds are reached but each of the undertakings concerned achieves more than two-thirds of its aggregate Community-wide turnover within one and the same Member State.

State aids

Any aid granted by a Member State or through State resources in any form whatsoever which distorts or threatens to distort competition in the common market by favouring certain undertakings or the production of certain goods is, in so far as it affects trade between Member States, incompatible with the common market. Generally, such aid is prohibited although some exceptions may apply. The most important of these exceptions are aid to promote the economic development of areas where the standard of living is abnormally low or where there is serious underemployment and aid to facilitate the development of certain economic activities or of certain economic areas. These are largely regional aids or aids to specific industrial sectors.

After the completion of the internal market, the Commission is particularly anxious that the abolition of non-fiscal barriers to trade should not be followed by increased fiscal distortion of competition. If the Commission finds that State aid which has been granted is not compatible with the common market, it must order the Member State in question to abolish or alter the aid. In certain circumstances an order may be made requiring that any aid already granted be repaid. Member States must inform the Commission of any plans to grant or alter aid and may not put their proposed measure into effect until the Commission has made a decision allowing it.

Social policy

Social policy has been a major source of legislation in the European Community. This aims to promote improved working conditions and the standard of living of workers. In particular, the Commission has the task of promoting close cooperation between Member States in the social field in matters relating to employment, labour law and working conditions, vocational training, social security, health and safety at work and the right of association and collective bargaining between employers and employees. Equal pay and equal treatment for men and women is guaranteed under Community law. Much legislation has already been adopted dealing with these matters and with health and safety at work. In addition, the Council has adopted a Social Charter which sets out a list of measures which are to be adopted by the Community in the social field and also operates as a declaration of fundamental rights for workers.

Environmental policy

Action by the Community relating to the environment is intended to preserve, protect and improve the quality of the environment, to contribute towards protecting human health and to ensure a prudent and rational utilisation of natural resources. It is based on the principles that preventive action should be taken, that environmental damage should as a priority be rectified at source and that the polluter should pay. Environmental protection requirements should be a component of the Community's other policies. Where there has been no action at Community level, national environmental protection measures may be permitted even though they restrict inter-State trade. In addition, where Community measures have been taken, this does not prevent any Member State from maintaining or introducing more stringent protective measures as long as they are otherwise compatible with Community law.

A significant amount of legislation has been adopted or proposed by the Community institutions in the field of environmental protection. These cover mainly air, water and land pollution as well as waste control, protection of the natural habitat and compulsory environmental assessment.

International trade

One aim of the customs union of the Community is to contribute to the harmonious development of world trade, the progressive abolition of restrictions on international trade and the lowering of customs barriers. A common commercial policy was established which is based on uniform principles in regard to tariff rates, the conclusion of tariff and trade agreements, the achievement of uniformity in measures of liberalisation, export policy and measures to protect trade such as anti-dumping measures.

Common EC rules of origin have been established for imports into the Community. These relate both to the common commercial policy and to the free movement of goods within the Community. Goods produced in two or more countries are regarded as originating in the country where the last substantial process or operation that is economically justified was performed, having been carried out in an undertaking equipped for the purpose, and resulting in the manufacture of a new product or representing an important stage of manufacture. For the purpose of these rules, the Community is considered as one territory.

The Council and the Commission have the power to impose anti-dumping duties in respect of imports from third countries. For the duty to arise there must be shown to be dumping or a subsidy whereby the dumped or subsidised goods cause or threaten to cause injury so that the interests of the Community need to be protected.

The institutional structure of the Community

There are four institutions of the European Community: the Council, the Commission, the Parliament and the Court of Justice. These institutions also cover the sectoral Communities dealing with coal and steel and atomic energy. In addition, the Heads of State or of Government and the President of the Commission meet at least twice a year as the European Council. Other Community bodies which are not official institutions as such, but which have a particular role to play include the Economic and Social Committee and various advisory and management committees. The offices of the Council, the Commission and the Parliament are situated mainly in Brussels and Luxembourg, with the Parliament having its plenary sessions in Strasbourg. The Court of Justice is based in Luxembourg.

The Council of the European Communities

The Council of the European Communities consists of representatives of the Member States, with each Government providing one of its members as a delegate. The office of President of the Council is held in turn by each of the Member States for a term of six months, in the following order:
- for a first cycle of six years: Belgium, Denmark, Germany, Greece, Spain, France, Ireland, Italy, Luxembourg, Netherlands, Portugal, United Kingdom;
- for the following cycle of six years: Denmark, Belgium, Greece, Germany, France, Spain, Italy, Ireland, Netherlands, Luxembourg, United Kingdom, Portugal.

In 1991 the Presidency will be held by Luxembourg and the Netherlands and in 1992 by Portugal and the United Kingdom respectively. The Council meets when convened by the President on his own initiative or at the request of one of its members or of the Commission. For general affairs, the Council will normally be composed of the ministers for foreign affairs, but when more specialist or technical matters are dealt with, it will normally be the ministers with responsibility for the particular sector who are present. Thus, for example, for agricultural matters, the ministers for agriculture will make up the Council. While it holds the Presidency, a Member State will provide the chairman for all of the Council meetings. The President is also the representative for the Community in its relations with third countries, a role which is also performed by the Commission. Although the Council is composed of the representatives of the Member States, it has its own separate permanent secretariat. In order to help the smooth running of the Council meetings and to ensure that time is not wasted at them, the Council is assisted by the Committee of Permanent Representatives (COREPER). Each Member State has a Permanent Representative to the Community, together with a support staff. Before the Council meets, COREPER will have discussed the matters which the Council is due to deal with. If COREPER reaches unanimous agreement on any matter, that matter is placed on Part A of the Council agenda and is adopted by the Council without further deliberation. Other matters are placed in Part B and will be discussed by the Council in order to reach agreement.

There are three methods of voting in the Council. In some instances, the Council acts by a simple majority of its members. More commonly, though, the Treaty provisions which enable the Council to act usually specify that it may only adopt measures either unanimously or by a qualified majority. An abstention by any member present in person or represented does not prevent the adoption of acts which require unanimity. Where the Council is required to act by a qualified majority, the vote of each member is weighted as follows:

France, Germany, Italy, United Kingdom	10
Spain	8
Belgium, Greece, Netherlands, Portugal	5
Denmark, Ireland	3
Luxembourg	2

For their adoption by qualified majority, acts of the Council require at least 54 votes in favour where the Treaty requires them to be adopted on a proposal from the Commission, with the additional requirement in other cases that these votes must be cast by at least eight members.

The Commission of the European Communities

If the Council is to be regarded as the Community legislature, the Commission of the European Communities is the executive body. The Commission consists of seventeen members who are appointed by common accord of the Governments of the Member States. The term of office of the Commission is four years and this is renewable. Only nationals of Member States may be members of the Commission. It must include at least one and not more than two nationals of each Member State. In practice, each of the larger States (France, Germany, Italy, Spain and the United Kingdom) has two Commissioners. The President and six Vice-Presidents of the Commission are appointed, also by common accord of the Member States. Until the end of 1992, the President of the Commission is Mr. Jacques Delors. Members of the Commission are chosen on the grounds of their general competence and each is given a portfolio of responsibilities although decisions of the Commission are taken by a majority vote. They are wholly independent of the national Governments once appointed and in the performance of their duties they must neither seek nor take instructions from any Government or from any other body. The Member States undertake to respect this principle and not to seek to influence the members of the Commission in the performance of their tasks. Members of the Commission may not, during their term of office, engage in any other occupation. Although the Parliament can vote to remove the entire Commission, an individual Commissioner cannot be dismissed, except by the Court of Justice either on grounds of serious misconduct or because he no longer fulfils the conditions required for the performance of his duties.

The European Parliament

The European Parliament is a directly elected body of members representing the peoples of the Member States. It exercises the advisory and supervisory powers conferred upon it by the Treaty. There are a total of 518 seats divided among each of the Member States as follows:

France, Germany, Italy, United Kingdom	81
Spain	60
Netherlands	25
Belgium, Greece, Portugal	24
Denmark	16
Ireland	15
Luxembourg	6

Members of Parliament sit in political groups reflecting their political opinions rather than nationality. The largest groups are the Socialists and the European People's Party (Christian Democrats). Other groups are the European Democrats, Communists and Allies, Liberals and Democratic Reformists, European Alliance for Renewal and Democracy, Rainbow Group, European Right and Independents.

The Court of Justice of the European Communities

The European Community has its own Court of Justice which sits in Luxembourg and which is charged with ensuring that Community law is observed. The Court consists of thirteen judges and is assisted by six Advocates General, all of whom are chosen from persons whose independence is beyond doubt and who possess the qualifications required for appointment to the highest judicial offices in their respective countries or who are jurisconsults of recognised competence. They are appointed by common accord of the Member States for a term of six years.

Actions can be brought to the Court in one of two ways: either the action is started before the Court itself or it is started before a national court and a question on interpretation or validity of Community law is referred by that court to the European Court. In direct actions, the applicant may be the Community institutions, a Member State or a natural or legal person. Different rules apply according to the nature of the action. If the Commission considers that a Member State has failed to fulfil an obligation under the Treaty, it delivers a reasoned opinion on the matter after giving the State concerned the opportunity to submit its observations. If the State does not comply with the Commission's opinion, the latter may bring the matter before the Court. In addition, a Member State which considers that another Member State has failed to fulfil a Treaty obligation may bring the matter before the Court, although the matter must first be brought before the Commission. If the Court finds that a Member State has failed to fulfil its obligations, the State is required to take the necessary measures to comply with the Court's judgment.

The Court may review the legality of acts of the Council and the Commission other than recommendations and opinions. It can hear actions brought by a Member State, the Council or the Commission on grounds of lack of competence, infringement of an essential procedural requirement, infringement of the Treaty or of any rule of law relating to its application, or misuse of powers. Any natural or legal person may, under the same conditions, institute proceedings against a decision addressed to him. This applies also to a decision which, although in the form of a regulation or a decision addressed to another person, is of direct and individual concern to him. Should the Council or the Commission, in infringement of the Treaty, fail to act, the Member States and the other institutions of the Community may bring an action before the Court to have the infringement established. Any natural or legal person may also complain to the Court that a Community institution has failed to address to him any act other than a recommendation or an opinion.

The Council may give the Court power to review penalties which have been imposed for a breach of Community law. Examples of such penalties are to be found in competition law and anti-dumping regulations. The Court may also in any cases before it prescribe any necessary interim measures.

Attached to the Court of Justice is a court of first instance which has jurisdiction to hear and determine, subject to appeal on a point of law to the Court of Justice, certain classes of action. At present, the only actions which may be heard by the court of first instance concern staff disputes within the Community institutions and appeals against Commission decisions in competition law matters.

The Economic and Social Committee

The Council and the Commission are assisted by the Economic and Social Committee which acts in an advisory capacity. The members of the Committee, who are appointed by the Council, are representatives of the various categories of economic and social activity, in particular, representatives of producers, farmers, carriers, workers, dealers, craftsmen, professional occupations and the general public. There are 189 members of the Committee as follows:

France, Germany, Italy, United Kingdom	24
Spain	21
Belgium, Greece, Netherlands, Portugal	12
Denmark, Ireland	9
Luxembourg	5

European Community law: legislation, procedures and effects

Although the Treaty sets out the basic rules for European Community law, a substantial body of secondary legislation has been adopted. The

Treaty provides that the Council and the Commission are to make regulations, issue directives, take decisions, make recommendations and deliver opinions. The main legislative measures are regulations, directives and decisions. Recommendations and opinions have no binding effect, although they do have a function in the Community legal system and are capable of producing legal effects. For example, before the Commission can bring an alleged infringement of the Treaty by a Member State before the Court of Justice, it must deliver a reasoned opinion on the matter after giving the State concerned the opportunity to submit its observations. Several provisions in the Treaty allow for the adoption of specific measures and lay down the procedures which are to be adopted in the particular case. In relation to the Treaty provisions which set out the basic prohibitions on restrictions to free movement, the Court has held many of these to be absolute and to give rise to rights and obligations for individuals as well as the Member States which the national courts are bound to protect.

The main body of the proposed legislation in the White Paper is concerned with directives. There are, though, other measures, including some regulations and decisions. Each of these types of measures has different consequences in the legal system, both in terms of the method of incorporation into the national and Community legal orders and in terms of the legal effects flowing from them.

Regulations

EC regulations have general application throughout the Community, are binding in their entirety and directly applicable in all Member States. They are published in the Official Journal of the European Communities and enter into force either on the day specified in them or, in the absence thereof, on the twentieth day following their publication. This legislative measure is self-executing in the legal order and needs no national implementing measure for it to come into effect. In certain cases, regulations affect the rights and obligations of individuals and may be relied upon before national courts.

Directives

EC directives are addressed to one or more Member States and are binding on them as to the result to be achieved. Each directive sets out provisions which the Member State is bound to incorporate into its legal order, although it is for the national authorities to choose the form and method by which this is done. Normally, a directive will result in a national legislative measure, such as an Act of Parliament, statutory instrument or Parliamentary decree. Directives are normally published in the Official Journal and take effect upon notification to the State or States to which they are addressed. The date for implementation of the provisions of the directive into national law is always stated in the directive itself. So as to promote legal certainty, it is now becoming common for directives to require that the national implementing legislation refer to the actual directive on which it is based.

Decisions

EC decisions are binding in their entirety on those to whom they are addressed and do not need to be implemented into the national legal order for them to take effect. The Council or the Commission may address a decision to a Member State authorising it, for example, to derogate from a certain rule of Community law. Decisions addressed to individuals or companies are most commonly found in those areas where the Commission has a role in regulating business practices, such as competition law, state aids and anti-dumping. As with directives, there is no Treaty requirement that these be published, although they often are and they also take effect upon notification to those to whom they are addressed.

Direct effect

EC regulations can be invoked before national courts in appropriate circumstances by an individual against either the national authorities or other individuals. That is because those provisions are automatically incorporated into the national legal order. Similarly, those provisions of the treaties which impose clear, precise and unconditional obligations may produce direct effects before national courts. When a directive has been properly implemented into national law, it is the national law which is the source in the national legal order of the rights and obligations which the directive establishes. However, if the directive is misimplemented or if it is not implemented at all, that does not prevent it from producing legal effects of its own which individuals may rely on even though it is addressed to a Member State. The Court has held that certain provisions of a directive will, if specific requirements are satisfied, be capable of producing direct effects in the national legal order. These requirements are as follows:

- the provision must impose a clear, precise and unconditional obligation on the Member State;
- the time limit for implementation of the provision must have expired;
- the obligation must not be subject to the adoption of any subsequent rules or regulations on the part either of the Community institutions or of the Member States, so that, in particular, Member States must not be left with any real discretion with regard to the application of the rule in question.

Directly effective provisions of directives, however, have more restrictive legal consequences than either regulations or directly effective provisions of the treaties. Because directives are not directly applicable, they do not themselves form part of the national legal order. The European Court, however, has consistently held that a Member State which has not adopted the implementing measures required by the directive may not rely, as against individuals, on its own failure to perform the obligations which the directive entails. Thus, an individual may rely upon the terms of a directive before the national court to establish the rights and obligations as against the national authorities which he would have had if the directive had been properly implemented. The Court has limited the application of the direct effect of provisions of directives so that it is not possible for one individual to rely on such provisions as against other individuals. Accordingly, whether a directive has been fully implemented or not, one individual in an action against another is limited to the national law in establishing the rights and obligations of one party to the other. However, the application of the concept of direct effect is extremely powerful. Most of the directives dealing with the abolition of obstacles to free movement are phrased in such a way that their essential provisions are directly effective. In addition to this, the Court has developed the notion of national authorities for these purposes very widely. Thus, any body, whatever its legal form, which has been made responsible, pursuant to a measure adopted by the State, for providing a public service under the control of the State and has for that purpose special powers beyond those which result from the normal rules applicable in relations between individuals is included in any event among the bodies against which the provisions of a directive capable of having direct effect may be relied upon.

Legislative procedure

Procedures for adopting Community legislation are set out in the Treaty with different procedures applying depending on the particular part of the Treaty which is in issue. Generally, the Treaty provides for the Council to act following a proposal from the Commission so that it is for the Commission to initiate the procedure with the Council being unable to act of its own volition. What happens thereafter depends on the rules applying to that proposal. In some cases, the Council is required to obtain the opinion of other bodies, such as the Parliament or the Economic and Social Committee. Unanimity is required of the Council in some matters, qualified majority in others. While in some cases the Parliament is merely entitled to give its opinion, in others, under the cooperation procedure, it is given a much fuller part to play.

Where the Council is to issue directives for the approximation of national laws which directly affect the establishment or functioning of the common market, with the major exception of a number of specified areas concerned with the completion of the internal market, it must act unanimously on a proposal from the Commission. The Parliament and the Economic and Social Committee must be consulted in the case of directives whose implementation would, in the case of one or more Member States, involve the amendment of legislation. If legislation should prove necessary to attain one of the objectives of the Community and the Treaty has not provided the necessary powers, the Council, acting unanimously on a proposal from the Commission and after consulting the Parliament, may take the appropriate measures. The Council is not obliged to accept a Commission proposal. It may refuse to adopt the proposed measure or it may amend it before adopting it. As long as the Council has not acted, the Commission may alter its proposal or it may withdraw it.

As well as the specific Treaty provisions allowing for legislation to be adopted in connection with the internal market, the Treaty provides that the Council, acting by a qualified majority on a proposal from the Commission, in cooperation with the European Parliament and after consulting the Economic and Social Committee, is to adopt measures for the approximation of laws which have as their object the establishment and functioning of the internal market. This does not apply to approximation of national laws covering fiscal provisions, to those relating to the free movement of persons or to those relating to the rights and interests of employed persons, all of which still require unanimity of the Council. Many specific provisions of the Treaty, including those dealing with new Community measures covering the free movement of persons and services, also enable the Council to adopt measures by qualified majority. If, after the adoption of a harmonisation measure by a qualified majority, a Member State deems it necessary to apply national provisions on exceptional grounds, such as public policy, public security or public health, or on grounds relating to protection of the environment or the working environment, it must notify the Commission of those provisions. The Commission will then confirm those provisions and verify that they are not a means of arbitrary discrimination or a disguised restriction on trade between Member States. If a Member State makes improper use of this power, the matter may be dealt with by the Court of Justice.

Where the Council acts on a proposal from the Commission, unanimity is required for an act constituting an amendment to that proposal. Although the Council must obtain the opinion of the Parliament and is not entitled to proceed without that opinion, where it is to act in cooperation with the Parliament, a quite different procedure applies. The Council, acting by a qualified majority on a proposal from the

Commission and after obtaining the opinion of the Parliament, adopts a common position. This common position is then communicated to the Parliament. The Council and the Commission must inform the Parliament fully of the reasons which led the Council to adopt the common position and also of the Commission's position in relation to it. If, within three months, the Parliament approves this common position or has taken no decision on it, the Council definitively adopts the act in question in accordance with the common position. Alternatively, the Parliament may, within the three months, by an absolute majority of its members, propose amendments to the Council's common position or reject it. If the Parliament rejects the common position, unanimity is required for the Council to act on a second reading.

If the Parliament has not accepted the Council's common position, the Commission, within one month, must re-examine the proposal on the basis of which the common position was adopted and take into account the amendments proposed by the Parliament. The Commission then forwards to the Council its re-examined proposal together with the amendments of the Parliament which it has not accepted. At this stage, the Council may adopt the re-examined proposal by a qualified majority, although if it wishes to incorporate any amendments, including those amendments of the Parliament which the Commission did not accept, it must act unanimously. The Council must act within three months. If no decision is taken within this period, the Commission proposal is deemed not to have been adopted.

The scheme of the Handbook

This Handbook follows exactly the order of the programme as set out in the White Paper. Some of the proposals which were listed at that time have been withdrawn or have been amended and others have been added. Accordingly, only those measures which continue to form the programme for the completion of the internal market are included. A detailed analysis of each measure is given and, where appropriate, previous legislation is also explained in order to place the whole matter in the proper context. Much of the legislation, however, is very technical. The nature of the Handbook is such that it can only summarise the major features of this kind of measure. Users are therefore advised that, while the Handbook seeks to give the fullest possible analysis, it is always useful to refer to the full legislation itself as contained in the accompanying encyclopedia entitled *Completing the Internal Market of the European Community: 1992 Legislation*. The annex contains a list of all of the published adopted and proposed measures contained in the programme to complete the internal market.

Part One

The Removal of Physical Barriers

I Control of Goods
1. Various Controls
2. Veterinary and Phytosanitary Controls
II. Control of Individuals

I. Control of Goods

1. Various Controls

Although customs duties and quantitative restrictions have been abolished for intra-Community trade, customs controls and formalities still exist for Community goods, thereby frustrating the completion of the internal market. The aim of the White Paper is to simplify the various controls and then to abolish them by 1992.

The introduction of common border posts

Customs formalities and controls are usually required both on leaving the Member State on exit and on entering the Member State of entry. This is known as banalisation. These formalities and controls are generally repetitive and result in loss of time and considerable expense arising from immobilisation. The Commission considers that as an intermediate step to completing the internal market additional simplification measures should be introduced through the introduction of common border posts. Such a measure would end the duplication of formalities and controls on both side of the border. The Council has, therefore, adopted Regulation 4283/88 on the abolition of certain exit formalities at internal Community frontiers - introduction of common border posts. The regulation provides that where goods cross an internal frontier, they need to be presented, for the purposes of the formalities and controls, to be carried out at the office of exit under the ATA carnet, the Community movement carnet or the

3

Form 302 procedure (laid down under the Convention between the parties to the North Atlantic Treaty on the status of their forces) only at the office of entry. The office of entry completes the formalities and controls that are incumbent upon the office of exit and immediately informs the latter thereof. Findings made by the office of entry have the same evidential force as findings made by the authorities in the Member State where the goods have just left. Any irregularities discovered are deemed to have been discovered in the Member State where the goods have just left.

The abolition of administrative documentation

The simplification of administration documentation

Prior to the publication of the White Paper, the Council had already adopted Regulation 678/85 which introduced a single administrative document (SAD) for the control of imports, exports and goods in transit throughout the Community and the Community Transit procedure had also been in force for some time. It was considered that the simplification of import and export documentation would encourage firms, in particular small firms, to view their business in terms of the whole of the internal market.

The SAD is also known outside the United Kingdom as the COM document. It greatly simplified the administrative forms applicable in intra-Community trade by replacing a multitude of documents, in particular forms T1 and T2, with a single document. The SAD is a form containing eight copies:

copy 1 - copy for the office of departure
copy 2 - statistical copy for the country of export
copy 3 - exporter's or consignor's copy
copy 4 - copy for the office of destination
copy 5 - community transit return copy
copy 6 - customs import declaration
copy 7 - statistical copy for the country of destination
copy 8 - copy for the consignee

Regulation 678/85 applied only to intra-Community trade in Community produced goods. Regulation 1900/85 introduced corresponding forms, EX and IM, for imports of non-Community produced goods and exports to third countries.

Abolition of the single administrative document

The effect of implementing the principle of the completion of the internal market is to eliminate all checks and all formalities in respect of

Community goods moving within the Community. This renders the single administrative document redundant since from 1993 there will be a presumption that all products on the Community market will have Community status that therefore there is no need to check the place of origin in intra-Community trade. Proof that a product originates in the Community will thenceforth be supplied solely by an invoice and not by any administrative documents. Consequently Regulation 717/91 abolishes the need for a SAD for imports and exports in respect of goods in free circulation within the Community.

The use of the SAD will continue in respect of intra-Community goods not in free circulation with the Community as well as imports into the Community and exports from the Community. The SAD will continue to be used also during the transitional period of the accession of Spain and Portugal to the Community in connection with trade between the Community and between Spain or Portugal in goods still liable to certain customs duties and charges having equivalent effect or which remain subject to other measures laid down by the Act of Accession.

Regulation 717/91 repeals Regulation 678/85, 679/85 and Regulation 1900/85 and will apply from 1 January 1993.

The Community Transit (CT) procedure

Initial steps

The introduction of the Community Transit (CT) procedure simplified the formalities that are carried out when internal frontiers in the Community are crossed. The CT procedure is used for the movement of goods within the customs territory of the Community and movements to and from Austria and Switzerland. The CT procedure is governed by Regulation 222/77 and Regulation 1062/87. Regulation 1901/85 amended Regulation 222/77 so that the SAD is now used in the CT procedure.

Briefly, the CT procedure is as follows. A person who wants to transport goods from one Member State to another is called a CT principal. He undertakes primary responsibility that the transportation will be properly carried out and must give a guarantee or cash deposit to ensure that duties or other taxes which each Member State is authorised to charge in respect of goods passing through its territory are paid. The CT principal should indicate on the SAD the status of the goods so that it can be determined whether customs duties are payable or a refund is due. The CT principal may describe the goods as T1 or T2: T2 means that the goods are of Community origin or are in free circulation within the Community; T1 means that the goods are not Community goods.

The customs authorities at the country of departure carry out any necessary control of the goods or documents and register the movement.

They stamp the relevant copies of the SAD, keep copy 1 and return the rest to the CT principal who keeps copy 3. Copies 4, 5 and 7 must travel with the goods and be produced at customs offices during the course of the transit. By virtue of Regulation 474/90 carriers are only obliged to give transit advice notes to each customs office at the point of exit from the Community when the consignment is leaving the territory of the Community in the course of a Community transit operation via a frontier between a Member State and a third country, and each office of transit at the point of entry into the Community, where the goods have passed through the territory of a third country. The obligation under Regulation 222/77 to lodge a transit advice note with the customs at each internal frontier of the Community has been abolished. As a general rule, identification of the goods is ensured by sealing and the offices of transit do not inspect the goods unless some irregularity is suspected or the seals are broken. The CT procedure is completed when the goods reach the customs office of destination which returns copy 5 to the customs office of departure certifying that the movement has been completed satisfactorily. The guarantee may then be discharged or the deposit repaid. The customs office of departure retains overall customs control and takes the necessary action if the customs office of destination certifies that there was an irregularity.

The necessity to provide a guarantee has now been abolished in certain circumstances. Regulation 1674/87 provides that customs authorities may grant a guarantee waiver to persons who:

- are resident in the Member State where the waiver is granted;
- who are regular users of the CT procedure;
- whose financial position is such that they can meet their commitments;
- who have not committed any serious infringement of customs or fiscal fraud; and
- who undertake to pay, upon first application in writing by the competent authorities of the Member States, any sums claimed in respect of their transit operations.

Moreover, the waiver is not available where the total value of the goods exceeds 50,000 ECU. The authorities must issue a guarantee waiver certificate, to which reference must be made on the T2 declaration and which may be withdrawn if the above requirements are no longer met.

Abolition of the procedure for Community goods

The application of the principle of completion of the internal market has the effect of eliminating all controls and all formalities in respect of Community goods moving within the Community and consequently of rendering, in principle, the procedure for internal Community transit devoid of any purpose. Consequently, by virtue of Regulation 2726/90

Community goods moving within the Community will no longer be subject to customs controls and formalities, goods will move freely, as they do at present within any one Member State and consequently the Community transit procedure will no longer be applicable. From 1 January 1993 the Community transit procedure will apply in the main to non-Community goods (external Community transit) and it will apply to Community goods (internal Community transit) only in quite specific cases: when goods are dispatched via the EFTA countries, or in trade between the Community of ten and Spain and Portugal, or between those two countries, in goods to which the special measures laid down by the Act of Accession continue to apply on a transitional basis. The regulation repeals Regulation 222/77, but reformulates most of the principles applicable to external transit.

The abolition of exit customs formalities: TIR

The TIR procedure allows goods in road vehicles or containers sealed by customs to cross one or more countries en route to their destination with the minimum of customs interference. TIR carnets are used for this purpose but they cannot be used for goods exported to other Member States unless they have to leave Community territory in order to reach their destination. For goods moving entirely within the Community, the CT procedure must be used.

Under the TIR procedure, virtually identical formalities must be completed, first at the customs office of exit and then at the customs office of entry. Regulation 3690/86 avoids duplication of checks on both sides of a frontier by providing that one check should be carried out at the office of entry into a Member State. The office of entry must, if necessary, send to the office of exit information relating to TIR consignments and to irregularities discovered. The Member State of exit, however, remains competent to take action to recover duties and taxes due to it. This regulation, therefore, constitutes an important step to achieving a single land border post at frontiers.

By virtue of Regulation 719/91 when goods are transported from one point in the Community to another under the procedure for the international transport of goods under cover of TIR carnets or under cover of ATA carnets the territories of the Member States of the Community shall, for the purposes of such transit, be considered to form a single territory. The regulation comes into force on 1 January 1992.

The abolition of postal fees for customs presentation

The completion of the internal market means that both customs formalities and customs charges are abolished when they apply to trade in Community goods between Member States. Regulation 1797/86 provides that postal fees for consignments of goods presented to customs can no longer be levied on goods sent from a Member State which either originate in a Member State or come from a third country and are in free circulation in the Community. Spain and Portugal may apply the same postal fees for customs presentation of goods coming from other Member States as are applied to goods from third countries until customs duties are finally eliminated in trade with other Member States at the end of 1992.

The removal of transport restrictions

Delays caused by physical inspections and administrative formalities constitute a significant hindrance to the completion of the internal market not only when they apply to the goods carried, but also when they apply to the means of transport itself. In this respect, Directive 68/297 laid down the minimum quantity of fuel contained in commercial motor vehicles which must be admitted duty-free at the internal frontiers. Directive 85/ 347 further facilitates frontier crossing by increasing this quantity to 600 litres for commercial passenger vehicles. The maximum quantity of duty free fuel for goods vehicles remains at 200 litres.

Further, the Council has adopted Regulation 4060/89 on the elimination of controls performed at the frontiers of Member States in the field of road and inland waterway transport. Pursuant to existing Community and national legislation in the field of road and inland waterway transport, Member States perform checks, verifications and inspections relating to technical characteristics, authorisations and other documentation that vehicles and inland waterway vessels must comply with. These checks, verifications and inspections continue in general to be justified in order to avoid disturbances to the organisation of the transport market and to ensure road and inland waterway safety. The regulation outlines the relevant controls; i.e., relating to weights, dimensions and other technical characteristics of road vehicles, roadworthiness tests for motor vehicles, certificates relating to the carriage of passengers by coach and by bus, driving licences, etc. These controls must no longer be performed at the frontier but solely as part of the normal control procedures applied in a non-discriminatory fashion throughout the territory of a Member State.

Statistics relating to intra-Community trade

The Commission has proposed a regulation which would oblige the Community and the Member States to draw up statistics relating to the trading of goods. A transitional period will operate from 1 January 1993 until the date on which a unified system of taxation in the Member State of origin is implemented and some of the details of the system will be altered at the end of the transitional period. All goods which move from one Member State to another will be the subject of statistics which shall categorised as transit, storage or trade statistics. A statistical collection system, known as Intrastat, will be set up. Statistics on trade between Member States shall cover, on the one hand, movements of goods leaving the Member State of dispatch and, on the other, movements of goods entering the Member State of arrival. The data to be recorded must include the name of the country of arrival and dispatch, the quantity and value of the goods, the nature of the transaction, the delivery terms and the presumed mode of transport.

2. Veterinary and Phytosanitary Controls

Border checks on plant and animal health

Customs posts are often used for making veterinary and plant health checks. These controls stem from differences in public, animal and plant health standards, which give national authorities grounds for checking that imported products conform to national requirements. These measures constitute quantitative restrictions on the import of goods but they may be justified under the Treaty.

As the internal market is created, these controls will have to be abolished in order to allow the free movement of animals, animal products and plants. The Commission has, therefore, set out to implement a programme for the harmonisation of essential health requirements which is a technically complex and procedurally slow process. Intra-Community trade of animals, animal products and plants would therefore become equivalent to national trade in these products. Many of the measures on veterinary and phytosanitary controls which are contained in the White Paper build upon previous measures. In the animal health sector, common rules have been established or proposed for intra-Community trade in cattle and pigs and their meat and meat products and for the control and eradication of certain major diseases: swine fever, brucellosis, tuberculosis and leucosis in cattle, foot and mouth. In the public health sector, standards have been established or proposed for intra-Community trade in certain products: meat, meat products, milk, eggs, fish. Also included are measures in such areas as the use of hormones and the control of pesticides and residues in animals and animal products. Common rules have also been established in respect of organisms harmful to plants or plant products and the certification of seeds.

Alongside these harmonising measures the Commission has proposed a new approach to veterinary and phytosanitary controls to facilitate the removal of frontier controls. The aim is that all veterinary controls of animals and animal products and phytosanitary controls of plants will be limited to the place of departure from a Member State and controls of veterinary and plant health certificates will be made at the place of destination. Imports from non-EEC countries would, upon arrival at a Community frontier, be checked to ensure that they complied with

Community standards. Compliance with these standards would enable these products to be traded freely within the Community.

VETERINARY CONTROLS

Abolishing veterinary controls at the frontier

The ultimate aim is that by 1992 veterinary checks will only be carried out at the place of dispatch. However, as a first step to the attainment of this objective, the Council has adopted two directives concerning veterinary checks in intra-Community trade in most animal products and certain live animals. The directives place the emphasis on the checks to be carried out at the place of dispatch and provide that certain checks can be carried out at the place of destination. The consequence is that veterinary checks at internal frontiers are abolished.

Directive 89/662 concerns veterinary checks in intra-Community trade of most animal products. Directive 90/425 concerns veterinary and zootechnical checks in intra-Community trade in certain live animals and products.

Checks at origin

Member States of origin must ensure that the animal products covered by the Community measures have been obtained, checked, marked and labelled in accordance with Community rules and are accompanied to the final consignee by a health certificate, animal health certificate or by any other document provided for by Community veterinary rules.

Similarly, Member States of origin must ensure that live animals (covered by Directive 90/425) satisfy the requirements of the relevant Community directives listed in the annex to the directive. These rules relate mainly to cattle and swine. In respect of sheep, goats, live poultry and domestic rabbits, these must fulfil the animal health requirements of the Member State of destination. All the animals must come from holdings, centres or organisations which are subject to regular official veterinary checks, they must be registered in such a way that the original or transit holding, centre or organisation can be traced, and they must when transported be accompanied by health certificates. The animals must be transported in suitable means of transport which satisfy hygiene rules. Where the transport operation involves several places of destination, animals and animal products must be grouped together in as many consignments as there are places of destination. Each batch must be accompanied by the relevant certificate.

Each Member State must notify other Member States of outbreaks of diseases likely to constitute a serious hazard to animals or to humans. Member States of origin should immediately implement precautionary or control measures provided for in Community rules, in particular the setting up of buffer zones. All dealers engaging in intra-Community trade in animals or products may be subject to registration.

Checks on arrival

Member States of destination may carry out non-discriminatory veterinary spot checks that the Community rules have been complied with. Where there is a strong suspicion of irregularity, the veterinary check could be carried out while the goods were being transported. Where Community rules or, national rules in areas which have not yet been harmonised, require that live animals be put into quarantine, the latter should normally take place at the holding of destination.

The directives provide for measures to be taken when controls made at the place of destination disclose irregularities. For example, if the authority of the Member State of destination establishes the presence of a contagious disease, it can order that the animals be slaughtered at once or that the consignment be destroyed. If the Community health rules or the health rules of the Member State of destination are not met, the consignor or his representative may be given the choice of returning the consignment to the Member State of origin, using the goods for other purposes or destroying the goods. In the case of livestock, the authorities of the Member State of destination could put the animals into quarantine. Any decision by the Member State of destination must be subject to a right of appeal by the consignor. Where the Member State of destination discovers breaches of the Community or national rules, it should contact the Member State of origin without delay. The Commission may send a mission of inspection to the establishment concerned to ascertain whether the rules are being complied with and may take the appropriate measures which may go as far as authorising the Member States of destination to prohibit provisionally the bringing into their territory of products or live animals coming from the establishment in the Member State of origin.

Both directives foresee the elimination of veterinary controls at internal Community frontiers by 31 December 1991 at the latest (with the exception of Greece which has until 31 December 1992). In the case of live animals Member States may maintain until 31 December 1992 documentary checks during transport of live animals in order to satisfy themselves that the specific requirements laid down by Community rules have been complied with. In the case of most animal products, Member States may until 31 December 1992 maintain documentary checks during transport to ensure that Community rules concerning foot and mouth disease and swine fever have been complied with.

Under Directive 89/608 Member States must co-operate fully in the correct application of the veterinary legislation. Thus at the request of the Member State of destination, the Member State of origin must keep a watch on establishments, on places where stocks of goods have been assembled, on notified movements of goods or on means of transport.

Veterinary checks on animals entering the Community from third countries

The Commission has proposed a Council regulation which would provide for the veterinary checks on animals entering the Community from third countries. Each consignment of animals from a third country would be subject to a documentary check by the customs' authorities of the Member States irrespective of the customs' destination of the animals. The animals would be conveyed directly, under customs' supervision, to an inspection post or to a quarantine centre. There they would be subject to a physical check and an identity check on a random basis. Thereafter intra-Community trade in the animals would be conducted in accordance with the rules laid down in Directive 90/425.

The Commission could, as a protective measure, prohibit imports or apply special conditions to imports of animals from a third country in which a disease threatening animal or public health had broken out. Representatives of the Commission could make an immediate visit to the third country concerned.

Each Member State would draw up a programme for the exchange of officials empowered to carry out the checks on animals originating in third countries. The regulation lays down the measures to be taken where one Member State considers that another Member State is not complying with the regulation. In such an event the Commission could send an inspection team to the defaulting Member State in question.

Health problems affecting intra-Community trade in meat products

Directive 88/658 amends directive 77/99 on health problems in order to take account of new scientific and technical developments and to include certain meat-based preparations and pre-cooked dishes not currently covered. Each Member State must ensure that only meat products complying with the conditions laid down in the directive are sent from its territory to the territory of another Member State. Meat products are products prepared from or with meat which has undergone treatment such that the cut surface shows that the product no longer has the characteristics of fresh meat. The meat products must have been prepared by heating, curing or drying, which process may be combined with smoking or maturing, possibly under specific micro-climatic conditions. They may also be associated with other foodstuffs and condiments. Meat which has undergone only cold treatment does not constitute a meat product.

Each Member State must draw up a list of the establishments where meat products are prepared. Each establishment will have a veterinary approval number and the list must be sent to other Member States and to the Commission. In an annex to the directive, detailed conditions are laid down which an establishment must satisfy before being approved. Commission veterinary experts may carry out regular inspections of approved establishments to ensure application of the directive.

Meat products must be wrapped and packaged in accordance with the directive, bear a health marking and be accompanied by a health certificate during transport to the country of destination. Member States of destination may check that all consignments of meat products are accompanied by the relevant health certificates. As a general rule, checks and inspections must be carried out at the place of destination of the goods or at any other suitable place, provided that the choice of the latter place causes as little interference as possible with the movement of goods. There must not be such delay that the quality of the meat products is impaired. If it is found that the requirements of the directive have not been complied with, the Member State of destination can give the consignor, the consignee or their representatives the choice between the reconsignment of the meat products, their use for other purposes or their destruction.

The Commission has proposed a regulation repealing and replacing Directive 77/99. The regulation when adopted will harmonise the health rules applicable to the production and placing on the market of meat products by extending the rules governing intra-Community trade laid down in the directive to domestic trade.

Health problems affecting Intra-Community trade in fresh meat

A directive of 1964 harmonised certain differences between the health requirements of Member States concerning meat which hinder intra-Community trade. Directive 88/288 amends this directive and harmonises health requirements concerning frozen meat, hygiene rules for intra-Community rules in sliced offal and harmonises rules for possible additional requirements for ante-mortem and post-mortem inspections. For example, the directive provides that offal may not be sliced except for livers of animals of the bovine species where such livers are sliced in an approved cutting plant. Sliced livers of these animals must be individually wrapped. During slicing, wrapping and packaging, the internal temperature of livers must be kept at a constant 3½°C or less. Fresh meat for freezing must come directly from an approved slaughterhouse or an approved cutting plant. Frozen meat must reach an internal temperature of -12°C or lower and may not be stored at higher temperatures thereafter. Fresh meat which has undergone a freezing process must bear an indication of the month and year in which it was frozen.

The Commission has proposed a regulation which will repeal and replace the 1964 directive. The regulation will harmonise the health rules applicable to the production and placing on the market of fresh meat by extending the rules governing intra-Community trade laid down in the 1964 directive to the domestic markets. A similar proposed regulation deals with health rules for the production and placing on the market of fresh poultry meat.

Public health and animal health problems affecting the importation of meat products from third countries

A Directive of 1972 laid down the relevant conditions applicable to imports of fresh meat from certain third countries. Directive 89/227 lays down the conditions as regards public health and animal health applicable to the importation from third countries of meat products with the exception of meat products containing poultry meat. The aim of this measure is to prevent imports of meat products from countries in which there are cases of contagious animal diseases from which the Community is free and which, therefore, would present a danger to the Community livestock.

Health requirements

Fresh meat intended for the manufacture of meat products must come from approved establishments which satisfy the conditions laid down in the 1972 directive. Member States may then authorise the importation of meat products which originates from third countries if imports of fresh meat are permitted from those countries. Where the importation of fresh meat is not authorised from a third country, the importation of meat products is, nevertheless, permitted if they have undergone a heat treatment process. If a contagious animal disease breaks out in a third country for which a list of establishments has been drawn up and the disease can be carried by meat products and is likely to endanger animal or public health, the Member State concerned or the Commission can prohibit the importation of those products coming directly or indirectly from the third country. In order to protect public health, the importation of meat products from third countries will not be authorised unless they have been obtained in an officially approved establishment and comply with a 1977 directive which deals with intra-Community trade in meat products.

Inspection and certification

Veterinary experts of the Member States and the Commission may carry out spot checks to verify that these provisions are being applied in practice. The importation of meat products is conditional upon the production of an animal health certificate and a public health certificate drawn up by an official veterinarian of the exporting third country. The animal health certificate must certify that the meat products comply with the animal health requirements. A specimen of the public health certificate is given in an annex to the directive. This certificate must be issued on the day in which the meat products are loaded with a view to consignment to the country of destination.

Each consignment of meat products may undergo a physical inspection by random sampling relating to both public health and animal health aspects before being released into the Community. If the meat products are not suitable for human consumption or the conditions laid down in the directive are not fulfilled, the meat products may either be returned or destroyed. Meat products which are authorised for circulation in the Community will have to be covered by a certificate corresponding in presentation and content to the specimen given in another annex to the directive. The cost of inspection of the meat products, storage costs and any costs of destroying the meat products is chargeable to the consignor or the consignee.

Trade in animal semen

Directive 88/407 (as amended by Directive 90/120) harmonises national rules relating to intra-Community trade in the semen and to imports of semen from third countries. Semen is defined as the prepared or diluted ejaculate of a domestic animal of the bovine species.

Intra-Community trade

Semen being sent from the territory of one Member State to the territory of another Member State must satisfy certain animal health conditions relating to the collection, processing and storage which are fully set out in annexes to the directive. For the purposes of artificial insemination, all semen must be collected and processed in an officially approved semen collection centre. All approved centres must be registered and a list of them sent to the other Member States. If a Member State fears that the requisite animal health conditions have not been satisfied, it should inform the Commission which may authorise it to prohibit temporarily the admission of semen coming from the centre in question.

The importation of semen is conditional upon production of an animal health certificate which is drawn up by an official veterinarian of the Member State of collection. A specimen certificate is annexed to the directive. The Member State of destination may prohibit the importation of the semen if the certificate reveals that the animal health conditions have not been satisfied in which case the semen may be returned to the Member State of collection or even destroyed.

Imports from third countries

Semen may be imported into the Community only from those third countries which appear on a list drawn up in accordance with the directive. Furthermore, semen may only be imported from semen collection centres in those third countries which reach certain standards and which are officially supervised. The semen must come from animals which, immediately prior to collection of their semen, remained for at least six months in the territory of a listed third country. Member States must not authorise the importation of semen from a third country on a list unless the semen complies with certain animal health requirements. The importation of semen from third countries is also conditional upon the production of a certificate. Protective measures, including storage in quarantine, may be taken in order to obtain definite proof in cases where semen is suspected of being contaminated by pathogenic organisms. If the semen does not satisfy any of the requirements relating to approved countries, approved centres, health certificates or animal health requirements, the semen may be returned to the third country or be destroyed.

Safeguard and control measures

A Member State may take the following measures if there is a danger of an animal disease spreading as a result of the introduction of semen into its territory from another Member State: in the event of an outbreak of an epizootic disease in the other Member State, it may temporarily prohibit or restrict the introduction of semen from the areas of that Member State where the disease has occurred; if an epizootic disease becomes widespread, or if there is an outbreak of a further contagious animal disease of a serious nature, it may temporarily prohibit or restrict the introduction of semen from the whole of the territory of that Member State.

If in a third country a contagious animal disease which can be carried by semen and is liable to endanger the health of livestock in a Member State breaks out or spreads, or if any other reason connected with animal health so justifies, the Member State of destination concerned should prohibit the importation of that semen, whether imported directly or indirectly through another Member State.

Veterinary experts from the Commission have power to make spot checks to ensure that the directive is being complied with.

Council Directive 90/429 lays down animal health requirements applicable to intra-Community trade in and imports of semen of pigs. Similar rules are laid down to those contained in Directive 88/407. Thus Member States must ensure that each consignment of semen is accompanied by an animal health certificate and that it is collected and processed in an officially approved semen collection centre. As regards precautionary and control measures it is provided that Directive 90/425 applies in particular with regard to checks at origin, the organisation and monitoring of checks to be carried out by the Member State of destination. Further, Member States may authorise importation of semen only from those third countries which appear on an approved list. Until 31 December 1992, Member States in which all collection centres contain only animals which have not been vaccinated against Aujeszky's disease may refuse admission to their territory of semen from collection centres which do not have that status.

Trade in bovine embryos

Directive 89/556 lays down animal health conditions governing intra-Community trade in and importation from third countries of embryos of domestic animals of the bovine species. Intra-Community trade in embryos is limited to those complying with conditions concerning conception, collection, processing, storage and certification, the requirements for which are laid down in the directive. There are also specific provisions for protection against foot and mouth disease. Imports of embryos for third countries are restricted to a list of authorised countries and have to comply with specified conditions relating, for example, to the state of health of livestock in the third country. Each consignment of embryos entering the customs territory of the Community will be subject to control before being put into free circulation.

Minced meat

Intra-Community trade in minced meat, meat in pieces of less than 100gm and meat preparations (i.e., which have been seasoned) is impeded by disparities in national health requirements. In order to combat this, Directive 88/657 sets out health requirements to be satisfied for the placing on the market of such meat.

Intra-Community trade

Directive 88/657 provides that such meat can only be dispatched from one Member State to another if the meat meets certain specified conditions. These are as follows:

- it must have been prepared from fresh meat which complies with earlier directives;
- it must have been prepared in establishments which comply with earlier directives and which fulfil special conditions which are contained in an annex to the directive;
- it must have been prepared, packaged, stored and inspected, marketed and transported in accordance with the specific conditions laid down in the directive;
- during transport to the country of destination, it must be accompanied by a health certificate.

Member States must ensure that minced meat containing offal and minced poultry meat is not sent to other Member States which do not authorise the production or marketing of such meat. Member States must ensure that production plants undergo official inspection in order to ensure that production hygiene requirements are fulfilled.

The Commission has proposed a regulation which will repeal Directive 88/657. This regulation will harmonise the health rules applicable to minced meat and mince preparations and other comminuted meat by extending to national markets the rules laid down in Directive 88/657.

Sheep and goats

Directive 91/68 defines the animal health conditions governing intra-Community trade in ovine and caprine animals. Sheep and goats may only be sent to another Member States under the following minimum conditions:

- there is no clinical sign of disease of day of loading;
- they are not intended for slaughter under a scheme for eradication of disease;
- they do not originate from a holding subject to prohibition on grounds of health (brucellosis, rabies, anthrax);
- they are not subject to restrictions under Directive 85/511 in respect of measures concerning foot and mouth disease;
- they must be accompanied by a health certificate signed by an official veterinarian in accordance with the model contained in an annex to the directive.

Further conditions (i.e., in relation to scrapie) are imposed for animals which are sent for fattening or breeding purposes. The rules laid down in

Directive 90/425 apply in particular to checks at origin, to the organisation of checks in the Member States of destination and the protective measures to be implemented. Veterinary experts from the Commission may carry out on-the-spot inspections to ensure application of the directive.

In respect of imports of sheep and goats from third countries, Directive 91/69 makes the importation of such animals subject to Directive 72/462 (as amended by Directive 90/425) which lays down health and veterinary inspection requirements for the importation of cattle and pigs, fresh meat and meat products from third countries.

Dogs, cats and rabies

The continued presence of rabies in certain areas of the Community presents obstacles to the freedom of movement of dogs and cats and other companion animals owing to quarantine restrictions in some Member States. The Commission considers that it would be premature to require the dismantlement of quarantine restrictions owing to the risk of spread of rabies. As an intermediate measure, therefore, the Commission has proposed the harmonisation of rabies vaccination and health certificates for dogs and cats on visits of less than one year in the Member States. Further, Council Decision 89/455 provides that Member States should draw up plans for large-scale pilot projects for the oral immunisation of foxes with a view to eradicating rabies in those Member States which have the disease.

Rodents

It is proposed that the placing of wild rodents (i.e., rabbits, hares, mice and rats) will be prohibited if they come from a zone of a radius of ten kilometres in which rabies, myxomatosis, haemorrhagic disease, tularaemia is present or suspected of being present. Inspections will be carried out by veterinary experts of the Commission to ensure that the proposed regulation is being applied. Pending the application of Community rules concerned, the conditions applicable to the import of rodents from third countries must not be more favourable than those governing intra-Community trade.

Horses

Directive 90/426 harmonises the animal health conditions governing the intra-Community trade in equidae. Directive 90/428 applies to equidae intended for competitions. Under Directive 90/426 intra-Community trade is subject to certain conditions. The equidae may not present any sign of disease when inspected during the 48-hour period preceding loading, and may not have been in contact with infected equidae during the 15-day period preceding loading. Equidae must be conveyed directly to the place of destination accompanied by an animal health certificate (a model of which is contained in an annex to the directive). Commission veterinary experts may carry out on-the-spot inspections.

Imports of equidae from third countries are also subject to certain rules. They must have originated in a third country included in a list drawn up by the Commission and they must have remained for a continuous period (of a duration yet to be specified) in the country of dispatch and must be accompanied by a certificate made out by an official veterinarian of that country. Inspections will be carried out by the national and Community veterinary experts. An annex to the directive lists diseases which are subject to compulsory notification.

Trade in fresh poultry meat and fresh meat of reared game birds

A proposed regulation will deal with animal health conditions governing intra-Community trade and imports from third countries of fresh poultry meat and reared game bird meat.

To be accepted for intra-Community trade, fresh meat will have to be obtained from poultry or reared game birds which:

- have remained in the Community since hatching or have been imported from third countries in accordance with Directive 90/539 on animal health conditions governing intra-Community trade in and imports from third countries of poultry and hatching eggs;
- come from a holding which has not been placed under animal health restrictions in connection with a poultry disease and is not situated in an area infected with avian influenza or Newcastle disease;
- have not been in contact, during transport to the slaughter house, with birds infected with avian influenza or Newcastle disease. Any fresh meat suspected of contamination at the slaughter house, cutting plant or storage depot, or during transport, must be excluded from intra-Community trade.

The rules on veterinary checks in intra-Community trade with a view to the completion of the internal market will apply as regards checks in the Member State of origin and checks in the Member States of destination. Commission veterinary experts may carry out on-the-spot inspections to ensure that the health requirements have been met.

Fresh meat imported into the Community must come from third countries included in a list drawn up by the Commission. The decision as to whether a third country is included is based in particular, on the state of health of the poultry, the existence of contagious animal diseases in its territory and rules of the country on the prevention and control of animal diseases, etc. Fresh meat must come from countries free of avian influenza and Newcastle disease. The meat must be accompanied by a certificate made out by an official veterinarian of the exporting third country.

Game and rabbit meat

Intra-Community trade of game meat will be subject to the appropriate animal health rules governing intra-Community trade of fresh meat. The slaughtering, cutting and processing establishments must be approved by the Member States. Veterinary experts from the Commission may make on-the-spot checks to ensure that the health rules are being complied with.

A survey of the health status of game and rabbits shall be performed at regular intervals in each Member State. The annexes to the directive contain provisions on health inspection of rabbits, health labelling, storage and transport.

Fish

Disparities in national health requirements concerning fish and fish products also hinder intra-Community trade. The Commission has, therefore, proposed a regulation which will lay down the health conditions for all production and placing on the market of fish and fishery products. The annexes to the regulation set out the conditions under which fish caught wild are to be handled, packed, prepared, processed, frozen, defrosted or stored. Fishery products will not be handled except in establishments conforming to the standards laid down in the annexes. The establishments must be inspected by the competent authorities and Commission experts may carry out on-the-spot inspections to ensure that the regulation is being applied. Fishery products which are marketed live must at all times be kept under the most suitable survival conditions and it is provided that certain species, namely those that are poisonous, will not be marketed. The provisions applicable to imports of fishery products from third countries will be applicable to those governing the placing on the market of Community products. The annexes to the regulation set out the requirements during and after the landing; relating to on-shore establishments, the handling of fishery products on shore, health control and supervision of production, wrapping, packaging, labelling, storage and transport of fishery products.

A proposed regulation would also harmonise health requirements so as to prevent the consumption of fish and fish products contaminated by nematodes. It provides that fresh fish and fish products intended for marketing would undergo the treatment laid down in an annex to the proposed regulation. For example, fresh fish would have to be cleaned and gutted immediately after having been caught and fresh fish intended to be consumed raw would be subjected to cold treatment in which the internal temperature of the fish would be at a maximum of -20°C for at least 24 hours. Establishments which carried out such treatment would be approved by the Member States and be subjected to regular controls and inspections.

The Commission has also proposed a regulation setting the health standards for the production and marketing of live molluscs (mussels, oysters). They will have to be harvested, transported, prepared for marketing and wrapped in accordance with the requirements set out in the annexes to the regulation.

Council Directive 91/67 has harmonised the animal health conditions governing the placing on the market of aquaculture animals and products (i.e., live fish, crustaceans or molluscs originating from a farm). The primary aim of the directive is to prevent the spread of infectious diseases and consequently, it provides for the designation of officially-approved Community zones with a favourable health status and the requirement of a movement document (i.e., a health certificate) for these products. Inspections will be carried out on the spot by veterinary experts of the Member States and the Commission to verify that the provisions of the directive have been complied with.

Eggs and egg products

The marketing of eggs and egg products within the Community has been hindered by disparities in national health requirements. Consequently the Council has adopted Directive 89/437 on hygiene and health problems affecting the production and the placing on the market of egg products and has adopted Directive 90/539 on animal health conditions governing intra-Community trade in, and imports from third countries of, poultry and hatching eggs.

The annex to Directive 89/437 lays down the hygiene and health requirements relating to: premises, equipment, staff, manufacture, packaging, storage and transport and marking of egg products. Thus the egg products must meet certain conditions before they can be placed on the market. They have to be prepared in approved establishments and under satisfactory hygiene conditions (i.e., micro-biological checks in order to ensure the absence of salmonella); they must have undergone health checks, be appropriately packed, stored and transported and bear the mark of wholesomeness (i.e., the official number of the establishment, the country of origin, the temperature at which the egg products have been maintained, the batch number and the place of destination). Random checks will be carried on egg products to detect any residues, antibiotics, pesticides, detergents or other substances which are harmful to health. Commission officials may carry out spot checks to ensure application of the directive. Member States of destination may also carry out inspections where they suspect irregularities. National provisions governing the importation of eggs from third countries must not be more favourable than those governing intra-Community trade.

Directive 90/539 provides that intra-Community trade in poultry and hatching eggs is subject to the following conditions:

- they must come from establishments approved by the Commission and not be located in areas declared as infected with avian influenza or Newcastle disease;
- at the time of consignment, they must present no clinical sign or suspicion of disease and satisfy vaccination conditions;
- the transport of animals in purpose-designed containers of cages conform with hygiene conditions laid down by the competent authority of the Member State concerned;
- an inspection by a veterinary expert of the Commission may be carried out to ensure that the conditions are being complied with.

The annexes to the directive contain a list of diseases which are compulsorily notifiable (avian influenza and Newcastle disease).

The eggs must during transportation to the place of destination be accompanied by a health certificate which conforms with the appropriate model contained in the annex. In respect of imports from third countries, the eggs must originate from a country included on a list which is drawn up by the Commission. In deciding whether a third country may be included on the list the Commission will look primarily to the state of health of the poultry in that third country. Eggs cannot come from countries which are not free from avian influenza or Newcastle disease. The eggs must also be accompanied by a certificate drawn up and signed by an official veterinarian of the exporting third country. On-the-spot inspections will be carried out by veterinary experts of the Member States and the Commission to ensure that all provisions of the directive are complied with.

Milk

Directive 85/397 aims to eliminate national differences in health requirements concerning heat-treated milk (pasteurised, UHT or sterilised milk) which hinder intra-Community trade in these products. Intra-Community trade in products derived from milk, other than heat-treated milk, is not affected by the directive.

Intra-Community trade

Heat-treated milk must satisfy the conditions which are laid down in the directive before it can be exported to another Member State. The milk must have been obtained from untreated milk (e.g., produced by secretion from the mammary glands of one or more dairy cows); the untreated milk must be obtained from cows which are free from infection and must come from production holdings which meet specific hygiene conditions; the heat-treated milk must come from a milk treatment establishment which fulfils the conditions laid down in an annex to the directive; the milk must also be treated, packaged, stored and transported in accordance with the rules and conditions laid down in the annex.

Milk tankers must be used exclusively for the transport of milk, milk products and portable water. Premises, installations and working equipment may not be used for purposes other than the collection, treatment and storage of milk and milk products. To the extent that Member States authorise the use of tankers and working equipment for the transport and manufacture of other liquid foodstuffs at different times, they must ensure that all appropriate measures are taken to prevent contamination or deterioration of milk or milk products. Each Member State is to draw up a list of its approved milk treatment establishments and, in so far as they are concerned with intra-Community trade in heat-treated milk, a list of approved collection centres and standardisation centres, each such establishment or centre having an approval number. A list of these establishments should be sent to the other Member States and to the Commission. If an establishment ceases to fulfil the requirements of the directive, it should be withdrawn from the list of approved establishments.

Where a Member State considers that the provisions governing approval are not being observed in an establishment in another Member State, it should inform the competent authority of that State accordingly. Where the two Member States cannot reach agreement the matter should be referred to the Commission which may instruct an expert to go to the place where the consignment under dispute is stored and/or to the consignor's establishment in order to propose appropriate interim protective measures. These measures may include a ban on the importation of heat-treated milk from that establishment. A consignment of heat-treated milk must be accompanied by a health certificate which conforms to the model contained in an annex to the directive. The country of destination may check that all consignments of heat-treated milk are accompanied by this health certificate. Where irregularities are suspected, the country of destination may carry out checks to verify whether the requirements of the directive have been met. If, during a check, it is found that the milk does not comply with these requirements, the consignee or the consignor should be given the choice of having the milk returned to the country of exportation or having the milk destroyed. Where the marketing of the consignment is banned, the consignor or the consignee should be allowed to obtain the opinion of an expert.

In the event of an outbreak of foot and mouth disease in a Member State, another Member State may ban the importation of pasteurised milk which is obtained in an approved establishment which collects untreated milk in the infected area. If the disease becomes widespread, the Member State of destination may prohibit the importation into its territory of pasteurised milk and UHT milk from the whole of the territory of the Member State of exportation.

Supervision

Provision is made for regular inspections of approved establishments and on-the-spot checks by veterinary experts from the Commission. Member States should also ensure that production holdings undergo periodic inspections in order to ensure that hygiene requirements are fulfilled. Checks should be effected to detect any residues of substances having a pharmacological or hormonal action, and of antibiotics, pesticides, detergents and other substances which are harmful or which might alter the organoleptic characteristics of milk or make its consumption dangerous or harmful to human health. If the milk examined does not comply with the directive and, in particular, shows traces of residues which exceed permitted tolerances, the heat-treated milk should be excluded from intra-Community trade.

The Commission has proposed a regulation which will repeal Directive 85/397. The regulation will harmonise health rules on the production and placing on the market of heat-treated drinking milk by extending to national markets the rules on intra-Community trade laid down by Directive 85/397.

The Commission has also proposed a regulation harmonising the health rules applicable to the production and marketing of raw milk, milk for the manufacture of milk-based products and milk-based products (excluding heat-treated drinking milk). The annex to the proposed regulation lays down standards for cows' milk and for milk-based products and lays down conditions governing labelling. It is proposed that the regulation would not apply to the direct sale to the consumer by the producer of raw milk produced on his farm. All restrictions on the free movement of milk within the Community would be abolished.

Birds and bees

The Council has laid down or the Commission has proposed animal health rules applicable to cattle, swine, sheep and goats, equidae, poultry and hatching eggs, fish and fish products, rodents, semen of bulls and boars, bovine embryos, fresh meat, poultry meat, meat products, game meat and rabbit meat. The Commission has proposed a regulation laying down animal health requirements for the placing on the market in the

Community of animals and products of animal origin not specifically covered by the above-mentioned rules. The regulation would lay down health requirements relating to cage birds, fur animals, bees, monkeys and ungulates.

Swine fever

The measures in the White Paper amend several previous measures designed to render the Community free from classical swine fever. By virtue of Decision 87/489, the Council will decide on further measures which may be adopted by a qualified majority.

Financial aid

Under a directive of 1980, Community aid was granted to Member States for the implementation of a plan to eradicate classical swine fever. Decisions 87/230 and 87/488 increase the amount of aid available. The latter decision, in particular, provides for specific reimbursement to Member States of, for example, 50% of the costs incurred in respect of compensation to owners for the slaughter and destruction of infected pigs. In addition, Directive 87/487 provides that Member States which are not officially free of swine fever must prepare new plans for completing the eradication of the disease.

Protective measures

In 1964 the Council adopted a directive on animal health problems affecting intra-Community trade in cattle and swine and in 1972 a directive was adopted on health problems affecting intra-Community trade in fresh meat. These provided that live pigs and fresh pig meat must fulfil certain conditions as regards classical swine fever before being traded within the Community. As a result of national programmes to eradicate classical swine fever, some Member States have totally eradicated the disease and can claim to be officially free of classical swine fever. Decision 87/231 amends these directives and gives Member States which are officially free of classical swine fever the possibility of maintaining their status by restricting the entry of pigs and pig meat into their territory.

Directive 87/486 amends an earlier directive on measures to be applied in the event of an outbreak of swine fever. This lays down rules concerning the prohibition of pigs being transported by road, the prohibition on the use of specific immune-serum or sero-vaccination and the requirement that vaccines be produced under official control and conform to the provisions of the European Pharmacopoeia. Rules are also laid down on the preventative vaccination of pigs in an area close to a contaminated area, on the systematic vaccination of pigs, on the vaccination of pigs for production and on emergency vaccination.

Some Member States are still not officially free of swine fever. As a result, Directive 85/320 lays down further protective measures to be applied in intra-Community trade in live pigs. A protection zone with a radius of 3 km should be established around an infected holding for a period of 30 days where the disease is swine fever and with a radius of 2 km for 15 days where other diseases are involved. A Member State in whose territory African swine fever has been recorded within the previous twelve months should not allow the export of live pigs to other Member States. Where there is an outbreak of African swine fever in a Member State where the disease has not been recorded for at least twelve months, that Member State should ensure the immediate prohibition of export to the other Member States of live pigs from the part of its territory in which the disease has been recorded. An outbreak of the disease in a Member State that has an official fever free status will result in that status being suspended. This status may be restored after a minimum period of:

- three months after eradication if there has previously been no vaccination;
- six months after eradication and elimination of vaccinated pigs if there has been previous vaccination.

Similar protective rules concerning export bans are laid down by Directive 85/321 on pig meat products which have not undergone treatment to destroy the virus of the disease and Directive 85/322 on fresh pig meat.

African swine fever

African swine fever has been present in Portugal and Spain for many years and they have received financial aid to eradicate the disease so as to stop it spreading to other Member States. Decisions 86/649 and 86/650 require Portugal and Spain respectively to draw up reinforced plans for the eradication of African swine fever and the restructuring of pig farms so as to protect the health of their livestock. The decisions specify in some detail the measures to be taken. Financial assistance of an estimated 10 million ECU is available to Portugal and an estimated 42 million is available to Spain to cover the cost of their plans.

The Council has in the past adopted measures which define the types of treatment likely to destroy agents responsible for livestock diseases in meat products with a view to permitting intra-Community trade in such products. Directive 87/491 continues this approach by approving a new heat treatment for preparing pig meat products in Member States in which African Swine fever is prevalent.

Aujesky's disease

Under a proposed directive, Aujesky's disease would be included within the scope of previous directives on diseases affecting pig herds.

Foot-and-mouth disease

Directive 85/511 lays down minimum control measures to be applied in the event of outbreaks of foot and mouth disease. Any outbreak of foot and mouth must be immediately notified to the authorities so that an official investigation can take place and preventative measures can be carried out. As soon as a suspected outbreak is notified, restrictions on the movement of animals, milk, vehicles and persons should be imposed. If the disease is confirmed, all animals liable to catch the disease must be slaughtered. As a result of Directive 90/423 the use of foot and mouth vaccines is now prohibited, save in extreme cases where emergency vaccination may be used. A protection zone with a minimum radius of three kilometres and a surveillance zone with a minimum radius of ten kilometres should be established around the infected farm which may have the effect of restricting within those areas the movement of animals, artificial insemination and the holding of fairs and shows. Member States must ensure that animals can be traced to their original holding and that laboratory testing to detect the presence of foot and mouth disease is carried out by one of the national laboratories listed in Directive 85/511.

Brucellosis, tuberculosis and leucosis

Final eradication of brucellosis, tuberculosis and leucosis constitutes an essential prerequisite for the establishment, with regard to trade in beef cattle, of the internal market in bovine animals. Decision 87/58 supplements earlier Community measures for the eradication of these diseases. Spain and Portugal are required to prepare eradication plans and other Member States are required in so far as is necessary to prepare accelerated eradication plans. These national plans must be approved by the Commission and Community financial aid is available in respect of the cost of their implementation. When all the new accelerated eradication plans have been executed, the Commission will submit a general report to the Council on the results obtained, with a proposal for further harmonisation of national preventive measures, should this be necessary.

In respect of sheep and goats, Council Decision 90/242 introduces a Community financial measure for the eradication of brucellosis to encourage Member States to draw up plans for the eradication of the disease involving partial compensation to flock owners for the compulsory slaughter of contaminated stock.

Microbiological controls

Previous directives have laid down the hygiene conditions under which fresh meat and fresh poultry meat must be produced in slaughter houses and cutting plants. Directive 85/323 and Directive 85/324 improve the required hygiene conditions under which fresh meat and poultry meat are produced in slaughter houses and cutting plants by requiring proprietors to conduct microbiological analysis as a means of achieving an objective assessment of the standard of hygiene. The microbiological controls should cover utensils, fittings and machinery at all stages of production and, if necessary, products. Regular checks will be made by officials, including the Commission's veterinary experts, to verify the frequency and results of these controls.

Medical examination of personnel

Three measures, Directives 85/325, 85/326 and 85/327, introduce new requirements for persons employed in handling fresh meat, poultry meat or meat products respectively. Any person employed to work with, or handle, fresh meat, fresh poultry meat or meat products is required to show, by a medical certificate, that there is no impediment to such employment. This medical certificate should be renewed every year. Any person who is a possible source of contamination, in particular through pathogenic agents, is prohibited from working with or handling fresh meat, fresh poultry meat or meat products.

Meat inspection personnel

At present only official veterinarians may be appointed to supervise the hygiene requirements imposed by the directives on health problems affecting intra-Community trade in poultry meat. A proposed directive would make it possible for Member States to authorise other suitably qualified officials who are charged at present with the responsibility for supervision and inspection in their territory to be responsible for supervision of the hygiene requirements provided for in the directives. In the United Kingdom, for example, the environmental health officer would be recognised as having a qualification suitable to carry out these particular tasks. A second proposed directive provides that veterinarians should supervise the hygiene and certification of meat products and also that certain tasks could be carried out by non-veterinary personnel with certain approved qualifications.

Growth-promoting hormones

Directive 85/358 provides that controls on farm animals, the meat of such animals and the meat products obtained therefrom should be carried out to detect the presence of prohibited substances which are administered to animals for fattening purposes. Where there is a justified suspicion of infringement, provision is made for the identification of the animal and the farm of origin. Investigation may also be made at the manufacturing, handling, storage, transport, distribution or sales stages. If analysis reveals the presence of prohibited substances, the animals may not be placed on the market for human or animal consumption.

Under Directive 88/146 producers of products having a hormonal effect must keep a register detailing, in chronological order, quantities produced or acquired and those sold or used for the production of pharmaceutical and veterinary products. A list of products which may be authorised by the Member States for therapeutic use will be made. Member States must ensure that no animals treated with hormonal substances or meat from such animals are exported from their territory. There is also a ban on importation from third countries of animals or meat containing similar substances.

Residues

Differing national laws concerning the examination of animals and fresh meat for the presence of residues result in major obstacles in intra-Community trade in animals and meat. Directive 86/469 provides a common approach for detecting and limiting residues in meat and meat products. Member States must ensure that examination of animals, their excrement and body fluids and of tissues and fresh meat for the presence of residues is carried out in accordance with the directive. Residue is defined as 'residue of substances having a pharmacological action and of conversion products thereof and other substances transmitted to meat and which are likely to be dangerous to human health'. National plans for the examination of residues should be submitted to the Commission for approval. Moreover, veterinary experts from the Commission may make on-the-spot checks to ensure that the directive is being complied with.

Where samples reveal the presence of residues exceeding allowable levels, the competent authorities of the Member States should seek to identify the animal and farm of origin. The Commission should be informed where the results indicate the need for investigation into other Member States or where one Member State suspects that another is not complying with the directive. Within a reasonable time, it should appoint an expert to investigate the matter and, if it is found that the directive is not being complied with, appropriate action should be taken. An annex to the directive lists the residue groups involved and lays down rules for residue levels and the frequency of sampling.

Pesticides

The composition of animal feeding stuffs is regulated by a directive of 1974 which controls the presence in feeding stuffs of undesirable substances. These are substances which are either found naturally in feeding stuffs or are present as residues from processing which if present in excessive quantities can endanger human health. The directive identifies such substances and specifies their maximum permitted levels in particular feeding stuffs but expressly excluded pesticide residues from its field of application. The presence of pesticide residues in feeding stuffs may also entail risks for human health, since in general toxic substances or preparations with dangerous effects are involved. A few Member States have already laid down maximum permitted levels for certain pesticide residues, but by virtue of the fact that levels differ the free circulation of feeding stuffs within the Community is not ensured. Directive 87/519, therefore, fixes in respect of feeding stuffs maximum levels for a group of very persistent and harmful active substances which are used in pesticides, namely organochlorine compounds. Until a Community decision is taken to fix a maximum level for other pesticides, Member States may retain their own national levels. Directive 86/363 fixes maximum levels for organochlorine compounds in meat and meat products and milk and milk products, which must be observed when these products are put into circulation within the Community. Consequently, Member States cannot prevent the sale of these products on the grounds that they contain pesticide residues if the quantity of such residues does not exceed the maximum levels specified in the directive. Member States must provide for suitable control measures. For example, check sampling should be applied to fresh milk and frozen cream. The levels laid down may be reduced temporarily if they unexpectedly prove to be dangerous to human or animal health. The directive does not apply to products intended for exports to third countries.

Medicated feeding stuffs

In order to safeguard public health from any dangers arising from the use of medicated feeding stuffs for animals intended for food production, the Council has adopted Directive 90/167 covering the manufacture and placing on the market and use of medicated feeding stuffs in the Community.

In principle, medicated feeding stuffs would be manufactured under the same conditions as those applying to veterinary medicinal products. Since simple mixing is usually the main process in the manufacture of medicated feeding stuffs, only authorised pre-mixes can be used. Furthermore, the manufacture of medicated feeding stuffs is subject to specified conditions:

e.g., the manufacturer must have suitable and adequate premises, technical equipment, storage and inspection facilities for the various stages in the preparation of medicated feeding stuffs.

Medicated feeding stuffs must be placed on the market only in packages or containers sealed in such a way that, when the package is opened, the closure or seal is damaged and they cannot be reused. Where road tankers or similar containers are used to place medicated feeding stuffs on the market, these must be cleaned before any re-use in order to prevent any subsequent undesirable interaction or contamination. The packages or containers must be clearly marked 'Medicated Feeding Stuffs'. Member States must take all necessary measures to ensure that medicated feeding stuff cannot be placed on the market unless it has been manufactured in accordance with the directive. Moreover, Member States must ensure that medicated feeding stuffs are not supplied to stock farmers or holders of animals except on presentation of a prescription from a registered veterinarian and then only under certain conditions. An annex to the directive provides a model of a prescription for a medicated feeding stuff and another annex provides a model for the certificate which must accompany medicated feeding stuffs.

Additives in animal nutrition

A directive of 1970 provided that only certain listed additives could be incorporated in feeding stuffs. Directive 87/153 states that the dossiers which accompany every request for the inclusion of an additive or the new use of an additive in the list should be compiled in accordance with certain guidelines.

Zootechnical considerations

Member States have endeavoured to promote the production of livestock of a limited number of breeds meeting specific zootechnical standards. These different standards, which vary from one Member State to another, hinder intra-Community trade.

A directive of 1977 partially liberalised intra-Community trade in pure-bred breeding animals of the bovine species (e.g., bovines entered or registered and eligible for entry in a herd book with parents and grandparents so entered or registered). This directive provides that intra-Community trade in the semen and embryos of pure-bred breeding animals of the bovine species should not be restricted on zootechnical grounds. However, until the entry into force of Community provisions for the approval of pure-bred breeding animals of the bovine species, the approval of bulls to be used for artificial insemination and the use of semen and embryos were to remain subject to national law as long as this was non-discriminatory. As a result of this partial harmonisation, Member States could still require import licences for the importation of, for example, semen intended for the artificial insemination of cattle. Directive 87/328 introduces further harmonisation in the pedigree requirements of cattle and their semen for breeding purposes. The directive aims to prevent national provisions relating to the acceptance for breeding purposes of pure-bred breeding animals of the bovine species and their semen from impeding intra-Community trade. As a result, the directive provides that Member States should ensure that there is no restriction on the acceptance of pure-bred female animals of the bovine species for breeding purposes and the acceptance of pure-bred bulls for natural service. A Member State may not restrict or impede the acceptance for official testing of pure-bred bulls or the use of their semen within the limits of the quantities necessary for approved organisation to carry out such official tests and a Member State may not restrict or impede the acceptance for artificial insemination within its territory of pure-bred bulls or the use of their semen when those bulls have been accepted for artificial insemination in a Member State on the basis of tests which are laid down by Community law. The use of pure-race bulls and their semen should subject to identification of the bulls concerned by analysis of the blood group. Semen for intra-Community trade must be collected, treated and stored in an officially approved artificial insemination centre.

Harmonising rules are contained in Directive 88/661, Directive 90/119 and Directive 90/118 which have harmonised standards for breeding purebred breeding pigs and hybrid breeding pigs. Thus, Member States must ensure that intra-Community trade in such animals, their semen, ova and embryos are not restricted on zootechnical grounds.

Similar rules have been laid down for purebred breeding sheep and goats (Directive 89/361) and for equidae (Directive 90/427). Similar rules have also been proposed in respect of the marketing of purebred animals and their semen, ova and embryos, other than those of bovine, porcine, ovine, caprine and equine species.

PHYTOSANITARY CONTROLS

Abolition of frontier checks

Directive 77/93 on protective measures against the introduction into the Member States of harmful organisms of plant or plant products provided that only occasional official inspections can be carried out by the Member State of destination. According to the final sentence occasional inspections were deemed so if they were made on no more than one-third of the consignments introduced from a given Member State and were as evenly spread as possible over time and over all products. The production of a phyto-sanitary certificate was made a general requirement. Directive 90/168 provides that the 33% figure should be gradually reduced to zero by the time that Member States have brought into effect new checking arrangements in compliance with provisions intended for the completion of the internal market. The directive also amends the safeguard clause of Directive 77/93 by providing that the principal responsibility for any protective measure is with the Member State of origin. Under Directive 89/439 it is provided that Commission health inspectors may carry out phyto-sanitary checks thereby increasing the credibility of inspections made in the consignor Member State.

A proposed Council directive would further amend Directive 77/93 by abolishing plant health checks at Community internal frontiers. Checks would be made mandatory at the place of production and would extend to all relevant plants and plant products grown, produced, used or otherwise present there. All producers would have to be officially registered. If the results of the checks were satisfactory, instead of the phyto-sanitary certificate used in international trade, a conventional mark (plant passport), would be attached to the product to ensure its free movement throughout the Community. Plants originating in third countries would in principle be subjected to plant health controls at the Community external frontiers and if the checks proved satisfactory, would also be issued with a plant passport, ensuring free movement within the Community. The proposal envisages the repealing of Directive 77/93 and the adoption of a consolidated text.

Plant protection products

One of the most important methods of protecting plants and plant products is to use plant protection products, but the effect of these products may not be wholly favourable for plant production and their use may involve risks for man and the environment. This is because in the main they are toxic substances or preparations having dangerous effects, and in the case of certain products these risks are so great that their use must be restricted.

A directive of 1979 provided that Member States must ensure that plant protection products containing active substances should not be placed on the market or used. It has now been established that the use of ethylene oxide as a plant protection product, in particular for the fumigation of plants or plant products in storage, leaves residues in foodstuffs which may give rise to harmful effects on human or animal health. As a result, Directive 86/355 prohibits the marketing and use of ethylene oxide as a plant protection product. Directive 90/533 has added five more groups of prohibited substances.

National rules which govern the approval of plant protection products differ from one Member State to another, thus hindering intra-Community trade. A proposed directive would harmonise these provisions so as to achieve the free circulation of plant protection products in the Community (e.g., pesticides and other active substances intended to destroy organisms harmful to plants or to increase the life process of plants). Thus Member States must allow plant protection products on their territory if they have been accepted in accordance with the directive. To be accepted, plant protection products would have to meet the following requirements:

- their active substances were listed in accordance with the annex to the directive;
- they are sufficiently effective;
- they have no unacceptable effect on plants;
- they have no harmful effect on human or animal health;
- they have no unacceptably adverse influence on the environment;
- their preparation is registered before they are placed on the market.

Member States would be obliged to compile files on each active substance listed in the annex. Inclusion on the list would be for a maximum of ten years, renewable for a period of five. The annex to the directive also lays down the requirements which the dossier must satisfy when a Member State wishes an active substance to be listed. Application for acceptance of a plant protection product could be made by the manufacturer, the importer or the distributor, if the plant protection product was to be placed on the market in the first instance by the distributor. Every applicant would be required to have a permanent office within the Community. Member States would inform the other Member States and the Commission immediately in writing of each plant protection product which had been accepted in accordance with the directive, indicating the conditions and the period of validity of such acceptance and attaching a copy of the label under which the plant protection product is to be placed on the market. Member States must draw up an annual list of plant protection products accepted in its territory and communicate that list to the other Member States and the Commission. Member States would require that applicants for acceptance of a plant protection product submit with their application a dossier satisfying the requirements set out in the Annex.

The proposed directive also contains detailed provisions concerning packaging and labelling of EC accepted plant protection products. All packages would have to show clearly the trade name or the designation of the plant protection product, the name and address of the holder and the name and amount of each active substance etc. Member States will have to make suitable arrangements for plant protection products which have been placed on the market to be officially checked by sampling to see whether they comply with the requirements of the directive.

Certification of seeds

Under various previous directives, the Council harmonised national rules relating to the marketing of certain seeds and materials so as to allow only those which satisfy common Community standards. These directives apply to the marketing within the Community of beet seed, fodder plant seed, cereal seed, seed potatoes, seed of oil and fibre plants and vegetable seed. Seeds must not be placed on the market unless they have been certified in accordance with the conditions laid down in these directives. Directive 88/380 amends these directives by adding further species to their scope of application; for example, owing to their increased importance in the Community, rescue grass, Alaska brome grass, California bluebell, triticale, Chinese cabbage, industrial chicory and certain additional cereal species and sunflower. The directive also improves rules on seed labelling in order to provide better information for seed users.

Organisms harmful to plants or plant products

Directive 77/93 has been amended by Directive 85/574 which gives a detailed definition of certain terms used in connection with the term 'plants'. For example, living parts of plants should be considered to include fruit (in the botanical sense), vegetables, tubers, corms, bulbs, rhizomes, cut flowers, branches with foliage, cut trees retaining foliage and plant tissue cultures. The directive also provides that the botanical names of plants should be indicated in Latin characters on the phytosanitary certificate which would be invalidated if it contained uncertified alterations. Any copies of the certificate should only be issued with the indication 'copy' or 'duplicate' printed or stamped on the certificate. In respect of the introduction of plants and plant products from third countries, the certificates must contain information which is in accordance with the model certificate contained in the International Plant Protection Convention of 1951.

Further amendments to Directive 77/93 were made by Directive 88/572 which clarifies the definition of 'wood' and adopts new rules on import inspections. The protective measures against the introduction of harmful organisms concern wood only in so far as it retains all or part of its natural round surface, with or without bark, or as it is in the form of chips, particles, sawdust, woodwaste or scrap. Wood in the form of dunnage, spacers, pallets or packing material may also be covered. A detailed description of wood is also contained in an annex and corresponds to the definition of wood used for the purposes of the common customs tariff. In addition to the inspections already permitted under the 1976 directive, phytosanitary inspections may be made where they are necessary to check the identity of the declared plants and plant products. They will not be considered necessary where official sealing of their packaging or officially approved and supervised equivalent safeguards have been taken in the forwarding Member State to ensure their identity. Member States must ensure that the carrying out of permitted phytosanitary checks at the border is gradually transferred to the place of destination. Forwarding Member States must be informed where consignments have been intercepted.

Pesticide residues

One of the most important methods of protecting plants and plant products from the effect of harmful organisms and weeds is the use of chemical pesticides. However, a large number of these pesticides may have harmful effects on consumers. In order to deal with these dangers several Member States have already fixed maximum levels for certain residues in and on cereals. The differences which exist between Member States as regards the maximum permissible levels for pesticide residues creates barriers to intra-Community trade in cereals. Consequently, Directive 86/362 fixes maximum levels for certain active substances in cereals which must be observed when these products are put into circulation in the Community. As a result, Member States may not restrict the sale of certain cereals on the grounds that they contain pesticide residues if the quantity of such residues does not exceed the maximum levels specified in the directive. Member States should take all necessary measures to ensure, at least by check sampling, that the maximum levels are complied with. Where a Member State considers that a maximum level endangers human health, and therefore requires swift action to be taken, that Member State may temporarily reduce the level in its own territory. In such an event, the Member State should immediately notify the other Member States and the Commission. Cereals intended for export to third countries are not covered by the directive.

Similar measures have been laid down by Directive 90/642 which deals with the fixing of maximum levels for pesticide residues in and on certain products of plant origin, including fruit and vegetables. This brings a number of products such as potatoes and oilseeds within the scope of Community measures for the first time. The list of pesticide residues concerned and their maximum levels will be established by the Council acting by qualified majority on a proposal from the Commission. Directive 90/642, therefore, essentially constitutes a framework directive.

The marketing of vegetables

The Commission has proposed a regulation aimed at harmonising the quality and plant health standards applicable to young plants and propagating material, excluding seeds, marketed in the Member States to ensure that material meeting these standards can move freely throughout the Community. Suppliers of young plants and propagating material would have to comply with the requirements laid down in the annex to the regulation: records must be kept, certain harmful organisms could not be present on any of the vegetables, official inspections would take place and the plants would be accompanied by an official plant health statement. Young plants and propagation material which complied with the requirements and conditions of the regulation and the rules adopted for its implementation could not be subject to any marketing restrictions as regard suppliers' obligations, characteristics, plant health, growing medium, packaging, the arrangement for their examination, other than those laid down in a regulation. Member States could, however, impose stricter requirements on suppliers established in their own territory.

The marketing of ornamental plants

The Commission has proposed a regulation aimed at harmonising the quality of plant health standards which would be met by ornamental plants, propagating material (including seeds) and all ornamental plants marketed in the Member States so as to guarantee that the material could move freely within the Community. A schedule will be established for each genus or species containing the conditions with which nucleus stock (basic propagating material), or propagating stock, or certified plants must comply, in particular those relating to harmful organisms, to the growing crop and to the varietal identity and varietal purity. Furthermore, the suppliers of propagating material and ornamental plants would have to comply with the requirements laid down in the annex to the regulation; for example, they must keep detailed records of such material. Member States will be obliged to carry out tests etc. to ensure that the conditions are being complied with. Materials complying with the requirements of the regulation and the implementing rules will be able to move freely within the Community.

The marketing of organic plants

The Commission has proposed a regulation on organic production of agricultural products. A product will be regarded as organic, for example, where there are indications referring to farming without the use of synthetic chemical pesticides, soil conditioners or fertilisers. The production of such products would comply with at least the requirements of the annex to the regulation (e.g., relating to the control of pests, diseases and weeds). Member States would ensure that a regular inspection system is set up and that the products are properly labelled and advertised. Thus, Member States would not be able, on grounds relating to the method of production or the presentation of that method, prohibit or restrict the marketing of organic products that met the requirement of the regulation.

The marketing of fruit plants

The Commission has proposed a regulation aimed at harmonising the quality and plant health standards which would be met by fruit plants, by material used for propagating fruit plants and by fruit plants intended for fruit production so as to ensure satisfactory results in the cultivation of such plants and to guarantee free movement within the Community.

Suppliers of propagating material and fruit plants would have to comply with the requirements laid down in the annex to the regulation; i.e., they must keep detailed records of such plants. Such material would be certified in one of the following categories: nuclei (basic propagating material), propagating stock and certified plants - material would be graded either as virus-free or virus-tested. A schedule would be established for each species containing a list of the serious viruses and virus-like pathogens occurring in the Community. The regulation would lay down rules concerning separation and homogeneity of lots, packing, sealing and marking of the material. Material which complied with these requirements and conditions would be able to move freely throughout the Community. Compliance with Community standards would be attested by official certification following examination of the material concerned.

II. Control of Individuals

Introduction

While it is anticipated that in the completed internal market individuals should be entitled to move freely throughout the Community, present border controls prevent the exercise of that freedom considerably. Accordingly, the Commission has proposed certain measures aimed at removing many of the reasons justifying these border controls.

Tax-free and duty-free allowances for personal goods and certain other goods lessen the need for controls at borders which aim to combat tax evasion. The higher the threshold for these allowances, the more persons can benefit from them and the less is the need for frontier controls. At the end of 1992 it is planned that these thresholds would be lifted completely for intra-Community travel, so that there would be no remaining justification of a fiscal nature for internal frontier controls. In the mean time, the Commission's proposals aim at increasing the thresholds which already exist and at enlarging the scope of the exemptions.

A series of other proposals are intended to replace the need for physical frontier controls by tackling certain problems dealing with checks that need to be carried out for the protection of society. Proposals have been made on the easing of border controls and formalities and on the legislation on the acquisition and possession of arms. Other proposals still to be published concern the rights of third country nationals, refugees, drugs, national visa policies and extradition.

Tax-free and duty-free allowances

Directives specifying compulsory tax-free and duty-free allowances on movement within the internal market deal with personal allowances in international travel, small private consignments, the final importation of certain goods, the temporary importation of vehicles, and imports of personal property.

Personal allowances in international travel

Common rules on tax-free and duty-free allowances for individuals in international travel were established by Directive 69/169. These allowances are reviewed regularly to ensure that inflation does not erode their effect. Directives 85/348, 87/198, 88/664 and 89/194 gradually increased the previous thresholds. A further proposal for increases in tax-paid allowances in intra-Community travel has been made by the Commission. Presently, the amount of tax-free goods that may be imported at any one time by an individual is not to exceed 390 ECU, or 100 ECU in the case of a child under 15 years. Denmark and Greece may exclude from the exemption goods the unit value of which exceeds 340 ECU and 310 ECU, respectively, and Ireland may exclude goods costing more than 85 ECU. The Commission has proposed that the full allowances be increased as from 1 January 1992 to 1600 ECU for adults and 400 ECU for children.

Specific limited quantitative allowances are set out for tobacco products, alcoholic beverages, perfumes, coffee and tea. For instance, the Commission proposes to increase the personal allowance on cigarettes in intra-Community travel to 600 as from 1 January 1992. Again, derogations for specific items are allowed for Denmark, Greece and Ireland. However, on 1 January 1993 the Commission proposes to abolish all of these limits so as to provide for unlimited freedom.

Small consignments of a non-commercial character

Goods dispatched from a Member State in small consignments of a non-commercial character by a private person intended for another private person in another Member State are not subject to taxes or duties on importation into the latter country. This applies, by Directive 74/651, to consignments of goods which:

- have been acquired subject to taxation in the Community;
- are not intended for commercial use and appear from their nature and quantity to be intended solely for the personal or family use of the recipient;
- are not sent against payment of any kind by the recipient; and
- do not exceed a specified value.

This specified value has been amended to take account of the increase in the cost of living. Directive 88/663 set it at 110 ECU from 1 July 1989, with a derogation being allowed to Ireland of 85 ECU. These limits are inapplicable in the case of personal duty-free exemptions. Where the value of goods contained in a small consignment exceeds the specified amounts, turnover taxes or excise duties need not be applied if the total amount to be levied is less than 3 ECU.

Final importation of certain goods

Contrary to the general rule, value added tax and excise duties are not to be levied on the final importation of certain goods into a Member State. Some of the rules governing this exemption, which are set out in Directive 83/181, apply only to importation from outside of the Community while others apply also to imports from another Member State. Only the latter are relevant in the context of the completion of the internal market. Some minor amendments have been introduced by Directive 88/331.

Imports of goods of a total value not exceeding 10 ECU are exempt from tax. Exemption may also be granted for goods exceeding 10 ECU but not exceeding 22 ECU. This exemption does not apply to alcoholic products, perfumes, toilet waters, tobacco or tobacco products. Other amendments apply to reference substances for the quality control of medical products, decorations and awards, advertising material, certain official publications, and fuels and lubricants in land motor vehicles.

Temporary importation of means of transport

Temporary importation of means of transport is exempt from turnover taxes and excise duty by virtue of Directive 83/182 as long as it has been acquired or imported in accordance with the general conditions of taxation in force in a Member State. This applies to motor vehicles, caravans, pleasure boats, private aircraft, bicycles, tricycles and saddle-horses. The exemption does not apply to commercial vehicles. This directive does not allow for residents of the Member State of importation to use an imported vehicle which has been exempted. The Commission has therefore proposed certain amendments.

Means of transport for private use

Where a vehicle is imported, it is exempt from tax for a period of not more than six months in any twelve months, provided that

- the individual importing the vehicle has his normal residence in another Member State and uses the vehicle for his private use;
- the vehicle is not disposed of or hired out in the Member State of temporary importation or lent to a resident of that State. Private vehicles belonging to a car-hire firm having its head office in the

Community may be re-hired to non-residents with a view to being re-exported if they are in the country as a result of a hire contract which ended in that country. They may also be returned by an employee of the firm to the Member State where they were originally hired, even if such employee is resident in the State of temporary importation.

It is proposed that the period of exemption would be extended to nine months in twelve when a person imports into the Member State where he has his occupational ties a private vehicle which is registered in the Member State where he has his normal residence. The prohibition on disposing of the car would be abolished and the provisions on car-hire would be extended to include hiring to residents. Where a vehicle was re-hired to a resident, it would have to be re-exported within eight days. Also, a resident would be entitled to use a vehicle registered in another Member State during periods when the individual who imported the vehicle is in the Member State of temporary importation.

Private vehicles for business use

A private vehicle imported temporarily for business use is exempt from tax, provided that:

- the individual importing the vehicle has his normal residence in another Member State and does not use the vehicle within the Member State of temporary importation in order to carry passengers for hire or material reward of any kind, or for the industrial or commercial transport of goods, whether for reward or not;
- the vehicle is not disposed of, hired out or lent in the Member State of temporary importation.

In certain cases involving business use, the period of exemption is increased to seven months in twelve.

Again, it is proposed that the prohibition on disposal be abolished. A private vehicle registered in one Member State which is temporarily imported by an individual who is resident in another Member State would be exempt from tax where it belonged to or was hired by an undertaking established in the State where it was registered. Members of the individual's family would also be entitled to use the vehicle in the Member State of temporary importation when the individual was in that State. The exemption relating to business use would not be subject to any time limit.

Travel to work

The exemption from tax already applies where a private vehicle is registered in the country of normal residence of the user and is used regularly for the journey from his residence to his place of work in an undertaking in another Member State. This exemption is not subject to any time limit.

Students

In the case of a student, exemption from tax applies where the vehicle is used in another Member State where the student is residing for the sole purpose of pursuing his studies. It is proposed that the vehicle might also be used by the student's spouse or the companion who has a stable relationship with the student where the legislation of the Member State applies this notion.

Vehicle breakdown

It is proposed that exemption from tax will apply where a resident of one Member State, following the temporary immobilisation of his own vehicle as a result of a breakdown or accident in another Member State, imports a private vehicle registered in the latter State. Such exemption would apply for the period during which the vehicle was being repaired up to a maximum of two months, unless the vehicle was retained in connection with police investigations.

Car-hire

In addition to the provisions on car-hire already stated, it is proposed that exemption for up to eight days would apply where a resident used a private vehicle hired from a car-hire firm and which is registered in another Member State.

Vehicles which have been irretrievably damaged

It is proposed that outright exemption would be granted for private vehicles registered in a Member State which have been badly damaged as a result of a duly proven accident or criminal or malicious act which occurred within the Member State into which they were temporarily imported. Outright exemption would also be granted where a private vehicle registered in a Member State has been immobilised as a result of a serious breakdown where the cost of the requisite repairs exceeds its market value. In order to qualify for exemption, the vehicle would have to be disposed of to a taxable person with a view to its being scrapped or demolished.

Permanent imports of personal property

Permanent imports of personal property, i.e., property for the personal use of the persons concerned or for the needs of their household, are exempt from turnover taxes and excise duties by Directive 83/183. Certain amendments to this were incorporated by Directive 89/604 to harmonise and relax certain formalities necessary for the grant of the exemption pending the abolition of fiscal frontiers.

Conditions for exemption

The exemption is granted for property which has been acquired under the general conditions of taxation in force in a Member State as long as the person concerned has had the actual use of the property before the change of residence is effected. In the case of motor vehicles (including their trailers), caravans, mobile homes, pleasure boats and private aircraft, Member States may require that the person concerned should have had the use of them for a period of at least six months before the change of residence. Such motor vehicles, etc., may not be disposed of, hired out or lent during the twelve months subsequent to importation except in circumstances duly justified to the satisfaction of the competent authorities of the Member State of importation. The duty-free goods covered by Directive 69/169 may be imported in quantities up to four times the limits set out above, except in the case of tobacco products.

Formalities on the transfer of normal residence

The exemption is granted in respect of personal property imported by a private individual when transferring his normal residence. The grant of the exemption is subject only to the drawing up of an inventory of goods accompanied, if required, by a declaration of transfer of residence. No reference to value may be demanded on the inventory. The last of the property must be imported not later than twelve months after the transfer of normal residence. Where the property is imported in a number of operations within this period, only on the occasion of the first importation may the Member State of importation require that a complete inventory be produced.

Secondary residences

The exemption is granted on the importation of property for a secondary residence provided that the property has actually been in the possession of the person concerned and that he has had the use of it before establishment of the secondary residence. This is also the case where such a residence has been relinquished and the property is imported to the normal residence or to another secondary residence.

Importation of property on marriage

On marrying, a person is entitled to exemption from turnover taxes and excise duties when importing into the Member State to which he intends to transfer his normal residence personal property which he acquired or which came into his possession provided that the importation takes place during the period commencing two months before the marriage date envisaged and ending four months after the actual marriage date.

Exemption is also granted in respect of presents customarily given on the occasion of a marriage which are sent to a private person by persons having their normal residence in another Member State. Each present may have a value up to 350 ECU, although any Member State may increase this limit to 1400 ECU.

Easing of border controls and formalities for Community nationals

The Commission has proposed a directive on the first stage of the abolition by 1992 of controls and formalities to which nationals of the Member States may be subjected at intra-Community borders. This applies to nationals of the Member States crossing an intra-Community border who comply with the provisions concerning both the movement of persons and the movement of goods and in particular as regards the value or quantities of goods admitted free of taxes. The controls and formalities covered are all those applicable to the intra-Community movement of persons and goods carried by them, including currency but excluding any carriage of a commercial nature.

Spot checks

Member States would be obliged to take the measures necessary for the controls and formalities applicable to those persons presenting themselves at an inter-State border to be operated according to the principle of free passage, whatever the mode of transport used. This principle of free passage would also apply to those persons presenting themselves on leaving a Member State in order to enter another Member State. However, security checks in airports are not to be affected. The proposed directive would not prevent Member States from carrying out spot checks on Community nationals in so far as such checks, to be carried out either at the border crossing or within a frontier zone of 15km from the border, affected only a minimal proportion of the persons for each border crossing point. More intensive controls of a temporary nature would be allowed in exceptional and specific cases, in particular for security purposes. This should not lead to an increase in the number of mobile units since that would be equivalent to relocating rather than abolishing border controls.

Crossing of borders by road

Where a person wished to cross a border by road in a private vehicle, the principle of free passage would mean that the vehicle should cross the border at a reduced speed in order to enable the authorities responsible for the border controls to carry out a simple visual check without requiring the vehicle to stop, except in specific cases. The same principle should apply to persons travelling on foot or by any other mode of transport. Signs should clearly indicate in good time the local speed restrictions. As far as possible, signs bearing the inscription 'Customs' are to be removed at border crossing points.

In order to facilitate free passage, Member States, wherever it was technically possible, would have to set up two separate channels at borders, one being for those who benefited from the rights of free passage and the other for all other travellers. Community nationals who benefited from these rights would show a disc bearing the letter E on a green background, which would be displayed, for instance, on a car windscreen, and which would be equivalent to a declaration by the driver of the vehicle that all the persons travelling with him were Community nationals to whom the rights of free passage pertained. This disc would be supplied free of charge by the Member States.

In the event of a vehicle being subjected to border controls, the necessary arrangements would have to be made so that the passage of the following vehicles is not hampered. Where possible, only one checkpoint for the two adjacent Member States should be allowed in each direction of traffic.

Airports and ports

Where persons present themselves at an airport or port on arrival in another Member State, the principle of free passage would allow them to cross the border without controls. Airports and ports open to international traffic and having a certain level of traffic would establish channels designated by green or red signs. The selection of the green channel by a traveller would be equivalent to a declaration that the principle of free passage is to apply in his case.

International trains and coaches and other travellers

Private individuals crossing a border between two Member States on board international trains or coaches and who benefit from the principle of free passage would be allowed to cross without being controlled. For such persons and for all other persons not covered by the above specific cases, the mere presentation, shut, by the person concerned, at his own initiative, of his passport or national identity card issued by a Member State, would, in the absence of any other indication by him, be equivalent to a declaration that he was entitled to benefit from the principle of free passage.

Acquisitions and possession of firearms

A proposal has been made for a directive on the control of the acquisition and possession of arms. This will not preclude Member States from implementing more stringent laws on weapons. However, Member States might prohibit residents from purchasing or acquiring a weapon in another Member State only where they prohibited the purchase or acquisition of such a weapon in their own territory. The possession of weapons by persons passing from one Member State to another would be prohibited, except in the circumstances allowed by the proposed directive. The proposed directive envisaged the adoption of a European firearms pass which would be issued to a person lawfully in possession of a firearm and which would be valid for five years. It is proposed that Member States would abstain from carrying out other controls on the possession of weapons at internal Community frontiers from 31 December, 1992, at the latest. Controls on the possession of weapons at external frontiers would be intensified and further controls would be allowed at the time of boarding a means of transport.

Sale of weapons and firearms

Any person whose trade or business consisted wholly or partly in the manufacture, sale, purchase, exchange, hiring out, repair or conversion of weapons would be required to be authorised to do so. Each such dealer would be required to keep a register in which information concerning all firearms received or disposed of by him was recorded, including such particulars as enable the weapon to be identified, such as the type, make, model, calibre and serial number thereof, and the names and address of the supplier and the person acquiring the weapons.

Firearms would be classified as Categories A, B, C and D. Category A firearms would be prohibited. Category B firearms could be sold only to authorised persons who would have to be at least 18 years old, have the necessary mental and physical capacity and be not likely to be a danger to public order or public safety. No one could be in possession in a Member State of a firearm classified in Category C which that State had not made subject to authorisation unless he had declared it to the authorities of that State. It would be unlawful to hand over a firearm to a person resident in another Member State unless that person was authorised to receive it in that country. No ammunition for a firearm could be handed over to a non-resident unless that person established by producing a European firearms pass that he lawfully possessed a weapon of a calibre for which that ammunition was intended.

Transfer of firearms out of a Member State

Firearms would be allowed to be transferred from one Member State to another or to a third country only in accordance with the procedure set out in the proposed directive. Before transferring the firearms to another Member State or to a third country, the exporter would have to supply the following particulars to the Member State in which the firearm was situated:

- the names and addresses of the person selling or disposing of the firearm and of the person purchasing or acquiring it or, where appropriate, of the owner;

- the address to which the firearm was to be sent;
- the number of firearms to be sent;
- the particulars enabling the firearm to be identified;
- the means of transfer;
- the date of departure and the estimated date of arrival.

Where the transfer was authorised, a licence incorporating all these particulars would be issued by the Member State and would accompany the firearm until it reached its destination. Each Member State might supply the others with a list of firearms whose transfer to its territory could not be authorised without its prior consent. As an alternative to the individual licence, Member States might grant a general licence to dealers, valid for up to three years, authorising the transfer of firearms to another territory. A certified copy of such a licence would have to accompany the firearm until it reached its destination.

Where a firearm was to be imported from a third country, the dealer would have to supply the Member State of importation with all the particulars. A licence would then be granted which would accompany the firearm until it reached its destination.

Possession of firearms while travelling

The same procedure as applies when transferring firearms out of a Member State would be followed in respect of possession of a firearm in the course of travel between two or more Member States. Alternatively, a person carrying arms from one Member State to another could be authorised in both those States. Hunters and marksmen could, without prior authorisation, be in possession of a Category C or D firearm with a view to engaging in hunting or taking part in a target-shooting event provided that they possessed a European firearms pass for each gun and could prove the reason for their journey.

Part Two

The Removal of Technical Barriers

I. Free Movement of Goods
II. Public Procurement
III. Free Movement for Labour and the Professions
IV. Common Market for Services
1. Financial Services
2. Transport
3. New Technologies and Services

V. Creation of Suitable Conditions for Industrial Cooperation
1. Company Law
2. Intellectual and Industrial Property
3. Taxation

I. Free Movement of Goods

Removal of remaining barriers to trade

Restrictions on the import or export of goods in intra-Community trade are prohibited, except in limited circumstances. This is based on the reasoning that the common market involves the mutual acceptance of goods throughout the Community. However, pending the approximation of various national laws affecting the production of goods, certain interests or values have to be protected. This results, in some cases, in permitting a Member State to refuse to allow the importation or sale of certain goods from other Member States.

In order to limit the circumstances in which these exceptions might apply, the Council issues directives for the approximation of national laws, regulations and administrative practices. In previous years, the policy had largely been to harmonise standards throughout the Community by detailed legislation. This led to many measures not being adopted since it was impossible in a number of areas to obtain agreement on common standards. A new standardisation policy, based on mutual recognition of standards rather than total harmonisation, was adopted by the Council in May 1985. Under this policy, essential safety requirements are laid down. As long as the relevant products conform with these requirements, they may be marketed throughout the Community. Measures in the programme to complete the internal market which follow this policy include those dealing with machinery, simple pressure vessels, personal protective equipment, toys and electromagnetic compatibility.

Other measures which harmonise the laws applicable to goods include some relating to motor vehicles, tractors, food products, pharmaceuticals, chemicals products, construction products and cosmetics. Also included are measures dealing with noise emissions, fire safety in hotels, good laboratory practice and consumer protection and safety.

New approach in technical harmonisation and standards policy

The Council adopted the following principles for a European standardisation policy:

- agreement by the Member States to keep a constant check on the technical regulations so as to withdraw those which are obsolete or unnecessary;
- agreement by the Member States to ensure the mutual recognition of the results of tests and the establishment, where necessary, of harmonised rules as regards the operation of certification bodies;
- agreement to early Community consultation at an appropriate level where major national regulatory initiatives or procedures might have adverse repercussions on the operation of the internal market;
- extension of the Community practice of entrusting the task of defining the technical characteristics of products to European or national standards where the conditions necessary for this purpose, particularly as regards health protection and safety, are fulfilled;
- a very rapid strengthening of the capacity to standardise, preferably at European level, with a view to facilitating harmonisation of legislation by the Community and industrial development, particularly in the field of new technologies, since this could in specific circumstances involve the Community in introducing new procedures to improve the drawing up of standards.

Harmonisation is limited to the adoption of directives setting out essential safety requirements (or other requirements in the general interest) with which products put on the market must conform and which should therefore enjoy free movement throughout the Community. The task of drawing up the technical specifications needed for the production and sale of products conforming to these essential requirements is entrusted to standardisation bodies. Once these standards have been recognised, national authorities are obliged to accept that products manufactured in conformity with them are presumed to conform to the essential requirements of the directive. Since the technical specifications are not mandatory, but maintain their status as voluntary standards, the producer has the choice of not manufacturing in conformity with the standards. In this event, he has an obligation to prove that his products conform to the essential requirements of the directive.

Standards will continue to be adopted at Community level and national level. The national standards must be approved by the Commission which is assisted by a standing committee composed of officials from national administrations. Community standards will gradually replace the national standards, the competent standardisation bodies at Community level being CEN (Comité Europeén de la Normalisation) and CENELEC (Comité Européen de la Normalisation Electrotechnique). For specific sectors of industrial activity other European bodies might be involved. All of these bodies are governed by their own internal rules, although the drafting and introduction of the harmonised standards are subject to guidelines agreed with the Commission. These guidelines include rules on the association of public authorities and interested parties, such as consumers bodies, trade associations and employees' and employers' organisations.

The harmonising directives have a common format covering general rules about placing the product on the market, essential safety requirements, the obligation on Member States to respect the free movement of goods, proof of conformity, management of the lists of standards, safeguard clauses and means of attestation of conformity.

Products which conform with the recognised standards, which will be published in the Official Journal of the European Communities, will be entitled to carry a means of attestation (the EC mark) declaring that they are in conformity with these standards. Where the manufacturer has not applied for a standard, his products will still be entitled to carry the attestation marks if he otherwise has satisfied the essential safety requirements. The means of attestation commonly used is a certificate or mark of conformity, the result of tests carried out, or a declaration of conformity issued by the manufacturer or his agent. Decision 90/683 sets out the various procedures for conformity assessment.

Where a Member State or the Commission decides that a standard is no longer satisfactory for the purposes for which it is required, the procedure for setting standards may be reopened. Also, where a Member State finds that a product might compromise the safety of individuals, domestic animals or property, it must take all appropriate measures to withdraw that product or prohibit its placing on the market or to restrict its free movement even if it is accompanied by a means of attestation. It must then inform the Commission of its objections to the product. If the complaint is substantiated, the Commission should inform the other Member States to prevent the product from being placed on the market.

The provision of information in the field of technical standards and regulations

Directive 83/189 lays down a procedure for the provision of information in the field of technical standards and information by which Member States must inform the Commission of new standards and regulations prior to their enactment. The scope of this directive has been extended by Directive 88/182 so as to cover industrially manufactured products and any agricultural product. If the Commission submits a proposal for a directive or a regulation covering a particular subject, the Member States may not adopt technical regulations on that subject for a period of twelve months from the date of its submission.

Machinery

Directive 89/392 as amended by Directive 91/368 on the approximation of the laws relating to machinery applies to any assembly of mechanically linked parts or components, at least one of which moves. Certain equipment is excluded from the scope of this proposal, but the Commission estimates that at least half of all machines in the Community are covered by it. The excluded sectors include mobile equipment, lifting equipment, machinery whose only power source is directly applied manual effort, machinery designed and constructed for medical use, special equipment for use in fairgrounds and amusement parks and all machinery which is covered by a directive containing technical design and construction requirements relating to health and safety. Separate directives are to apply to many or all of these excluded sectors.

The manufacturer, or his authorised representative in the Community, in order to certify the conformity of machinery to the essential safety requirements in the directive must draw up a declaration including the following information:

- name and address of the manufacturer or his authorised representative in the Community;
- description of the machinery;
- all relevant provisions complied with by the machinery;
- the relevant harmonised or national technical standards.

The manufacturer would then be entitled to place the EC mark on the machinery. The safety requirements listed in the annexes to the directive deal with such aspects of safety as reliability of controls, protection against mechanical and other hazards, warning devices and maintenance.

The Commission intends to strengthen the content of Directive 89/392 and has already produced a proposal for a directive to amend it in certain respects, in particular in relation to the health and safety requirements of equipment entailing specific risks due either to its mobility or its ability to lift loads.

Mobile machinery

A separate directive has been proposed for the approximation of the laws dealing with mobile machinery. This covers machinery which operates in working areas and whose operation requires either mobility while working, or continuous or semi-continuous movement between a succession of fixed working points. The machinery may be self-propelled or towed, pushed or carried by other mobile machinery or tractors. The proposed directive excludes from its ambit lifting machinery, mobile machinery whose only power source is directly applied manual effort, means of transport, machinery with a medical usage, and any machinery covered by other directives relating to essential safety requirements.

Special safety requirements which are particular to this type of machinery are set out in the proposed directive. For instance, the driving position must be so designed and constructed that all manoeuvres necessary for the operation of the machinery can be performed by the driver from the driving position without risk or excessive fatigue. The machinery would have to be so designed that it was sufficiently stable, under the intended operating conditions, without risk of overturning, falling or unforeseeable movement.

Simple pressure vessels

Directive 87/404 on the harmonisation of the laws relating to simple pressure vessels manufactured in series applies to any welded vessel subjected to an internal gauge pressure greater than 0.5 bar which is intended to contain air or nitrogen and which is not intended to be fired. The parts and assemblies contributing to the strength of the vessel under pressure must be made either of non-alloy quality steel or of non-alloy aluminium or non-age hardening aluminium alloys. The maximum working pressure of the vessel may not exceed 30 bar and the product of that pressure and the capacity of the vessel (PS.V) may not exceed 10,000 bar/litre. Also the minimum working temperature must be no lower than -50°C and the maximum working temperature must not be higher than 300°C for steel and 100°C for aluminium or aluminium alloy vessels. The following vessels are excluded from the scope of the directive:

- vessels specifically designed for nuclear use, failure of which may cause an emission of radioactivity;
- vessels specifically intended for installation in or the propulsion of ships and aircraft;
- fire extinguishers.

Vessels in respect of which the PS.V exceeds 50 bar/litre must satisfy the essential safety requirements set out in the directive. Those vessels with a lower PS.V must be manufactured in accordance with sound engineering practice in one of the Member States.

The manufacturer must send to the appropriate national authority a document which includes:

- a description of the means of manufacture and checking appropriate to the construction of the vessels;
- an inspection document describing the appropriate examinations and tests to be carried out during manufacture, together with the procedures therefor and the frequency with which they are to be performed;
- an undertaking to carry out the examinations and tests in accordance with the inspection document and to have a hydrostatic test or a pneumatic test carried out on each vessel manufactured at a test pressure equal to 1.5 times the design pressure;
- the addresses of the places of manufacture and storage and the date on which manufacture is to commence.

In addition, when PS.V exceeds 200 bar/litre, manufacturers must authorise access to the places of manufacture and storage for inspection purposes by the competent authority and must supply it with all the necessary information, in particular, the design and manufacturing schedule, the inspection report, the EC type examination certificate or certificate of adequacy and a report on the examinations and tests carried out.

Personal protective equipment

Directive 89/686 on the approximation of the laws relating to personal protective equipment (PPE) applies to any device or appliance designed to be worn or held by an individual for protection against one or more safety and health hazards. It also covers units constituted by several devices or appliances which have been integrally combined by the manufacturer for the protection of an individual against one or more potentially serious risks, protective devices or appliances combined with personal non-protective equipment and interchangeable PPE components which are essential to its satisfactory functioning. Any system marketed in conjunction with PPE for its connection to an external device shall be regarded as an integral part of that equipment even if the system is not intended to be worn or held permanently by the user for the entire period of risk exposure. Certain specified PPE is excluded from the scope of the directive, including PPE designed and manufactured for use by the armed forces or in the maintenance of law and order, PPE for private use in bad weather and PPE for self-defence.

Before marketing a PPE model, the manufacturer would have to assemble certain documentation for submission, if necessary, to the competent authorities. In most cases, prior to the series production of PPE, the manufacturer or his representative would have to submit a model for EC type-examination. This is not required in the case of PPE models of simple design where the user can himself assess the level of protection provided against the minimal risks concerned which can be safely identified in good time owing to the gradual nature of their effects. This category includes PPE such as gardening gloves, gloves affording protection against diluted detergents and certain seasonal clothing or footwear.

Series-manufactured PPE is subject to the EC quality control procedure in the case of PPE of complex design intended to protect the user against mortal danger, the immediate effects of which cannot be identified in sufficient time. Included in this category are certain respiratory devices, equipment providing limited protection against chemical attack or against ionising radiation, emergency equipment for use in high-temperature environments in which the atmospheric temperature is liable to exceed 100°C and which may or may not be characterised by the presence of flames or the projection of large amounts of molten material, and emergency equipment for use in low-temperature environments in which the atmospheric temperature is liable to be below -50°C.

Safety of toys

Directive 88/378 on the approximation of laws concerning the safety of toys defines a toy as any product or material designed or clearly intended for use in play by children of less than 14 years of age. Toys may be marketed only if they do not jeopardise the safety or health of users or third parties when they are used as intended or in a foreseeable way, bearing in mind the normal behaviour of children. The following are not covered by this directive:

- Christmas decorations;
- detailed scale models for adult collectors;
- equipment intended to be used collectively in playgrounds;
- sports equipment;
- aquatic equipment intended to be used in deep water;
- folk dolls and decorative dolls and other similar articles for adult collectors;
- 'professional' toys installed in public places (shopping centres, stations, etc.);
- puzzles with more than 500 pieces or without picture intended for specialists;
- air guns and air pistols;
- fireworks, including percussion caps;
- slings and catapults;
- sets of darts with metallic points;
- electric ovens, irons or other functional products operated at a nominal voltage exceeding 24 volts;

- products containing heating elements intended for use under the supervision of an adult in a teaching context;
- vehicles with combustion engines;
- toy steam engines;
- bicycles designed for sport or for travel on the public highway;
- video toys that can be connected to a video screen, operated at a nominal voltage exceeding 24 volts;
- babies' dummies;
- faithful reproduction of real firearms;
- fashion jewellery for children.

The essential safety requirements for toys are related to risks which are connected with the design, construction or composition of the toy or which are inherent in the use of the toy and cannot be completely eliminated by modifying the toy's construction and composition without altering its function or depriving it of its essential functions. The degree of risk present in the use of a toy must be commensurate with the ability of the users, and where appropriate their supervisors, to cope with it. This applies in particular to toys which, by virtue of their functions, dimensions and characteristics, are intended for use by children of under 36 months. A minimum age for users of toys and/or the need to ensure that they are used only under adult supervision must be specified where appropriate. Labels on toys and/or their packaging and the instructions for use which accompany them must draw the attention of users or their supervisors fully and effectively to the risks involved in using them and to the ways of avoiding such risks. Particular rules are laid down regarding physical and mechanical properties, flammability, chemical properties, electrical properties, hygiene and radioactivity.

Toys which do not conform in whole or in part with the harmonised standards must be subjected first to the EC type examination procedure in order to certify that they comply with the essential safety requirements. This procedure requires the submission to the competent authority of:

- a description of the toy together with a model;
- the name and address of the manufacturer or of his authorised representative and the place of manufacture of the toy;
- comprehensive manufacturing and design data.

Electromagnetic compatibility

Electric or electronic appliances together with equipment and installations containing electrical or electronic components which are liable to cause electromagnetic disturbance are covered by Directive 89/336 on the approximation of the laws relating to electromagnetic compatibility. The electromagnetic disturbance generated by this apparatus must not exceed a level which prevents radio and telecommunications equipment or other apparatus from operating as intended and the apparatus must have an adequate level of intrinsic immunity to electromagnetic disturbance. Special measures may be taken by the national authorities in order to protect reception in the case of public-service stations or emergency operations.

Active implantable medical devices

Directive 90/385 on the approximation of the laws relating to active implantable medical devices applies to any instrument, apparatus, device material or other article relying for its functioning on a source of electrical energy which is intended to be wholly or partially introduced into the human body permanently. The devices must be designed and manufactured in such a way that their use does not compromise the clinical condition or safety of the patient and they must not present any risk to the person implanting them or to any other person. Any side effects or undesirable conditions must constitute acceptable risks when weighed against the intended performance.

Appliances burning gaseous fuels

Directive 90/396 on the approximation of laws relating to appliances burning gaseous fuels deals with appliances burning gaseous fuels used for cooking, heating, hot water production, refrigeration, lighting or washing and having a normal water temperature not greater than 105 degrees. Appliances specifically designed for use in industrial processes carried out on industrial premises are excluded. The appliances covered by the directive must be so designed as to operate safely and present no danger to persons, domestic animals or property when normally used. When placed on the market, they must be accompanied by technical instructions intended for the installer, instructions for use and servicing intended by the user and they must bear all appropriate warnings. This information must be in the language of the country into which the appliance is to be sold. The warning notices must clearly state the type of gas used, the gas supply pressure and any restrictions on use, in particular any restriction whereby the appliance must be installed only in areas where the is sufficient ventilation. Materials must be appropriate for their intended purpose and must withstand the technical, chemical and thermal conditions to which they will foreseeably be subjected.

Non-automatic weighing instruments

Nationals laws relating to non-automatic weighing instruments are harmonised by Directive 90/384. This deals with any weighing instrument requiring the intervention of an operator during weighing. Various design and construction requirements are set out, such as that the indication of the weighing results and other weight values must be accurate, unambiguous and non-misleading.

Motor vehicles

So that the free movement of motor vehicles throughout the common market should be assured, a system of EC type approval was instituted by Directive 70/156. A vehicle manufactured in one Member State may not be refused entry into and use in another Member State on the grounds of its construction or functioning if a model of it has been granted EC type approval. The type approval certificate is granted if the vehicle meets the requirements of any other directives setting out technical standards. Member States are required to verify that they have adequate arrangements to ensure that vehicles in production conform to the approved type. Various amendments have been made to Directive 70/156 by Directive 87/358.

Engines

Specific technical standards which must be complied with in the manufacture of engines include those relating to:

- maximum net power and torque;
- fuel tanks and reserve fuel tanks;
- interference suppressor complying with the technical requirements adopted by the United Nations Economic Committee for Europe;
- sound level and silencers;
- air pollution;
- fuel consumption.

Directive 88/76 introduced a large number of amendments to these requirements in respect of measures to be taken against air pollution by gases from the engines of motor vehicles. From 1 July 1988, no Member State may, on grounds relating to air pollution by gases from an engine or to engine fuel requirements, refuse to grant type approval to or prohibit the entry into service of motor vehicles which comply with the new requirements.

Member States may, from 1 October 1988, in the case of engines over two litres, from 1 October 1990, in the case of engines below 1.4 litres, and from 1 October 1991, in the case of other engines, refuse type approval where the engine emits gaseous pollutants at levels which do not comply with the directive. In the case of types of vehicles which have an engine capacity between 1.4 and 2 litres and which are fitted with compression ignition engines of the direct-injection type, the relevant date is 1 October 1994. Also Member States may prohibit the entry into service of such vehicles from 1 October 1989, in the case of engines over two litres, from 1 October 1991, in the case of engines below 1.4 litres, from 1 October 1993, in the case of engines between 1.4 and 2 litres, and from 1 October 1996, where engines in the latter case are fitted with compressor engines of the direct–injection type. Type approval may be refused, from 1 October 1988, for 2 litre vehicles and from 1 October 1990, for other types, where the vehicle is fitted with a positive ignition engine whose fuel requirements do not meet the provisions of the directive. Such vehicles may be prohibited from entry into service from 1 October 1990. Further special provision in relation to engines under 1.4 litres are proposed by the Commission.

Directive 88/77 provides that from 1 July 1988, no Member State may, on grounds related to the gaseous pollutants emitted from an engine, refuse type approval, registration, sale, entry into service or use of new diesel engines or vehicles fitted with them where the requirements of the directive are met. If these requirements are not met, type approval may be refused, except, until 30 September 1990, in the case where the engine is of a type which has already been approved.

Specific provisions were deemed necessary to extend the laws relating to air pollution which already applied to engines in motor vehicles to diesel engines. Directive 70/220 laid down limit values for emissions of carbon monoxide and unburnt hydrocarbons. Directive 88/436 extends the scope of this directive to particulate pollutant emissions from diesel engines. Where the requirements are not met, Member States may refuse type approval from 1 October 1989, except in the case of direct-injection engines where the date is postponed until 1 October 1994. Member States may prohibit the entry into service of motor vehicles equipped with engines which fail to comply with the directive from 1 October 1990, and from 1 October 1996 in the case of direct-injection engines.

In line with the general policy of environmental protection, the Commission has now proposed further tightening of these limitations.

Weights and dimensions

The proposal for a directive on the approximation of the laws relating to the weights and dimensions of certain motor vehicles with a permissible laden weight of 3,500 kg provides that Member States could not refuse type approval or prohibit the use of a vehicle on grounds relating to its weights and dimensions if the requirements set out in the proposed directive were satisfied.

Tyres

The proposed directive on the approximation of laws relating to tyres of motor vehicles and their trailers lays down detailed mandatory requirements for the manufacture of new radial or belted cross-ply tyres designed for a maximum speed up to 210km/h or new cross-ply tyres intended for vehicles having a maximum speed up to 200km/h. A separate proposal deals with pneumatic tyres.

Directive 89/459 requires that all tyres of certain categories of vehicles have, throughout their service life on the road, a tread depth in the main grooves of at least 1.6 mm.

Lateral protection

Directive 89/297 on the approximation of national laws relating to the lateral protection of motor vehicles lays down common technical and safety requirements which are to be met in the manufacturer of motor vehicles and trailers. Certain categories of vehicles must be constructed or equipped so as to offer effective protection to unprotected road users (i.e., pedestrians, cyclists and motorcyclists) against the risk of falling under the sides of the vehicle and being caught under the wheels.

Safety glass

The proposed directive on the approximation of laws relating to safety glass for motor vehicles would require the mandatory use of laminated safety glass and sets out various detailed technical specifications. EC type approval would replace national type approvals for certain types of safety glass, in particular, windscreens. Glass conforming with this type approval would carry an EC mark and could be marketed throughout the Community. In addition, any vehicle with safety glass bearing an EC mark could not be refused entry into a Member State on grounds relating to safety glass.

A further proposed directive sets out mandatory structural and testing requirements for safety glazing. All types of glass, in particular glass intended for use in windscreens, would have to be of a quality enabling the risk of corporal damage in the event of breakage to be reduced as much as possible. The glass would have to offer adequate resistance to any stressing which may arise during accidents occurring under normal traffic conditions, and similarly to atmospheric and thermal factors, chemical agents, fire and abrasion. In addition, safety glass would have to be adequately transparent, cause no noticeable deformation of objects seen through the windscreen, nor cause any confusion between the colours used on road signs. In the event of windscreen breakage, the driver must continue to be able to see the road clearly enough in order to be able to brake and bring his vehicle to a halt in complete safety.

Motorcycles

Motorcycles are also subject to EC type approval or, in some Member States, national type approval. Directive 78/1015 deals with the permissible sound level and exhaust system of motorcycles and has now been amended by Directive 89/235, the effect of which is that those Member States which have national type approval should apply the harmonised technical requirements which are set out in the directive.

Tractors and agricultural machines

A similar type approval system established by Directive 74/150, as amended, applies to tractors as to motor vehicles. A number of factors are taken into account on the type approval certificate and many of these have already been the subject of technical standards directives. Further harmonising directives were proposed in the White Paper.

Directive 89/173 on the approximation of the laws relating to certain components and characteristics of wheeled agricultural or forestry tractors provides that no Member State it permitted to refuse type approval of a tractor or prohibit it on grounds relating to:

- dimensions and masses;
- speed governors, protection of drive components, projections and wheels;
- windscreens and other glazing;
- mechanical linkages between tractor and trailer;
- location and method of affixing statutory plates and inscriptions to the body of the tractor;
- brake control for towed vehicles; where these complied with the requirements set out in the directive.

Directive 87/402 on roll-over protection structures mounted in front of the driver's seat on narrow-track tractors applies to tractors having the following characteristics:

- ground clearance of not more than 600mm beneath the lowest points of the front and rear axles, allowing for the differential;
- fixed or adjustable minimum track width with one of the axles less than 1150mm fitted with tyres of a larger size;
- mass of 600 and 3000 kilograms, corresponding to the unladen weight of the tractor.

All such tractors must be fitted with a roll-over protection structure. Member States must grant component type approval for any type of roll-over protection structure and its tractor attachment which satisfies the construction and testing requirements set out in the directive.

Food

National rules on the health and safety of food present some of the greatest problems in the free movement of these products. Much Community legislation has already been adopted in order to harmonise these rules. The completion of the internal market required a number of further measures to be taken.

Additives

Directive 89/107 on the approximation of laws concerning food additives applies to additives used or intended to be used as ingredients during the manufacture or preparation of a foodstuff and still present in the final product, even if in altered form. An additive is defined as any substance not normally consumed as a food by itself and not normally used as a characteristic ingredient of food whether or not it has nutritional value. This does not include substances added to food as nutrients. Excluded from the scope of the directive are processing aids, substances used in the protection of plants and plant products which are covered by other Community rules, and flavourings for use in foodstuffs which are covered by a separate directive.

Particular provisions relating to various categories of additives are to be laid down in a comprehensive directive which is to be drawn up in stages. This will include the list of substances, the use of which would be authorised to the exclusion of all others of the same kind, the criteria of purity for the substances and the foodstuffs to which they might be added. In respect of any of these categories for which lists were drawn up, only those additives included in the lists could be used in the manufacture and preparation of foodstuffs and only under the conditions of use specified therein.

Food additives not intended for sale to the consumer could be marketed only if the packaging or container bore the following information, which must be conspicuous, clearly legible and indelible:

- for additives sold singly or mixed with each other, for each component, the name laid down by any Community provisions applying to the product in question and its EC number or, in the absence of such provisions, a description of the product that was sufficiently precise to enable it to be distinguished from products with which it could be confused;
- either the statement 'for use in food' or a more specific reference to its intended food use;
- if necessary, any special storage conditions or conditions of use;
- instructions for use, if the omission thereof would preclude appropriate use of the additive;

- an identifying batch or lot number;
- the name or business name and address of the manufacturer or packager, or of a seller established within the Community;
- an indication of the percentage of any component which is subject to a quantitative limitation in a food or adequate compositional information to enable the purchaser to comply with any provisions applying to the food;
- the net quantity.

Where the food was sold for manufacturing purposes and not for retail sale, some of this information might be put on the relevant trade documents instead of the packaging. Additives intended to be sold to the ultimate consumer may be marketed only if their packaging or containers bore this information, with the exception of the component percentage, together with the date of minimum durability and certain other information.

Materials and articles in contact with foodstuffs

Directive 89/109 on the approximation of the laws relating to materials and articles which are intended to come into contact with foodstuffs applies to such products and also to materials and articles which are in contact with water intended for human consumption. Coverings or coating substances, such as the substances covering cheese rinds, prepared meat products or fruit, which form part of foodstuffs and may be consumed together with the food, are not subject to the directive. This directive amends and codifies the previous law contained in Directive 76/893.

Materials and articles must be manufactured in compliance with good manufacturing practice so that, under their normal or foreseeable conditions of use, they do not transfer their constituents to foodstuffs in quantities which could endanger human health or bring about an unacceptable change in the composition of the foodstuffs or a deterioration in their organoleptic characteristics. Special provisions apply to plastics, regenerated cellulose film, elastomers and rubber, paper and board, ceramics, glass, metals and alloys, wood, textile products, paraffin wax and microcrystalline wax.

When placed on the market, materials and articles not already in contact with foodstuffs must be accompanied by:

- the words 'for food use', or a specific indication as to their use, or a special symbol denoting use;
- any special conditions to be observed when they are being used;
- the name and address, or trade mark, of the manufacturer or processor or of a seller established within the Community.

These particulars must be conspicuously, legibly and indelibly shown:

- at the retail stage, on the materials and articles or on the packaging, or on labels affixed to them, or, if that was not possible, on a sign in their immediate vicinity which was clearly visible to the purchaser;
- at other marketing stages, on the accompanying documents, on the labels or packaging, or on the materials and articles themselves.

Retail trade in these materials and articles must be prohibited if these particulars are not given in a language easily understood by purchasers unless the purchaser is informed by other means.

Directive 82/711 laid down the basic rules necessary for testing migration of the constituents of plastic materials and articles intended to come into contact with foodstuffs. The list of simulants to be used for testing migration is set out in Directive 85/572.

Foodstuffs intended for particular nutritional uses

Directive 89/398 on the approximation of the laws relating to foodstuffs intended for particular nutritional uses applies to foodstuffs which, owing to their special composition or manufacturing process, are clearly distinguishable from foodstuffs for normal consumption. A particular nutritional use must fulfil the particular nutritional requirements of certain categories of persons whose digestive processes or metabolism are disturbed, or of certain categories of persons who are in a special physiological condition and who are therefore able to obtain special benefit from a controlled consumption of certain substances in foodstuffs, or of infants or young children in good health. These products, other than baby foods, may be characterised as 'dietetic' or 'dietary'. In the labelling, presentation and advertising of foodstuffs for normal consumption, the use of these words, or any other markings or presentation likely to give the impression that the foods were dietetic or dietary, is prohibited. However, it should be possible for foodstuffs for normal consumption which are suitable for a particular nutritional use to indicate such suitability. This amends and codifies the pre-existing law contained in Directive 77/94.

The nature and composition of these products must be such that the products are appropriate for the particular nutritional use intended. Specific additional directives deal with, for example, infant formulae, follow-up milk and other follow-up foods, baby foods and low-energy and energy-reduced foods.

In the labelling, presentation and advertising of the products, there may not be attributed to them properties for the prevention, treatment or cure of human disease, except in specific clearly defined cases. This should not prevent the dissemination of any useful information or recommendation exclusively intended for persons having qualifications in medicine, nutrition or pharmacy.

The labelling of products for which no special provisions apply must include the particular elements of the qualitative and quantitative composition of the special manufacturing process which gave the product its particular nutritional characteristics. It must state the available energy value expressed in kJ and kcal and the carbohydrate, protein and fat content per 100g or 100ml of the product as marketed and, where appropriate, per specified quantity of the product as proposed for consumption. If the energy value is less than 50kJ (12kcal) per 100g (or 100ml) of the product as marketed, these particulars may be replaced either by the words 'energy value less than 50kJ (12kcal) per 100g (100ml)'.

Infant formulae and follow-up milks

A proposal for an directive on the approximation of the laws relating to infant formulae and follow-up milks has been made. Infant formulae are foodstuffs intended for particular nutritional use by infants during the first four to six months, while follow-up milks are intended for use after four months of age and constitute the milk element of a progressively diversified diet. The compositional criteria which must be met and the substances which might be used for enrichment purposes are set out. To take account of scientific or technical developments subsequent to the adoption of the directive, a Member State could authorise for a maximum period of three years within its territory other criteria and substances.

Various conditions are to be imposed in relation to labelling, presentation and advertising in addition to those that are required of foodstuffs generally. Labelling would have to bear:

- in the case of infant formulae generally, a statement to the effect that the product is suitable for particular nutritional use by infants from birth in cases in which breast-feeding is not advised, sufficient or possible, or the mother chooses not to breast-feed;

- in the case of infant formulae that do not contain added iron, a statement to the effect that, when the product is given to infants over the age of six months, their total iron requirements must be met from other additional sources;

- in the case of follow-up milks, a statement to the effect that the product is only suitable for particular nutritional use by infants over the age of four months, that it should form only part of a diversified diet and that it is not to be used as a replacement for breast milk during the first four months of life;

- the available energy value, expressed in kJ and kcal, and the content of proteins, lipids and carbohydrates per 100ml of the product ready for use;
- the average quantity of each mineral substance and of each vitamin mentioned in the directive and, where applicable, of choline per 100ml of the product ready for use;
- instructions for appropriate preparation of the product and a warning against the health hazards of inappropriate preparation;
- information to enable batch identification.

The labelling of infant formulae would in addition have to bear the following particulars, preceded by the words 'Important Notice' or their equivalent:

- a statement concerning the superiority of breast-feeding;
- a statement recommending that the product be used only on the advice of persons having the qualifications in medicine, nutrition or pharmacy;
- a warning concerning the negative effect on breast-feeding of introducing partial bottle-feeding;
- a warning concerning the difficulty of reversing a decision not to breast-feed.

The use of terms such as 'humanised', 'maternalised' or 'adapted' shall be prohibited. Labelling could not include pictures of infants or other pictures or text which might idealise the product. These rules would also apply to articles for use in conjunction with infant formulae, such as teats, feeding bottles, bottle heaters and other specially designed feeding equipment.

Advertising of infant formulae, which is also subject to these rules, would be restricted to publications specialising in baby care. There would be a ban on point-of-sale advertising, giving of samples or any other promotional device to induce retail sales directly to the customer, such as displays, discount coupons, premiums, special sales, loss leaders and tie-in sales. Manufacturers and distributors would not be allowed to provide, to the general public or to pregnant women, mothers or members of their families free or low-priced products, samples or any other promotional gifts, either directly or indirectly via the health care system or health workers.

Labelling, presentation and advertising of foodstuffs

When Directive 79/112 on the approximation of laws relating to the labelling, presentation and advertising of foodstuffs for sale to the ultimate consumer was adopted, there were a number of matters that could not be definitively settled and so provision was made for national derogations. Amendments have now been made to that directive by Directives 86/197 and 89/395. Its scope has been extended to cover foodstuffs intended for supply to restaurants, hospitals, canteens and similar mass caterers. Other amendments cover irradiation, designation of ingredients, flavourings, date of minimum durability or of last consumption, spices and herbs, milk bottles and small packages and additives.

A separate directive deals with nutritional labelling rules for foodstuffs intended for sale to the ultimate consumer. Under Directive 90/496, nutritional labelling is compulsory when a nutrition claim, i.e., that a foodstuff has particular nutrition properties, is made in labelling or advertising and is optional in all other cases. The labelling must state the energy value and the amounts of protein, carbohydrate, sugars, fat, dietary fibre and sodium and it might also include the amounts of starch, sugar alcohols, saturates, monosaturates and polyunsaturates and certain vitamins or minerals. Information would have to be expressed per 100mg or per 100ml or per package where the package contained only a portion of less than 100mg.

Identification of the lot to which a foodstuff belongs

The indication which allows the identification of the lot to which a foodstuff belongs is covered by Directive 89/396. Foodstuffs may not be marketed unless the indication is properly made in accordance with the directive. This does not apply to agricultural products when they are sold for certain processing purposes. Nor does it apply to some foodstuffs which, at the point of sale to the ultimate consumer, are not prepackaged, are prepackaged at the request of the purchaser or are prepackaged for immediate sale.

Official inspection of foodstuffs

Directive 89/397 on the official control of foodstuffs lays down general rules to be followed when national authorities carry out controls on the conformity of foodstuffs and materials and articles intended to come into contact with them with the provisions which ensure the protection of the consumer against health risks and fraud in the matter of labelling and presentation. It does not apply to metrological inspections.

Inspections must carried out regularly or where non-conformity is suspected. These inspections cover all stages of production, manufacture, import into the Community, processing, storage, transport, distribution and trade and centre on:

- the state and use which is made of the site, premises, offices, plant, means of transport, machinery and equipment;
- raw materials, ingredients, additives and technological aids used for the manufacture of foodstuffs;
- finished and semi-finished products;

- materials and articles intended to come into contact with foodstuffs;
- cleaning and maintenance products and procedures;
- processes used for the manufacture or processing of foodstuffs;
- labelling and presentation of foodstuffs;
- preserving methods.

Sampling and analysis

Directive 85/591 concerning the introduction of Community methods of sampling and analysis for the monitoring of foodstuffs intended for human consumption applies where it is necessary to introduce Community methods for the purpose of determining the composition, conditions of manufacture, packaging or labelling of a foodstuff. This is a framework directive and the intention is that further directives will be adopted under it, taking account of the state of scientific and technical knowledge. The introduction of these measures shall not preclude Member States from using other tested and scientifically valid methods provided that this does not hinder the free movement of products recognised as complying with Community rules. The methods of analysis are to be examined with respect to specificity, accuracy, precision, limit of detection, sensitivity, practicability and applicability, together with any other criteria which may be required.

Ionising radiation

The process and marketing of foodstuffs treated by ionising radiation is the subject of a proposed directive which provides that only those foodstuffs which complied with the rules laid down in it could be sold. This proposal does not apply to foodstuffs exposed to ionising radiation emitted by measuring or inspection devices as long as the dose does not exceed 0.5Gy at a maximum energy level of 5MeV or where the foodstuffs are irradiated under medical supervision for patients requiring sterile diets. Foodstuffs authorised for irradiation treatment as well as the maximum allowable doses are listed in the proposed directive.

Irradiated foodstuffs could not be imported from third countries unless they complied with the directive. The Commission could enter into arrangements with third countries regarding the mutual notification of irradiation plants and arrange for Community inspection of irradiation plants in those countries.

Quick-frozen foods intended for human consumption

Directive 89/108 deals with the approximation of laws relating to quick-frozen foodstuffs for human consumption. Ice cream and other edible ices are not included in the scope of this directive.

Any raw materials used must be of sound merchantable quality and the quick-freezing operation must be carried out immediately after preparation of the product to be processed. The cyrogenic media authorised, to the exclusion of all others, for use in direct contact with quick-frozen foodstuffs, is limited to air, nitrogen and carbon dioxide. Until 31 December 1992, the use of dichlorodifluoromethane is also permissible.

During storage and transport and in retail display cabinets, the temperature of the foodstuffs must be maintained at -18½C or lower. Brief upward fluctuations in temperature in accordance with good storage and distribution practices may be permitted on condition that they do not exceed 3½C during storage and transport other than local distribution and 6½C during local distribution and in retail display cabinets. Random official checks are to be carried out on the equipment used for quick-freezing and on the temperatures of the foodstuffs.

Retail sales must be identified as 'quick-frozen' or 'quick-frozen foodstuff' and the labelling must also state the period during which they could be stored in the home of the ultimate consumer, together with the storage temperature or type of storage equipment required.

Flavourings

Directive 88/388, supplemented by Directive 91/71, deals with the approximation of laws relating to flavourings for use in foodstuffs and to source materials for their production. 'Flavouring' means flavouring substances, flavouring preparations, process flavourings, smoke flavourings or mixtures thereof. This directive does not apply to edible substances and products intended to be consumed as such, substances which have exclusively a sweet, sour or salt taste, or material of vegetable or animal origin, having inherent flavouring properties, where they are not used as flavouring sources. Flavourings may not be marketed or used if they do not comply with the rules laid down in the directive. The directive applies to flavouring and foodstuffs imported into the Community, but not to those intended for export outside of the Community.

National regulations must ensure that:

- flavourings do not contain any element or substance in a toxicologically dangerous quantity;
- flavourings do not contain more than 3mg/kg of arsenic, 10mg/kg of lead, 1mg/kg of cadmium and 1mg/kg of mercury;
- the use of flavourings and other ingredients with flavouring properties does not result in the presence of certain substances in quantities greater than those specified in the directive.

A list is to be adopted of substances or materials authorised in the Community as additives necessary for the storage and use of flavourings, products used for dissolving and diluting flavourings and additives necessary for the production of flavourings where such additives are not covered by other Community provisions. Methods of sampling and analysis are to be established together with criteria of purity for flavourings.

Flavourings not intended for sale to the final consumer may not be marketed unless their packaging or containers bear certain information which must be easily visible, clearly legible and indelible. Those intended for sale to the final consumer must also clearly show certain information, such as the date of minimum durability.

Extraction solvents

Directive 88/344 on the approximation of the laws on extraction solvents applies to extraction solvents used in the production of foodstuffs and food ingredients but excludes those used in the production of food additives, vitamins and other nutritional additives, unless these are listed in the directive. However, the use of these other solvents must not result in foodstuffs containing extraction solvent residue levels dangerous to human health. This directive does not affect the laws of the Member States relating to the use of methanol, propan-1-ol, propan-2-ol and trichloroethylene as extraction solvents.

A list of substances and materials which the Member States must authorise is set out in the directive together with conditions of use and maximum residue limits. Certain purity criteria are established. The solvents may not contain a toxicologically dangerous amount of any element or substance, nor may they contain more than 1mg/kg of arsenic or 1mg/kg of lead. Sampling and analysis procedures are to be established. The solvents may not be sold unless their packaging, containers or labels carry certain information which must be easily visible, clearly legible and indelible.

Preservatives

A list of preservatives which may be used for the protection of foodstuffs intended for human consumption against deterioration caused by micro-organisms was established by Directive 64/54, as amended. A further amendment has been made to this list by Directive 85/585 so as to include potassium acid sulphite (potassium bisulphite) which may be used in wine production as an alternative to other sulphites already permitted by the directive.

Emulsifiers, stabilisers, thickeners and gelling agents

Directive 74/329, as amended, lays down a list of emulsifiers, stabilisers, thickeners and gelling agents which may be authorised for use in foodstuffs. Certain amendments are made to this by Directives 86/102 and 89/393. These deal with temporary authorisation of Tragacanth gum, Karaya gum and thermally oxidised soya bean oil interacted with mono- and di-glycerides of fatty acids, pectin and amidated pectin.

Polyoxethylene (8) stearate, polyoxethylene (40) stearate, lactylated fatty acid esters of glycerol and propylene glycol, and dioctyl sodium sulphosuccinate are no longer to be allowed in foodstuffs and the marketing of foodstuffs containing any of these substances is prohibited.

Modified starches intended for human consumption

The proposal for a directive on the approximation of the laws relating to modified starches intended for human consumption deals with products obtained by one or more chemical treatments of edible starches which may have previously undergone a physical or enzymatic treatment. The marketing and use as foodstuffs ingredients of the modified starches listed in the proposed directive would be allowed under the conditions laid down in it. All other modified starches would be prohibited. Use as an ingredient of foodstuffs intended specifically for infants and young children would be subject to special rules. In order to take account of scientific or technical developments which might occur after the adoption of the proposed directive, a Member State could authorise the marketing and use within its territory for up to three years of a modified starch not listed in the directive.

The labelling of modified starches would consist solely of the following mandatory wording:

- the denomination under which the product is sold;
- the words 'for human consumption' or an indication of the specific intended use of the modified starch;
- the net quantity, except in the case of products put up in bulk;
- the date of manufacture or identification of the production batch;
- the name and address of the manufacturer, packer or a seller established in the Community.

Coffee extracts and chicory extracts

Directive 77/436 on the approximation of the laws relating to coffee extracts and chicory extracts has been amended by Directive 85/573. The amendments allow for the existence of a concentrated product in the case of chicory extract, abolish any requirements as to the minimum quantity of raw coffee and the maximum content of insoluble substances used in coffee extract, and reduce the minimum dry matter content required for both chicory extract and coffee extract.

Fruit juices and similar products

Directive 89/394 amends Directive 75/726 on the approximation of the laws concerning fruit juices and certain similar products. The series of quite minor amendments allows fruit nectars to be produced without the addition of sugar, fruit purée to be used in the manufacture of certain fruit juices and sugar to be replaced by honey in all fruit nectars. The option of using sugars and honey together in certain nectars is deleted and certain rules are introduced regarding sweeteners and the option of adding citric acid to correct the natural acidity of some juices.

Fruit jams, jellies, marmalades and chestnut purée

Directive 88/593, amending Directive 79/693 on the approximation of the laws relating to fruit jams, jellies, marmalades and chestnut purée, is largely concerned with minor technical amendments and the clarification of certain provisions whose interpretation is unclear. This includes amendments dealing with residual sulphur dioxide, sugar content, identity and purity criteria, sampling and analysis and colouring.

Spirit drinks

Regulation 1576/89 lays down general rules on the definition, description and presentation of spirits drinks. To be marketed for human consumption in the Community under one of the names listed in the regulation, an alcoholic spirits beverage would have to comply with the definition and requirements applicable to the category to which it belongs. The addition of any substance other than those expressly authorised would disqualify the beverage from the use of the restricted name. However, the restricted name might be used for beverages which were flavoured or sweetened or which contained certain additives.

The minimum alcoholic strength by volume is:

- for whisky, whiskey or pastis, 40%;
- for rum, spirits, gin, vodka, grappa, aquavit, ouzo, Roggenbrand, Kornbrand and Weisanbrand, 37.5%;
- brandy, 36%;
- anis, 35%;
- for Korn, 32%;
- for caraway-flavoured spirits drinks, 30%;
- for fruit spirits drinks, 25%;
- for aniseed-flavoured spirits drinks (except ouzo and pastis), 15%.

Water may be added in the preparation of spirituous beverages as long as it met Community quality standards. Ethyl alcohol used must be solely of agricultural origin and meet certain specifications. Only natural aromatic substances, substances identical to these and natural aromatic preparations may be used as flavouring.

Only those beverages which meet the requirements of the regulation may be sold under these names and these names must be used to describe these beverages in the Community. A list is given of geographical ascriptions, e.g., armagnac, which might be used in addition to or instead of these names, provided that the production stage during which the product acquired its character and its definitive qualities took place in the geographical area concerned. Special provisions may be adopted on the use of certain words, initials or signs, the use of certain composite names such as 'brandy', and the names of mixed beverages. Where the labelling referred to the raw material used to produce the ethyl alcohol of agricultural origin, each type of alcohol must be mentioned in decreasing order of quantity used. A maturation period may be specified only where it referred to the youngest alcoholic component and provided that the product was aged under revenue supervision or other supervision affording equivalent guarantees.

Vermouths and aromatised wines

A separate proposal has been made for a regulation laying down general rules on the definition, description and presentation of vermouths and other aromatised wines. Vermouth is defined as aromatised wine, the characteristic taste of which is obtained by the use of appropriate substance always including wormwood. It may not contain any colouring matter and may be sweetened only by means of sugar and rectified concentrated grape must. Aromatised wine is defined as a beverage which is produced from wine and/or must to which, except in certain cases, spirit of viticultural origin and/or alcohol of agricultural origin has been added, which has been flavoured and to which sugar may have been added.

In the preparation of aromatised wines only the following might be used:

- wine which may be offered or released for direct human consumption within the Community, in accordance with Community law, excluding aerated sparkling or aerated semi-sparkling wines;
- grape must, grape must in fermentation, grape must with fermentation arrested by the addition of alcohol and concentrated grape must.

It is proposed that these must, after a maximum enrichment of 2% by volume, have a minimum total alcoholic strength of 10% by volume and, before enrichment, be present in the finished product in a proportion of not less than 75%. This proportion would be 70% for dry aromatised wines and certain sweet aromatised wines.

The addition of water might be authorised in the preparation of aromatised wines as long as it met Community quality standards. Ethyl alcohol used to extend or dissolve colouring matters, flavourings or other authorised additives would have to be of agricultural origin and meet the quality specifications set out in the proposed regulation. Only natural aromatic substances, substances identical to these and natural aromatic preparations could be used as flavourings.

To be released for human consumption in the Community under one of the names listed in the proposed regulation, the aromatised wines would have to have a minimum actual alcoholic strength of 15% vol. The minimum strength would be fixed at 17% vol. where the aromatised wine was described as dry and at 18% where it was described as bitter. In the case of products treated with carbon dioxide, the alcoholic strength would be between 8% and 12% vol. The total alcoholic strength by volume of aromatised wines would be not less than 17.5% vol., except in certain cases.

The names used in the proposed regulation would have to be used to describe the wines in the Community and any wines not meeting the necessary requirements could not bear those names. A list is given of geographical ascriptions, e.g., Turin vermouth, which might be used in addition to or instead of these names, provided that the production stage during which the product acquired its character and its definitive qualities took place in the geographical area concerned.

Pharmaceuticals and high-technology medicines

An important sector for the completion of the internal market relates to those rules governing the placing on the market of medicinal products and veterinary products. By virtue of Directive 65/65, no proprietary medicinal product may be placed on the market unless an authorisation has been issued by the competent authority in that Member State. Directive 75/319 on the approximation of laws relating to proprietary medicinal products set up a committee consisting of representatives of the Member States and the Commission which allowed for the coordination of national decisions relating to the placing on the market of such products. A similar procedure was established for veterinary medicinal products by Directive 81/851. A series of directives have now been adopted amending and supplementing these basic directives. These extend their application to ready-made medicinal products, vaccines, toxins, serums and allergens, medicinal products derived from human blood and radiopharmaceuticals. Another directive relates to the transparency of measures regulating the pricing of medicinal products for human use and their inclusion within the scope of the national health insurance system. Other measures relate to labelling, legal status for the supply of medicinal products,the manufacture of substances used in illicit drugs and a European Agency for the Evaluation of Medicinal Products.

Placing on the market of high-technology medicines

Directive 87/22 on the approximation of national measures relating to the placing on the market of high-technology medicinal products introduces various improvements into the system. It was felt that the existing procedures were not sufficient to open up to high-technology medicinal products the large Community-wide market which they required. The scientific expertise available to each of the national authorities was not always sufficient to resolve problems posed in this sector. Accordingly, now, before taking a decision on a marketing authorisation or suspension of a marketing authorisation in respect of the medicinal products listed in the directive, Member States' authorities must refer the matter to the committee established in Directive 75/319 or Directive 81/851. As soon as it receives an application for marketing authorisation relating to a medicinal product covered by the directive, the competent authority must, at the request of the person responsible for placing the product on the market, bring the matter before the committee for an opinion. Where the product is developed by means of new biotechnological processes an opinion must be sought, regardless of whether a request is made by the responsible person. This is not the case if the applicant certifies that neither he nor any person connected with him has sought, during the preceding five years, or intends to seek, in the following five years, authorisation to place a product containing the same active principles on the market of another Member State.

Testing of proprietary and veterinary medicinal products

Detailed rules on testing proprietary medicinal products and veterinary medicinal products were established by Directives 75/318 and 81/852 on the approximation of laws relating to analytical, pharmaco-toxicological and clinical standards and protocols. Directives 87/19 and 87/20 have introduced certain amendments designed to adapt the procedures in the light of scientific and technical progress. Other amendments are made to the existing rules on physico-chemical, biological or microbiological tests of proprietary and veterinary medicinal products. Directive 90/677 extends the provisions of Directive 81/851 to cover immunological veterinary medicinal products, i.e., those products administered to animals in order to produce active or passive immunity or to diagnose the state of immunity. In addition, Directive 90/676 amends Directive 81/851 at some length in order to adapt it to scientific progress.

A series of notes for guidance intended to prevent differences of interpretation in the conduct and evaluation of the tests provided for in

Directive 75/318 have been amended by Recommendation 87/176. These deal with:

- single-dose toxicity;
- testing of medicinal products for their mutagenic;
- cardiac glycosides;
- clinical investigation of oral contraceptives;
- user information on oral contraceptives;
- data sheets for antimicrobial drugs;
- clinical testing requirements for drugs in long-term use;
- non-steroidal anti-inflammatory compounds for the treatment of chronic disorders;
- anti-epileptic/anti-convulsant drugs;
- investigation of bioavailability;
- clinical investigation of drugs for the treatment of chronic peripheral arterial diseases;
- pharmacokinetic studies in man;
- anti-anginal drugs;
- corticosteroids intended for use on the skin.

In Directive 65/65, it was provided that various types of proof of the safety and efficacy of a proprietary medicinal product may be put forward in an application for marketing authorisation depending on the objective situation of the product in question. Directive 87/21 has amended this to the effect that an applicant shall not be required to provide the results of these tests or trials if he can demonstrate either:

- that the product is essentially similar to a product authorised in the country concerned by the application and that the person responsible for the marketing of the original product has consented to the pharmacological, toxicological or clinical references contained in the file on the original product being used for the purpose of examining the application in question; or
- by detailed references to published scientific literature presented in accordance with Directive 75/318 that the constituents of the product have a well established medicinal use with recognised efficacy and an acceptable level of safety; or
- that the product is essentially similar to a product which has been authorised within the Community, in accordance with Community provisions in force, for not less than six years (ten years in the case of high-technology medicines and certain other products) and is marketed in the Member State for which the application is made. A Member State may extend this period to ten years for all products marketed in its territory where it considers it necessary in the interest of public health.

Where the product is intended for a different therapeutic use from that of the other products marketed or is to be administered by different routes or in different dosages, the results of tests and trials must be provided. In the case of new products containing known constituents not hitherto used in combination for therapeutic purposes, the results of tests and trials relating to that combination must be provided, but it is not necessary to provide references relating to each individual constituent.

Vaccines, toxins, serums and allergens for human use

Directive 89/432 extends the scope of Directive 65/65 and Directive 75/319 to immunological medicinal products for human use consisting of vaccines, toxins and serums and allergens. Processes used in the manufacture of immunological products must be properly validated and attain batch-to-batch consistency. The competent authority may require the person responsible for marketing a product to submit samples from each batch of the bulk and/or finished product for testing by a State laboratory or a laboratory designated for that purpose before release onto the market. That person might be required to submit to the competent authority all the control reports signed by a qualified person. These provisions cover the marketing of live vaccines, immunological medicinal products used in the primary immunisation of infants or of other groups at risk or used in public health immunisation programmes, and new immunological medicinal products for a transitional period.

Medicinal products derived from human plasma

Directive 89/381 extends the scope of Directive 65/65 and Directive 75/319 to medicinal products derived from human plasma and applies to products based on blood constituents which are prepared industrially by public or private establishments and include, in particular, albumin, coagulating factors and immunoglobins of human origin. It does not apply to whole blood, plasma or blood cells of human origin.

The processes used in the manufacture of medicinal products derived from human plasma must be properly validated, attain batch-to-batch consistency and guarantee, in so far as the state of technology permitted, the absence of viral contaminants. Manufacturers must notify the competent authorities of the method used to reduce or eliminate pathogenic viruses liable to be transmitted by medicinal products derived from human blood or plasma. Similar rules on the validation of manufacturing processes apply as in the case of immunological medicinal products.

Radiopharmaceuticals

Directive 89/343, extending the scope of Directive 65/65 and Directive 75/319 to radiopharmaceuticals, applies to radiopharmaceuticals for human use, excluding radionuclides in the form of sealed sources. Authorisation is required for generators, kits, precursor radiopharmaceuticals and industrially prepared radiopharmaceuticals. However, authorisation is not required for a radiopharmaceutical prepared at the time of use by a person or by an establishment authorised by national law to use it in an approved health care establishment exclusively from authorised generators, kits or precursor radiopharmaceuticals in accordance with the manufacturer's instructions.

In addition to the requirements set out in Directive 65/65, an application for authorisation to market a generator must contain a general description of the system together with a detailed description of the components of the system which might affect the composition or quality of the daughter nucleid preparation and qualitative and quantitative particulars of the eluate.

The outer carton and the tin containing radionuclides must be labelled in accordance with the regulations for the safe transport of radioactive materials laid down by the International Atomic Energy Agency. The label on the shielding must explain in full the codings used on the vial and indicate, where necessary, for a given time and date, the amount of radioactivity per dose or per vial and the number of capsules or, for liquids, the number of millilitres in the container. The labelling on the vial must also contain certain stipulated information and a detailed instruction leaflet must be enclosed with the packaging of radiopharmaceuticals, generators, kits or precursor radiopharmaceuticals.

Homeopathic medicinal products

Directives 65/65, 75/319 and 81/851 are to be amended so as to cover homeopathic medicines. Since such medicines are not fully recognised throughout the Community, the Commission proposed that it was appropriate, while harmonising certain provisions relating to their control, to recognise certain national traditions without imposing them. Two directives have been proposed to alter the basic directives in this respect. These products would be subject to a simplified registration procedure if they were administered orally or externally, were marketed without any specific therapeutic indication and if there was a sufficient degree of dilution to guarantee the safety of the preparation.

Tolerances for residues of veterinary medicinal products

A regulation is proposed laying down a Community procedure for the establishment of tolerances for residues of veterinary medicinal products.

This would establish maximum levels or residues of such products which might be acceptable and which do not present a health hazard. A list of permissible products and levels would be established. Member States would not authorise the marketing of a product intended for administration to food-producing animals containing an active substance which was not authorised in accordance with the regulation. In order for a product to be authorised, the person responsible for marketing it would make an application to the Commission which would forward it to the Committee for Veterinary Medicinal Products for authorisation.

Pricing of medicinal products

National measures on the marketing of medicinal products have included some aimed at controlling or reducing public health expenditures by direct or indirect controls on the prices of medicinal products and limitations on the range of products covered by the national health insurance system. Directive 89/105 relating to the transparency of measures regulating the price of medicinal products for human use and their inclusion within the scope of the national health insurance system seeks to remedy some of the problems associated with this area.

If the marketing of a product is permitted only after a national authority has approved the price at which it is to be sold or if an increase in this price is allowed only after prior approval has been obtained, a decision on the price which might be charged must be adopted and communicated to the applicant within 90 days. In the absence of such a decision, the applicant is entitled to market the product at the price applied for. Should a decision be made not to permit this price, a detailed statement of reasons must be given.

In the event of a price freeze being imposed on all medicinal products or on certain categories of such products, prices must be reviewed at least once every year. Any person who was responsible for marketing a product may apply for a derogation from a price freeze, stating his reasons in detail. A decision on this application must be made within 90 days by the competent authority, otherwise the applicant is entitled to apply in full the price increase requested.

A Member State which adopts a system of direct or indirect controls on the profitability of manufacturers and importers of medicinal products is required to publish the following information:

- the methods used to define profitability, return on sales and/or return on capital;
- the criteria according to which target rates of profit are set for individual manufacturers or importers together with the criteria according to which manufacturers or importers will be allowed to retain profits above their given targets;

- the range of target profit currently permitted;

- the maximum percentage profit which any manufacturer or importer is allowed to retain above his target.

Where a medicinal product is covered by the national health insurance system only after the competent authorities have decided to include it in a positive list of products covered by the system, a decision on an application made for inclusion in the list must be adopted within 90 days. Alternatively, the competent authorities might be empowered to exclude products from the coverage of the national health insurance system. A decision refusing to include the product in a positive list or a decision to include it in a negative list must state in detail the reasons upon which it was based.

Wholesale distribution of medicinal products

A directive has been proposed on the wholesale distribution of medicinal products setting out minimum rules. Member States would have to ensure that only those products in respect of which a marketing authorisation had been granted could be distributed. Wholesalers would be subject to a system of authorisation and checks would be carried out periodically on them and their premises. In order to obtain an authorisation, applicants would have to show that they possessed suitable premises and that they had qualified personnel to deal with the products. All pharmacists and other persons authorised to supply medicinal products to the public would be required to keep accurate records showing, in respect of each individual transaction of medicinal products received, the date, the name and form of the medicinal product, the quantity received and the name and address of the supplier.

Labelling of medicinal products

Directive 65/65 (as amended) established a list of particulars to be given on the packaging and outer packaging of medicinal products. Similarly, Directive 75/319 established a list of the particulars to be stated on the package insert leaflets. Both of these lists are to be supplemented. Accordingly, the Commission has proposed a wholly new directive which would consolidate all of these provisions, including the new provisions. The leaflet would have to identify the medicinal product, detail any therapeutic indications, give any information which is useful before taking the product and set out the proper method of use. It must be written in clear and understandable terms for the patient, in the official language of the State where the product is put on the market.

Legal status for the supply of medicinal products

The conditions for supply of medicines to the public differ appreciably from one Member State to another so that, for example, medicines on free sale in one country may only be available on prescription in another. The Commission has proposed a directive concerning the legal status for the supply of medicinal products seeking to harmonise the situation throughout the Community. Medicinal products would be classified as subject to or not subject to medical prescription and those subject to prescription would be subdivided into categories depending on whether the prescription might be automatically renewed or not. Medical products which contained substances which were likely to present a direct or indirect danger to human health, even under normal conditions of use, would not be supplied to the public without prescription.

Substances in the manufacture of illicit narcotic drugs

A directive has been proposed to harmonise the national provisions dealing with the manufacture and placing on the market of substances used in the illicit manufacture of narcotics drugs and psychotropic substances and intending to monitor such drugs so as to prevent unlawful use of them. All transactions leading to the placing on the market of scheduled substances would be properly documented. In particular, commercial documents would contain sufficient information to identify the substance and the names and addresses of the supplier and customer. The competent authorities would be given the power to obtain information on any orders or transactions in scheduled substances, to enter and search professional premises of operators and obtain evidence of irregularities and to seize and scheduled substance if there is sufficient evidence that it is to be used in the illicit manufacture of narcotics.

The European Agency for the Evaluation of Medicinal Products

In order to achieve the full benefits of the harmonised legislation in the pharmaceuticals field, the Commission proposed that a Community body be set up to resolve disagreements between Member States about the quality, safety and efficacy of medicinal products. It thus proposes the establishment of the European Agency for the Evaluation of Medicinal Products whose primary task would be to provide scientific advice of the highest possible quality in relation to authorisation and supervision. The Agency would have two committees, one dealing with proprietary medical products and the other with veterinary medicinal products. Each committee would have a permanent technical and administrative staff and would be assisted by working parties and expert groups. The Agency would undertake the following tasks:

- coordination of scientific evaluation;

- assessment reports on products, labels and packaging;
- continuing supervision of authorised products;
- coordination of supervisory responsibilities;
- maintenance of a data base on medicinal products available for public use;
- promotion of technical cooperation;
- provision of information to the public.

Chemical products

Community law provisions on the marketing and use of certain dangerous substances and preparations were set out in Directive 76/769. The purpose of these provisions is to protect the public and other persons who come into contact with them and also to protect the environment.

PCBs and PCTs

Directive 85/467 amends Directive 76/769 so as to provide special rules for polychlorinated biphenals (PCBs) and polychlorinated terphenals (PCTs). Given the serious risks presented by PCBs and PCTs and since substitutes had been developed which were considered less dangerous, the continued marketing of PCBs and PCTs is permitted only in certain exceptional cases. In addition to the other labelling requirements for dangerous substances, equipment and plant containing PCBs and PCTs may also be required to display instructions concerning the disposal of these substances and the maintenance and disposal of equipment and plant containing them. These instructions must be capable of being read horizontally and the inscription must stand out clearly from its background.

Asbestos

Directive 85/610 amends Directive 76/769 in respect of the provisions dealing with asbestos. The use of asbestos and certain products containing it can, by releasing fibres, cause asbestosis and cancer. Directive 76/769 prohibited, with a few exceptions, the placing on the market and use of crocidolite and required specific labelling to draw attention to the hazards inherent in the use of products containing asbestos fibres. Under the amended provisions, the placing on the market and use of products containing the types of asbestos fibres specified in the directive are prohibited for:

- toys;
- materials or preparations intended to be applied by spraying. Butiminous compounds containing asbestos intended to be applied for spraying as vehicle undersealing for anti-corrosion protection may be allowed;

- finished products which are retailed to the public in powder form;
- items for smoking such as tobacco pipes and cigarette and cigar holders;
- catalytic filters and insulation devices for incorporation in catalytic heaters using liquefied gas;
- paints and varnishes.

Polybromobiphenyl ether

Directive 76/769 is to be amended so as to include polybromobiphenyl ether in the substances subjected to restrictions. This substance, used as fire retardant in certain plastic polymers and in certain plastic products may, under the uncontrolled condition of a fire, during plastics manufacture or processing and during waste disposal involving incineration, lead to the emission of polyhalogenated dibenzo dioxins which are dangerous to man and the environment.

Detergents

Damage to the environment and to public health caused by detergents was tackled by Directive 73/404 which prohibits the placing on the market and use of detergents where the average level of biodegradability does not comply with particular requirements. Certain exemptions were allowed for non-ionic surfactants contained in detergents. The scope of these exemptions was restricted by Directive 86/94. Until 31 December 1989, Member States could have exempted the following products:

- low-foaming alkene oxide additives on such substances as alcohols, alkylphenols, glycols, polyols, fatty acids, amides or amines, used in dish-washing products;
- alkali-resistant terminally blocked alkyl and alkylaryl polyglycol ethers and substances of the type referred to above used in cleaning agents for the food, beverage and metal-working industries.

Classification, packaging and labelling of dangerous preparations

Rules were established on the classification, packaging and labelling of dangerous preparations by Directive 73/173 and other directives which applied to solvents, pesticides, printing inks, paints and varnishes. Directive 88/379 extends this so as also to apply to preparations which are placed on the market in a Member State and which contain at least one substance classified and regarded as dangerous. Certain products which are covered by other provisions of Community law are excluded from the ambit of the directive.

Specific provisions list the criteria to be adopted in deciding whether a preparation is to be regarded as dangerous and how certain health hazards should be ascertained. Dangerous preparations may not be placed on the market unless their packaging complies with the necessary requirements with respect to strength, leak-tightness and fastening systems. Containers for holding dangerous preparations which are offered or sold to the general public must not have either a shape or graphic decoration likely to attract or arouse the active curiosity of children or to mislead consumers. Nor may these containers have a presentation or designation used for human and animal foodstuffs or medicinal or cosmetic products. Certain containers must be fitted with child-resistant fastenings and carry a tactile warning of danger.

The following information must be clearly and indelibly marked on any package:

- the trade name or designation of the preparation;
- the name and full address, including the telephone number, of the person established in the Community who is responsible for placing the preparation on the market, whether it be the manufacturer, the importer or the distributor;
- the chemical name of the substances present in the preparation;
- the symbols for and indications of the dangers involved in the use of the preparation;
- standard phrases indicating the special risks arising from such dangers (R phrases);
- standards phrases indicating the safety advice relating to the use of the preparation (S phrases);
- the nominal quantity of the contents in the case of preparations sold to the general public.

Information such as 'non-toxic', 'not harmful' or any other statement indicating that the preparation is not dangerous is prohibited.

Fertilisers

Directive 88/183 extends the scope of Directive 76/116 on the approximation of the laws relating to designation, composition, labelling and packaging of solid fertilisers to cover fluid fertilisers. The designation 'EEC fertiliser' may be used only for fertilisers belonging to one of the types listed in the directive and complying with the requirements laid down in it. In addition to the rules on packaging which apply to all fertilisers, fluid fertilisers may be marketed only if suitable directions are provided, covering, in particular, storage temperature and prevention of accidents during storage.

Directives 89/284 and 89/530 extend Directive 76/116 to cover the trace elements contained in fertilisers. These apply to the calcium, magnesium, sodium and sulphur content of fertilisers and to solid or fluid fertilisers containing one of the trace elements boron, cobalt, copper, iron, manganese, molybdenum and zinc. As long as these met the requirements set out in the annex to the proposed directive, they might be marked 'EEC fertiliser'.

Construction products

Different national rules on construction products have a direct influence on the nature of the products employed in any construction project. Directive 89/106 on the approximation of laws relating to construction products applies to products which are produced with a view to their incorporation in construction works, including buildings and civil engineering works.

The products must be fit for their intended use, that is, they must have such characteristics that the construction works in which they are incorporated in accordance with defined rules and conditions can meet the essential requirements regarding safety, health and certain other aspects in the general interest set out in the directive which concern:

- mechanical resistance and stability;
- safety in case of fire;
- hygiene, health and environment;
- safety in use;
- durability;
- protection against noise;
- energy economy and heat retention.

National standards need not cover all of the essential requirements, but any additional national requirements must not involve modifications to products that complied with the directive.

Technical specifications define the required characteristics of products in their particular uses, such as the levels of quality or performance, reliability or dimensions. Where these specifications distinguish between different performance classes corresponding to different requirement levels, Member States may determine, according to their climatic conditions, the requirement levels to be respected on their territory within the classifications adopted at Community level.

Pending the adoption of European standards, national standards which comply with the essential safety requirements suffice. Where there is no harmonised standard or relevant national standard, application may be made for European technical approval, whereby a favourable technical assessment of the fitness for use of the product may be made, based on fulfilment of the essential requirements for building works, by means of the inherent characteristics of the product and the defined conditions of application and use.

Products that benefit from the presumption of conformity with the essential requirements are dependent on the manufacturer having a factory production control system to ensure that production conforms with the relevant technical specifications or an approved certification body being involved in assessment and surveillance of production control or of the product itself. The choice of procedure for a given product or family of products is determined by the Commission according to the nature of the product, the variability of its characteristics and the importance of the part played by the product with respect to the essential requirements. In each case the simplest possible procedure would be chosen.

Importing Member States must attach the same value to reports and attestations of conformity issued in the producing Member State as they do to their own corresponding national documents.

Permissible sound power level of tower cranes

Noise emission standards of construction plant and equipment is governed by Directive 79/113, as amended. Directive 84/532 established the procedures for an EC type approval system for such equipment, but left it to separate directives to specify the details for particular categories of plant and equipment. One of these, Directive 84/534, which has been amended by Directive 87/405, dealt with the approximation of the laws relating to the permissible sound power level of tower cranes. The directive now applies to the permissible sound power level of airborne noise emitted into the environment and the permissible sound pressure level of airborne noise emitted at the operator's position for tower cranes used to perform work on industrial and building sites. A method is introduced for measuring the airborne noise emitted at the operator's position.

An EC type examination certificate is to be issued for each type of tower crane which conforms to the noise level requirements. Each tower crane built in accordance with the type so certified must bear a clear and permanent mark indicating the sound power level and, in the case of a type of tower crane with an operator's position fixed to its structure, the sound pressure level.

Airborne noise emitted by household appliances

Common rules on airborne noise emitted by household appliances were introduced by Directive 86/594. This applies to any machine, portion of a machine or installation manufactured principally for use in dwellings, including cellars, garages and other outhouses. It does not apply to

- appliances, equipment or machines designed exclusively for industrial or professional purposes;
- appliances which are integrated parts of a building or its installations such as equipment for air conditioning, heating and ventilating (except

household fans, cooker hoods and free-standing heating appliances), oil burners for central heating and pumps for water supply and sewage systems;

• equipment components such as motors;

• electroacoustic appliances.

Member States may require the publication, for certain families of appliances, of information on the noise emitted by such appliances. The general test method used to determine the airborne noise must be accurate enough for the measurement uncertainties to produce standard deviations not exceeding 2dB in the case of A-weighted sound power levels. Spot checks on the accuracy of the information published may be carried out.

Permissible sound power level of lawnmowers

Directive 84/538 on the approximation of laws relating to the permissible sound power level of lawnmowers has been amended by Directives 88/180 and 88/181 so as to apply to lawnmowers except agricultural and forestry equipment, non-independent devices (e.g., drawn cylinders) with cutting devices actuated by the wheels or by an integrated drawing or carrier component, or multi-purpose devices, the main motorised component of which has an installed power of more than 20kW.

Lawnmowers might not be sold unless their sound power levels, as measured under the conditions specified in the directive, do not exceed the permissible level. This level is 96 dB/pW where the cutting width is less than 50cm, 100dB/pW where the cutting width is up to 120cm. Lawnmowers with a cutting width in excess of 120cm may have a sound power level up to 105dB/pW and a sound pressure level of airborne noise up to 90dB.

Tyre pressure gauges for motor vehicles

In several Member States, the construction and methods of control of pressure gauges intended to measure the inflation pressure of motor vehicle tyres were subject to differing mandatory provisions. Directive 86/217 on the approximation of laws relating to tyre pressure gauges provides that no Member State may prohibit the sale or use of tyre inflation equipment on grounds relating to its metrological qualities if it bears the EC pattern approval sign and the EC initial verification mark. Detailed provisions covering metrological and technical requirements describe the equipment eligible for EC marks and signs.

Noise emitted by earth-moving machines

Directive 86/662 applies to the sound-power level of airborne noise emitted in the environment and the sound-pressure level of airborne noise emitted at the operator's position of hydraulic excavators, rope-operated excavators, dozers, loaders and excavator-loaders used to perform work on civil engineering and building sites. An EC type examination certificate must be issued for every type of earth-moving machine covered by the directive where the level of noise emitted in the environment does not exceed the permissible level. For every machine built in conformity with the type certified, the manufacturer must complete a certificate of conformity and indicate on it the net installed power and the corresponding swivel system. Each such machine must bear a clear and permanent mark indicating the sound-power level and the sound-pressure level at the operator's position. The provisions of the directive do not affect the national rules limiting noise levels at the operator's position provided that this does not entail any obligation to adjust earth-moving machines which meet the requirements of the directive to different emission specifications. Measures may be taken to limit the use of these machines in sensitive areas.

Fire safety in existing hotels

Rules governing fire safety in hotels exist in Member States to differing degrees of strictness. With the rapid expansion of tourism and business travel, it was felt that travellers were entitled to adequate protection in other Member States and to be informed of the nature and extent of that protection. Accordingly, Recommendation 86/666 urges Member States to take all appropriate measures, in so far as existing laws are not already sufficient to meet the necessary requirements, to ensure that fire precautions in existing hotels are intended to:

- reduce the risk of fire breaking out;
- prevent the spread of flames and smoke;
- ensure that all occupants can be evacuated safely;
- enable the emergency services to take action. In order to meet these objectives, all necessary precautions should be taken within the hotel so that:
- safe escape routes are available, are clearly indicated and remain accessible and unobstructed;
- the building's structural stability in the event of fire is guaranteed for as long as is needed for the occupants to evacuate the building safely;
- the presence or use of highly flammable materials in wall, ceiling or floor coverings and interior decorations is carefully limited;

- all technical equipment and appliances (electrical, gas. heating, etc.) operate safely;
- appropriate systems are installed and maintained in proper working order for alerting the occupants;
- safety instructions and a plan of the premises with an indication of the escape routes are displayed in each room normally occupied by guests or staff;
- emergency fire-fighting equipment (extinguishers, etc.) is provided and maintained in proper working order;
- the staff is given suitable instruction and training.

In applying these provisions to existing commercially operated establishments which occupy all or part of a building and which, under the name of hotel, boarding house, inn, tavern, motel or other equivalent designation, can offer accommodation to at least 20 paying guests, Member States should take into account the technical guidelines set out in the recommendation. These guidelines cover:

- escape routes;
- construction features;
- coverings and decorations;
- electric lighting;
- heating;
- ventilation systems;
- fire-fighting, alarm and alerting equipment;
- safety instructions.

Different or more stringent measures may be used if they achieve at least an equivalent result. In particular, if any of the provisions in the guidelines cannot be implemented for economic or technical (including anti-seismic and architectural) reasons, the alternative solutions adopted must ensure the overall minimum safety standard which the guidelines seek to establish.

For establishments offering accommodation to fewer than 20 paying guests, appropriate measures should be adopted which guarantee their safety in conformity with the principles set out in the recommendation, taking into account the size of the risk.

Indication of the prices of products

Community programmes for consumer protection and information policy provide for the establishment of common principles for indicating prices. Separate provisions apply to foodstuffs and to non-food products.

Rules on the indication of prices on foodstuffs were introduced by Directive 79/581. This has been amended by Directive 88/315. These rules do not apply to foodstuffs sold in hotels, restaurants, cafs, public houses, hospitals, canteens and similar establishments and consumed on the premises, to foodstuffs bought for a trade or commercial activity, nor to foodstuffs supplied in the course of the provision of a service. In addition, Member States may provide that the rules do not apply to foodstuffs sold on the farm or to private sales.

Directive 88/314 relates to the indication of the selling price and the price per unit of measurement of non-food products offered to the final consumer or advertised indicating the price, whether they are sold in bulk or pre-packaged in pre-established or variable quantities. The directive does not apply to:

- products bought for the purpose of a trade or commercial activity;
- products supplied in the course of the provision of a service;
- private sales;
- sales by auction and sales of works of art and antiques.

Both foodstuffs and non-food products must bear an indication of the selling price. Where these are pre-packaged and where they are sold in bulk, they must also bear an indication of the unit price, although this requirement may be waived for specific products or where it would be meaningless. Both the selling price and the unit price must be unambiguous, easily identifiable and clearly legible. National regulations may lay down specific rules relating to indication, e.g., by means of posters, labels on shelves or on packaging. Where a written or printed advertisement or a catalogue mentions the selling price of a product, the unit price shall also be indicated.

The unit price must be expressed as a price per litre or per cubic metre for products sold by volume, per kilogram or per tonne for products sold by weight, per metre for products sold by length and per square metre for products sold by area. For foodstuffs, smaller measurements, e.g., 100ml or 100g may be allowed. Ireland and the United Kingdom may retain, on a transitional basis, the imperial system of units of measurement.

Member States may exempt pre-packaged products which are sold by certain small retail businesses and handed directly by the seller to the purchaser from the obligation to indicate the unit price, where this is likely to constitute an excessive burden for such businesses or where it appears to be impracticable owing to the number of products offered for sale, the sales area, its layout or the conditions peculiar to certain forms of trading, such as particular types of itinerant trading.

Products which endanger the health or safety of consumers

Provisions in force in various Member States relating to products which, appearing to be other than they are, endanger the health or safety of consumers, were found to distort competition without necessarily ensuring effective protection for consumers. Directive 87/357 on the approximation of these laws applies to products which, although not foodstuffs, possess a form, odour, colour, appearance, packaging, labelling, volume or size, such that it is likely that consumers, especially children, will confuse them with foodstuffs and, in consequence, place them in their mouths or suck or ingest them, which might be dangerous and cause, for example, suffocation, poisoning, or the perforation or obstruction of the digestive tract. All necessary measures must be taken to prohibit the marketing, import and either manufacture or export of these products.

Good laboratory practice

The Organisation for European Cooperation and Development (OECD) adopted principles of good laboratory practice (GLP) in its Decision of 12 May 1981. These principles were accepted within the Community and are specified in Directive 87/18 on the harmonisation of laws relating to the application of the principles of GLP and the verification of their applications for tests on chemical substances.

Directive 88/320 on the inspection and verification of GLP applies to the inspection and verification of the organisational processes and the conditions under which laboratory studies are planned, performed, recorded and reported for the non-clinical testing of all chemicals in order to assess the effect of such products on man, animals and the environment. This covers, for example, cosmetics, industrial chemicals, medicinal products, food additives, animal feed additives and pesticides.

In order to avoid the duplication of tests on chemicals and the resultant waste of specialist manpower and testing laboratory resources, a procedure was introduced whereby designated national inspection authorities verify compliance with GLP of any testing laboratory within their territory claiming to use GLP in the conduct of tests on chemicals. Each year, national reports relating to the implementation of GLP are to be made, containing a list of the laboratories inspected, the date on which the inspection took place and a summary of the conclusions of the inspection. The results of inspections and study audits on GLP carried out by a Member State shall be binding on the other Member States, although there is a safeguard clause where one of the latter has sufficient reason to believe that GLP is not in fact being complied with. Thus, normally, test data generated by laboratories in one Member State will be recognised by the other Member States.

Cosmetic products

A comprehensive body of rules on the manufacturing and marketing of cosmetics is set out in Directive 76/768. A number of amendments to this directive have been made over the years, including Directive 88/667. The Commission has now proposed that the law be consolidated into one text. Cosmetic products are defined as any substance or preparation intended for placing in contact with the various external parts of the human body, i.e., epidermis, hair, nails, lips and external genital organs, or with the teeth and the mucous membranes of the mouth, with a view exclusively or principally to cleaning them, perfuming them or protecting them in order to keep them in good condition, change their appearance or correct body odours. Cosmetic products placed on the market must not be liable to harm human health when applied normally.

Cosmetics which comply with the directive may only be marketed if they also comply with the rules on labelling. The proposed amending directive tightens up these rules so that cosmetic products could be marketed only if the container and packaging bore the following information in indelible, easily legible and visible lettering:

- the name or style and address of the manufacturer or the person responsible for marketing the product within the Community;
- the nominal content;
- the date of minimum durability;
- the conditions of use and warnings;
- the batch number of manufacture or the reference for identifying the goods.

Any text, names, marks, pictures and figurative or other signs used in the labelling or advertising of these products will not be allowed if they imply that the products have characteristics which they do not have.

Tobacco and cigarettes

Directive 89/622 on the approximation of laws concerning the labelling of tobacco products seeks to harmonise health warnings. All unit packets of tobacco must carry, on the most visible surface the warning that 'Tobacco seriously damages health'. The warning must be clear and legible and printed in bold letters on a contrasting background. The Commission has also proposed a further directive strengthening the force of Directive 89/622 so as to include warnings about cancer and addiction.

Directive 90/239 harmonises the national provisions concerning the maximum tar yield of cigarettes, taking as a basis a high level of public health protection. The tar yield of cigarettes marketed in the Community shall not be greater than 15 mg per cigarette as from 31 December 1992 and 12 mg per cigarette as from 31 December 1997. Greece is allowed certain provisional derogations until 2006.

II. Public Procurement

Public procurement in the European Community

The opening up of government procurement is a key component of the internal market programme. Estimates of the Commission put such contracts at an average of 9% of national GDP if only contracts placed by central and local government are considered and as much as 15% if nationalised industries are included. Despite the free movement rules of the Treaty, especially with respect to goods and services, national governments have continued to use procurement policies as a method of sustaining their own industries through buy-national policies. Differences in national regulations regarding specifications help to sustain the divisions in the Community.

Community law has long sought to deal with the problems associated with public procurement tendering in the fields of public works and public supplies by seeking to make the tendering procedures more transparent. In particular, two directives, the 'Works' Directive 71/305 and the 'Supplies' Directive 77/62, as amended, contain detailed rules regarding advertising, technical specifications, tendering procedures and the criteria for disqualifying applicants and awarding contracts. The Commission estimates that only about 25% of public contracts are advertised in accordance with the directives. Accordingly, a series of directives amending and strengthening these rules have been adopted and others are in the pipeline in order to make their operation more effective. In addition, the scope of operation of the rules has been extended to include four major sectors which had previously been excluded: transport, water, energy and telecommunications. In order to improve the means of redress available to injured parties after a breach of the public procurement rules, a directive has been adopted on remedies in national courts and a further directive is proposed for the four special sectors. Finally, a directive has been proposed relating to procurement of services.

The 'Works' Directive and the 'Supplies' Directive

Two separate pieces of Community legislation were adopted because of the different characteristics of works and supplies. However, many of the basic rules are much the same in both directives. They are based on three main principles:

- Community-wide advertising of contracts so that firms in all Member States have an opportunity of bidding for them;
- the banning of technical specifications liable to discriminate against foreign bidders;
- application of objective criteria in tendering and award procedures.

The 'Works' Directive applies to public works contracts with an estimated value of at least 1,000,000 ECU, before VAT and the 'Supplies' Directive applies to public supply contracts with an estimated value of at least 200,000 ECU, before VAT. The authorities whose contracts are covered by the directives are the State, regional and local authorities and legal persons governed by public law or their equivalent. In each directive, a list is set out of the various national bodies included in this definition. Certain contracts awarded under international agreements are excluded from the scope of the directives.

Advertising tenders

All contracts subject to the directives must be advertised in the Supplement to the Official Journal of the European Communities. In the notices advertising tenders, certain specified items of information must be included. Contracts must be set out in accordance with the models contained in the directives. There are two types of tenders: open tenders and restricted tenders. In open tenders, any interested contractor may immediately bid for the contract, while in restricted tenders, a selection is made from the contractors who reply to the tender notice and the selected contractors only are invited to bid. Among the items which must be specified in the tender notice are the following:

- the date on which the tender notice was sent for publication to the Office for Official Publications of the European Communities;
- the tendering procedure;
- in works contracts: the site; the nature and extent of the work and the general nature of the project; if the contract is divided into several lots, the approximate size of the various lots and the possibility of tendering

for one, for several, or for all of the lots; if the contract involves design as well as construction work, sufficient information about the project to enable contractors to understand the requirements and prepare a tender accordingly;

- in supply contracts: the place of delivery, the nature and quantity of the goods to be supplied, and, if the contract is divided into several lots, whether suppliers may tender for some and/or all of the goods required;
- any delivery date or time limit for the completion of the work;
- the address of the body awarding the contract;
- in open tenders, the address from which the tender documents and additional documentation may be obtained and the final date for requesting the documentation, as well as the amount and terms of payment of any sum payable for the documentation;
- the closing date for receipt of tenders or of applications to tender, the address to which they must be sent and the language or languages in which they must be submitted;
- in restricted tenders, the final date on which invitations to tender will be issued;
- the persons authorised to be present at the opening of tenders and the date, time and place of opening;
- information about deposits and any other guarantees, whatever their form, that may be required;
- the main terms of financing and payment and/or references to the legislation in which these are laid down;
- the legal form which a consortium of contractors will be required to take if awarded the contract;
- the minimum financial and technical standards which contractors are required to meet;
- the length of time during which tenders must remain open for acceptance;
- the criteria, other than the lowest price, on which the contract is to be awarded.

Time limits must be clearly specified in the tender notice so that it is not more difficult for contractors from other countries to determine the closing date for submission of tenders than for contractors from the awarding authority's country. Thus, the Commission would not accept references to the date of publication of the notice in the national or regional official gazettes, access to which is much more difficult for foreign contractors. So that contractors throughout the Community can compete for contracts on equal terms, the national advertisement may not contain information other than that published in the Official Journal and tenders may not be advertised nationally before the date of dispatch of the tender notice for Community-wide publication. All government tenders published in the Official Journal are also on the TED (Tenders Electronic Daily) computerised system, which is accessible through various host organisations.

Technical specifications

Authorities are required to state in the general documentation on the tender and in the actual contract documents the technical specifications for the work or products and, in the case of works contracts, a description of the testing, inspection, acceptance and calculation methods to be used. Technical specifications include all the technical requirements objectively describing a job, material, product or supply suitable for the purpose for which it is required. They include all the mechanical, physical and chemical properties, classifications and standards and testing, inspection and acceptance requirements for the works and the materials and parts used in their construction. Specifications that would have the effect of discriminating against contractors in other Member States are prohibited. This covers any specifications that mention products of a specific make or source or a particular process and thereby eliminate or favour certain firms, unless such specifications are justified by the subject of the contract. In particular, it is not permitted to refer to trademarks, patents or types, or to specific origins or makes unless the awarding authority is unable to describe the subject using specifications that are sufficiently precise and intelligible to all interested parties without such references, in which case the references must be accompanied by the words 'or equivalent'. It is up to the authority using such specifications to show that they are justified. Technical specifications may be defined by reference to Community, international, national or other standards, but if there are no Community standards, authorities must consider on equal terms with products meeting the prescribed standards products from other Member States manufactured to a different design but having equivalent performance.

Tendering procedures

Time limits for bids and applications to bid are specified depending on the nature of the tender. An accelerated form of restricted tender with shorter than normal time limits is permitted in cases of urgency where observance of the normal time limits is impracticable. The requirement for contracts to be put out to competitive tender is waived in, and only in, the following special circumstances which are to be construed restrictively;

- where no suitable contractor was found in a previous tender because no or only irregular bids were received or because the bids submitted were unacceptable under national provisions that are consistent with the directives, provided that the original terms for the contract are not substantially altered;

- where, for technical or artistic reasons or because of the existence of exclusive rights, there is only one contractor in the Community able to carry out the work;
- for works carried out for purposes of research, experiment, study or development;
- in cases of extreme urgency resulting from unforeseen circumstances not attributable to the action of the awarding authority, where the normal time limits cannot be observed;
- where the works or supplies are classified as secret or where their execution must be accompanied by special security measures or where the protection of the basic interests of the State's security so requires;
- for additional work not included in an earlier project or in the contract awarded for that project which has become necessary as a result of unforeseen circumstances, where the additional work is to be done by the contractor awarded the earlier contract and is either not separable from the earlier project or is strictly necessary for its later stages. The total value of the additional work may not exceed 50% of the value of the earlier contract;
- for new work consisting in a repetition of work similar to that carried out under an earlier contract awarded to the same contractor by the same authority, provided that the work conforms to a basic project and the earlier contract was awarded after an open or restricted tender;
- for additional deliveries by the original supplier required either as part replacement of regular supplies or equipment, or to extend existing supplies or equipment, where a change of supplier would compel the authority to purchase equipment having different characteristics which would result in incompatibility or disproportionate technical difficulties of operation or maintenance;
- for goods purchased on a commodity market in the Community;
- in exceptional cases, where the nature of the work or the risks attaching to them make it impossible to estimate their total cost.

Grounds for disqualification or elimination

Safeguards are included in the system to prevent the arbitrary selection of contractors on discriminatory criteria. Contractors may be disqualified on certain grounds pertaining to their solvency, record and integrity and may be eliminated on the grounds of their financial and technical capacity to undertake the work. Any contractor may be immediately disqualified who:

- is bankrupt or, being wound up, has ceased trading or is operating under court protection pending a settlement with creditors;
- is the subject of proceedings for bankruptcy, winding-up or court protection;

- has been convicted of an offence concerning his professional conduct;
- can be shown by the authority awarding the contract to have been guilty of grave professional misconduct;
- has not fulfilled obligations relating to payment of taxes or social security obligations in either his country of residence of the country of the awarding authority;
- has been guilty of serious misrepresentation in supplying information about his current standing or past record or his financial or technical capacity.

Contractors not disqualified on any of these may only be eliminated if they fail to satisfy certain financial or technical criteria. Evidence of the contractor's financial capacity may be provided by bankers' statements, company balance sheets or a statement of the firm's total turnover for the past three years. Other evidence may be required if it is objectively necessary to show that the contractor has the capacity to undertake the work. The technical evidence that may be required for a works contract is concerned with the professional qualifications of the contractor and/or his senior employees, the satisfactory completion of other works carried out over the past five years, and particulars of the tools, plant and equipment to be used, of the workforce and managerial staff of the firm, and of the technical resources available to the contractor. For a supplies contract, the technical evidence required may cover details of the supplier's main deliveries over the last three years, a description of the supplier's technical plant, quality control procedures and research and design facilities, and particulars of the technical resources available to the supplier. In addition, the supplier may be required to produce samples, descriptions and/or photographs of the products and certificates of official authorities that the product conforms to certain specifications or standards. Where the products required are complex or are required for a special purpose, an inspection may be required of the supplier's production, design and research facilities and of his quality control procedures.

Award criteria

The only criteria on which authorities may award contracts are the lowest price and the economically most advantageous tender overall. This means that the awarding authority may consider the price, period for completion, running costs, profitability, technical merit, aesthetic and functional characteristics, after sales service and technical assistance. Only objective criteria may be used which are strictly relevant to the particular contract and uniformly applicable to all bidders.

If a bid appears to be abnormally low given the contract specifications, the authority awarding the contract is entitled to check the costing of the bid before awarding the contract to the bidder. For this purpose, it is obliged to give the bidder an opportunity of justifying the bid and, if it considers any of his explanations unsatisfactory, to tell him so. Otherwise, no bid may be rejected on this ground. In evaluating whether or not a bid is abnormally low, authorities must base themselves on the conditions in the bidder's country, having regard to the extra costs involved in supplying to another country.

The only exception to the rule that contracts be awarded to the lowest bidder or to the bid offering the most advantageous terms is where legislation provides for certain preference to be given by way of aid, as long as such legislation is compatible with Community rules on State aid.

Public works concession contracts

Public sector concession contracts under which the contractor's consideration includes a franchise to operate the completed works, such as a toll-road or bridge, are excluded from the normal Community rules on public works contracts. However, the work done under such contracts is not entirely outside the scope of the 'Works' Directive. Authorities are required to stipulate in the contract with the firm awarded the franchise that it must not discriminate on grounds of nationality when it itself awards contracts to third parties. Of course, if the organisation operating the franchise is a public authority, it will in any case be subject to the directive. The Member States have agreed voluntarily on a code of practice for these contracts. Authorities wishing to award a contract with an estimated value exceeding 1,000,000 ECU in return for a franchise to operate the works are required to advertise the contract in the Official Journal. The tender notice must describe the subject of the contract in sufficient detail to enable potentially interested contractors to make a valid assessment. It must list the personal, technical and financial conditions to be fulfilled by applicants and must state the main criteria on which the contract is to be awarded and give the closing date for submission of tenders. Furthermore, it should be stipulated in the principal contract that the contractor must subcontract out a certain percentage of the work to third parties and must advertise such subcontracts.

Amendments to the 'Supplies' Directive

Directive 88/295 has established a number of amendments to the procedures to be applied in the award of public supply contracts. This was to be implemented by 1 January 1989, except in Greece, Spain and Portugal where the date for implementation is 1 March 1992. The definition of the types of contract covered is widened. The directive now applies to contracts for pecuniary interest concluded in writing involving the purchase, lease, rental or hire purchase, with or without option to buy, of products between a supplier and one of the authorities subject to the directive. Certain amendments are made to the provisions dealing with excluded sectors and the methods of calculating the value of contracts for the purpose of applying the threshold.

Open tenders, which offer the widest possible access to contracts, are now the rule. Restricted tenders are only allowed in justified cases, such justification being constituted by, for example, a need to maintain a balance between contract value and procedural costs or the specific nature of the products to be acquired. A new procedure, called the negotiated procedure, whereby contracting authorities consult suppliers of their choice and negotiate the terms of the contract with one or several of them, may be allowed in the case of irregular tenders in response to an open or restricted procedure or in certain other limited cases. In the case of restricted and negotiated procedures, the contracting authority must draw up a written report containing the justification for the use of that procedure and details of the outcome. This report, or the main features of it, is to be communicated to the Commission at its request.

The rules on technical specifications are brought into line with the new standards policy. Without prejudice to legally binding national technical rules in so far as these are compatible with Community law, such technical specifications are to be defined by reference to national standards implementing Community standards or by reference to common technical standards. Some exceptions to this rule continue to apply.

Amendments to the 'Works' Directive

Directive 89/440 amends the 'Works' Directive resulting in an extensive revision of the provisions governing the award of public construction contracts. This was to be implemented by 19 July 1990, with an extension until 1 March 1992 for Greece, Spain and Portugal.

The threshold of 1,000,000 ECU has been replaced by 5,000,00 ECU. This will be reviewed every two years. Where a work is divided into several lots, the total value will be accumulated for the purpose of determining the applicability of the directive. It is unlawful to split up a contract with the intention of avoiding the application of the rules.

Contracts may be subject to one of three tendering procedures: 'open procedures' whereby all interested contractors may submit tenders; 'restricted procedures' whereby only those contractors invited by the contracting authority may apply; and 'negotiated procedures' whereby contracting authorities consult contractors of their choice and negotiate the terms of the contract with one or more of them. Those instances in which negotiated procedures may be used are set out in the directive. For instance, this may apply in the absence of tenders or of appropriate tenders in response to an open or restricted procedure as long as the original terms of the contract are not substantially altered or where, for technical or artistic reasons or for reasons connected with the protection of exclusive rights, the works may only be carried out by a particular contractor. For each contract awarded, the contracting authority must draw up a written report specifying the details of the contract and the reasons for choosing the contractor and for rejecting the other applicants.

Until 31 December 1992, the directive does not prevent the application of existing national provisions on the award of public works contracts which have as their objective the reduction of regional disparities and the promotion of job creation in regions whose development is lagging behind and in declining industrial regions as long as they are compatible with Community law, in particular with the principles of non-discrimination on grounds of nationality, freedom of establishment and freedom to provide services and the Community's international obligations.

Water, energy, transport and telecommunications sectors

Directive 90/531 extends the rules on public procurement to entities operating in the water, energy, transport and telecommunications sectors. It is intended to be implemented by 1 July 1992, although any Member State may postpone it until 1 January 1993, and further until 1 January 1996 in the case of Spain and 1 January 1998 in the case of Greece and Portugal. The directive applies to public authorities or public undertakings and to other bodies which operate on the basis of special and exclusive rights granted by a Member State. The activities covered by the directive are:

- the provision or operation of fixed networks intended to provide a service to the public in connection with the production, transport or distribution of drinking water, electricity, gas or heat or the supply of these to such networks;
- the exploitation of a geographical area for the purpose of exploring for or extracting oil, gas, coal or other solid fuels, or for the provision of airport, maritime or port facilities;
- the operation of networks providing a service to the public in the field of transport by railway, automated systems, tramway, trolley bus, bus or cable;
- the provision or operation of public telecommunications networks or the provision of one or more public telecommunications services.;

In certain situations the provisions of the directive will not apply. For instance, it will not apply to contracts awarded for purposes of re-sale or hire to third parties, provided that the contracting entity enjoys no special or exclusive right to sell or hire the subject of such contracts and other entities are free to sell or hire it under the same conditions as the contracting entity. Nor shall it apply to contracts with telecommunications entities for purchases intended exclusively to enable them to provide one or more telecommunications services where other entities are free to offer the same services in the same geographical area and under substantially the same conditions.

The threshold for the application of the directive to contracts is 400,000 ECU in the case of supply contracts in the water, transport and energy sectors, 600,000 ECU in the case of telecommunications supply contracts and 5,000,000 ECU in the case of all works contracts.

Public service contracts

Public service contracts will be covered by a separate directive which has been proposed by the Commission. 'Services' is defined very broadly and includes all contracts which are not covered by the existing directives on works and supplies. Another separate proposal will deal with services in the water, transport, energy and telecommunications sectors. The full procedural and other rules contained in the proposed directive will apply only to services which are of priority interest from the point of view of cross-border operations. Some services will be exempted from the rules while others will be subject only to basic transparency requirements so that there is sufficient information for those providing services to be aware of market opportunities. The classification of services as being of priority interest is to be based on a number of factors, including the current proportion of public contracts in the overall turnover of the industry concerned, the potential for increased cross-border transactions in the Community and the positive effects in terms of market opening and competition which application of the procurement rules could yield. Those services which have been identified as being of priority interest include certain types of intellectual services such as those in the fields of engineering and architecture, some telecommunications services, insurance and banking, publishing, transport and maintenance, repair and similar services. Public service concessions whereby a public authority delegates to an enterprise the provision of a service to the public are included.

For most service categories, the threshold of ECU 200,000 applies as in the Supplies Directive. Generally, the value of the contract will be equal to the total remuneration of the supplier. However, certain financial services are treated differently. For instance, insurance services which command an annual premium of ECU 100,000 are included. Services related to the design of public works are included only where the cost of the project will be not less than ECU 5,000,000.

Remedies for breach of the Community rules

Anyone who believes that a Member State or public authority has breached its obligations under the Community rules on public procurement may complain direct to the Commission or may bring an action before the national authorities, including a national court.

Complaints to the Commission

There is no specific form in which complaints should be submitted, but it is essential to give the Commission full details of the complaint and all the evidence in the complainant's possession. The Commission can then investigate the case quickly without having to ask for further information from the national authorities, thereby enabling it to take appropriate action against the Member State in time for this to be of some use to the complainant. It is vital that the complaint should be made as soon as the complainant becomes aware of the alleged breach, so that, if the award procedure is still in progress, the Commission might be able to act before the contract is awarded. The matter may end up in the Court of Justice which has the power to take interim measures ordering the Member State not to proceed with the tender pending the Court's judgment.

Actions before the national court

Complainants may also bring an action against the awarding authority in the national courts in order to establish their rights under Community law. This may be a much more effective method of ensuring compliance with the law, since the remedies available from the national court can include an injunction against the awarding authority or, possibly, damages. However, different national legal rules apply. Accordingly, a directive has been adopted coordinating the national laws relating to the application of Community rules on procedures for the award of public contracts.

Under Directive 89/665, to be implemented by 1 December 1991, Member States are to take the measures necessary to ensure that decisions taken by the contracting authorities may be reviewed effectively and as rapidly as possible. They must ensure that the review procedures are available at least to any person having or having had an interest in obtaining a particular contract and who has been or who risks being harmed by an alleged infringement. New review bodies may be established for these purposes. The complainant may be required to have previously notified the contracting authority of the alleged infringement and of his intention to seek review. Among the powers of the review body are the ability to take interim measures, including suspension of the award procedure, the setting aside of unlawful decisions and the award of damages to injured persons. However, review procedures need not have an automatic suspensive effect.

The Commission, where it considers that a clear and manifest infringement of the rules has been committed, may notify the Member State and the contracting authority concerned accordingly. Within 21 days, the Member State must communicate to the Commission either its confirmation that the infringement has been corrected, or a reasoned submission as to why no correction has been made, or a notice that the award procedure has been suspended. Where the procedure has been suspended, the Member State must subsequently notify the Commission when the suspension is lifted or if a new award procedure has been initiated.

In addition to this directive, the Commission has proposed a further directive on the application of the procedural rules in the special sectors of water, transport, energy and telecommunications. This calls for Member States to take the measures necessary to ensure that decisions taken by the contracting entities may be reviewed effectively and as rapidly as possible and lays down the framework for taking such decisions.

III. Free Movement for Labour and the Professions

Obstacles to free movement of persons and services

Free movement of persons within the European Community is one of the most fundamental objectives of the EEC Treaty. The ability of nationals of one Member State to move freely through the Community without hindrance is the most potent expression of European Union. Although the Treaty rules are concerned largely with the rights of nationals to be employed in another Member State or with rights of establishment and freedom to provide services, the developments in Community law have not been limited to the ability to work. Progress has been made in related areas, such as the social security arrangements for workers and their dependants, vocational training, and rights of residence.

In the White Paper, the Commission stated that it intended to make the necessary proposals to eliminate any remaining obstacles standing in the way of the free movement of workers and rights of residence. Two proposed directives deal with the taxation of migrant workers and their families and with the removal of cumbersome administrative procedures relating to residence permits. As regards the free movement of workers in general, comparability of vocational training qualifications is a high priority. The Council has adopted a decision on this with the aim of enabling workers to make better use of their qualifications, in particular for the purposes of obtaining suitable employment in another Member State. The intention is that a European vocational training card will serve as proof that the holder has been awarded a specific qualification. In addition, the Council has adopted the COMETT programme on cooperation between universities and enterprises regarding training in the field of technology.

Substantial barriers remain in the field of rights of establishment of the professions, the main problem being the harmonisation of professional qualifications. Action in this field concerns recognition of vocational or professional qualifications generally and also specific qualifications in the pharmacy, medical and technological sectors.

Finally, it was recognised that differences in national laws on commercial representation substantially affected conditions of competition within the Community. A directive has therefore been adopted with the aim of coordinating certain provisions of national laws relating to self-employed commercial agents.

Income tax provisions for workers who live in one Member State and work in another and certain other payments

It is common in income tax systems for tax liability to be assessed differently according to whether the taxpayer is a resident or non-resident of the country. These differences may serve to penalise workers who live in one Member State but work in another. This is especially the case with frontier workers. In order to ensure greater freedom of movement for workers within the Community, it is essential to reduce the differences that exist in the taxation of the employment income of resident and non-resident workers. The balance between direct and indirect taxes must also be seen as an operating factor in this barrier to free movement. A frontier worker returns usually on a daily basis to the Member State where he resides and pays his indirect taxes for the most part in that State. The Commission has proposed a directive concerning the harmonisation of income tax provisions with respect to freedom of movement for workers within the Community. This proposed directive deals with certain provisions concerning the taxation of the income of frontier workers and of other non-resident employed persons and the taxation treatment of certain other payments. For the purposes of the directive, the term 'resident' is to be interpreted according to national tax provisions and the relevant double taxation treaty.

Frontier workers

A frontier worker means any individual deriving income from employment who exercises that employment in a Member State where he is not resident and who is resident in another Member State to which he returns as a rule daily. A frontier worker who is posted by his employer to a place inside the Community other than his usual place of work so that he is prevented from returning daily to the place where he resides would not lose his status as a frontier worker, provided that the posting did not exceed in aggregate one third of the days in the calendar year for which he has the status of a frontier worker.

Employment income of a frontier worker would be subject to tax in the Member State in which he was resident. The Member State in which the employment was exercised might, however, levy a tax on that income, but only by means of a withholding tax. The withholding tax would then be credited against the tax due in the Member State of residence. To the extent that the withholding tax exceeded the tax due in the Member State of residence, that State would refund the excess to the frontier worker. It would then be for the two Member States to agree upon the apportionment between them of the tax receipts and the amounts of refund.

Non-residents

Other provisions apply to individuals, other than frontier workers, who are resident in one Member State and taxed in another on income from dependent personal services and pensions and other similar remuneration received in consideration of past employment. This income would not be subjected in the taxing State to any more burdensome taxation than if the taxpayer were resident in that State. The taxing State could restrict the allowances, exemptions, deductions and other general tax reliefs reserved for resident taxpayers to the proportion that the net income bore to the total net income of the taxpayer.

Tax allowances

Where a Member State grants a tax advantage for the purposes of income tax, whether by way of deduction from the tax base or otherwise, for payments made by a natural person to an insurance company, bank, pension fund, building society or any other recipient, such a tax advantage could not be refused solely because that recipient was situated, established or resident in another Member State.

Right of residence in another Member State

A number of directives have been adopted or proposed relating to the right of residence for nationals of one Member State in the territory of another Member State. Such a right is essential for the proper exercise of the rights needed for the free movement of persons. Although Directive 64/221 coordinated special measures concerning the movement and residence of Community nationals, the exercise of the right of residence was largely concerned with those instances where it was necessary to carry out work, whether this was employed or self-employed. The new measures seeks to extend this to situations which are independent of the pursuit of an economic activity. Directive 90/364 grants a conditional right of residence throughout the Community, Directive 90/365 deals with the right of residence for employees and self-employed persons who have ceased their occupational activity and Directive 90/366 covers the rights of residence of students. In addition, proposals have been made to amend Directive 68/360 and Regulation 1612/68 relating to free movement of workers and their families and a further proposal has been made for a directive on voting rights for Community nationals in local elections in their Member State of residence.

Right of residence

Where a person does not have the right of free movement under other provisions of Community law, Member States must grant the right of residence to other Community nationals and to members of their families, provided that they are covered by sickness insurance in respect of all risks in the host State and have sufficient resources to avoid becoming a burden on the social assistance system of the host State during their period of residence. These resources will be deemed sufficient when they are higher than the level of resources below which social assistance may be granted. Exercise of the right of residence shall be evidenced by means of a residence permit, the validity of which may be limited to five years on a renewable basis. In certain cases, revalidation may be necessary after two years. The spouse and the dependent children of the person entitled to this right of residence shall be entitled to take up any employed or self-employed activity anywhere within that State, even if they themselves are not Community nationals.

Persons who have ceased occupational activity

Under Directive 90/365, from 1 July 1992, the right of residence must be granted to Community nationals who have pursued an activity as an employee or self-employed person and members of their families, provided that they are recipients of an invalidity or early retirement pension, or old age benefits, or of a pension in respect of an industrial accident or disease of an amount sufficient to avoid becoming a burden on the social security system of the host State during their period of residence and provided that they are covered by sickness insurance in respect of all risks in the host State. As with the right given by Directive 90/364, sufficient resources will be deemed available where they are higher than the level for the grant of social assistance and evidence of the right of residence is to be given by the residence permit which is valid for five years on a renewable basis. Similar rights of employment apply to non-Community dependents.

Students

In order to facilitate access to vocation training, Directive 90/366 provides that students who are Community nationals and who do not enjoy the right of free movement under other Community law provisions must be granted the right of residence, along with their spouse and dependent children, where the student assures the relevant national authority that he has sufficient resources to avoid becoming a burden on the social assistance system of the host State during his period of residence, provided that he is enrolled in a recognised educational establishment for the principal purpose of following a vocational training course. The right of residence is limited to the duration of the course of studies in question. It shall be evidenced by a residence permit which may be limited to the duration of the course or to one year where the course lasts longer, in which case it shall be renewed annually. The spouse or dependent children shall be entitled to take up employment even where they are non-Community nationals. This directive does not entitle the student to any right to the payment of maintenance grants.

Ancillary rights to freedom of movement

Regulation 1612/68 and Directive 68/360 are to be strengthened so as to further the implementation of the right to free movement for Community nationals. A number of amendments have been proposed by the Commission to these measures. For instance, where national provisions attribute legal effect or make social or tax advantages subject to the occurrence of certain facts or events, those facts or events occurring in other Member States would have to be taken into account as if they occurred in the national territory. A residence permit would be valid for five years but renewable for ten years at a time.

Right to vote in local elections

A directive has been proposed on voting rights for Community nationals in local elections in their Member State of residence. The Commission proposes that Community nationals residing in another Member State should have the right to vote and to stand for election in local elections in the municipality in which they are resident. The putative voter would have to produce a document from the consulate of his State of origin certifying that he had not been deprived of his civic rights in that country and that he could no longer exercise the right to vote in local elections there because of non-residence. He would be entitled to be registered to vote following a period of continuous residence in the host State of not less than the term of office of the municipal council in the case of the right to vote and two terms if he wishes to stand for election. Applications for entry on the electoral register would be made only in the municipality in which the applicant was actually resident and would be subject to the rules laid down by national legislation, in particular as regards the minimum period of residence in the municipality and the deadlines for applying for entry on the electoral register.

The offices of Mayor, Deputy Mayor or other equivalent position could be restricted to nationals of the host State. Where members of a municipal council were, by virtue of that membership, electors of a parliamentary assembly, national law could provide that nationals of other Member States who were members of the council could not take part in the election.

Comparability of vocational training qualifications

The absence within the Community of a system of mutual recognition of vocational training qualifications was a factor inhibiting the freedom of movement of workers in so far as it restricted the possibility for workers seeking employment in one Member State from relying on vocational qualifications which were obtained in another Member State. Under the Treaty, the Council was required to lay down general principles for implementing a common vocational training policy. Decision 63/266 established general principles in this area and called for a common vocational training policy to be framed to enable levels of training to be harmonised progressively. However, there remains a substantial degree of diversity in the vocational training systems in the Community. This was recognised in the Council's Resolution of 11 July 1983, in which it also affirmed the need for a convergence of these policies.

Decision 85/368 on the comparability of vocational training qualifications between the Member States requires expedited common action by the Member States and the Commission, so as to enable workers to make better use of their qualifications, in particular for the purpose of obtaining suitable employment in other Member States. The Commission, in close cooperation with the Member States, is to undertake work in respect of specific occupations or groups of occupations, particularly those of skilled workers. Employers' and employees' organisations at Community level are to be involved. Whenever possible, the SEDOC register, used in connection with the European system for the international clearing of vacancies and applications for employment, is to be used as the common frame of reference for vocational classifications.

The procedure to be adopted is as follows:

- selection of the relevant occupations or groups of occupations on a proposal from the Member States or the competent employer or worker organisation at Community level;

- drawing up mutually agreed Community job descriptions for these occupations or groups of occupations;
- matching the vocational training qualifications recognised in the various Member States with the job descriptions;
- establishing tables incorporating information on:
  - the SEDOC and national classification codes;
  - the level of vocational training;
  - for each Member State, the vocational title and corresponding vocational training qualifications;
  - the organisations and institutions responsible for dispensing vocational training;
  - the authorities and organisations competent to issue or to validate diplomas, certificates or other documents certifying that vocational training has been acquired;
- publication of the mutually agreed Community job descriptions and the comparative tables in the Official Journal;
- establishment of a model standard information sheet for each occupation or group of occupations, to be published in the Official Journal;
- dissemination of information on the established comparabilities to all appropriate bodies at national, regional and local levels, as well as throughout the occupational sectors concerned.

If experience shows the need for it, this action could be supported by the creation of a Community-wide database. Each Member State must designate a coordination body responsible for ensuring, in close collaboration with the social partners and the occupational sectors concerned, the proper dissemination of information to all interested bodies. These bodies are to establish appropriate arrangements with regard to vocational training information for their competent national, regional or local bodies as well as for their own nationals wishing to work in other Member States and for workers who are nationals of other Member States. These bodies may supply on request the model occupational information sheet which the worker may present to the employer together with his national certificate. The Commission, meanwhile, will continue studying the introduction of a common European vocational training pass.

Cooperation between universities and enterprises regarding training in the field of technology -- COMETT

The Community has adopted a number of industrial projects aimed at strengthening the connections between industry and training institutions.

These plans, such as ESPRIT (information technology), BRITE (industrial technology) and other programmes dealing with biotechnology and scientific and technical information, increase the potential for university research and vocational and other training to be more industry orientated and for better use of human resources. A further programme was adopted by Decision 86/365 on cooperation between universities and enterprises regarding training in the field of technology – COMETT. This was extended into a second stage by Decision 89/27.

COMETT II aims at reinforcing training in, in particular, advanced technology, the development of highly skilled human resources and the competitiveness of European industry. It is centred on the changing skill requirements of industry and its personnel. It will facilitate innovation and technology transfer as well as the balanced economic and social development of the Community. In this context, its objectives are:

- to improve the contribution of advanced technology training at the various levels concerned and thus the contribution of training to economic and social development;
- to foster the joint development of training programmes and the exchange of experience and also the optimum use of training resources at Community level, notably through the creation of transnational sectoral and regional networks of advanced technology training projects;
- to respond to the specific skill requirements of SMEs;
- to promote equal opportunities for men and women in initial and continuing training in advanced technology;
- to give a university dimension to cooperation between universities and industry in initial and continuing training relating to technologies and their applications and transfer.

The funds estimated as necessary for the programme, which the Commission administers, amount to 200 million ECU for 1990-1994. COMETT II comprises a range of transnational projects, including a European network of university-industry training partnerships (UITPs), with the objective of identifying and resolving training needs. Specific incentives are to be developed to promote transnational exchange through the allocation of grants for students and others to train abroad and for personnel to be seconded from universities and industry to bodies in other Member States. Other projects deal with initiatives with regard to multimedia training systems and other advanced technology applications. Finally, a part of the budget is to be spent on measures concerning exchange of information, analysis and monitoring of the skills needed by industry and its consequent training needs, and an examination of the obstacles hindering the further development of university-enterprise cooperation.

Recognition of higher education proposals

Rather than provide individual directives covering each professional activity, the Council has adopted Directive 89/48 on a general system for the recognition of higher education diplomas. This is designed to help those who have acquired their higher education in a Member State other than that in which they wish to carry on their professional activity. It applies in the case of any diploma, certificate, or other evidence of formal qualifications which shows that the holder has successfully completed a post-secondary course of at least three years duration, or of an equivalent duration part-time, at a university or establishment of higher education or another establishment of similar level and, where appropriate, that he has successfully completed the professional training required and which shows that the holder has the professional qualifications required for the taking up or pursuit of a regulated profession in the Member State where the diploma was acquired. The education and training attested by the diploma must have been received mainly in the Community or the holder must have three years' professional experience certified by the Member State which recognised the diploma of a third country. In addition to this directive, the Commission has proposed a complementary directive for the recognition of professional education and training covering secondary education and post-secondary courses of less than three years' duration.

Directive 89/48 applies to any national of a Member State wishing to pursue a regulated profession in a host Member State in a self-employed capacity or as an employed person. It does not apply to those professions which are governed by separate directives on mutual recognition of qualifications.

Where, in a host Member State, the taking up or pursuit of a regulated profession is subject to possession of a diploma, the competent authority in that State may not, on grounds of inadequate qualifications, refuse to authorise a Community national to take up or pursue that profession on the same conditions as apply to its own nationals:

- if the applicant holds the diploma required in another Member State for the taking up or pursuit of that profession in its territory, such diploma having been awarded in a Member State; or;
- if the applicant has pursued the profession full-time for two years during the previous ten years in another Member State which does not regulate that profession. In this case, he must possess evidence of formal qualifications which have been awarded in a Member State, which show that the holder has successfully completed a post-secondary course of at least three year' duration or its equivalent part-time together with any necessary professional training, and which have prepared him for the pursuit of the profession.

The host State might also require the applicant to provide evidence of professional experience where the duration of the education and training adduced in support of his application is at least one year less than that required in the host State. In this event, the period of professional experience required:

- may not exceed twice the shortfall in duration of education and training where the shortfall relates to post-secondary studies and/or to a period of probationary practice carried out under the control of a supervising professional person and ending with an examination;
- may not exceed the shortfall where the shortfall relates to professional practice acquired with the assistance of a qualified member of the profession.

In addition, the host State may require the applicant to complete an adaptation period not exceeding three years or to take an aptitude test where the matters covered by the education and training received differ substantially from those covered by the diploma required in the host State. This is also the case where the profession regulated in the host State comprises activities which are not included in the professional activities of the State from which the applicant comes and that difference corresponds to specific education and training required in the host State covering matters which differ substantially from those covered by the applicant's diploma or other qualifications. It is to be for the applicant to choose between an adaptation period and an aptitude test, except for professions whose practice requires precise knowledge of national law and in respect of which the provision of advice and/or assistance concerning national law is an essential and constant aspect of the professional activity, in which case the choice lies with the Member State.

A host State may allow the applicant, with a view to improving his possibilities of adapting to the professional environment of that State, to undergo there, on the basis of equivalence, that part of his professional education and training represented by professional practice acquired with the assistance of a qualified member of the profession which he has not undergone in the State from which he comes. Where the host State requires of persons wishing to take up a regulated profession proof that they are of good character or repute or that they have not been declared bankrupt or suspends or prohibits the pursuit of that profession in the event of serious professional misconduct or a criminal offence, that State would be required to accept as sufficient evidence the production of documents issued by the competent authorities of that person's home State showing that the requirements were met. If the home State does not issue such documents, they are to be replaced by a declaration on oath or a solemn declaration made before a competent judicial or administrative authority or, where appropriate, a notary in the home State. Where the host State required of its own nationals a certificate of physical and mental health, the equivalent document from the home State would suffice. Host States might require that these documents and certificates be presented no more than three months after their date of issue.

Persons carrying on a profession in a host State must be allowed the right to use their lawful professional or academic title. If the latter might be confused with an academic title of the host State, that State might require that it be followed by the name and location or examining board of the country which awarded it.

A complementary directive is proposed which would apply to those wishing to pursue a regulated profession either in a self-employed or employed capacity and covers secondary education and post-secondary courses of less than three years' duration. Essentially, it applies the same rules mutatis mutandis to qualifications for that level of education as Directive 89/48 applies to higher education.

Pharmacy

Progress has been made in the mutual recognition of qualifications in the field of pharmacy, although not all conditions of access to and pursuit of such activities have been coordinated. Directives 85/432 and 85/433 contain various provisions dealing with this area. Since training courses in the Member States were broadly comparable, the intention was to allow Member States freedom of organisation as regards teaching, subject to minimum standards being observed, coupled with a system of mutual recognition of qualifications.

Access to pharmacy activities

Member States must ensure that the holders of a diploma, certificate or other university or equivalent qualification in pharmacy are entitled at least to access to the following activities, subject, where appropriate, to the requirement of additional professional experience:

- the preparation of the pharmaceutical form of medicinal products;
- the manufacturing and testing of medicinal products;
- the testing of medicinal products in a laboratory for the testing of medicinal products;
- the storage, preservation and distribution of medicinal products at the wholesale stage;
- the preparation, testing, storage and supply of medicinal products in pharmacies open to the public;
- the preparation, testing, storage and dispensing of medicinal products in hospitals;
- the provision of information and advice on medicinal products.

These pharmacy qualifications must meet certain minimum conditions in that training leading to the award of the qualification must ensure adequate knowledge of:

- medicines and the substances used in the manufacture of medicines;
- pharmaceutical technology and the physical, chemical, biological and microbiological testing of medicinal products;
- the metabolism and the effects of medicinal products and of the action of toxic substances and of the use of medicinal products;
- how to evaluate scientific data concerning medicines in order to be able to supply appropriate information on the basis of this knowledge;
- the legal and other requirements associated with the practice of pharmacy.

With minor exceptions, the training must cover a period of at least five years comprising at least four years of full-time theoretical and practical training in a university or a higher education institution of equivalent status and at least six months of in-service training in a pharmacy or hospital. The training must include at least the following subjects:

- plant and animal biology;
- physics;
- general and inorganic chemistry;
- organic chemistry;
- analytical chemistry;
- pharmaceutical chemistry, including analysis of medicinal products;
- general and applied biochemistry (medical);
- anatomy and physiology—medical terminology;
- microbiology;
- pharmacology and pharmacotherapy;
- pharmaceutical technology;
- toxicology;
- pharmacognosy;
- legislation and, where appropriate, professional ethics.

The balance between theoretical and practical training must give sufficient importance to theory to maintain the university character of the training.

Mutual recognition of diplomas in pharmacy

Member States must give mutual recognition to diplomas, certificates and other formal pharmacy qualifications. However, since there is as yet no convergence of views among the Member States on the appropriate requirements for additional professional experience, the qualifications need not be recognised in the case of the establishment of new pharmacies open to the public and those which have been in operation for less than three years. These provisions do not apply to Greece, except in the case of employed pharmacists. Professional experience is also evidenced by the issue of a certificate by the competent authorities in each Member State. Qualifications which were awarded and which do not satisfy all of the above requirements are to be treated as if they did so if they are evidence of training which was either completed before, or commenced before but completed after, the implementation of the directive and the holder has a certificate stating that he has been lawfully and effectively engaged in practice for at least three of the preceding five years.

Academic titles may be used in other Member States provided that, if the title might be confused with other qualifications of the host State which would require additional training and which the holder has not undergone, the host State may require a suitable wording to be used. Where in the host State the use of the professional title is regulated, nationals of other Member States who fulfil the conditions of the directive are entitled to use the professional title of the host State.

Any requirement of proof of good character, good repute or physical or mental health shall be satisfied in the host State by a certificate of the Member State of origin, which must be presented within three months of issue. If a host State requires of its own nationals an oath or solemn declaration and the form of that oath or declaration cannot be used by nationals of other Member States, the host State is obliged to ensure that an appropriate and equivalent form is offered to the persons concerned. The competent authorities of the Member States are to cooperate with each other in the provision of information regarding evidence of professional misconduct and other relevant matters.

General medical practice

Rules on freedom of movement for medical practitioners were established by Directives 75/362 and 75/363. Any person wishing to take up and pursue a medical profession must hold a diploma, certificate or other evidence of formal qualification in medicine which guarantees that, during the complete training period, he has acquired:

- adequate knowledge of the sciences on which medicine is based and a good understanding of the scientific methods including the principles of measuring biological functions, the evaluation of scientifically established facts and the analysis of data;
- sufficient understanding of the structure, functions and behaviour of healthy and sick persons, as well as relations between the state of health and the physical and social surroundings of the human being;
- adequate knowledge of clinical disciplines and practices, providing him with a coherent picture of mental and physical diseases, of medicine

from the point of view of prophylaxis, diagnosis and therapy and of human reproduction;
- suitable clinical experience in hospitals under appropriate supervision.

The complete period of medical training is to comprise at least a six-year course or 5,500 hours of theoretical and practical instruction given in or under the supervision of a university.

Mutual recognition of diplomas in specific training

These directives contained no provisions regarding the mutual recognition of diplomas attesting to specific training in general medical practice or the criteria to which such training should conform. However, Directive 86/457 provides that specific training in general medical practice must comply with certain minimum requirements as follows, thus allowing for mutual recognition of qualifications:

- entry shall be conditional upon successful completion of at least six years' study on a course recognised in Directive 75/363;
- it shall be a full-time course lasting at least two years;
- it shall be practically rather than theoretically based; practical instruction shall be for at least six months in an approved hospital or clinic and six months in a general medical practice or centre;
- it shall entail the personal participation of the trainee in the professional activities and responsibilities of the persons with whom he works.

If a Member State currently provides training by means of experience in a general medical practice acquired by the medical practitioner in his own surgery under the supervision of an authorised training supervisor, this may be retained on an experimental basis as long as certain other conditions are fulfilled.

Part-time training may be authorised as long as it is of a quality equivalent to that of full-time training. The total duration of the course must be at least as long as a full-time course and the weekly duration of a part-time course must be at least 60% of that of a full-time course. It must include a certain number of full-time training periods, both for the training conducted at a training or clinic and for the training given in an approved medical practice or centre. Irrespective of any acquired rights they recognise, Member States may issue their diploma, certificate or other evidence of medical qualification to a medical practitioner who holds the equivalent qualification from another Member State. From 1 January 1995, and subject to the acquired rights it has recognised, each Member State is to make the exercise of general medical practice under its national social security scheme conditional on possession of these qualifications. Persons who are undergoing specific training in general medical practice may be exempted from this scheme. Each Member State shall specify the acquired rights that it recognises. However, it must recognise the right to exercise the activities of general medical practitioner under its national social security scheme without evidence of the relevant qualifications having been acquired by all those doctors who on 31 December 1994, possess such a right and who are established in its territory on that date. The competent authorities of each Member State will issue on request a certificate granting doctors possessing acquired rights the right to practise as general medical practitioners under its national social security system without the need for the evidence of the relevant qualifications. These provisions do not prejudice the possibility, which is open to Member States, of granting, in accordance with their own rules and in respect of their own territory, the right to practise as general practitioners to persons who possess qualifications obtained in a non-member country. Certificates granted in the Federal Republic of Germany stating that qualifications obtained in the German Democratic Republic are recognised as equivalent shall also be recognised.

Academic titles may be used in the host State, although the holder may be required to state the name and location of the establishment or examining board which established it. If the title might be confused with a title in the host State requiring additional training which the person concerned has not undergone, the host State may require that person to use the title in a suitable form.

Activities in the field of technical research, invention and consultancy and their application

Pending the adoption of general measures for the mutual recognition of qualifications, the Commission proposed a directive for transitional measures for activities in the field of technical research, invention and consultancy and their application. A Member State would be obliged to recognise the qualifications listed in the proposed directive as being equivalent to the qualifications available in that State. Three different categories of qualifications are listed. The first covers those which are acquired on completion of a course of at least four years in a university or equivalent institution. The second covers those gained after three years in a higher technical college. The third covers those which are gained after 13 years education which must have ended in at least two years full-time technical training. In each case, the qualification must be accompanied by a further two years' practical experience.

A further directive was proposed specifically dealing with transitional measures of mutual recognition in the training of engineers. Member States would be obliged to ensure that their rules on the training of engineers correspond to the requirements of the second category of the general proposed directive. They would further have to ensure that those who held that qualification would be allowed access to the university course in the first category. To this end, they could decide on any complementary education necessary taking account of the studies already completed.

Self-employed commercial agents

Differences in national laws concerning commercial representation substantially affect the conditions of competition within the Community and are detrimental both to the protection available to commercial agents and to the security of commercial transactions. Often, those differences are such as to inhibit substantially the conclusion and operation of commercial representation contracts where principal and commercial agent are established in different Member States. Directive 86/653 on the coordination of the laws relating to self-employed commercial agents concerns laws governing some of the relations between commercial agents and their principals. Such provisions shall apply at least to contracts concluded after the entry into force of the directive and shall apply to all contracts in operation by 1 January 1994, at the latest.

A commercial agent is defined as a self-employed intermediary who has continuing authority to negotiate the sale or the purchase of goods on behalf of a principal or to negotiate and conclude such transactions on behalf of and in the name of that principal. It does not include a person who, in his capacity as an officer, is empowered to enter into commitments binding on a company or association, or a partner who is lawfully authorised to enter into commitments binding on his partners. Nor does it include a receiver, a receiver and manager, a liquidator, or a trustee in bankruptcy. The directive does not apply to commercial agents whose activities are unpaid or to operations on the commodity exchanges or in the commodity market. In the United Kingdom, the Crown Agents are excluded. Specific provisions of the directive deal with the rights and obligations of the parties, remuneration and conclusion and termination of the agency contract.

Rights and obligations

In performing his activities, the agent must look after his principal's interests and act dutifully and in good faith. He must make proper efforts to negotiate and conclude the transactions he is instructed to take care of, he must communicate to his principal all necessary information and he must comply with reasonable instructions given by the principal. The principal must also act dutifully and in good faith. He must provide his agent with the necessary documentation relating to the goods concerned and obtain for him the information necessary for the performance of the contract. In particular, he must notify the agent once he anticipates that the volume of commercial transactions will be significantly lower than that which the agent could normally have expected. Also, the principal must inform the agent of his acceptance, refusal or any non-execution of a commercial transaction which the agent has procured for him.

Remuneration

In the absence of specific agreement between the parties, a commercial agent is entitled to the remuneration that would be customary for a contract dealing in such goods or, if there is no such custom, to reasonable remuneration. Where the agreement provides for payment on commission, the agent is entitled to commission where a transaction has been concluded as a result of his action or is concluded with a third party whom he has previously acquired as a customer for transactions of the same kind. Where the agent is entrusted with, or has an exclusive right to, a specific geographical area or group of customers, he is entitled to a commission where a transaction has been entered into with a customer belonging to that area or group. If the transaction is concluded after the termination of the agency agreement, the agent is entitled to commission where the transaction is mainly attributable to his efforts during the period of the agreement and it was entered into within a reasonable period after the contract terminated.

Termination

An agency contract for a fixed period which continues to be performed by both parties after that period has expired shall be deemed to be converted into a contract for an indefinite period. Where a contract is concluded for an indefinite period, either party may terminate it by notice. The directive lays down rules for ascertaining the period of notice. This shall not affect the laws which permit immediate termination of the contract because of the failure of one party to carry out all or part of his obligations or where exceptional circumstances arise. Certain provisions deal with the circumstances in which, and the amounts by which, the principal must indemnify the agent or pay him compensation where the contract is terminated. A clause in the agreement restricting the business activities of the agent following termination of the contract is valid only if it is in writing and it relates to the group of customers and/or the geographical area entrusted to the agent and to the kind of goods covered by his agency under the contract. Such a restriction may be valid for not more than two years.

IV. Common Market for Services

1. Financial Services

Free Movement and Financial Services

The Commission considers that the free movement of financial products should follow the same pattern as the free movement of goods. In the *Cassis de Dijon* judgment, the European Court stated that a product lawfully manufactured in one Member State should, in principle, be allowed to be marketed in another Member State. In the same way, insurance policies, home ownership savings contracts and unit trusts, once authorised in one Member State, should be allowed to be marketed in another.

There are three key elements underlying the Commission's approach to achieving unified financial markets and to facilitating the movement of these financial products:

- harmonisation of essential standards for prudential supervision and for the protection of investors, depositors and consumers;
- mutual recognition of the way in which each Member State applies those standards;
- based on the first two elements, home country control and supervision of financial institutions operating in other Member States.

The aim is, therefore, to obtain sufficient harmonisation to enable the internal market in financial services to be completed on the basis of mutual recognition of control and supervision. The Commission's proposals in the White Paper range across banking, insurance and transactions in securities.

BANKING

Background

Progress on the harmonisation of the banking sector was slow with only three directives being adopted before the publication of the Commission's White Paper in 1985. The first of these, Directive 73/183, aimed to abolish discrimination against banks and other financial institutions seeking to establish themselves or provide services in other Member States. For example, the directive required certain Member States to abolish nationality requirements which were imposed on managers and directors of banks. However, the directive did not seek to coordinate national laws which applied both to domestic and foreign banks and was of minor importance.

The First Banking Directive

It was not until 1977 that the Council embarked on the course of harmonising the different banking laws when it adopted its First Banking Coordination Directive 77/780. This constituted the first step towards a common market for credit institutions. The primary aim of this directive is to lay down minimum requirements which must be fulfilled by credit institutions before they can be authorised to operate. As a result national authorities can only grant authorisation when the following condition(s) are met:

- the credit institution must have separate capital (e.g., separate from the resources of the proprietors);
- it must possess adequate minimum own funds;
- at least two persons must effectively direct the business of the institution and they must be of 'sufficient repute' and possess 'sufficient experience'.

Although this directive led to a system of prior authorisation being introduced, its practical effect was limited. Whilst it is true that the authorisation requirements reduced to some extent the discretionary powers of national supervisory authorities, authorisation in one Member State does not imply automatic authorisation in another. Indeed, the authorisation procedure does not prevent Member States from requiring that more stringent conditions be fulfilled and in practice national laws do lay down further criteria. As a result, national regulatory rules still differ widely. Another serious drawback is that branches of banks established in other Member States remain subject to the authorisation procedure of the host Member State.

Whereas Directive 73/183 applies to financial institutions, Directive 77/780 only applies to credit institutions. The distinction is important because different rules apply. The distinction may be summarised as follows: a financial institution's principal activity is merely to grant credit facilities (including guarantees) or to make investments; credit institutions, such as banks, receive deposits or other repayable funds from the public and grant credits for their own account. A list of the credit institutions covered by the directive is published by the Commission in the Official Journal of the European Communities.

Supervision on a consolidated basis

A step towards home country control was made by Directive 83/350 which provides that supervision on a consolidated basis should be exercised by the competent authorities of the country in which the parent credit institution has its head office. A parent credit institution is deemed to participate in other credit institutions if it directly or indirectly owns 25% or more of the other's capital. 'Supervision' means the techniques employed by the supervisory authorities in order to monitor prudential aspects of a credit institution's business. Supervision on a consolidated basis enables the authorities supervising a parent institution to make a more soundly based judgement about the financial situation of that credit institution. The Commission has proposed a further directive which aims to consolidate supervision of all banking groups including those whose parent is not a credit institution.

The White Paper proposals on banking

As a result of the Commission's White Paper, considerable progress has been made in the banking sector. The legislation necessary complete the internal market in banking has been adopted. The Council has adopted directives on the annual accounts of banks and their branches, own funds, solvency ratios and minimum capital needed for authorisation and continuing business. Recommendations on large exposures and deposit-guarantee schemes have been made. Essentially, the approach has been to harmonise the essential supervisory and prudential rules necessary to secure mutual recognition of national authorisation and supervisory systems. This will enable the application of the principle of home country control and the granting of a single licence recognised throughout the Community. The single banking licence, which lies at the very heart of completing the internal market in banking, will permit banks licensed in one Member State to open branches and provide services in another.

The annual accounts and consolidated accounts of banks and other financial institutions

Directive 86/635 aims to ensure that the content, format and layout of accounts of credit and financial institutions in different Member States are comparable. As more such institutions operate across national borders the need to coordinate accountancy rules has become important for two reasons: first, it enables creditors, debtors and members of the general public to compare accounts of various credit and financial institutions which may be in competition with each other; secondly, the coordination of rules relating to accounts and consolidated accounts make it easier for national authorities to authorise and supervise these institutions.

The directive fills the gap left by the Fourth and Seventh Directives on company law. The Fourth Directive coordinates the rules relating to the presentation and content of annual accounts and reports and valuation methods of companies in general. This was supplemented by the Seventh Directive which coordinates the national laws on the consolidation of accounts (e.g., within a group). Directive 86/365 broadly applies the rules contained in those directives to credit institutions and certain financial institutions which were specifically excluded from the two company directives. It applies to all banks whether they are incorporated or not (e.g., partnerships are included) and all limited financial institutions not covered by the Fourth Company Directive. Certain credit institutions, e.g., Central Banks, may be exempted. Unlike the Fourth Directive, there is no exemption for small and medium sized undertakings.

Balance sheet

Whereas the Fourth Directive allows for a vertical and a horizontal balance sheet for companies, credit and financial institutions may only adopt a horizontal format of balance sheet. There are sixteen main asset captions which are to be classified in order of decreasing liquidity and fourteen liability captions. A change in presentation for some banks will be the disclosure of contingent liabilities and banking commitments on the face of the balance sheet but below the balance sheet totals. This information is often only contained in the notes on the accounts. There are special provisions for certain balance sheet items, e.g., cash in hand, treasury bills, debt securities and amounts owed to banks.

Profit and loss account

The profit and loss account may follow a vertical or a horizontal layout or both. The directive contains special provisions relating to certain items in the profit and loss account and, in particular, provision is made for the introduction of a liabilities item entitled 'Fund for general banking risks' which should include amounts put aside to cover risks particularly associated with banking.

Valuation rules

The valuation rules broadly follow the Fourth Directive on company law, but regard is had to the special characteristics of credit institutions. There are valuation rules for assets, fixed financial assets, debt securities, transferable securities, loans and advances, variable-yield securities, and foreign exchange assets and liabilities. For example, assets and liabilities denominated in foreign currency are translated at the spot rate of exchange ruling on the balance sheet date.

Notes and publication

As a result of the directive, the contents of the notes of the accounts for banks, etc., will be more detailed and transparent than is often the case. Accounts and annual reports must be drawn up on a consolidated basis in accordance with the Seventh Directive and must be published in accordance with the First Directive on company law in every Member State in which the institution has branches.

For many banks, in particular those in the United Kingdom, Ireland and the Netherlands, the directive will lead to more disclosure on the face of the accounts, rather than in the notes which themselves are subject to new disclosure requirements. With some exceptions, the practice of offsetting assets and liabilities and income and expense items will be virtually eliminated.

The annual accounts of branches

Some Member States still require branches of credit institutions and financial institutions having their head office outside that Member State to publish annual accounts relating to the activities of that branch. This is regarded by the Commission as an obstacle to the right of establishment which is unjustified following the adoption of Directive 86/365 which provides that annual accounts should be drawn up in accordance with uniform principles and published in every Member State where the institution has a branch.

The completion of the internal market presupposes that branches of credit and financial institutions having their head office in other Member States should be treated in the same way as branches of institutions having their head office in the same Member State. The Commission considers that it is in general sufficient for the branches of such institutions to publish the annual accounting documents of the institution as a whole, although it recognises that branches must publish a limited amount of additional information.

Abolition of branch accounts

Directive 89/117 provides that branches may not be required to publish annual accounts relating to their own activities. Host Member States must, however, require branches of credit institutions and financial institutions to publish the documents specified in Directive 86/365: annual accounts, consolidated accounts, annual reports, consolidated annual reports and auditors' reports. Member States may require branches to provide additional information relating to the income and costs of the branch, the average number of staff employed, the total claims and liabilities attributable to the branch, and certain other matters relating to assets and liabilities.

Branches of credit and financial institutions having their head office in non-member countries are under a similar obligation to provide annual accounts, consolidated accounts, annual reports, consolidated annual reports and audits. Where these documents, which are drawn up outside the Community, conform with the requirements of Directive 86/635 and the conditions of reciprocity for Community credit institutions and financial institutions are fulfilled, branches would not be required to publish annual accounts relating to their own activities. The Member State can also require the same additional information which may be required from branches of Community institutions.

Member States may require that all the relevant documents are published in their official national languages and that translations be certified.

Winding up of credit institutions

The Commission has proposed a directive which would coordinate national rules relating to the reorganisation and the winding up of credit institutions. This proposal envisages the situation where a credit institution runs into financial difficulties which has repercussions on its branches in other Member States. The proposed directive would aim at achieving the principle of mutual recognition by Member States of each other's reorganisation and winding-up rules so that home country control was ensured. A list of reorganisation measures and winding-up procedures in force in each Member State would be set out in an annex to the proposed directive.

Reorganisation

'Reorganisation measures' are measures designed to safeguard or restore the financial situation of a credit institution. They are, therefore, designed to prevent credit institutions from becoming insolvent as soon as financial difficulties become apparent and to maintain savers' confidence in the banking system.

Consistent with the principle of home country control, in the case of credit institutions having their head office within the Community, the authorities or the courts of the home country would be responsible for the reorganisation of a credit institution or its branches. These measures would be fully effective as against governing bodies and creditors of branches situated in other Member States, even if they were contrary to or different from the host country's rules on reorganisation. Moreover, it would preclude the application of reorganisation measures by the host country, unless the home country otherwise consented. Rules are laid down relating to the exchange of information between the national authorities and to the notification of such measures to creditors and shareholders established in the host country. Where the credit institution had its head office outside the Community, the host country would apply its reorganisation measures to the branch situated in its territory and notify these to the authorities in other host Member States in which the institution had set up branches. These authorities could then decide that the notified reorganised measures should take effect as against the creditors of branches situated in that host country.

Winding up

Any winding up of a credit institution which had its head office within the Community would be carried out in accordance with the winding-up procedures of the home country. This would be effective against the credit institution's branches situated in other Member States and would preclude the commencement of any winding-up procedure in respect of them. Where the credit institution had its head office outside of the Community, it would be the winding-up procedures of the host country which would apply to the branch. Further provisions of the proposed directive would concern voluntary winding up, the appointment of liquidators and the notification of the winding-up procedure.

Deposit-guarantee schemes

A deposit-guarantee scheme means all provisions designed to guarantee appropriate compensation for depositors or to protect them against any loss. The proposal envisages the introduction of a deposit-guarantee scheme which would be coordinated by a future directive in the light of the experience gained as a result of the Commission's recommendation concerning the introduction of a deposit-guarantee scheme in the Community. In the mean time, Member States would be obliged to ensure that the deposit-guarantee scheme existing in their territory covered the deposits of branches of institutions having their head office in another Member State. Furthermore, a Member State, in whose territory a credit institution had its head office, would be obliged to extend the benefit of its deposit-guarantee scheme to branches set up in host Member States which had no such scheme.

Own funds of credit institutions

Directive 89/299 on own funds is important because it provides the legally-binding definition of capital on which the harmonised solvency ratios are based. Own funds serve to absorb losses which are not matched by prospective profits of sufficient volume. Own funds are funds which are the property of a bank, as opposed to client funds which are on deposit with the bank and are essentially the property of the client.

The First Co-ordination Directive defines own funds as a credit institution's own capital. This includes items defined as capital under national rules which currently use a variety of different methods to calculate a credit institution's capital resources. The Commission considers that common standards for the own funds of credit institutions are an important cornerstone in building up an internal market in the banking sector since they ensure the continuity of credit institutions, protect savings and improve comparability between credit institutions which in a common banking market engage in direct competition with each other.

The Directive provides that the unconsolidated own funds of credit institutions should consist of the following items:

- paid-up share capital plus share premium accounts;
- reserves and revaluation reserves;
- funds for general banking risks (provisionally without limit);
- value adjustments;
- certain commitments of members of credit institutions set up as co-operative societies;
- fixed-term cumulative preferential shares and subordinated loan capital (if in the event of bankruptcy or liquidation of the credit institution, they rank after the claims of all other creditors and are not to be repaid until all other debts outstanding at the time have been settled);
- certain securities of indeterminate duration and other types of cumulative preferential shares;
- other items provided that they are freely available to the credit institution to cover normal banking risks where revenue or capital losses have not yet been identified, their existence is disclosed in internal accounting records and their amount is determined by the management of the credit institution and verified by independent auditors.

Directive 89/299 lays down certain deductions and limits. Thus the total of revaluation reserves, value adjustments, other items, commitment of members of co-operative societies and fixed-term cumulative preferential shares and subordinated loan capital must not exceed a maximum of 100% of the sum of the paid-up capital and reserves (minus own shares at book value held by the credit institution, intangible assets and material losses of the current financial year). The total of the commitments of members of co-operative societies, fixed-term cumulative preferential shares and subordinated loan capital must not exceed a maximum of 50% of paid-up capital and reserves (minus own shares, intangible assets and material losses). Further, certain holdings in other credit and financial institutions are deducted and Member States must not include in the own funds of public credit institutions guarantees which they or their local authorities extend to such entities.

Solvency ratio for credit institutions

Directive 89/647 on a solvency ratio for credit institutions has two main objectives. First, the harmonisation of essential prudential rules is necessary for the achievement of mutual recognition. Secondly, average solvency standards among credit institutions should be strengthened in order to protect both depositors and investors. The directive accompanies Directive 89/299 on own funds in particular, as own funds form the numerator of the solvency ratio.

The directive seeks to establish a uniform method of assessing the capacities of credit institutions to withstand losses incurred by their clients going bankrupt–i.e., credit risk. The capital adequacy directive will harmonise the national rules relating to interest rate, foreign exchange and other market risks in relation to credit institutions.

The solvency ratio constitutes the relationship between a credit institution's own resources (the ratio numerator) and the total of its assets and its unpublished reserves weighted against different degrees of risk (the ration denominator). The ratio expresses the own funds of each credit institution as a proportion of the risk-adjusted value of its assets and off balance sheet business. Degrees of credit risk are assigned to asset and off-balance sheet items. These 'risk weights' are expressed as percentages: 0%, 20%, 50% or 100%. Thus, cash in hand is given a zero weighting, cash items in the process of collection are given a 20% weighting, whereas asset items representing claims on some foreign governments are given a 100% weighting. The competent authorities can establish higher weights as they see fit. The risk-adjusted value, e.g., the denominator, is then obtained by multiplying the value of each item by the relevant percentage.

For the purpose of assigning risk weights to various assets and off-balance sheet items, borrowers are grouped in a number of categories, e.g., central banks, central governments, credit institutions and the non-banking sector. An element of country risk in bank lending is also introduced.

With effect from 1st January 1993 credit institutions must not allow their ratios to fall below 8%. This means that the amount of a credit institution's own funds cannot fall below one-twelfth of the value of its assets and off-balance sheet items as adjusted for risk. As an intermediate measure until 31st December 1992 credit institutions whose ratios are below 8% must not allow their ratios to fall any further. The 8% figure is in line with the Basle capital convergence accord signed by the governors of the group of ten central banks in July 1988. The accord provides that banks are to have capital equivalent to at least 8% of their risk-weighted assets.

Large exposures

The monitoring and controlling of exposures of a credit institution is an integral part of prudential supervision, since an excessive concentration of exposures to a single client or a group of connected clients may result in an unacceptable degree of risk which is prejudicial to the solvency of the credit undertaking. The Commission has, therefore, made a recommendation that Member States monitor and control the large exposures of credit institutions authorised in the Community.

The recommendation contains an indicative list of the elements that the Commission considers to constitute an exposure. For example, on-balance sheet items include loans and off-balance sheet items include guarantees. An exposure is considered to be large when its value has reached or exceeded 15% of the credit institution's own funds. A report of every large exposure should be made by the credit institution at least annually. Furthermore, credit institutions may not incur an exposure to a client or group of connected clients when its value exceeds 40% of own funds. Groups of connected clients are covered where their cumulated exposure represents to the credit institution a single risk. In addition, credit institutions may not incur large exposures which in the aggregate exceed 800% of own funds.

These limits may only be exceeded in exceptional circumstances, in which case the credit institution should be required to increase the volume of own funds or take other remedial measures. There is provision for these limits to be exceeded where the exposure is to certain public authorities or the exposure is an interbank exposure having a maturity of six months or less. The application of the recommendation may also be deferred where certain specialised credit institutions are concerned. Where a credit institution owns at least 25% of the capital of another credit institution, the exposures of the former must be monitored and controlled on a consolidated basis. However, this does not preclude the exposures of the individual credit institution being monitored and controlled on a non-consolidated basis in addition.

The competent authorities in a Member State of a branch having its head office in a third country may require the branch's exposures to be reported to them in order that it can be monitored and controlled.

Deposit-guarantee schemes

Before adopting a directive on the mandatory introduction of deposit-guarantee schemes in the Community, the Commission has made a recommendation that Member States should check that their schemes fulfil certain conditions in the event that the winding up of a credit institution reveals insufficient assets. The schemes should:

- guarantee compensation for depositors who do not possess the means of properly assessing the financial policies of the institutions to which they entrust their deposits;
- cover the depositors of all authorised credit institutions, including the depositors of branches of credit institutions that have their head office in other Member States;
- distinguish sufficiently clearly between intervention prior to winding up and compensation after winding up;
- clearly set out the criteria for compensation and the formalities to be completed in order to receive compensation.

Member States which do not operate a deposit-guarantee scheme must draw up plans for such a scheme which should be implemented by 1 January 1990.

Mortgages

A proposed directive would abolish restrictions on all credit institutions from undertaking mortgage business throughout the Community. This would provide for mutual recognition of financial techniques authorised in different Member States. Member States would be required to allow credit institutions from other Member States to apply their own domestic techniques in its market, even if such techniques did not in every respect comply with the rules of the host State.

This proposal applies to credit institutions which carry on mortgage credit activities, i.e., the receiving of funds from the public and the granting of loans to the public secured by mortgage on real property for the purpose of acquiring or retaining property rights in building land or in existing or projected buildings or for renovating or improving buildings. The receipt of funds could be in the form of deposits or the proceeds from the issuing of mortgage bonds or other bonds or securities or reimbursable shares. Mortgages cover any other legal instruments having equivalent effect, e.g., a charge. 'Financial techniques' means the funding and lending techniques of the designated credit institutions.

Mutual recognition of financial techniques

The home Member State (e.g., where the credit institution had its head office) would be obliged to allow credit institutions to undertake mortgage credit activities in any other Member State and to allow them to use any financial techniques which were permitted in the home Member State. Therefore, home Member States could not restrict credit institutions from lending on the security of property situated in another Member State.

The host Member State (e.g., where a credit institution had a branch or into which it supplies services) would have to repeal all legal and administrative provisions which obstructed a credit institution, which had its head office in another Member State, from undertaking mortgage credit activities in the host State in accordance with the financial techniques permitted under the law of its home State. The proposal, therefore, goes further than the First Coordination Directive, which submits branches of credit institutions in other Member States to the host country's rules of operation. An exception would relate to the issue of bonds secured by mortgages where host Member States would retain the right to require that their own national rules were complied with. This is due to the large number of types of bonds secured by mortgage issued under different conditions in the various Member States. Bonds are commonly used in Denmark, France and Germany. Where the importation of new financial techniques adversely affected the competitive position of the credit institutions in the host State, that State would be under an obligation to adopt similar techniques. Public assistance measures, such as tax breaks, would be extended to mortgages and credit activities provided by credit institutions from other Member States.

Supervisory responsibilities

Different supervisory rules would apply depending on whether a credit institution wished to establish itself or provide services in another Member State. A credit institution which established itself in the host Member State would be supervised by the competent authority of that State. Branches would, therefore, be supervised in the host Member State. Close cooperation with the home Member State would be necessary especially with regard to the imported financial techniques. The main supervisory role with respect to the supply of cross-border services would be carried out, in accordance with the principle of home country control, by the authority of the home State. Before providing cross-border mortgages in a host Member State for the first time, a credit institution would provide its own competent authority with certain information, e.g., the host Member State, the type of activity. The authority would then carry out a preliminary investigation aimed at ascertaining the financial soundness of the institution. The home authority would supply the host authority with a report on the credit institution's financial soundness and the host country would then have three months in which to prepare its supervision which basically would be limited to determining whether the new service complied with the host Member State's laws for the protection of the public.

Transitional provisions

There are important transitional provisions. For a maximum of seven years after the adoption of the proposed directive, host Member States could require that both funding and lending be in its currency, or where it allowed transactions to be in another national currency, that assets and liabilities in each national currency be matched. The institution could always use the ECU as an alternative. For a similar period, the home Member State could require matching between assets and liabilities in each national currency, or the ECU, in order to prevent the institution under its supervision from incurring a foreign exchange risk. Finally, for a similar period, the home Member State could limit the supply of mortgage credit services to other Member States to 25% of the total domestic mortgage lending of the relevant credit institution in the previous year. This proposed limitation in volume is due to the fact that supervisory authorities do not have sufficient experience in supervising transactions carried out abroad.

This proposal should be read with the directive on capital movements because the activities concerned are still subject in some Member States to exchange control restrictions. Mortgage lending is also dealt with in the Second Banking Directive.

The Second Banking Directive--the single banking licence

The Second Banking Directive, Directive 89/646, is the centre-piece of the programme to complete the internal banking market. It aims to abolish the remaining restrictions which were left untouched by the First Banking Directive and were primarily the following:

- a bank wishing to set up a branch still needs to be authorised by the supervisors of the host Member State;
- a bank remains subject to supervision by the host Member State and its range of activities may be constrained by host country laws;

- most Member States stipulate that branches of banks established in other Member States make provision for 'endowment capital' as if it were a new bank.

The crux of the Directive 89/646 is to ensure that all credit institutions, duly authorised in the home Member State, are able to establish or supply services throughout the Community without further authorisation from the host State. They can undertake specified banking activities provided that those activities are not prohibited under the terms of their home country authorisation. The supervision of credit institutions, including their branches in other Member States, is undertaken by the supervisory authorities of the home Member State.

Minimum capital

The First Directive merely provides that credit institutions have adequate minimum capital, the level of which differs in the Member States. Directive 89/646 provides that in order for most credit institutions to obtain authorisation they must have an initial capital of at least 5m ECU (reduced to 1 million in some cases) to be met by means of paid-up capital or something similar to equity. A credit institution's own funds, as defined in the own funds directive should not fall below the initial capital required for authorisation. Member States may decide that credit institutions already in existence when the directive is implemented, the own funds of which do not attain the levels prescribed for initial capital, may continue to carry on their activities. In that event, their own funds must not fall below the highest level reached after the date of the notification of the directive.

Supervisory control of major shareholders

Prior to being granted authorisation, credit institutions must inform the national supervisory authorities of the identity of shareholders or members so that their suitability can be appraised. Moreover, anyone considering taking an interest in a credit institution which gives it a 10% holding or which enables it to exert a significant influence over the institution (a 'qualified participation'), must first inform the competent authorities of its intention. Credit institutions are also under an obligation to provide the competent authorities on an annual basis with the names of major shareholders and members and the size of their holding. If the competent authorities consider that a holding is likely to be to the detriment of the prudent and sound management of the banking activities of the institution, they may order appropriate remedies, such as the divesting of the shares or suspension of the voting rights. There is also a requirement for the vetting of the acquisition by credit institutions of substantial shareholdings in non-financial business. In this respect, two limits are provided: a credit institution cannot hold a participation exceeding 15% of its own funds in an undertaking which is neither a credit nor a financial institution, e.g., an insurance company; and the total value of such participations cannot exceed 60% of own funds. These limits do not apply in the case of the acquisition of shares held temporarily during a financial rescue or restructuring operation or for underwriting purposes or if the shares were held by nominees. Nor do the limits apply to such participations if the investment made was deducted in the calculation of the bank's own funds.

Sound accounting and internal control mechanisms

The competent authorities of the home Member State must ensure the existence within each credit institution of sound administrative and accounting procedures and adequate internal control mechanisms.

The single banking licence

Credit institutions authorised and supervised in their home Member State can freely undertake throughout the Community all the listed activities either through a branch or by supplying services. Member States can, however, require adherence to their own laws or regulations in the case of an institution which is not a credit institution or in the case of a credit institution pursuing activities which are not on the list. A financial institution may also pursue the listed activities either through a branch or through the provision of services when it meets the following conditions:

- it is at least 90% owned by a credit institution which is authorised in a Member State;
- the activities in question are carried out in that Member State;
- its commitments are guaranteed by the parent undertaking;
- it is included in the consolidated supervision of the parent credit institution.

The core banking activities which are listed in the proposed directive are as follows:

- deposit-taking and other forms of borrowing;
- lending (including consumer credit, mortgage lending, factoring);
- financial leasing;
- money transmission services;
- issuing of credit cards, travellers' cheques, etc.;
- guarantees;
- trading for own or for customers' account in money market instruments (e.g., bill), foreign exchange, financial futures and options, exchange and interest rate instruments and securities;
- participation in securities issues;

- advice relating to mergers and acquisitions;
- money broking;
- portfolio management and advice;
- safekeeping of securities;
- credit reference services;
- safe custody services.

As a result, any credit institution authorised in its home country is able to exercise such activities in the host country through mutual recognition, provided that its licence covers the relevant activities, even if similar credit institutions in the host country are not permitted to carry on the same activities. On the other hand, the directive does not allow a credit institution to exercise through mutual recognition an activity that is not on the list (e.g., bullion dealing). Likewise, an institution which has not been authorised by its home State to undertake an activity cannot benefit from mutual recognition in the host country, even if the activity is included on the list. In short, for there to be mutual recognition, the activity must at least be authorised by the home Member State and be included on the list.

Branches

A branch means a place of business which forms a legally dependent part of a credit institution and which conducts directly all or some of the operations inherent in the business of credit institutions. The introduction of the single banking licence means that host Member States may no longer require authorisation for branches of credit institutions which are authorised in other Member States. Until the abolition of authorisation, or, at the latest by 1 January 1990, Member States cannot require, as a condition for authorisation, that branches provide initial endowment capital which is greater than 50% of the initial capital required by national rules for authorisation of credit institutions of the same nature. Branches which have already commenced their activities and required to provide initial capital are allowed to reduce their initial capital accordingly and to recover the free use of any surplus. All branches must be able to recover any sums paid by way of initial capital once the requirement for authorisation is abolished.

Subsidiaries

Where a credit institution seeks to establish a subsidiary in another Member State, the competent authorities in the host Member State is obliged to consult the supervisory authorities in the other Member States before authorising the subsidiary to carry on banking activities.

Reciprocity and non-EEC banks

Credit institutions authorised in third countries, wishing to set up a branch in a Member State, will still be subject to authorisation by that Member State. These branches do not enjoy the freedom to provide services under Article 59 or the freedom of establishment in Member States under Article 52.

A subsidiary of a credit institution authorised in a third country can pursuant to Article 58 of the Treaty take advantage of the single banking licence, provided that the subsidiary is a credit institution authorised in one of the Member States. However, the directive provides that requests for authorisation of such subsidiaries are subject to a procedure intended to ensure that Community credit institutions receive reciprocal treatment in third countries. Whenever it appears to the Commission that a third country is not granting Community credit institutions effective market access comparable to that granted by the Community to credit institutions from that third country, the Commission may submit proposals to the Council with a view to rectifying the matter. The Council may take the appropriate measures acting by qualified majority. Whenever it appears to the Commission that Community credit institutions in a third country do not receive national treatment offering the same competitive opportunities as are available to domestic credit institutions and the conditions of effective market access are not fulfilled, the Commission may negotiate directly with the third country to rectify the matter. The Commission may also order the competent authorities of the Member States to limit or suspend for a maximum of three months their decisions regarding requests for authorisation or the takeover of a Community credit institution. Before the end of the three-month period the Council may decide by qualified majority whether the suspension should continue. Such suspension cannot apply to the setting-up of subsidiaries by credit institutions duly authorised in the Community or to the acquisition of holdings in Community credit institutions by such institutions or subsidiaries.

Supervisory responsibilities

Home country supervisors are responsible for the application and monitoring of all the essential harmonised standards, in particular, those on capital and solvency. However, pending further harmonisation, host country supervisors retain primary responsibility for the supervision of liquidity and exclusive responsibility for monetary policy. Pending adoption of the Capital Adequacy Directive host countries can also require credit institutions to make sufficient provision to guard against risks on the securities market. This is considered necessary because the solvency ratio directive only covers credit risks and not risks inherent in the securities market. In order to accomplish their supervisory roles, the competent authorities from the home and host States must be authorised to carry out on-the-spot investigations of branches and to exchange information which must be kept confidential.

If the competent authority of the host Member State ascertains that an institution having a branch or providing services in its territory is infringing its laws for the protection of the public interest or is infringing the provisions of the directive, that authority can take appropriate steps to terminate the infringement.

Notification procedure

The right freely to establish branches and provide services is subject to certain notification and reporting requirements. Credit institutions wishing to establish a branch in the host Member State must first provide the home Member State with the following information:

- the address in the host Member State in whose territory it wished to establish a branch;
- the type of business envisaged and the structural organisation;
- the amount of the own funds and solvency ratio of the credit institution;
- the names of those responsible for controlling the activities of the branch.

The information allows the home Member State to decide whether to block the establishment of the branch on the ground that the credit institution does not have adequate organisational structure. The home Member State has three months in which to communicate this information to the host Member State which then has two months to prepare for its own supervision of the institution. If there had been no communication at the expiry of that period the branch is free to establish itself and commence business.

Any credit institution wishing to supply services to another Member State for the first time has merely to notify the home State of the activities which it intends to undertake. Home Member States then have one month in which to notify the host State of this information.

INSURANCE

Background

Community legislation on insurance covers both the right of establishment and the freedom to provide services with respect to reinsurance, retrocession and co-insurance. However, legislation on direct life and non-life insurance only concerns the freedom of establishment and did not seek to liberalise the provision of services, (e.g., the sale of an insurance policy in another Member State without the intermediary of a branch or agency).

Although the directives on direct life and non-life insurance do not deal with the provision of services, the Treaty provisions on services continue to have full effect. In December 1986, the Court of Justice shed light on the degree to which host Member States were entitled to impose authorisation requirements and other obstacles to insurance companies wishing to provide cross-border services from other Member States in which they were established. The Court held that, pending further Community legislation in the field of insurance, host Member States were entitled to impose their own authorisation requirements on insurers from other Member States. These rules had to be justified to protect the public interest and in particular the consumer and would not be justified if they were discriminatory (e.g., the rules were not applicable to their own nationals) or merely duplicated rules which were applicable in the home Member State. Moreover, such rules would not be justified where large commercial clients were concerned because they did not need the same degree of consumer protection.

In 1973, the Council adopted the First Coordination Directive on direct non-life insurance. The classes of insurance covered by the First Directive are defined in an annex. The classes are:

- accident;
- sickness;
- land vehicles;
- railway rolling stock;
- aircraft;
- damage to ships;
- goods in transit;
- fire and natural forces;
- other damage to property;
- motor vehicle liability;
- aircraft liability;
- liability for ships;
- general liability;
- credit;
- suretyship;
- miscellaneous financial loss;
- legal expenses;
- assistance.

Importantly, the provisions of the directive do not apply to life assurance, supplementary insurance carried on by life insurers (e.g., health insurance) and export credit insurance for the account of or with the support of the State.

In order to facilitate the taking up and pursuit of the business of insurance, it was essential to eliminate certain divergences in national supervisory legislation. The system established by the directive is that supervisory control is exercised partly by the host Member States and partly by the home Member States.

The directive required Member States to make the taking up of the business of direct insurance in its territory subject to an official authorisation. The conditions for authorisation were coordinated and insurers establishing their head office or opening branch or agency had to submit a 'scheme of operations' containing certain information on the nature of the risks it proposed to cover, tariffs, provision for re-insurance, details of the minimum guarantee fund and set-up and administrative costs.

Member States, in whose territory insurers carry on business, must require them to establish sufficient technical reserves to meet their underwriting liabilities. National rules determine the amount of such reserves, the type of assets included and its value, although the directive provides that the technical reserves should be covered by equivalent and matching assets localised in each country where business is carried on, although some relaxation of these rules is permissible.

Over and above the technical reserves, Member States, in whose territory insurers have their head office, must require them to establish an adequate solvency margin in order to safeguard against business fluctuations in respect of their entire business. The directive coordinates the method of calculation of the solvency margin and states that it must be represented by free assets and must not fall below a stipulated minimum. The solvency margin is determined on the basis either of the annual amount of premiums or contribution, or the average burden of claims for the past three or seven years depending on the nature of the risk covered.

One-third of the solvency margin should constitute a guarantee fund which is related to the size of the risk in the classes of insurance undertaken and is intended to establish a sufficient initial and working capital for the insurer.

Each Member State must also make access to insurance business by insurers whose head office is outside of the Community subject to official authorisation. Such insurers are generally subject to stricter conditions, e.g., each branch or agency must calculate their own separate solvency margin.

The Council also adopted another directive in 1973 which sought to abolish restrictions on the freedom of establishment in the business of direct insurance other than life assurance. Thus, all discriminatory treatment of nationals from other Member States as regards establishment in the business of direct insurance other than life insurance was unlawful. For example, Ireland was obliged to abolish a rule which provided that at least two-thirds of the shares in an insurance company had to be owned by Irish citizens. The lifting of restrictions on the setting up of branches and agencies of direct insurance undertakings was considered dependent upon the coordination of conditions achieved by the First Directive. Strictly speaking, since the Treaty provisions abolishing restrictions of the freedom of establishment are directly effective, this directive is of limited effect.

In 1979 the Council adopted the First Directive on the coordination of laws on direct life assurance. The provisions on authorisation, technical reserves, supervisory measures and non-Community insurers generally mirror the First Directive on non-life insurance. Differences on the solvency margin concern its composition and level. One important provision was the general prohibition on underwriting life and non-life insurance business simultaneously.

The Commission's White Paper

In order to achieve the internal insurance market it is imperative that insurers having their head office in the Community be able to provide services in the Member States, thus making it possible for policy-holders to have recourse not only to insurers established in their own country but also to insurers which are established in other Member States.

In common with other areas of financial services, the general approach is to harmonise essential standards and provide for mutual recognition by the national supervisory authorities of the controls operated by each other. On this basis the principle of home country control can be accepted in respect of the provision of certain types of insurance activities.

Progress on completing the internal market in insurance has been slow compared to the banking sector. The Council has adopted the Second Non-Life Insurance Directive and the Second Life Assurance Directive, but they only liberalise the provision of cross border services to a limited extent. It is only when the proposed Third Directives are adopted will there be a true internal market in insurance.

The Second Directive on direct non-life insurance

The Second Directive on direct non-life insurance, Directive 88/375, further coordinates the rules and regulations relating to direct insurance other than life assurance. Its primary objective is to supplement the First

Directive on direct non-life insurance and to liberalise the provision of services in this area.

At present in order to provide services in the insurance market dual authorisation is invariably required–from the authorities in the Member State where the insurance company is situated and from the Member State where the policy holder or the risk is situated. The Second Directive implements the principle of home country control in respect of insurance for large risks. Insurers will only need a licence in their home country (e.g., where they are established) to sell policies to large companies in other Member States. Only large companies will be able to shop around on the grounds that they are big enough to forego dual protection.

Extended definition of establishment

An insurer will be 'established' in the Member State where it has its head office, a branch or agency, and also in the Member State where it has any permanent presence even if that presence does not take the form of a branch or agency, but consists merely of an office managed by the insurers' own staff or by a person who is independent but has permanent authority to act for the insurer as an agent would.

Definition of provision of services

The directive defines the provision of services by reference to where the risk is situated. The situation of the risk is as follows;

- where the insurance relates to buildings (and their contents), it is the Member State where the building is situated;
- where the insurance relates to vehicles, it is the Member State where the vehicle is registered;
- where the insurance relates to travel or holidays, it is the Member State where the policy-holder took out the policy;
- otherwise, it is the Member State where the policy-holder has his habitual residence.

The freedom to provide cross-border insurance services

The freedom to provide services only covers the classes of risk covered by the First Directive on direct non-life insurance. Some risks are, however, excluded, notably as regards accidents at work, carriers' liability arising out of the use of a motor vehicle, nuclear civil liability and pharmaceutical products' liability and compulsory insurance of building works.

The directive draws an important distinction between providing services in the insurance market in general and underwriting large risks, for it is only in the latter case that it can be said that the freedom to provide services has been effectively liberalised. Large risks are classified as those covering railway rolling stock, aircraft, ships, goods in transit and liability arising out of the use of aircraft and ships. Certain other classified risks (fire and natural forces, other damage to property, general liability, miscellaneous financial loss) are treated as large risks if the policy-holder's balance sheet or turnover or the number of staff employed by him exceeds certain limits. Other categories of classified risks (credit and suretyship) are treated as large risks where the policy-holder is engaged in an industrial, commercial or professional activity and the risks relate to such activity.

An insurer established in one Member State cannot be prevented from underwriting large risks in another Member State once he has lodged with the host Member State the following documents:

- a certificate issued by the competent authorities of the Member State where the insurer has his head office to the effect that he satisfies the solvency margin;
- a certificate from all the Member States where he is established (e.g., head office branch, agency or permanent presence) to the effect that he is authorised to carry out the insurance activities in question;
- a statement of the risks which he proposes to cover.

Where an insurer established in one Member State wishes to provide services in another Member State by underwriting risks, which are not large risks, the host Member State may, if it wishes, subject the insurer to prior authorisation whereby the insurer may be required to produce the same two certificates as the above, and also submit a scheme of operations containing particulars of the nature of the risk, any general and special conditions in the policy, premium rates and any other documents that he intends to use. This information may be required in the language of the host state which has six months from receipt in which to grant or refuse authorisation. If no decision is made within that time, authorisation is deemed to be refused, but the insurer must be allowed to challenge any refusal before the courts. If the host Member State does not make access to such activities subject to this administrative authorisation, the insurer can commence activities once he has produced the same documentation as that required for underwriting large risks.

Every insurance contract concluded by way of services is subject exclusively to the indirect taxes and parafiscal charges on insurance premiums in the Member State where the risk is situated.

Non-Community branches

The directive excludes non-Community branches from the freedom to provide services. This would appear lawful given that the Treaty provides that the Council may extend the freedom to provide services to nationals of third countries who are established within the Community.

Supervision

Where insurers wish to provide services by underwriting large risks in other Member States, those host Member States cannot lay down provisions requiring approval or systematic notification of general policy conditions, scales of premiums, forms and other printed documents. They may only require non-systematic notification. In the case of risks which are not large risks, approval may be demanded by the host Member State provided that the supervisory rules are not disproportionate and do not duplicate similar rules in force in the Member State where the insurer is established.

In respect of the underwriting of large risks or the provision of services for which there is no authorisation, the supervision of technical reserves, their covering by equivalent and matching assets and the localisation of those assets is carried out by the competent authorities of the Member State where the insurer is established. Otherwise, where a Member State subjects the provision of services to authorisation, it is the competent authority of that host Member State which determines the amount of technical reserves.

The directive contains provisions which allow the host Member State to prevent an insurer providing services from infringing its 'legal rules', a term which is undefined. The host Member State should inform the Member State of establishment which should attempt to put an end to the infringement. If this fails, the host Member State may take appropriate action.

Amendments to the First Directive

The directive amends the First Directive in a number of ways, in particular as regards matching rules for technical reserves, the applicable law to insurance contracts, compulsory insurance, approval of insurance contracts, supervisory powers, and the transfer of portfolios of contracts.

Matching rules for technical reserves

Whereas Member States were allowed a certain discretion in the way the technical reserves were covered by matching assets, they are now bound to comply with detailed rules which are contained in an annex to the directive.

The applicable law of insurance contracts

The directive lays down lengthy provisions on the applicable law of insurance contracts. These essentially provide as follows:

- where the policy-holder has his habitual residence or central administration in the Member State in which the risk is situated, the applicable law is the law of that Member State, unless under that law the parties are free to choose another law;

- where the policy-holder does not have his habitual residence or central administration in the Member State in which the risk is situated, the parties to the contract may choose to apply either the law of the Member State in which the risk is situated or the law of the State where the policy-holder has his habitual residence or central administration;

- where a policy-holder pursues a commercial or industrial activity or a liberal profession and where the contract covers two or more risks which are related to these activities and are situated in different Member States, the parties may choose the law applicable either in those different Member States or the country where the policy- holder has his habitual residence or central administration;

- where the risks covered by the contract are limited to events occurring in one Member State which is different to the Member State where the service is provided, the parties may choose the law of the former;

- where the risks relate to the transport sector, the parties may choose any law;

- where the contract covers risks situated in more than one Member State, the contract is considered as constituting several contracts each relating to one State;

- when in the case of compulsory insurance the law of the Member State in which the risk is situated and the law of the Member State imposing the obligation to take out insurance contradict each other, the latter prevails;

- the provisions on the applicable law cannot restrict the rules of the law of the forum in a situation where they are mandatory.

Compulsory insurance

Insurers may offer and conclude compulsory insurance under the conditions set out in the directive, which provides inter alia that the contract must be in accordance with the specific provisions relating to the compulsory insurance laid down by the Member State imposing the obligation to take out insurance.

Approval of insurance contracts

The First Directive provided that it was acceptable that as a condition for authorisation, Member States could require that managers and directors be qualified and that policies and premiums could be subject to approval. The Second Directive provides that as regards large risks, Member States may not require the prior notification and systematic approval of such information. They may only require non-systematic notification which cannot be made a pre-condition for the grant of authorisation.

Supervisory powers

The First Directive required every insurer whose head office was in the territory of a Member State to produce annual accounts covering all types of operations, of its financial situation and its solvency. It further provided that branches and agencies should render returns together with statistical documents necessary for the purpose of supervision. The Second Directive adds to these supervisory powers by requiring that the supervisory authorities be able to make detailed inquiries about the insurer's business, to demand the production of documents and to carry out on-the-spot investigations.

The transfer of portfolios of contracts

The Second Directive reinforces the First Directive in this respect and covers the situation where an undertaking established in one Member State wishes to transfer its portfolio to an accepting office established in another Member State. There are also provisions specifically covering the transfer to an accepting office of the portfolio of contracts concluded by the provision of services.

Motor vehicle liability insurance

Directive 90/618 provides for the possibility of treating risks in both Class 10 (motor vehicle liability) and Class 3 (damage to or loss of land motor vehicles or other land vehicles) as large risks within the meaning of the definition inserted in Article 5 of the First Directive by Article 5 of the Second Directive. It will thus be possible for such risks to be covered by way of the provision of services subject to the relevant provisions of the Second Directive.

The reason for the exclusion of third party motor insurance, which is compulsory in all the Member States by virtue of the First Motor Insurance Directive 72/166, is that there are special considerations peculiar to this class of insurance. These relate to the operation of national guarantee funds, to the operation of the green card system, and in particular of the supplementary agreement between the national motor insurers' bureau, and to the need to safeguard the interests of accident victims in their position as third party claimants. Directive 90/618 deals with these issues.

Directive 90/618 provides that where an insurer through an establishment situated in one Member State covers a risk in Class 10 (motor vehicle liability other than carrier's liability), which is situated in another Member State, the insurer will be required to become a member of and participate in the financing of the national bureau and the national guarantee fund of the Member State of provision of services. Moreover, the Directive provides that a 'services insurer' must nominate a claims settlement representative resident or established in the host Member State and possessing the necessary powers to bind the undertaking. The representative must limit his activities on behalf of that insurer to handling and settling claims. It is specifically provided that the representative is not to be considered as an establishment of the insurer and that his nomination will not constitute the opening of a branch or an agency of that insurer.

Reciprocity

Directive 90/619 inserts in the First Non–Life Insurance Directive reciprocity provisions for non–life insurance generally. Whenever it appears to the Commission that a third country is not granting Community insurers effective market access comparable to that granted by the Community to insurers from that country, the Commission may submit proposals to the Council of Ministers with a view to rectifying the matter. The Council may take the appropriate measures acting by qualified majority. Further, whenever it appears to the Commission that Community insurers in a third country do not receive national treatment offering the same competitive opportunities as are available to domestic insurers and the conditions of effective market access are not fulfilled, the Commission may negotiate directly with the third country to rectify the matter. The Commission may also order the competent authorities of the Member States to limit or suspend for a maximum of three months their decisions regarding requests for authorisation or the takeover of a Community insurer. Before the end of the three-month period the Council of Ministers may decide by a qualified majority whether the suspension should continue.

The third non-life insurance directive

In the direct non–life insurance sector, the Second Directive substantially amended the First Directive and facilitated the freedom to provide services in respect of direct non–life insurance covering large risks based on home country control. Major restrictions remain, however;

- the insurance of mass risks remains subject to the supervisory rules of the host country (i.e., where the risk insured is located);
- in respect of large risks, authorisation is still needed from the host country for the establishment there of an office, branch or agency.

No single authorisation system has been put in place for insurance and there is no genuine home country control. Consequently, the Commission has proposed a Third Directive to fill the gaps left by the First and Second Directives and to complete the internal market for direct non–life insurance. The structure of the proposal is similar to the Second Banking Directive. It aims to harmonise the essential requirements for the protection of the consumer and consequently to provide that an insurance undertaking with its head office in one Member State is able freely to provide non-life insurance business in another Member State either by setting up a branch there or by providing cross-frontier services.

The authorisation provisions contained in the First Directive will be substantially amended. Authorisation to take up the business of direct non-life insurance will be granted by the home Member State (i.e., where the insurer has its head office) and this will be valid for the whole Community. It will permit an insurer to carry on business in any host Member State either by way of establishment or by way of the provision of services. No separate authorisation from the host Member State will be needed. The proposed directive brings the authorisation requirements for insurance companies engaging in mass risks in line with those for large risks as set out in the Second Directive. Thus the host Member State will no longer be able to require in respect of mass risks prior approval of policy conditions or premium rates. Insurers will no longer need to state in their scheme of operations the tariffs which they propose to apply for each category of business they engage in. In common with the Second Banking Directive, the competent authorities of the home Member State would be informed of the identities of major shareholders before granting an authorisation.

The choice of law provisions contained in the Second Directive will also be amended. The proposed Third Directive will permit Member States to apply their law to contracts relating to mass risks located in their territory. The Second Directive leaves complete freedom of choice to the parties only in respect of transport risks. The Third Directive will extend this freedom of choice to all large risks.

The principle of home country control will be introduced for non-life insurance. Thus home Member States will have sole responsibility to supervise the solvency of the insurer even where the insurer establishes a branch or agency in another Member State or provides cross-frontier services. It would be the task of the home Member State to require every insurer to establish sufficient technical provisions in respect of its entire business and to cover these by matching assets. In respect of business written in the European Community, these assets would be localised in the Member State of the Community. However, Member States would not be able to require insurers to invest in particular categories of assets or to localise their assets in a particular Member State. The list of assets recognised for the purpose of covering the solvency margin will be updated to include, for example, subordinated loan capital. The amount of such technical provisions will be determined according to the proposed Directive on the annual accounts and the consolidated accounts of insurance undertakings.

Host Member States would retain only limited supervisory powers. They will be able to intervene where an insurer concludes a contract of insurance which infringes the host Member State's rules relating to the general good (for example cold calling). They could also require systematic notification of policies relating to compulsory insurance and health insurance. Further, no Member State will be able to continue to prohibit the simultaneous carrying on of insurance business in its territory under conditions of establishment and under conditions of freedom to provide services. The option given to Member States in this connection by the Second Directive will be abolished.

The notification procedure for large risks contained in the Second Directive will be extended to mass risks.

Compulsory motor insurance

Disparities in national laws on liability in respect of the use of motor vehicles are liable to impede the free movement of motor vehicles and persons within the Community. Consequently the Council has adopted three Directives on the approximation of the laws of the Member States relating to insurance against civil liability in respect of the use of motor vehicles.

The First Directive of 1972 provided for the abolition of checks on green cards and also provided that each Member State should take all appropriate measures to ensure that civil liability in respect of motor vehicles was covered by insurance. The Second Directive adopted in 1983 introduced certain minimum requirements to reduce the differences in compensation provided by compulsory insurance in the various Member States. The Third Directive of 1990, Directive 90/232, goes further and provides comparable treatment irrespective of where in the Community an accident occurs. The directive provides that compulsory motor insurance should cover liability for personal injuries to all the passengers, other than the driver, arising out of the use of a vehicle. Member States are obliged to ensure that all policies of compulsory insurance covering civil liability in respect of motor vehicles, cover, on the basis of a single premium, the entire territory of the Community and provide, in addition to the cover required by law in the Member State in which the vehicle is normally based, at least the cover required by law in each of the other Member States. Further, in the case of an accident caused by an uninsured vehicle, Member States must abolish national rules which allow the compensation body to make compensation conditional upon the victim's establishing that the person responsible is unable or unwilling to pay.

The Second Directive on direct life assurance

The Second Directive on direct life assurance, Directive 90/619, further co-ordinates the rules and regulations relating to direct life assurance. Its primary objective is to supplement the First Directive on life assurance and to liberalise the provision of services in this area. As regards the latter, the directive distinguishes between passive (own initiative) business, where the policy-holder takes the initiate in approaching an insurer in another country, and active business, where the insurer actively seeks business in other countries.

Definition of establishment

The Member State of establishment means the Member State in which the establishment covering the commitment is situated. Establishment means the head office, agency or branch and any permanent presence of an undertaking in the territory of a Member State.

Member State of provision of services

This means the Member State where the commitment is covered by an establishment situated in another Member State. The Member State of the commitment means the Member State where the policy-holder has his habitual residence or, if the policy-holder is a legal person, the Member State where the latter's establishment. This equates to "Member State where the risk is situated" in the Second non-life insurance Directive.

The freedom to provide cross-border life assurance services

The freedom to provide services covers the same classes of risk covered by the First Directive on life assurance, with some notable exceptions relating to the management of group pension funds and operations relating to the length of human life prescribed by or provided for in social insurance legislation. The directive draws an important distinction between providing active business and passive business in the insurance market for it is only in the latter case that it can be said that the freedom to provide services has been effectively liberalised.

Active business: Host Member States may require official authorisation for active services business. To this end the host Member State may require the insurer to produce the following documents:

- a certificate certifying that the insurer has the necessary solvency margin and is permitted to operate outside the Member State of establishment;
- a certificate showing the classes in respect of which the insurer is authorised to write and stating that its supervisors do not object to it underwriting services business;

- a scheme of operations concerning the nature of the commitments, the general and special conditions of the assurance policies, the premium rates which the undertaking envisages.

The host Member State can require the scheme of operations to be supplied in its official language. If no decision has been taken by the end of six months by the host Member State, authorisation is deemed to be refused. A right to appeal to the courts must be provided in respect of a refusal of authorisation.

Passive business: the policy-holder is deemed to have taken the initiative in the following cases:

- where the contract is entered into by both parties in the Member State in which the undertaking is established or by each of the parties in that party's own state of establishment or of habitual residence, and where, the policy-holder has not been contacted in his state of habitual residence by the undertaking or through an insurance intermediary or any person authorised to act for it or by means of any solicitation for business addressed to him personally;
- where the policy-holder approaches an intermediary established in the Member State in which the policy-holder has his habitual residence in order to obtain information on life assurance offered by insurers established in other Member States. Member States are allowed to prohibit the use of local intermediaries for passive services business for three years from the coming into force of the directive.

Insurers wishing to write passive services business need only supply to the host Member State the two certificates. No scheme of operations is required and no second authorisation is necessary. The insurer may commence business as from the certified date on which the host Member State is in possession of the two certificates. The insurer cannot write a type of business in another Member State if it is not authorised in the Member State of establishment.

If the insurer has an establishment in the host Member State, the latter must allow the insurer to write passive services business from an establishment in another Member State (the question of cumul). Further, for passive services business, host Member States can require only non-systematic notification of general and special policy conditions, scales of premiums, forms and other printed documents which the insurer intends to use. This requirement cannot constitute a prior condition in order for the insurer to commence activities. In the case of passive services business, the amount of the technical reserves, including mathematical reserves, and the rules on profit sharing and on the surrender and paid-up values of the contracts concerned will be determined under the supervision of the Member State of establishment. The Member State of establishment must ensure that the reserves relating to all the contracts which the undertaking concludes through the establishment concerned are sufficient and covered by equivalent and matching assets.

Member States must prescribe that a policy-holder who concludes an individual life assurance contract by way of freedom of services must have a period of between 14 and 30 days from the time when he was informed that the contract had been concluded within which to cancel the contract. Where an operation is offered by way of freedom to provide services, the policy-holder must, before any commitment is entered into, be informed of the Member State in which the head office, agency or branch with which the contract is to be concluded, is established.

The directive contains provisions on sanctions which are similar to those contained in the Second non-life insurance Directive. Thus host Member States may prevent an insurer providing services from infringing its legal rules, a term which is undefined. The host Member State should first inform the Member State of establishment which should attempt to put an end to the infringement. If this fails, the host Member State may take appropriate action.

Amendments to the first directive

The directive amends the First Directive in a number of ways, in particular as regards the applicable law to insurance contracts, supervisory powers, the transfer of portfolios of contracts and reciprocity.

Applicable law

The directive lays down the following principles:

- as a general principle, the law applicable is that of the Member State of the commitment, although the parties may choose the law of another country if this is permitted by the Member State of the commitment.
- Where the policy-holder is a natural person and the countries of his nationality and habitual residence are different, the parties may choose between the law of these two countries.
- The directive does not restrict application of the law of the forum in a situation where this is mandatory irrespective of the law otherwise applicable to the contract.

Increased powers of the supervisory authorities

Each Member State must take all steps necessary to ensure that the supervisory authorities have the powers, in particular, to make detailed enquiries about the insurer's whole business, to gather information, to carry out on-the-spot investigations and to ensure that measures required by the supervisory authorities are carried out, if need by, by enforcement through judicial channels.

Transfer of portfolios of contracts

The First Directive provisions on transfer of portfolios are reinforced and supplemented by provisions specifically concerning the transfer to another undertaking of the portfolio of contracts concluded by way of freedom to provide services.

Reciprocity provisions

The directive contains provisions on reciprocity and third countries which are almost identical to those provisions contained in Directive 90/618 on non-life insurance.

The proposed third life assurance directive

The proposed Third Directive on life assurance is similar in many respects to the proposed Third Directive on non-life insurance. Thus, the taking up and pursuit of the business of life assurance will be subject to the grant of a single official authorisation issued by the authorities of the Member State in which the insurer has its head office. Such authorisation will enable the insurer to carry on business everywhere in the Community, whether under conditions of freedom of establishment (i.e., agency or branch) or under conditions of freedom to provide services (whether active or passive business).

The host Member State will no longer be able to require the insurers who have been authorised in the home Member State and who wish to carry on assurance business there to seek a fresh authorisation. The responsibility for monitoring the financial health of the insurer, including its state of solvency, the establishment of sufficient technical provisions and the covering of those provisions by matching assets, will lie with the competent authorities of the home Member State.

The conditions for authorisation will be amended. For example, it will be necessary for the managers and directors of an insurer to possess adequate technical qualifications and general soundness. Home Member States will not be able to require prior approval or systematic notification of general and special policy conditions, scales of premiums, or forms and other printed documents which the undertaking uses in its dealings with policy-holders. The suitability of shareholders will also be vetted. The current restrictions on composite insurers providing life assurance and non-life insurance at the same time would be abolished.

The proposed directive aims to co-ordinate rules concerning the valuation of assets used to cover technical provisions and their diversification, the rules on localisation and currency matching in order to facilitate mutual recognition. The calculation of technical provisions would be based for the most part on actuarial principles. The directive contains a list of assets in which the home Member State might allow insurers to invest their technical provisions. The list is similar to that in the proposed Third non-life insurance Directive.

The Member State of commitment will no longer be able to require the prior approval of premium rates or policy conditions. The Commission considers that a system of prior authorisation is inconsistent with the logic of a single market since it confers on the host Member State the right to prevent the marketing of financial products developed and already distributed in other Member States. The Directive would not, however, deny the supervisory authorities of the host Member State the right to protect its consumers: it could still be proved ex post facto that a particular clause freely entered into was not in keeping with a legal provision protecting the general good. The Commission considers that this approach is consistent with the co-insurance cases and essentially it amounts to shifting the burden of proof onto the host Member State.

The notification provisions relating to the setting up of a branch in another Member State or providing services is similar to the notification procedure contained in the proposed third non-life insurance Directive.

Legal expenses insurance

The purpose of Directive 87/344 is to coordinate legal expenses insurance. Legal expenses insurance is defined as an undertaking to bear the costs of legal proceedings and to provide other services directly linked to insurance cover, in particular, those with a view to:

- securing compensation for the loss, damage or injury suffered by the injured person, by settlement out of court or through civil or criminal proceedings;
- defending or representing the insured person in civil, criminal, administrative or other proceedings or in respect of any claim made against him.

Certain categories of legal expenses insurance are excluded, for example, where it concerns risks arising out of the use of sea-going vessels. Subject to limited exceptions, legal expenses insurance cannot be regarded as ancillary to any other class of risk which means that an undertaking already authorised to cover wishes to cover legal expenses insurance.

Protection of the insured

The directive seeks to protect the insured and in particular attempts to resolve any conflict of interests that may arise when the insurer is covering the insured in respect of legal expenses and another class of risk. Thus, the directive provides that legal expenses cover should be contained in a separate contract from that drawn up for other classes of insurance or be dealt with in a separate section of a single policy. As a further measure of protection, Member States should either oblige insurers to have separate management for legal expenses insurance policy or to afford the insured the right to choose a lawyer of his choice from the moment that he has the right to claim from his insurer. Moreover, any contract of legal expenses insurance must expressly recognise that whenever a conflict of interest arises, the insured shall be free to choose a lawyer. There are certain exemptions to this obligation, notably in respect of motor vehicle or breakdown insurance. The contract must also state that the insured has the right to have recourse to arbitration or to the courts in the event that the insured and insurer cannot agree.

In the light of these provisions, all Member States must abolish all provisions which prohibit an insurer from carrying out within their territory legal expenses insurance and other classes of insurance at the same time. This provision is primarily directed at the Federal Republic of Germany which was allowed to retain such a restriction under the First Directive on direct non-life insurance.

Credit and suretyship insurance

Directive 87/343 amends the First Directive on direct non-life insurance as regards credit and suretyship in a number of ways.

Additional financial guarantees

Insurers undertaking credit insurance are subjected to financial guarantees additional to those contained in the First Directive on non-life insurance.

Insurers which accept credit insurance must set up a special equalisation reserve which is for the purpose of offsetting any technical deficit or above-average claims ratio arising in that class for a financial year. The equalisation reserve must be calculated in accordance with one of four fairly complex methods which are set out in an annex to the directive. Methods 1 and 2 concern the provision for any technical benefit and methods 3 and 4 concern the provision for above average claims. The amount contained in this reserve must be disregarded for the purposes of calculating the solvency margin. Member States may, but are not bound to, exempt insurers from the obligation to set up an equalisation reserve for credit insurance business where the premiums or contributions receivable in respect of credit insurance are less than 4% of the total premiums or contributions receivable by them and less than 2,500,000 ECU. The conditions for exemption are cumulative.

Due to the cyclical nature of claims in credit insurance, a period of seven years must be taken when calculating the solvency margin on the basis of the average burden of claims.

Subject to certain exceptions, the directive has increased the guarantee fund for credit insurance by 1,000,000 ECU to 1,400,000 ECU. This increase only applies to insurers for which the annual amount of premiums or contributions due in respect of credit insurance for each of the last three financial years exceeded 2,500,000 ECU or 4% of the total amount of premiums or contributions receivable by the insurer concerned. The conditions of 2,500,000 ECU and 4% are no longer cumulative but alternative so that companies which only satisfy one of the two conditions will have to increase their guarantee fund. The increase may be staggered over a period of seven years.

Exemptions

The First Directive provided that export credit insurance operations for the account of or with the support of the State would be excluded from the scope of the First Directive for a period of four years. This exemption has now been extended indefinitely to export credit insurance operations for the account of or guaranteed by the State, or where the State is the insurer. However, the directive abolishes the special dispensation granted to the Federal Republic of Germany which was allowed to prohibit the simultaneous undertaking of credit and suretyship insurance with other classes of insurance.

Insurance contracts

A proposed directive would coordinate certain national rules and regulations governing insurance contracts. Contracts of insurance covered by the directive would relate to the classes of insurance contained in the First Directive on direct non-life insurance, although the following would be excluded: marine, aviation and transport insurance because of their widely international character, life insurance, sickness insurance, credit and suretyship insurance which display special technical features. As a result of an amendment to the proposed directive, only risks situated in the Community would be covered

The proposal lays down circumstances in which the insurance contract could be terminated or renewed. For example, if a provision was made in the contract for automatic renewal, such renewal would take effect for a period not exceeding one year in each case. However, the proposal is primarily concerned with the rights and obligations of the insurer and the policy-holder. It attempts to maintain the fairest balance between the interests of the insurer on the one hand and the protection of the insured on the other, although the parties could agree on terms which were more favourable to the policy-holder, insured person or injured third party than were provided for in the directive.

Insurer's obligations

The insurer would be under an obligation to disclose in the insurance contract at least the following information:

- the name and address of the policy-holder; name and registered office of the insurer including any co-insurers and the address to which the policy-holder should send his declarations and premiums;
- the subject-matter of the insurance, any exclusions and a description of the risk covered;
- the amount insured or the method of calculating it;
- the amount of the premium or the method of calculating it;
- the dates on which premiums become due;
- the duration of the contract and the time at which cover commences and expires.

Pending the issue of the policy the insurer would be obliged to issue a cover note containing at least the information in the first three indents. If any provisional cover was required, the policy-holder would in addition be entitled to information in the last indent. The information contained in the insurance contracts would not be conclusive. A simplified form of insurance contract could be provided where it was for less than six months.

Insurance contracts would be drafted in the language of the Member State whose law was applicable according to the Second Directive on direct non-life insurance. Essentially this means that the policy-holder would be able to choose between the language of the Member State where the risk was situated or the language of the Member State where he habitually resided.

Policy-holder's obligations

When concluding the insurance contract, the policy-holder would be obliged to declare to the insurer any circumstances of which he ought reasonably to have been aware and which he ought to expect to influence a prudent insurer's assessment or acceptance of the risk. Any circumstance about which the insurer had specifically asked questions would be presumed to have influenced the assessment and acceptance of the risk. The obligation on the policy-holder to declare the risk would, therefore, be defined by reference to:

- knowledge of the risk on the part of a reasonable policy-holder; and
- assessment of the risk by a prudent insurer.

Within two months from the date on which he became aware that the policy-holder had failed in this obligation, the insurer would be entitled to propose an amendment to or to terminate the contract. If the policy-holder did not accept the proposed amendment, the insurer would be entitled to terminate. On termination, the insurer would refund to the policy-holder the proportion of the premium in respect of the period for which cover was not provided. Where a claim arose before the contract was amended or terminated, the insurer would only be obliged to provide limited cover (a sum equal to the ratio between the agreed premium and the premium which would have been fixed). However, if the insurer could show that no prudent insurer would have accepted the risk regardless of the rate of premium if he had been aware of the circumstances, he would not be obliged to pay any claim. Moreover, where the policy-holder had intended to deceive the insurer, in addition to his right of termination, the insurer would be entitled by way of damages to payment of all premiums due which would be without prejudice to damages for any additional losses incurred by the deceit and he would not be liable for any claims.

If both parties were unaware of a material fact or the policy-holder failed to declare circumstances of which he was aware but which he did not expect to influence a prudent insurer's assessment of the risk, the insurer or the policy-holder would be entitled to amend or terminate the contract. Either party would be entitled to terminate the contract if he rejected the other's proposed amendment. Specific time periods would be laid down for amendment and termination.

From the time of the conclusion of the contract the policy-holder would be obliged to declare to the insurer any new material circumstance, in which case similar provisions on amendment and termination of the contract would apply. On the other hand, if the risk diminished appreciably and permanently because of circumstances other than those covered by the contract, the policy-holder could ask for the premium to be reduced. If the insurer refused to reduce the premium the policy-holder would be entitled to terminate the contract and to be refunded a proportion of the premium corresponding to the period for which cover was not provided.

The policy-holder would be under an obligation to take all reasonable steps to avoid or reduce any loss that might arise. Any costs incurred by the policy-holder in mitigating the loss would, in principle, be borne by the insurer. Where the policy-holder was not a consumer, reimbursement might be limited to the sum insured. The policy-holder would be obliged to notify the insurer of any claim within a reasonable time.

There would also be a degree of coordination of the rights and obligations of insured persons who were not policy-holders, e.g., beneficiaries. Such persons would be under similar duties to disclose material facts to the insurer, to take steps in mitigation and to notify the insurer of any claim provided that they had knowledge of the contract and were able to fulfil these obligations. Where they took steps in mitigation, they would have a right to be reimbursed for costs incurred.

Compulsory winding up of insurance undertakings

The directives on direct non-life insurance and on direct life assurance sought to coordinate the provisions for the withdrawal of authorisation, but did not seek to harmonise the role of supervisory authorities, the effect on insurance contracts and the distribution of assets in the event of the winding up of the insurance company. A proposed directive on the compulsory winding up of direct insurance undertakings would fill these gaps. It would only apply to compulsory winding up (e.g., imposed by a court or administrative authority) of direct insurance undertakings. It would not, therefore, apply to voluntary winding up nor to insurance undertakings which deal only in re-insurance.

This proposal provides that every insurer would, in each Member State in which it had its head office, agency or branch, keep a register of the assets representing its technical reserves. Any charge or mortgage would be recorded in the register and that part of the value which was not available for the purpose of covering commitments would not be included in the total value of the assets. The register would be kept with the insurer in question. However, where the insurer was not free to dispose of its assets, the register would be lodged with certain supervisory authorities.

The proposed directive would provide for two types of winding up: normal compulsory winding up (NCW), which would be the automatic consequence of the withdrawal of authorisation, and special compulsory winding up (SCW), which would be opened when the undertaking was in a state of proven or provable insolvency. Once authorisation had been withdrawn, the undertaken could no longer be wound up voluntarily.

Normal compulsory winding up

The NCW would be carried out by the insurer under the supervision of the supervisory authority of the Member State in which the head office was situated. The NCW would be carried out according to the law of that Member State and would have full effect in all the Member States. The management of the insurers could be replaced by an administrator if this was necessary for the proper implementation of the NCW, although the insurer would be given a right of appeal to a court against the appointment. Publication of the withdrawal of authorisation and, if necessary, the appointment of the administrator would be published in the Official Journal of the European Communities. The primary aim of the

NCW would be to put an end to the insurance relationship while at the same time protecting the insured. Thus, the supervisory authorities would ensure that transfers of portfolios were sought, rights to terminate contracts were exercised and that reserves in respect of claims which had been incurred but not yet reported were lodged with a trustee. Insurance contracts would not be automatically terminated by the initiation of a NCW, but the policy-holder would be given a right of termination when the annual premium fell due.

Special compulsory winding up

The SCW of an insurer would either be ordered by the supervisory authority or the Courts where the insurer had its head office. The SCW would be carried out according to the law of that Member State and would have full effect in all the Member States. A SCW would be carried out by a liquidator who might appoint assistant liquidators in other Member States where the undertaking had a branch or agency.

SCW would automatically terminate contracts for non-life insurance 30 days after its publication, although this time-period might be extended in certain circumstances. The initiation of a SCW would not automatically terminate contracts for life-assurance. The liquidator's powers to transfer portfolios would be restricted; for example, they would be obliged to obtain authorisation first and the transfer could not prejudice the interests of the insurance creditors. Provided he was so authorised, the liquidator might reduce the obligations of the insurer arising from life-assurance contracts (e.g., to facilitate a transfer) or terminate them if termination was in the interests of the body of life-assurance creditors (e.g., because the management of these contracts would result in a substantial increase of winding up expenses).

After the initiation of the SCW, the insurer could not renew the acceptance of reinsurance cover, although the liquidator could seek such cover. The initiation of the SCW would not preclude the offsetting of reinsurance claims and liabilities.

The composition of the assets entered in all the registers could not be changed once the SCW was opened. The proceeds from the realisation of those assets would constitute a non-life asset fund and a life asset fund. A list of the claims eligible to participate in the asset funds are:

- claims, other than insurance claims, arising out of the opening of the SCW (e.g., the liquidator's emoluments). These claims would be met out of the non-life or life asset fund to the extent that they related to either branch of insurance business, or, if their allocation was impossible, in proportion to the size of each asset fund. If these claims could not be allocated specifically to the business of insurance, but had been incurred in the interests of all the creditors, only an equitable share would be charged to the separate assets funds;

- indemnity and lump-sum insurance claims and claims for unused portions of premiums for direct life assurance or direct non-life insurance;
- claims in respect of reinsurance acceptances arising from life or non-life reinsurance business to the extent that they were not offset;
- claims in respect of wages and salaries (including redundancies) arising before or after the opening of the SCW. These claims would be met out of the non-life or life asset fund to the extent that they related to either branch of insurance business, or, if their allocation was impossible, in proportion to the size of each asset fund.

The provisions on the distribution of assets would reflect the need to guarantee the rights of policy-holders, whose premiums supplied the funds of insurance undertakings, with the legitimate interests of other creditors, in particular, employees. Broadly speaking, the asset funds would be distributed in the order of the claims set out above, except that claims for unused portions of premiums paid would rank last.

Non-Community insurers

As regards non-Community insurers, it would be the supervisory authorities or the courts of the Member State which authorised the branch or agency which would be responsible for the supervision of the NCW or the SCW. NCW of such an agency or branch established in one Member State would not entail the NCW of agencies or branches established in other Member States.

Annual accounts and consolidated accounts of insurance undertakings

A directive has been proposed concerning the annual and consolidated accounts of insurance undertakings. Its purpose is similar to the Directive 86/635 on the annual and consolidated accounts of banks. The Fourth and Seventh Directives on company law, which deal respectively with the annual accounts and consolidated accounts of companies, specifically excluded insurance companies from their scope. However, improved comparability of accounts is of crucial importance to those who deal with insurers who are often in a different legal form but nevertheless pursue insurance activities in competition with one another. Improved comparability also makes it easier for supervisory authorities to authorise and supervise the insurer. As a result, this proposal would broadly apply the rules contained in the two company law directives to insurance undertakings, particular regard being had to their special characteristics.

The proposed directive would apply to all insurance undertakings whatever their form (companies or firms) and covers specialist reinsurance undertakings and Lloyd's underwriters. In respect of the latter, special adaptation might be made in the way that accounts of the various syndicates were drawn up. It would not apply to small mutual associations. Exemption would not be made for small and medium insurance undertakings such as is provided for under the First Directive on company law.

Balance sheet

The proposed directive would set out the structure and the item designations for the balance sheet and coordinates the presentation of certain transactions in the balance sheet. Only a horizontal form of balance sheet would be permissible. As compared with the Fourth Directive, the assets side of the balance sheet would be substantially modified to take account of the fact that by far the greater part of the assets of insurers consists of investments which cannot be readily separated between fixed and current assets. A new main heading, 'Investments', would be introduced. On the liabilities side, an important item would be the 'Technical provisions', which would represent amounts set aside to enable the insurer to meet its future obligations to policy-holders, but which could not be known with accuracy at the balance-sheet date. Both the gross amount of technical provisions and the reinsurance amount would have to be disclosed.

Profit and loss account

The proposed directive would lay down the composition and definition of certain items in the profit and loss account. Only a vertical format would be permissible. The profit and loss account would be divided into technical accounts and non-technical accounts. In the case of non-life insurance the technical account would be regarded as reflecting the result of the underwriting activity before taking into account investment income, which would appear in the non-technical account. However, in the case of life assurance the technical account would include the investment income which was used to calculate the participation of the policy-holders in any surplus.

Valuation rules

Rules would be provided which concern the valuation of the assets and liabilities which were entered in the balance sheet. In particular, there would be three methods of valuation where information about premiums or claims was insufficient to enable accurate estimates to be made. There would also be provision for the disclosure of the current value of investments as well as their value based upon the principle of purchase price or production costs.

Notes and publication

Certain changes are also proposed to the notes on the annual and consolidated accounts. Insurers would indicate in the notes on the accounts gross premiums broken down by categories of activity and into geographical markets (e.g., accident and health, motor marine, aviation and transport, etc.). Insurers would draw up consolidated accounts in accordance with the Seventh Directive and the rules in the Fourth and Seventh Directives concerning the publication of accounts would also apply to insurers. Where the insurer was not incorporated and was not required by national law to publish these documents, it would be obliged to make them available to the public at its registered office.

TRANSACTIONS IN SECURITIES

Completion of the internal market in securities

In the securities sector, the ultimate aim is to create a European securities market. Barriers between national stock markets would be removed and a Community-wide trading system for securities would be created. Stock exchanges would be linked electronically, so that members could execute orders on the stock exchange market offering the best conditions to their clients. It is considered that such an interlinking would substantially increase the depth and liquidity of Community stock exchange markets and would permit them to compete more effectively with stock exchanges outside the Community.

Although the above scenario is still in the distance, as a consequence of the liberalisation of capital movements the number of cross-border applications for admission to official listing is likely to increase. This has been made easier by three directives which have taken steps to coordinate the conditions for admission to official listing. In 1979, the Council adopted a directive which was aimed at harmonising the minimum conditions for such admission. This lays down certain minimum conditions for the admission of shares and debt securities to official listing, such as the legal position and size of the company and the negotiability of the shares and their distribution. It also lays down certain obligations on the issuers of such securities, in particular the publishing of information to the public. In 1980, these provisions were supplemented by a directive which coordinated the requirements for the drawing up, scrutiny and distribution of an information sheet known as listing particulars. These listing particulars aim to enable investors to make an informed assessment of the financial position of the issuer and of the rights attaching to such securities. The precise layout of the listing particulars depends on whether they are for the admission of shares, debt securities or certificates representing shares. After being approved by a competent authority, the listing particulars must be published in at least one newspaper or in a brochure freely available to the public. An important amendment to this directive was made in 1987 when the mutual recognition of listing particulars was recognised. This means that an issuer of securities can be admitted to stock exchanges throughout the Community so long as its listing particulars have been approved by the supervisory authorities in one Member State. The competent authorities of the other Member States cannot subject the listing particulars to prior approval or demand additional information to be included in the particulars. Mutual recognition does not, however, in itself confer a right to admission. Furthermore, Member States may restrict such mutual recognition to listing particulars of issuers having their registered office in a Member State, thus excluding third countries such as the USA. The directives on minimum conditions for admission and listing particulars were complemented by a further directive on interim financial information which must be disclosed by companies whose shares are listed on a stock exchange. Companies must at least every six months provide sufficient information to enable the public to evaluate its overall financial position and its general progress.

In the securities sector, therefore, an information policy has been established at Community level. This information policy is aimed at protecting the investor and increasing investors' confidence in the securities market. This in turn will enable companies to penetrate the securities market of the Member States and ultimately to establish a true European capital market.

Within the context of the White Paper, the Council has adopted a directive on the coordination of laws applicable to collective investment undertakings for transferable securities. Continuing the policy of coordinating rules applicable to stock exchanges, it has adopted a directive on information to be published when a major holding in a listed company is acquired or disposed of, a directive on the prospectus for unlisted securities and a directive on insider trading. The Commission has proposed a directive on investment services in the securities field.

Undertakings for collective investments in transferable securities (UCITS)

The directives on minimum conditions concerning admission and listing particulars do not apply to units issued by collective investment undertakings other than the closed end type (which essentially do not sell their units to the public). However, Directive 85/611 on the coordination of the laws on UCITS has made it easier for UCITS to be marketed in other Member States. It deals with the authorisation, supervision, structure, investment policies and obligations of UCITS and provides that the application of these common rules is a sufficient guarantee to permit UCITS situated in one Member State to market their units throughout the Community without the need for further approval.

For the purposes of the directive, UCITS are undertakings:

- the sole object of which is the collective investment in transferable securities of capital raised from the public and which operate on the principle of risk-spreading; and
- the units of which are, at the holder's request, repurchased or redeemed out of the undertaking's assets.

Action taken by a UCITS to ensure that the stock exchange value of its units does not significantly vary from their net assets value is regarded as equivalent to repurchase or redemption. The 'units' mean securities which represent the holder's right to participate in the assets. The undertakings may be constituted under the law of contract (as common funds managed by management companies) or trust law (unit trusts) or under statute (as investment companies). UCITS are not covered by the directive if they are of the closed-end type or raise capital without offering their units to the public, or the units may only be sold to the public in non-Member States.

Authorisation of UCITS

No UCITS should be able to carry on activities unless it has been authorised by the competent authorities of the Member State where it has its head office and such authorisation is valid for all other Member States. Before authorising a unit trust, the competent authorities must approve the management company, the fund rules and the choice of depositary. Before authorising an investment company, the competent authorities must approve its instruments of incorporation and the choice of depositary. In both cases they must verify that the managers or directors are of sufficiently good repute and have the necessary experience.

Structure of UCITS

A management company must have sufficient financial resources and an investment company must have sufficient paid up capital at its disposal to conduct its business effectively and meet its liabilities. No management company or investment company may engage in activities other than relating to unit trusts. Management companies may, however, be authorised to issue bearer certificates representing registered securities of other companies.

The assets of a unit trust or an investment company must be entrusted to a depositary for safe-keeping. The depositary, which is subject to public control, must carry out the instructions of the management company or the investment company and ensure that the units are dealt with in accordance with the fund rules or the instruments of incorporation. Failure to perform its obligations may render the depositary liable for any loss suffered by the management or investment company or the unit-holders. No single company can at the same time act as a management company and depositary or as an investment company and a depositary. In certain circumstances, investment companies may be exempted from the requirement of having a depositary. This is the case, for example, where an investment company markets its units exclusively through a stock exchange.

Investment policies of UCITS

The investments of a unit trust or of an investment company must consist of transferable securities admitted to an official listing of a stock exchange of a Member State or dealt on another regulated market which operates regularly and is recognised and open to the public. A UCITS may invest in other transferable securities (and in certain circumstances debt instruments) provided that this does not exceed 10% of its assets. A UCITS may invest no more than 5% of its assets in transferable securities issued by the same body, although this limit may be increased to 10%. However, the total value of the transferable securities held by a UCITS in the issuing bodies in each of which it invests more than 5% of its assets must not exceed 40% of the value of its assets. These limits are designed to limit the impact on the UCITS's assets of a possible bankruptcy on the part of an issuer whose securities are included in the portfolio.

By virtue of the fact that the State cannot normally become bankrupt, the directive provides that the limit on the UCITS investing in securities issued or guaranteed by the State may be raised to a maximum of 35% (and under certain conditions 100%) of the UCITS' assets. An amendment made in 1988 also increases these limits for certain types of transferable security which offer similar guarantees as regards their servicing. As a result, Member States may provide that a UCITS can invest no more than 25% of its assets in certain bonds which are issued by a credit institution having its registered office in a Member State. The issuing of such bonds must be subject by law to special public supervision designed to protect bond holders who must, in particular, be treated as preferential creditors should the issuer become bankrupt. Where a UCITS invests more than 5% of its assets in such bonds, the total value of these investments may not exceed 80% of the UCITS's assets. The amendment primarily arose in order to accommodate mortgage credit bonds issued in Denmark.

UCITS may not acquire the units of other UCITS. However, it may invest, up to a limit of 5% of its assets, in other UCITS which are covered by the directive. Investment in the units of a unit trust managed by the same management company is only allowed in the case of a trust which has specialised in investment in a specific geographical or economic sector. A management company cannot charge any fees on account of transactions relating to such units. These provisions have the effect of excluding parallel UCITS from the ambit of the directive. Parallel UCITS, often known as 'managed funds', invest in units issued by other UCITS managed or controlled by the same management company or by the same group of companies.

Subject to certain limited exceptions, an investment or management company may not acquire any shares carrying voting rights which would enable it to exercise a significant influence over the management of an issuing body and neither may it acquire more than 10% of the non-voting rights or debt securities of any single issuing body, nor may it acquire more than 10% of the units of a UCITS which is covered by the directive.

UCITS are not allowed to borrow, although, on a temporary basis, an investment company may borrow up to 10% of its assets and a management company may borrow up to 10% of the value of the fund. UCITS may not grant loans or act as guarantor for third parties. UCITS may not invest in precious metals.

Management companies must repurchase or redeem their units at the request of any unit-holder. The rules for the valuation of assets and the rules for calculating the price of the units must generally be laid down in the fund rules or the investment company's instruments of incorporation. A unit may not be issued unless the equivalent of the net issue price is paid into the assets of the UCITS.

Disclosure obligations of UCITS

An investment company and, for each of the trusts it manages, a management company must publish a prospectus, an annual report for each financial year and a half yearly report covering the first six months of the financial year. The prospectus and the annual reports must include the information necessary for investors to be able to make an informed judgement of the investment proposed to them or of the UCITS developments. The information which is to be contained in these documents is specified in the directive. A management company must periodically make public the price of its units.

Marketing of UCITS

Once UCITS have been authorised and have fulfilled all the obligations imposed on them by the directive, they are then allowed to market their units in other Member States. UCITS situated in one Member State but marketing their units in another Member State must, however, comply with the latter's laws on advertising. UCITS are also obliged to comply with those national rules and regulations which do not fall within the field governed by the directive. A Member State may also apply to UCITS situated within its territory requirements which are stricter than or additional to those laid down in the directive.

UCITS which market their units in another Member State must ensure that facilities are available in that country for making payment to unit-holders, repurchasing or redeeming units and making available the information which UCITS are obliged to provide. In addition, UCITS must inform the supervisory authorities in the other Member States that they intended to market their units there, and provide them with a certificate that it complies with the directive, a copy of its fund rules or instruments of incorporation, its prospectus, its latest annual reports and details of its marketing arrangements. After two months UCITS can commence operations, unless the authorities in the host Member State decide that they do not comply with its laws which fall outside of the directive. In accordance with the principle of home country control, the authorities of the Member State in which a UCITS has its head office is responsible for supervising it and that it is not in breach of its obligations under the directive.

Publication of major shareholdings in listed companies

The directive on minimum conditions for admission to a stock exchange already obliges companies to inform the public when a significant block of its shares change ownership. However, companies are often unaware that a change has taken place or do not know the identity of the mystery seller or purchaser of the shares. Directive 88/627 on the publication of major shareholdings in listed companies, therefore, helps a company to comply with its disclosure obligation by imposing a disclosure obligation on buyers and sellers.

The directive only applies to the dealings of shares which are officially listed on a stock exchange in the Community and does not apply to the dealing of shares in collective investment undertakings.

Disclosure obligations of purchasers and sellers

Where a person (natural or legal) acquires or disposes of a holding in a company such that the proportion of his voting rights exceeds or falls below 10%, 20%, 33.3%, 50%, 66.6%, he must notify the company and the competent authorities within seven calendar days of the proportion of the voting rights he holds following that acquisition or disposal. At the first annual general meeting of a company, any shareholder having 10% or more of the voting rights must disclose that fact. The acquisition of a holding means not only purchasing, but also acquiring a holding by any means whatsoever. Nominee shareholdings are caught so that someone who purchases a significant block of shares through a nominee is subject to the disclosure requirement. A person must also disclose any major dealing by a company that he controls. The acquisition or disposal of major holdings by brokers and members of the stock exchange may be exempted from the disclosure requirements in so far as they act in their professional capacity and do not intervene in the management of the company concerned.

Disclosure obligations of the company

The disclosure obligations of the company itself are also strengthened. Where the company learns that there has been a major dealing in its shares, it must disclose this fact to the public (e.g., in a newspaper) in each of the Member States in which its shares are officially listed within nine calendar days. The company may be exempted from this obligation where disclosure would be contrary to the public interest or seriously detrimental to the company.

Sanctions

Sanctions for breach of the directive are a matter for the Member States.

The publication of a prospectus when securities are offered to the public

The Listing Particulars Directive and the Admissions Directive co-ordinate the information to be published when securities are admitted to stock exchange listing. Directive 89/298 complements these directives by establishing equivalent rules concerning the publication of prospectuses for offers of unlisted securities to the public. The directive provides that Member States should ensure that any offer of transferable securities to the public within their territories is subject to the publication of a prospectus by the person making the offer.

Certain types of security issue are exempted from the directive, in particular, units issued by UCITS other than the closed-end type, securities issued by the State, securities issued in connection with a merger or division of a company, securities allotted to shareholders free of charge or to employees and shares issued in substitution for shares provided that the share capital is not increased. The directive does not apply to securities which have already been admitted to an official listing or to Eurobond issues or to transferable securities offered in individual denominations of at least ECU 40,000.

The prospectus must contain information which is sufficient for an investor to make an informed assessment of the assets and liabilities, financial position, profits and losses, and prospects of the issuer and of the rights attaching to the securities. The information is detailed in the directive and relates to the following:

- information concerning those responsible for the prospectus and the auditing of accounts;
- information concerning the offer for subscription or sale to the public and the shares being offered;
- general information about the issuer and its capital;
- information concerning the issuer's activities;
- information concerning the issuer's assets and liabilities, financial position and profits and losses;
- information concerning administration, management and supervision;
- information concerning the recent development and prospects of the issuer.

The directive provides for the mutual recognition of prospectuses. A prospectus prepared in accordance with the directive and approved by the competent authorities of the issuer's home Member State must, subject to certain limited exceptions (i.e., relating to income tax), be deemed to comply with the laws of all Member States in which the related securities are to be offered simultaneously or within a short interval of one another. Mutual recognition of a public offer prospectus as listing particulars where admission to official stock exchange listing is requested within a three-month period of the public offer is provided by Directive 90/211.

There is no general requirement for a prospectus to be subject to prior scrutiny by the competent authorities of the Member States. However, where a public offer relates to transferable securities which at the time of the offer are the subject of an application for admission to official listing on a stock exchange situated or operating within the same Member State, the contents of the prospectus and the procedures for scrutinising and distributing it, are determined in accordance with the Listing Particulars Directive. Further, Member States may provide that the person making a public offer should have the possibility of drawing up a prospectus, the contents of which is determined in accordance with the Listing Particulars Directive.

Insider trading

Insider trading benefits certain investors at the expense of others and is, therefore, likely to undermine investors' confidence in the financial markets. In many Member States there are no rules prohibiting insider trading, whereas the rules that do exist differ appreciably between Member States. The ultimate aim of a Community-wide trading system for securities would seriously be impeded if it were possible to circumvent the insider trading laws of one Member State by acting through an intermediary in another Member State. Consequently, Directive 89/592 introduces in all Member States a minimum set of rules on insider trading. It adopts a minimalist approach in that Member States might lay down more stringent rules provided that they were not discriminatory.

For the purposes of the directive inside information means information 'which has not been made public of a precise nature relating to one or several issuers of transferable securities or to one or several transferable securities, which, if it were made public, would be likely to have a significant effect on the price of the transferable security or the securities in question.' Transferable securities covers shares and debt securities, futures contracts, options and index contracts, etc. when traded on a regulated market.

Each Member State must prohibit any person who possesses inside information:

- by virtue of his membership of the administrative, management or supervisory bodies of the issuer, or
- by virtue of his holding in the capital of the issuer, or
- by virtue of the exercise of his employment, professional duties,

from taking advantage of that information with full knowledge of the facts either for his own account or for the account of a third party. These persons must be prohibited from disclosing inside information to any third party unless such disclosure is made in the normal course of the exercise of his or her employment, profession or duties and from recommending a third party, on the basis of that inside information, to acquire or dispose of transferable securities admitted to trading on a regulated market.

Companies the transferable securities of which are admitted to trading on a regulated market must inform the public as soon as possible of any major new development in its sphere of activity which are not public knowledge and which may, by virtue of their effect on its assets and liabilities or financial position or on the general course of its business, lead to substantial movements in the prices of its shares. The competent authorities may, however, exempt the company from this requirement, if the disclosure of particular information is such as to prejudice the legitimate interests of the company.

The penalties to be applied for infringement of the insider dealing rules are for the Member States to determine.

Investment services in the securities field

Under the Second Banking Directive credit institutions (e.g., deposit-taking institutions) may undertake securities business throughout the Community. Once a credit institution is authorised by its home Member State to undertake securities business, it may under the single licence provide services in host Member States. Investment firms are not covered by the directive. Consequently the Commission has proposed a directive on investment services to ensure that non-credit institutions not covered by the Second Banking Directive are not put under an unfair competitive disadvantage in comparison with credit institutions. Consequently the aim of the proposed directive is to achieve essential harmonisation sufficient to secure mutual recognition of authorisation and of prudential supervision systems, making possible a single authorisation recognised throughout the Community.

Prior authorisation

Credit institutions have been obliged to be authorised since the First Banking Directive of 1977. The proposed directive on investment services introduces for the first time an obligation on investment firms to be authorised in the home Member State (where the person has his principal place of business or where the firm has its registered office or head office). An investment firm means any natural or legal person whose business is to provide investment services. Investment services mean any of the services relating to any of the instruments set out in the annex to the proposed directive. The annex refers to brokerage, dealing as principal, market making, portfolio management, underwriting, professional investment advice, safekeeping and administration. The instruments referred to are transferable securities, money market instruments, financial futures and options, exchange rate and interest rate instruments. The minimum conditions for authorisation are that the investment firm must have sufficient minimum capital (set in accordance with the rules described in the proposed directive on capital adequacy), its managers and directors must be of good repute and experience and it must have suitable shareholders.

Conditions governing the pursuit of investment services

To continue pursuing the business of investment services, the investment firm must satisfy the following requirements:

- its own funds (as defined as by the Own Funds Directive 89/299) must not fall below the amount of the initial capital required at the time of authorisation;

- the shareholders must continue to be suitable in view of the need to ensure sound and prudent management;
- the firm must comply with the prudential rules set out in the Directive; these relate to sound administrative and accounting procedures and internal control mechanisms, the separation of securities belonging to investors from its own securities, the separation of clients' money from its own account, general compensation schemes designed to protect investors, the keeping of adequate records, and the avoidance of any conflict of interest between the firm and the client;
- the investment firm must make sufficient provision against market risk in accordance with the rules prescribed in the Capital Adequacy Directive.

The supervision of the conditions governing pursuit of the business of investment firms would be within the exclusive competence of the home Member State. Investments firms once authorised to provide the relevant service listed in the annex by the home Member State would be entitled to provide that service in the host Member State either by establishing a branch there or by way of provision of services, unless the host member States law relating to the public good were infringed. Host Member States could not make the establishment of a branch subject to further authorisation or to a requirement to provide endowment capital.

The proposed directive would provide that host Member States should ensure that investment firms (including credit institutions) which were authorised to provide broking, dealing or market-making services by the home Member State could have access to membership of stock exchanges and organised securities markets of host Member States. In these cases membership would be on the basis that the rules governing the structure and organisation of the relevant host stock exchange or organised securities market and clearing and settlement systems were complied with.

Notification procedure

An investment firm wishing to establish a branch in a territory of another Member State would have to notify the competent authorities of its home Member State and provide it with the following information:

- the Member State within the territory of which it plans to establish a branch;
- a programme of operations setting out inter alia the types of business envisaged and the structural organisation of the branch;
- the address in the host Member State from which documents may be obtained;
- the names of the managers of the branch.

The home Member State would have three months in which to communicate this information to the host Member State. On receipt, the host Member State would have two months to prepare for the supervision of the investment firm; i.e., to ensure compliance with host Member State rules justified by reference to the public good. If there had been no communication before the expiry of this period, the investment firm would be free to establish itself and commence business. As regards the operation of cross-border services, the investment firm would notify the competent authorities of the home Member State who would, within one month of receipt of this notification, send the notification to the competent authorities of the host Member State. The investment firm could commence its activities after the expiry of this one-month period.

Investment firms having their head office or registered office outside the Community

The procedure for the authorisation of branches of investment firms authorised in third countries will continue to apply to such firms. The setting up of subsidiaries or the acquisition of Community investment firms would be subject to reciprocity requirements similar to those contained in the Second Banking Directive; namely those relating to comparable access and discrimination.

Capital adequacy of investment firms and credit institutions

The proposed Council directive on investment services in the securities field has as its main object that of allowing investment firms authorised by the competent authorities of the home Member State and supervised by those same authorities to establish branches and provide services freely in other Member States. The directive does not however establish common standards for the own funds of investment firms, nor does it establish a common framework for the monitoring of market risks incurred by the firms. These are essential aspects of the harmonisation necessary for the achievement of mutual recognition and consequently the Commission has proposed a directive on capital adequacy of investment firms and credit institutions.

Initial capital

The proposed Investment Services Directive provides that one of the conditions necessary for authorisation is that the investment firm has sufficient initial capital. The proposed Capital Adequacy Directive provides that investment firms which were neither credit institutions, nor local firms, nor firms engaged purely in the business of supplying investment advice would be obliged to have an initial capital (i.e., paid-up share capital) of at least ECU 500,000. This sum could be reduced to ECU 100,000 in the case of firms who hold clients' monies or securities in acting as agents or portfolio managers, but who do not hold trading positions of their own. Furthermore, this sum could be reduced by the competent authorities to ECU 50,000 where a firm was authorised neither to hold customers' monies or securities, nor to act as a market-maker nor to underwrite. Under a grandfather clause, the competent authorities could continue the authorisation of investment firms in existence before the directive was implemented, where the own funds were less than the initial capital levels specified.

Provision against risks

Investment firms would be obliged to provide at all times a certain amount of own funds to cover each of the various risks associated with their particular activities. The sum of these amounts would be calculated in accordance with the methods outlined in the annexes to the directive: Annex 2 refers to position risk (long and short positions after allowance for hedging and netting); Annex 3 deals with counter-party settlement risk (transactions in which one or other party has not paid for the securities it has contracted to buy or not delivered the securities it has contracted to sell; or merely the malfunctioning of the settlement system); foreign exchange risk (i.e., adverse exchange rate movements); Annex 5 deals with other risks.

As regards position risk and counterparty/settlement risk for credit institutions, the competent authorities would be entitled to choose between two alternative approaches. Either the capital requirements set out in the solvency ratio could apply to all the credit institutions' business (the Annex provides that the overall net foreign exchange position should be assigned an 8% capital requirement). Alternatively the credit institutions could meet the capital requirements laid down in Annexes 2 and 3 on their trading books, and the requirements of Directive 89/647 on the rest of their business. The latter alternative allows credit institutions to have their capital requirements in this area of business measured in the same way as for investment firms which are not credit institutions. Thus the trading book option is consistent with the goal of ensuring a broadly level playing field between investment firms and credit institutions.

Under both of these options, all credit institutions would be required to provide, in addition to the requirements set out in the solvency ratio Directive (Directive 89/647), own funds to cover their foreign exchange risk, the amount of which would be calculated in accordance with the method outlined in Annex 4 of the directive. This requirement is necessary because the Solvency Ratio Directive does not expressly take account of foreign currency risks and the risk of losses from interest rates and exchange rate movements apply to credit institutions' traditional activities such as deposit-taking and lending as well as their investment business.

2. Transport

The common transport policy

The free movement of goods cannot be effectively achieved if the transport cost of moving those goods is seriously distorted. The Commission states in the White Paper that transport represents more than 7% of the Community's GDP which means that the development of a free market in this sector would have considerable economic consequences for industry and trade..

The Treaty obliges the Council to introduce a common transport policy. However, the liberalisation of the transport sector has proved a politically sensitive area and, as a result, the Council has been extremely slow in adopting a framework of measures necessary for a common transport policy. The necessity of making rapid progress in this area was highlighted by a judgment of the European Court in 1985. The Court held that although the absence of a common transport policy did not in itself constitute a breach of the Treaty, the Council was in breach of its Treaty obligations in failing to ensure freedom to provide services in the sphere of international travel.

The measures for completing the internal market in transport centre on the freedom to provide services, the liberalisation of which has now been given new impetus in the light of the Court's judgment. The principle of freedom to provide services means that any carrier in a Member State should be allowed to provide national transport services in another Member State without having to be established there under the same conditions as national carriers. These measures must be read in conjunction with those discussed in the chapter dealing with physical barriers to transport (e.g., frontier checks in road haulage traffic) and other measures which form part of the common transport policy (e.g., infrastructure planning and investment) but which are not strictly relevant to the completion of the internal market.

The freedom to provide services in the transport sector is to some extent dependent on the absence of any distortion of competition in the transport sector. In 1962 the Council adopted Regulation 17 which lays down detailed rules for the implementation and enforcement of the competition rules contained in the Treaty. However, it was considered advisable to exempt the transport sector from the ambit of this regulation until the

Council had implemented a common transport policy. Therefore, in the same year the Council also adopted Regulation 141 which provided that Regulation 17 would not apply to agreements, decisions or concerted practices in the transport sector which had as their object or effect the fixing of transport rates and conditions, the limitation of control of the supply of transport or the sharing of transport markets; nor was it applicable to an abuse of a dominant position in the transport sector. In 1968, the Council adopted Regulation 1017 which laid down detailed rules, with some qualifications, to transport by road, rail and inland waterway, but not to transport by air or sea. The competition rules in the Treaty continued to apply to transport by air and sea, but in the absence of any implementing regulations their enforcement was ineffective. The Council has now filled this gap by adopting implementing regulations covering the air and sea transport sectors.

AIR TRANSPORT

The completion of the internal market in air transport

The air transport sector has to date been governed by a network of international agreements, bilateral agreements between States and bilateral and multilateral agreements between air carriers. The purpose of the measures envisaged in the White Paper is to deregulate air transport and in this respect the Council has adopted measures concerning scheduled air fares, capacity sharing and increased market access for Community carriers. Although it was considered essential that the international regulatory system be opened up to increased competition and that the airlines should be subject to the Community competition rules, it was thought prudent that the air transport sector be given time to adapt to the more competitive environment. For this reason, the Council adopted a regulation granting the Commission power to adopt regulations exempting certain categories of agreement from the competition rules.

Fares for scheduled air services

Council Directive 87/601 made a first step towards the liberalisation in respect of air fares. Regulation 2342/90 constitutes the second phase of the liberalisation of air fares and revokes Directive 87/601. The regulation introduces a more flexible, simpler and more efficient system of zones within which air fares meeting particular conditions qualify for automatic approval by the aviation authorities of the States concerned. The regulation, therefore, makes a significant step towards a system of double disapproval of air fares (i.e., fares are deemed accepted unless both aviation authorities object) by 1 January 1993.

The regulation lays down the criteria and procedures which are to be applied with respect to the establishment of scheduled air fares charged on routes between Member States.

Criteria

Member States must approve scheduled air fares of Community air carriers if they are reasonably related to the applicant air carrier's long-term fully allocated relevant costs, while taking into account the need for a satisfactory return on capital and for an adequate cost margin to ensure a satisfactory safety standard. Member States should also take into account other relevant factors, the needs of consumers and the competitive market situation, including the fares of other air carriers operating on the route and the need to prevent dumping. 'Community air carrier' means an air carrier which has and continues to have its central administration and principal place of business in the Community, the majority of whose shares are and continue to be owned by Member States and/or nationals of Member States and which is and continues to be effectively controlled by such States or persons. Alternatively a Community air carrier means an air carrier which at the time of the adoption of the regulation (24 July 1990) either has its central administration and principal place of business in the Community and has been providing scheduled or non-scheduled air services in the Community during the 12 months prior to adoption of the regulation or has been providing scheduled air services between Member States on the basis of third and fourth freedom traffic rights during the 12 months prior to adoption of this regulation.

A third freedom traffic right means the right of an air carrier licensed in one State to put down in the territory of another State, passengers, freight and mail taken up in the State in which it is licensed. A fourth freedom traffic right means the right of an air carrier licensed in one State to take on, from the territory of another State, passengers, freight and mail for off-loading in the State in which it is licensed. These rights should be distinguished from a fifth freedom right which means the right of an air carrier to undertake the air transport of passengers, freight and mail between two States other than the State in which it is licensed.

The fact that a proposed air fare is lower than that offered by another air carrier operating on the route cannot be sufficient reason for withholding approval. Member States must permit Community air carriers of another Member State operating a direct or indirect scheduled air service within the Community to match an air fare already approved for scheduled services between the same city pairs. Only third and fourth freedom air carriers can act as price leaders.

Approval procedures

Scheduled air fares are subject to approval by the Member States concerned. To this end, an air carrier must submit its proposed air fare in the form prescribed by the aviation authorities of such Member States. Aviation authorities cannot require air carriers to submit their fares in respect of routes within the Community more than 45 days before they come into effect. Until 31 December 1992 Member States must, however, permit third, fourth or fifth freedom air carriers to charge air fares of their own choice provided that the fares come within certain zones of flexibility and meet the conditions set out in Annex II of the regulation (i.e., relating to the necessity for round trips, the length of stay, the time of flight). There are three zones of flexibility: normal economy fare zones, discount zones, and deep discount zones.

Fares which come within the zone of flexibility and which satisfy the conditions set out in Annex II qualify for automatic approval by the aviation authorities of the States concerned. Until 31 December 1992, fares not satisfying these conditions still require approval by both aviation authorities concerned. If neither of the Member States has expressed disapproval within 21 days of the date of submission of a fare, it is considered approved. Where the States disagree on a fare, there is a 21-day period for consultation and if disagreement still persists, the matter is referred to arbitration.

Agreements with non-member countries

Where a Member State has concluded an agreement with one or more non-member countries which gives fifth freedom rights for a route between Member States to an air carrier of a non-member country, and in this respect contains provisions which are incompatible with the regulation, the Member State must attempt to eliminate the incompatibility. It is specifically provided however that the regulation does not affect the rights and obligations *vis-à-vis* non-member countries arising from such agreements.

Capacity sharing and increased market access

Directive 83/416 laid down the procedure for automatically authorising scheduled inter-regional air services within the Community for a minimum distance by aircraft which have a limited capacity. Decision 87/602 expanded on the directive by allowing schedule air services to be operated by larger aircraft, between hub and regional airports and allowed certain aircraft to pick up and set down passengers, freight and mail en route to the final destination (defined as the fifth freedom under the 1944 Chicago Convention). These initial liberalising measures have been revoked by Regulation 2343/90 which constitutes the second phase of the liberalisation of air transport in these areas.

Third and fourth freedom traffic rights

Member States must authorise air carriers licensed in another Member State to provide third and fourth freedom air services between airports in one Member State and airports in another Member State and use, within the Community, the same flight number for combined third and fourth freedom services. Where an air carrier of one Member State has been licensed to operate a scheduled air service, the State of registration of that air carrier cannot raise any objection to an application for the introduction of a scheduled air service on the same route by an air carrier of the other state concerned. In respect of air services to a regional airport in a Member State's territory, that Member State may impose a public service obligation upon an air carrier to take all necessary measures to ensure the fixed standards of continuity, regularity and capacity.

Fifth freedom rights

Community air carriers must be permitted to exercise fifth freedom traffic rights between combined points in two different Member States on the following conditions:

- the traffic rights are exercised on a service which constitutes and is scheduled as an extension of a service from, or as a preliminary of a service to, their State of registration;
- the air carrier cannot use, for fifth freedom service more than 50% of its seasonal seat capacity on the same third and fourth freedom service of which the fifth freedom service constitutes the extension of the preliminary.

Combination of points

In operating scheduled air services to or from two or more points in another Member State or States other than its State of registration, a Community air carrier must be permitted by the States concerned to combine scheduled air services and use the same flight number.

Multiple designation

A Member State must accept multiple designation on a country -pair basis by another Member State. It must also accept multiple designation on a city-pair:

- from 1 January 1991 on routes on which more than 140,000 were carried in the preceding year, or on which there are more than 800 return flights per annum,
- from 1 January 1992 on routes on which more than 100,000 passengers were carried in the preceding year or on which there are more than 600 return flights per annum.

Limitations on carriers' rights

Notwithstanding these liberalising measures, the exercise of traffic rights is subject to published Community, national, regional or local rules relating to safety, the protection of the environment and the allocation of slots. Moreover, limitations may be imposed where the airport does not have sufficient facilities to accommodate air services or navigational aids are not sufficient.

Capacity sharing

Bilateral rules concerning capacity shares are not compatible with the principles of the internal market which should be completed by 1993 in the air transport sector. Thus, from 1 November 1990, a Member State must permit another Member State to increase its capacity share for any season by 7.5% compared to the situation during the previous corresponding season, it being understood that each Member State may in any event claim a capacity share of 60%. The Council must adopt, for implementation not later than 1 January 1993 measures to abolish capacity sharing restrictions between Member States. Capacity sharing limitations do not apply to a service between regional airports. These measures relating to capacity sharing may be suspended by the Commission if a Member State shows that the measures have led to serious financial damage for an air carrier. The regulation does not affect the relationship between a Member State and air carriers licensed by that State regarding market access and capacity sharing. It is intended that the Council will adopt further measures of liberalisation including cabotage in respect of market access and capacity sharing by 30 June 1992.

Air cargo services

Regulation 2342/90 (air fares for scheduled air services) and Regulation 2343/90 (access for air carriers) only liberalise air services for cargo in combination with passenger services. The air cargo industry still encounters national barriers which hamper the free movement of goods and the provision of services by air. The Commission has therefore proposed a Regulation removing certain barriers to market access for air cargo services thereby encouraging the development of express parcel services, door-to-door services, and just-in-time services etc.

Operating licences

It is proposed that the Council will adopt on the basis of a future Commission proposal common rules concerning the grant of air cargo licences to undertakings established in the Community. Until such common rules enter into force Member States would be obliged, on a non-discriminatory, equal opportunities and fair treatment basis, to grant such licences to air cargo carriers established on their territory and ensure that they apply technical, operational, economic, social and safety requirements. Air carriers would be able to appeal to the Commission against a decision refusing an operating licence.

Market access

Duly authorised Community air cargo carriers would be allowed to exercise third, fourth and fifth freedom traffic rights between Member States. Moreover, in operating intra-Community air cargo services, Community air cargo carriers would be allowed to exercise cabotage between points within one Member State. Community air cargo carriers would be allowed to exercise traffic rights on routes between Member States without calling at their State of registration. The carriers would be able to change aircraft at any point on a route and freely position aircraft. There would be no restrictions on frequency of service, aircraft type and/ or the amount of cargo and mail that could be carried.

Limitations on the exercise of traffic rights

The exercise of traffic rights would be subject to published Community, national, regional or local operational and technical rules relating to the protection of the environment, social conditions, allocation of slots and safety. Moreover, access for Community air carriers to certain routes could be limited where the airport facilities or the navigational aids were insufficient to accommodate the service.

Pricing

Air carriers operating in the Community would be obliged to publish all available cargo rates thus creating more transparency in the market place. Air carriers operating air cargo services, or cargo services in combination with passengers with the Community would be obliged to inform the States concerned of their cargo rates applicable to the carriage of cargo and/or mail on an airport-to-airport basis thirty days before their introduction. The States concerned would in particular examine in detail a cargo rate which was 20% lower than the corresponding rate in force during the previous corresponding season. If a cargo rate was 20% higher or lower the Commission could reject the rate. Thus, whilst air carriers need flexibility in setting cargo rates in accordance with their own commercial judgment in order to be better able to compete, it will also necessary to ensure that cargo rates include a sufficient margin to guarantee satisfactory technical and safety standards.

Allocation of slots at Community airports

The Commission considers that the present system of slot allocation gives preference to grandfather rights, but that the future evolution of the air transport market should allow for the entrance of new carriers into the Community market.

The Commission has proposed a regulation which would provide that in the case of congested airports (i.e., an airport where the capacity for more than one hour on any day does not meet the demand or forecast demand) Member States should consider designating the airport as a coordinated airport. This means that in order to land or take off, it would be necessary for an air carrier to have a slot allocated by an airport coordinator whose neutrality should be beyond any doubt.

The regulation would lay down the general rule that a slot that has been operated by an air carrier would entitle that air carrier to the same slot in the equivalent period and days of operation of the next equivalent season. This historical precedence should only apply to scheduled services and programmed non-scheduled services.

At a coordinated airport a pool would be set up containing newly created slots, unused slots and slots which have been given up by a carrier during or by the end of the season. Any slot not utilised more than 65% of the allocated period could be withdrawn and placed in the slot pool for re-allocation, unless the non-utilisation could be justified. The slots placed in the pool would be distributed among applicant carriers. At least 50% of these slots would be allocated to new entrants in accordance with the priority rules set out in the annex to the regulation. If slots could not be distributed to new entrants in this way, some slots might be reclaimed from other air carriers which operated more than six slots on one particular route per day. Slots would be reclaimed on a priority basis from those services which operated with aircraft of less than 200 seats.

New entrant air carriers from third countries would be given comparable treatment to that offered by those countries to Community air carriers. Where third countries do not grant Community air carriers comparable treatment to air carriers from that country or do not grant Community air carriers national treatment or otherwise discriminates against Community air carriers, the Commission could decide to suspend wholly or partially the obligations of an airport coordinator in respect of an air carrier of a third country.

Application of anti-trust rules to air transport

By virtue of Regulation 141, Regulation 17 does not apply to air transport services. Consequently, the Commission had no means of investigating directly cases of suspected infringement of the competition rules of the Treaty in air transport and the Commission lacked the powers of its own to take decisions and to impose penalties necessary to terminate an infringement. This position has now changed with the adoption of Regulation 3975/87 which lays down detailed rules for the application of Articles 85 and 86 to air transport services between Community airports. In short the regulation is the equivalent of Regulation 17.

Enforcement of Articles 85 and 86

The Commission may investigate a possible breach of Articles 85 or 86 either on its own initiative, or acting on a complaint by a Member State or by someone who claims a legitimate interest. The Commission has similar powers to determine whether an infringement has occurred. It may grant a negative clearance by holding that Article 85 does not apply to the agreement or conduct in question or it may order that an infringement be terminated.

The Commission has power to request information from parties and, to this end, Commission officials are empowered to examine and take copies of books and other business records, ask for oral examinations on the spot and enter any premises. Information obtained is subject to professional secrecy and should only be used for the purposes of the investigation. Provision is made for the relevant parties to be heard before the Commission adopts a decision which should be published and is subject to review by the European Court.

The Commission may impose fines for breach of the anti-trust rules of:

- between 100–5000 ECU if it finds that an undertaking has intentionally or negligently supplied incorrect or misleading information;
- between 1000–1,000,000 ECU or a sum in excess thereof but not exceeding 10% of the undertakings worldwide turnover if it finds that any undertaking has intentionally or negligently infringed Article 85 or Article 86;
- between 50–1000 ECU per day in order to compel an undertaking to terminate an infringement.

Agreements not falling within Article 85

Provision is made for agreements or conduct to be excepted from Article 85 altogether. A non-exhaustive list of agreements which may be excepted is contained in an annex to the regulation. These are agreements which achieve technical improvements or cooperation: e.g., technical standards for aircraft parts and for fixed installations for aircraft, technical communication networks, arrangements for the sale of tickets and the settling of accounts between air carriers.

Exemption from Article 85

The Commission has sole power to grant an exemption from Article 85 although national authorities, including national courts, have jurisdiction to declare that any case falls under Article 85 or Article 86. In order for an agreement to be exempted from Article 85 it must be notified to the Commission. Thereafter the Commission should publish in the Official Journal a summary of the notification and invite comments from interested parties within 30 days. If the Commission has not informed the parties to the contrary, the agreement is deemed to be exempt after 90 days of the publication of the summary. This provisional validity lasts for a period of six years during which time it is open to the Commission to reopen the investigation. Where the Commission decides that an agreement merits exemption, it may decide that the date from which the exemption is to take effect is prior to the date of notification. Any decision granting exemption should indicate the period for which it is valid. Normally, such period should not be less than six years. Conditions and obligations may be attached to the decision.

Block exemptions

Regulation 3976/87 grants the Commission power to adopt block exemptions covering certain categories of agreement so that Article 85 does not apply with retroactive effect. In accordance with this delegated power, the Commission has adopted three regulations which exempt under certain conditions agreements on the following areas;

- sharing of capacity and of revenue, tariffs on scheduled air services and slot allocation at airports;
- computer reservation systems for air transport services;
- ground handling services.

Interim measures

Regulation 3975/87 has been amended by Regulation 1284/91 which gives the Commission power to take interim measures in the air transport sector. The Commission may take action against practices which amount to a clear prima facie breach of Article 85 and 86 and which jeopardise the existence of an air service.

International air transport between Community airports and non-Member States

Regulation 3975/87 is limited to international air transport between Community airports. The Commission has therefore no means of investigating directly suspected infringements of Article 85 and 86 of the Treaty in respect of air transport within a Member State or between a Community airport and an airport in a third country; the Commission lacks the power to take decisions or impose penalties as are necessary for it to bring to an end infringements established by it. The Commission has proposed a regulation amending Regulation 3975/87 to extend the latter to these other areas of air transport.

If the application of the competition rules to third countries resulted in a conflict of international law, the Commission would consult with the competent authorities of the third country to resolve the conflict.

The Commission has also proposed regulations on the application of Article 85(3) to certain categories of agreements and concerted practices in the air transport sector relating to air transport within a Member State or between a Community airport and an airport in a third country.

Civil aviation licences

The Commission has proposed a directive on mutual recognition of personal licences for the exercise of functions in civil aviation. The draft Directive provides that the Commission shall at the latest by 31 December 1992 adopt measures establishing harmonised requirements for licences and training programmes. Until Community requirements have been adopted, Member States would have to meet at least the level of those requirements laid down in the eighth edition (July 1988) of Annex 1 to the Convention on International Civil Aviation. There would be mutual recognition of a licence complying with these standards.

The proposed directive applies to licensing procedures and requirements of Member States in the field of civil aviation with respect to flying crew, personnel employed in aircraft maintenance, air traffic control, flight operations and aviation station operations. The provisions of the directive would only apply to nationals of a Member State. Where a Member State issued a licence on the basis of a licence issued by a third country, this would be recorded in the licence. Other Member States would not be obliged to accept any such licence.

Until Community requirements have been laid down or until Member States comply with the Convention on International Civil Aviation, Member States would not be obliged to recognise a licence issued in another Member State which was based on requirements which were not equivalent.

Harmonisation of technical requirements and procedures applicable to civil aircraft

Several European civil aviation authorities have established the Joint Aviation Authorities Organisation (JAA) as an associated body of the European Civil Aviation Conference, to cooperate on the development and implementation of joint aviation requirements (JARs) in all the fields related to safety of aircraft and their operation. The Commission has proposed a directive which would harmonise safety levels by establishing common requirements and procedures on the basis of JAA codes. To facilitate harmonisation, all Member States would be obliged to become members of the JAA.

Under the proposed directive Member States would be obliged to accept the certification of products, organisations or persons concerned with the design, manufacture, maintenance and operation of products, without further technical work or evaluation, when the product, organisation or person had been certified in accordance with the common requirements or procedures. Member States would be obliged to adopt JAR codes as their sole national codes. However, where a specific JAR code had not been adopted, Member States would be allowed to use the relevant part of their existing national codes.

Baggage checks for passengers taking an Intra-Community flight

The checking of baggage of passengers flying from one Member State to another is contrary to the notion of a single European market. Consequently the Commission has proposed a regulation which would provide that no controls or formalities could be carried out in respect of cabin and checked baggage of passengers taking an intra-Community flight. The elimination of such controls and formalities applicable to baggage on an intra-Community flight does not rule out the possibility of maintaining safety checks. Intra-Community flight means a flight for which the airport of departure and the airport of arrival are situated in Community customs' territory. The regulation would not apply to the following:

- the cabin and checked baggage of passengers taking a flight in an aircraft that began its journey at a non-Community airport and which pursues it between two Community airports;
- the cabin or checked baggage of passengers taking a flight in an aircraft which, after a leg between two Community airports, continues its journey by proceeding from the second Community airport to a non-Community airport or to a final destination which is a non-Community airport.

Baggage would be subject to controls at the airport of destination of the intra-Community flight where it had come from a non-Community airport and had been transferred at a Community airport to another aircraft proceeding on an intra-Community flight. Baggage would be subject to controls at the airport departure of the intra-Community flight, where it was loaded onto an aircraft proceeding on an intra-Community flight for transfer at another Community airport to an aircraft whose destination was a non-Community airport

ROAD HAULAGE

The completion of the internal market in road haulage transport

The road haulage sector has been subjected to strict national regulations designed to protect domestic hauliers and the carriage of goods by railway. The carriage of goods by road has traditionally been governed by a system of bilateral agreements concluded between Member States which fix a quota for the volume of goods which may be carried between them. This rather inflexible system of bilateral quotas allows for a limited number of authorisations – usually journey authorisations – to be issued by the Member States to road hauliers which results in increased administrative expense and unladen return journeys.

As regards the freedom to provide road haulage services, Community legislation has concentrated on three areas: the exemption of the carriage of certain types of goods from quotas and authorisations; the framework in which Member States negotiate bilateral quotas; and the introduction of a Community quota system. The system of Community quotas is governed by Regulation 3164/76. They are by nature multilateral and provide for the freedom to provide haulage services throughout the Community under authorisations. The regulation provides that Community authorisations are made out in the name of the carrier and cannot be transferred to a third party. They are usually valid for one year, but as a result of an amendment in 1979 they may be converted into short-term authorisations lasting 30 days. Only a maximum of 15% of Community authorisations may be so converted. In 1984, a regulation was adopted which automatically increased the number of Community authorisations by 15% a year (this figure was subsequently increased to 40%). The authorisations are allocated to each Member State and those resulting from the increase in the quota are allocated among the Member States on the basis of 50% allocated across the board and 50% on the basis of the use made of the Community authorisations granted. The aim is that authorisations are to a certain extent divided between Member States in proportion to the use which is made of them. Therefore, Member States whose hauliers have made heavy (or little) use of Community authorisations will receive more (or fewer) authorisations the following year.

In order to complete the internal market in road haulage traffic, the White Paper envisages the phasing out of quotas and the establishment of conditions under which non-resident carriers may operate transport services in another Member State (cabotage).

The abolition of quotas

Regulation 1841/88 confirms the Council's intention to bring into being a free market in the intra-Community carriage of goods by road without quotas. All Community quotas, bilateral quotas and quotas for transit traffic to and from Member States are to be abolished by 1 January 1993, for Community hauliers. As from that date, access to the market for the transfrontier carriage of goods by road within the Community will be governed by a system of Community licences issued on the basis of qualitative criteria (e.g., the suitability of the haulage company).

By virtue of the fact that this liberalisation will inevitably cause a number of adjustment difficulties, certain transitional provisions are applicable during the period up to 1 January 1993. Regulations have been adopted laying down the total number of Community authorisations allocated to the Member States and for each year there is a 40% increase on the previous year. Additional allocations of Community authorisations for 1991 and 1992 have been made in view of the enlargement of the Community through the unification of Germany.

Cabotage

The internal market in road haulage transport would not be complete if non-resident carriers could not pick up and set down goods in another Member State (cabotage). The Council has therefore adopted Regulation 4059/89 which constitutes a significant first step towards liberalising the conditions under which non-resident carriers can operate cabotage services within another Member State.

In order for the freedom to provide cabotage services to be implemented smoothly and flexibly, the regulation introduces a transitional cabotage system which provides for the introduction of a Community cabotage quota comprising a number of specific authorisations (permits). With effect from 1 July 1990 any Community haulage carrier for hire and reward who is established in one Member State and is authorised in that Member State to operate international road haulage services and is in possession of the relevant authorisation will be entitled to operate cabotage services in a host Member State. The Regulation provides that the total cabotage quota should consist of 15,000 cabotage authorisations, each valid for two months (although these could be converted into two short duration authorisations of one month each) and the quota is allocated amongst the Member States. A further regulation has increased the quota allocation by 10% and another Regulation has increased the quota to take account of the unification of Germany.

The cabotage authorisation must correspond to the specimen in the regulation, it must be made out in the name of the carrier and is non-transferable. It can only be used for one vehicle at a time. Transport operations effected under a cabotage authorisation must be entered in a book of record sheets which are returned with the authorisation, within eight days of the expiry of the validity of the authorisation, to the competent authorities of the Member State of establishment which issued them. A specimen of the book of record sheets is also given in the regulation.

The Regulation introduces certain safety clauses for certain regions in order to prevent authorisations being used exclusively for trading in only one or a few Member States. Limitations on the use of such permits may occur where 30% of the total number of permits are used in any one Member State.

The performance of cabotage transport operations remain subject to the host Member State laws relating to rates and conditions governing transport contracts, weights and dimensions of road vehicles, requirements relating to the carriage of certain categories of goods (dangerous or perishable goods, live animals), driving and rest time, VAT on transport services and technical standards.

Before 1 July 1992 the Council acting on a proposal from the Commission should adopt a regulation laying down the definitive cabotage system which should enter into force on 1 January 1993.

Rates for the carriage of goods by road between Member States

By Council Regulation 4058/89 the Council has provided that with effect from 1 January 1990 the rates for the carriage of goods between Member States should be set by free agreement between the parties to the haulage contract. This applies even if, at the time of the carriage operations in question, part of the journey is performed in transit through a third country or by a road vehicle which is carried by another means of transport, without intermediate reloading of the goods.

ROAD PASSENGER TRANSPORT

The completion of the internal market in road passenger transport

The international carriage of passengers by coach and bus services is at present governed by three regulations (one adopted in 1966 and two in 1972). These regulations set out common rules for the international carriage of passengers, including standard definitions of the various types of service. These regulations would be superseded by a proposed regulation which would largely repeat the present regime, but at the same time makes some changes: for example, the definitions of the various types of transport service would be modified and the administrative procedures simplified. There is also a proposed regulation which lays down the conditions under which non-resident carriers could operate national road passenger services (cabotage).

Common rules for the international carriage of passengers by coach and bus

The proposed regulation would apply to the international carriage of passengers by road, using vehicles which were registered in a Member State and which were intended to carry more than eight passengers. The notion of international carriage would cover journeys from one Member State to another and extends to journeys which departed from a Member State to a third country or which departed from a third country with a Member State as destination, crossing in either case other Member States. The freedom to provide services would cover the provision of shuttle services, regular services and occasional services.

Conditions that the carrier must fulfil

Any carrier would be permitted to operate coach and bus services for the carriage of passengers between Member States if the following conditions were satisfied:

- he was established in a Member State in conformity with the legislation of that country;
- he was authorised in that country to carry out the international carriage of passengers by means of regular services or occasional services or shuttle services by coach or bus;
- he satisfied the conditions laid down in Directive 74/562 on admission to the occupation of carrier of passenger by road in national and international travel;
- he met national and international legal requirements on road safety;
- in the case of natural persons, the carrier would have to be a national of one of the Member States;
- in the case of legal persons (e.g., companies), the carrier would have be under the continuous and effective management of persons the majority of whom would be nationals of Member States and would have to be constituted in such a way that the persons participating in the majority of the financial results or having a majority of the shares were nationals of Member States.

Shuttle, regular and occasional services

'Shuttle services' would mean services whereby, by means of repeated outward and return journeys, previously formed groups of passengers were carried from a single place of departure to a single place of destination and subsequently carried back to the place of departure. Passengers might, under certain circumstances, make the return journey with another group or be taken up and set down during the journey. A journey would not cease to be a shuttle service because an empty journey was carried out. Shuttle services could be made with accommodation (e.g., package holidays).

'Regular services' would mean services which provided for the carriage of passengers at specific intervals along specified routes, passengers being taken up and set down at predetermined stopping points. The carriage of workers to and from work and of school children to and from school would be called 'special regular services'. Carriers providing regular services would be obliged to display the route of the service, the bus stops, the timetable, the fares and the conditions of carriage.

'Occasional services' would be services which did not fall within the definition of shuttle or regular services. They would be largely of a touristic nature and include, in particular, closed-door tours (e.g., the same vehicle would carry the same passengers throughout the journey, although passengers could be taken up in several places and set down in the same places, provided this happened in the Member State where the journey began). Occasional services would also include the making of an outward journey carrying passengers and the return journey unladen and *vice versa*. Local excursions could be provided in the context of an international occasional service.

Authorisation of the services

Regular services and shuttle services without accommodation would be subject to authorisation. Authorisations (permits) would be issued in the name of the transport undertaking and would be non-transferable although the service could be sub-contracted. The period of validity of an authorisation could not exceed seven years for regular services and special regular services and two years for shuttle services without accommodation. Authorisations should specify the type of service, the route of service, giving in particular the place of departure and the place of destination, the service timetable, the schedule of driving and rest periods for drivers, the period of validity of the authorisation and for regular services and special regular services the stops and fares. The transport undertakings would be entitled to operate the services in the territories of all Member States over which the routes of the services would pass. Applications would be made to the Member State in whose territory the place of departure was situated (the authorising authority). Authorisation should be given unless it could be shown that the service would compete unfairly with existing services in the area concerned. Authorisations could be refused where it was considered that the applicant was not suitable e.g., if he was guilty of previous breaches of road safety laws. The authorising authority would issue an authorisation in agreement with the competent authorities of all the Member States in whose territories passengers were taken up or set down. If agreement could not be reached, the decision would be referred to the Commission for arbitration. The authorisation or control document would be carried on the vehicle and presented at the request of any authorised inspecting officer. The authorising authorities could withdraw any authorisation where the holder no longer met the requirements of the regulation or repeatedly committed serious breaches of road safety laws, for example.

A flexible regime would apply to occasional services and shuttle services with accommodation. Thus, occasional services and this type of shuttle service would not require authorisation and this dispensation would extend to unladen journeys connected with occasional services so that a transport company could go to any other Member State in order to pick up passengers. Transport companies wishing to supply these services would obtain a control document from the Member State where they were established. The control document would indicate, for example, the type of service, the schedule of driving and rest periods for drivers and the main itinerary.

Cabotage

A proposed regulation would lay down the conditions under which non-resident carriers could operate cabotage road passenger services. The regulation would provide that any carrier should be allowed to provide regular, shuttle or occasional services (in vehicles which are suitable for carrying at least eight passengers) in the domestic market of a different Member State provided that he:

- was established in a Member State in conformity with the legislation of that country;
- was authorised in that State to carry out the international carriage of passengers by means of regular services or occasional services or shuttle services by coach or bus;
- satisfied the conditions laid down in Directive 74/562 on admission to the occupation of carrier of passenger by road in national and international travel.

Regular, shuttle and occasional services would be defined in accordance with the regulation on common rules for the international carriage of passengers by coach and bus. These 'international' definitions would therefore be used for the purpose of defining national or domestic transport of passengers.

By virtue of the fact that domestic markets of the Member States might be disturbed as a result of non-Community firms gaining access to cabotage operations, the proposed regulation would protect the domestic markets from such carriers by stipulating that they have a genuine link with a Member State. The criteria would be identical to the criteria laid down in the proposed regulation dealing with national road haulage services and would generally mean that carriers would have to be nationals of Member States.

Non-resident carriers would then be allowed to perform cabotage operations under the same conditions as resident carriers which means that they would still be obliged to comply with the laws, regulations and administrative provisions in force in the Member State in which they operated, e.g., as regards insurance. These rules could not, however, discriminate against non-carriers on the grounds of nationality or the place of establishment.

INLAND WATERWAY

The completion of the internal market in the transport of goods and passengers by inland waterway

Cabotage

A proposed regulation would lay down the conditions under which non-resident carriers could operate cabotage services by inland waterway. Any carrier of goods or passengers by inland waterway should be allowed to provide such services in a different Member State provided that:

- he was established in a Member State in conformity with the legislation of that country;
- he was authorised in that country to carry out the international transport of goods and persons by inland waterway;
- in the case of natural persons, the carrier and boat-owner would be obliged, if they were not the same person, to be a national of one of the Member States;
- in the case of legal persons (e.g., companies), the carrier and boat owner would be obliged, if they were not the same person, to be under the continuous and effective management of persons the majority of whom were nationals of Member States and to be constituted in such a way

that the persons participating in the majority of the financial results or having a majority of the shares were nationals of Member States.

Member States would issue certificates to carriers who fulfilled these conditions although a document showing that a boat belonged to the Rhine Navigation would be sufficient. Non-resident carriers would then be allowed to perform cabotage operations under the same conditions as resident carriers which means that they would still be obliged to comply with national rules in the Member States in which they operated, e.g., as regards insurance. These rules could not, however, discriminate against non-carriers on the grounds of nationality or the place of establishment.

MARITIME TRANSPORT

The completion of the internal market in maritime transport

The maritime transport sector has also been governed by a network of unilateral and bilateral measures which restrict the freedom to provide services and distort competition in the maritime sector. The purpose of the measures envisaged in the White Paper is to deregulate maritime transport and open it up to increased competition. In this respect, the Council has adopted measures guaranteeing the freedom to provide maritime transport services and prohibiting cargo sharing arrangements operated by Member States. Moreover, the maritime sector has traditionally been tied up by cartels. Shipping conferences are liable to disturb trade patterns within the Community primarily because they distort competition between ports in different Member States by altering their respective catchment areas. The Council has, therefore, adopted a regulation which subjects these agreements to the competition rules of the Treaty. At the same time, it has made provision for a block exemption for liner conferences which are considered to have a stabilising effect assuring shippers of reliable services. The Council has also adopted two regulations aimed at protecting the maritime sector in the Community from unfair practices by third countries.

Freedom to provide sea transport services

Regulation 4055/86 provides that nationals established in a Member State may freely provide maritime transport services. The services that may be freely provided are:

- the carriage of passengers or goods by sea between any port of a Member States and any port or off-shore installation of another Member State (intra-Community shipping services);
- the carriage of passengers or goods by sea between the ports of a Member State and ports or off-shore installations of a third country (third-country traffic).

The regulation has not liberalised the carriage of passengers or goods by sea between ports in any one Member State (cabotage).

Due to the structure of the Community shipping industry, the provisions of the regulation also apply to nationals of the Member States established outside the Community and to shipping companies established outside the Community and controlled by nationals of a Member State, if their vessels are registered in that Member State in accordance with its legislation. The Council may, although it is not bound to, extend the freedom to provide maritime services to nationals of a third country which are established in the Community.

Derogations

Derogations are granted for unilateral national restrictions, which were in existence before 1 July 1986, on the carriage of certain goods wholly or partly reserved for vessels flying the national flag. These should be phased out in accordance with a timetable laid out in the regulation.

Existing cargo-sharing arrangements contained in bilateral agreements concluded by Member States with third countries should either be phased out or adjusted in accordance with the regulation. Where the Code of Conduct for Liner Conferences is applicable, the cargo sharing arrangements should be adjusted to comply with the Code and with the obligations of Member States under Regulation 954/79. This provides for reservations to the code and sets out the conditions under which Member States could ratify the Code, e.g., it ensures that each shipping line established in the territory of a Member State is treated in the same way as lines which have their head office there. Where the Code is not applicable, the cargo sharing arrangements should be adjusted as soon as possible and in any event before 1 January 1993, so as to provide for fair and free and non-discriminatory access by all Community nationals to the cargo shares due to all the Member States concerned.

Notification of future cargo-sharing arrangements

Cargo-sharing arrangements in any future agreements with third countries are strictly prohibited save in those exceptional circumstances where Community liner shipping companies would not otherwise have an effective opportunity to ply for trade to and from the third country concerned. In such a case the Member State should inform the

Commission which would propose to the Council any appropriate action to be taken. This may include the negotiation and conclusion of cargo-sharing arrangements. In September 1987, the Council decided that Italy could ratify a bilateral agreement with Algeria which was designed to secure an equal share of traffic on routes linking the two countries. The permission is conditional on Italy acceding to the Code of Conduct for Liner Conferences and that the provisions of the agreement would be implemented in accordance with this regulation.

Cabotage

The Commission has proposed a regulation applying the principle of freedom to provide services to maritime transport within Member States. It is proposed that restrictions on freedom to provide maritime transport services within Member States should be abolished in respect of Community ship owners who are established in a Member State of the Community when using vessels registered in the Community Ship Register and not exceeding 6,000 GRT and provided that the vessels were allowed to operate such services within the State where they were registered.

The maritime transport services covered would include in particular:
- the carriage of passengers or goods by sea between ports in any one Member State, including overseas departments of that State (cabotage);
- the carriage of passengers or goods by sea between any port in a Member State and installations or structures on the continental shelf of that Member State (off-shore supply services).

Member States would be allowed to require that vessels used for these services are manned with nationals of the Member States to the same degree as is required in respect of the vessels flying its own flag which are used for the services. Further, they would be allowed to impose on ship-owners public service obligations as a condition for the right to provide such services; i.e., obligations aiming to guarantee the continuity, regularity and efficiency of certain services.

Such cabotage or off-shore supply services could be suspended by the Commission in the event of severe market disruption or serious imbalances between supply and demand in a given geographical area of a Member State.

Definition of Community ship-owner

Since many of the measures adopted or proposed for the completion of the internal market in maritime transport apply only to Community ship-owners, it is necessary to have a definition of a Community ship-owner.

Consequently the Commission has proposed a regulation on such a definition. The proposed regulation would define ship-owner as: a natural or legal person providing a liner or tramp service in the field of maritime transport of passengers or goods by one or more sea-going vessels which he or it owns or has chartered on the basis of a bare-boat charter, time charter or voyage charter. The following ship-owners would be regarded as Community ship-owners:

(A) a national of a Member State who has his domicile or usual residence in a Member State;

(B) a company or firm which is formed in accordance with the law of the Member State and which complies with the following conditions:

    (1) the principal place of business is situated and the effective control is exercised in a Member State; and

    (2) a majority of the members of the Board or of the directors are nationals of Member States having their domicile or usual residence in the Community or in which nationals or Member States participate by more than 50% or are company shareholders controlling more than 50% of the overall company capital;

(C) a national of a Member State who has his domicile or usual residence outside the Community if he is the owner of a vessel registered in a Member State in accordance with its legislation;

(D) a company or firm formed in accordance with the law of a third country in which nationals of Member States participate by more than 50% or are shareholders controlling more than 50% of the overall company capital provided that it is the owner of a vessel registered in a Member State in accordance with its legislation.

Community Ship Register

The Commission has proposed a regulation establishing a Community Ship Register and providing for the flying of a flag by sea-going vessels. The Commission considers that the establishment of a Community Ship Register would serve the purpose of creating a channel through which national efforts could be converged and would constitute a focus for the employment of Community sea-farers and constitute a trade-mark guaranteeing shippers a high-quality service

The Community Ship Register would be called Euros in which sea-going merchant vessels could be registered in addition to the Member States' national registers. The following vessel owners could apply for registration:

- nationals of Member States;
- companies formed in accordance with the law of a Member State and having their principal place of business in, and effective control within, the Community, provided that a majority of the members of the Board or of the directors of these companies are nationals of the Member States having their domicile or usual residence in the Community;
- companies formed in accordance with the law of a Member State or of a third country in which nationals of Member States participate by more than 50% or are Community shareholders controlling more than 50% of the overall company capital;
- nationals of certain third countries which allow vessels registered in Euros to be registered in their register.

The vessels which would be eligible for registration would be any sea-going merchant vessel with a tonnage of at least 500 grt, and be no more than twenty years old. Vessels operated by Community ship-owners on the basis of a bare-boat charter for a period of at least 12 months could be registered in Euros under certain conditions.

The deletion of a vessel from the national register of a Member State and its registration in the national register of another Member State at the same time, would not affect its registration in Euros. The Community vessel owner would apply to the Commission for registration of a vessel in Euros.

The proposed regulation also lays down requirements relating to safety, manning and crew. For example, on vessels registered in Euros all officers and at least half of the rest of the crew would have to be nationals of a Member State. Guidelines concerning the manning of vessels registered in Euros would be laid down by the Commission on the basis of the principles set out in Resolution No. A481(XII) of 19 November 1981 of the Assembly of the International Maritime Organisation (IMO) after consultation with the Joint Committee on Maritime Transport in Member States. The qualifications and licences of sea-farers who are nationals of a Member State would be recognised by the competent authorities of each Member State for the purposes of employment of any vessel registered in Euros, subject to minimum requirements for professional training and experience in the function concerned as required in future directives.

Vessels registered in Euros would be obliged to fly the European flag in addition to their national flag. Moreover a vessel registered in Euros would identify its port of registry on its stern.

Abolition of baggage checks on passengers taking an intra-Community sea crossing

The application of the principle of freedom of movement must result, inter alia, in the elimination of controls on the baggage of passengers making an intra-Community sea crossing. Consequently the Commission has proposed a regulation which would eliminate such controls or formalities. An intra-Community sea crossing means a sea crossing where the port of departure and port of arrival are situated in the Community customs' territory and the journey is made by a vessel crossing regularly between two or more specified Community ports. The regulation would not apply to:

- the baggage of passengers using a maritime service effected in one vessel and comprising successive legs departing from, terminating in or calling at non-Community ports;
- the baggage of passengers aboard a pleasure craft, i.e., private boats intended for recreational use or whose itinerary depends on the wishes of the user.

Application of anti-trust rules to maritime transport

According to Council Regulation 141, Regulation 17 does not apply to transport services. Consequently, the Commission had no means of investigating directly cases of suspected infringement of Articles 85 and 86 of the Treaty in maritime transport. The Commission lacked the powers of its own to take decisions or impose penalties necessary to terminate an infringement. This position has now changed with the adoption of Regulation 4056/86 which lays down detailed rules for the application of Articles 85 and 86 to maritime transport. In short, the regulation is the equivalent of Regulation 17.

The regulation applies to international maritime transport services from or to one or more Community ports, other than tramp vessel services. Tramp vessel services are excluded from the regulation on the grounds that the rates for these services are freely negotiated on a case-by-case basis in accordance with supply and demand conditions. Tramp vessel services means the transport of goods in bulk or in break bulk in a vessel chartered to shippers for non-regularly scheduled or non-advertised sailing.

Agreements falling outside Article 85

Certain types of technical agreements are excepted from the prohibition in Article 85 where their sole object is to achieve technical improvements or cooperations. These agreements concern the following:
- the uniform application of standards or types in respect of vessels, equipment, supplies or fixed installations;
- the exchange or pooling of vessels, space on vessels, equipment or fixed installations;
- the organisation of supplementary maritime operations and the fixing of their inclusive rates and conditions;

- coordination of timetables;
- consolidation of individual consignments;
- establishment of uniform rules for transport tariffs.

Exemption of liner conferences

Provision is made for the exemption under Article 85 of liner conferences on the ground that they have a stabilising effect, assuring shippers of reliable services. It was considered that as a result of the application of the Code of Conduct for Liner Conferences, there would be a considerable number of conferences serving the Community. The regulation therefore supplements the code by exempting liner conferences which have as their object the fixing of rates and conditions of carriage and one or more of the following objectives:

- the coordination of shipping timetables, sailing dates or dates of call;
- the determination of the frequency of sailing or calls;
- the coordination or allocation of sailing or calls among members of the conference;
- the regulation of the carrying capacity offered by each member;
- the allocation of cargo or revenue among members. Exemption is also granted to agreements between transport users or between users and conferences concerning rates, conditions and quality of liner services on the grounds that they secure a more efficient operation of maritime transport services.

These types of agreement are exempted subject to the condition that they do not, within the common market, cause detriment to certain ports, transport users or carriers by applying rates and conditions of carriage which are differentiated solely by reference to the country of origin or destination of the goods carried. The exemption of liner conferences is subject to further conditions, in particular the following:

- any loyalty arrangement must: (i) be subject to express agreement; (ii) offer transport users a system of immediate rebates or the choice between such a system and a system of deferred rebates; (iii) set out lists of cargo which are excluded; and (iv) set out the circumstances under which users are released from the loyalty arrangement;
- there must be no restriction on transport users as to their choice of inland transport operations and quayside services not covered by the freight charge on which the shipping line and the transport user have agreed;
- users must at all times be in a position to acquaint themselves with the rate and conditions of carriage applied by members of the conference;
- arbitration awards relating to the practice of conferences must be notified to the Commission.

The regulation provides that the benefit of the block exemption may be withdrawn by the Commission in particular where the conference infringes Article 86 which prohibits an abuse of a dominant position.

Rules of procedure

The Commission may investigate a possible breach of Articles 85 or 86 either on its own initiative or acting on a complaint by a Member State or by someone who claims a legitimate interest. The Commission has sole power to grant an exemption from Article 85, although national authorities, including national courts, have jurisdiction to declare that any case falls under Article 85 or 86. In order for an agreement to be exempted from Article 85, it must be notified to the Commission. Thereafter the Commission should publish in the Official Journal of the European Communities a summary of the notification and invite comments from interested parties within 30 days. If the Commission has not informed the parties to the contrary, the agreement is deemed to be exempt after 90 days of the publication of the summary. This provisional validity lasts for a period of six years during which time it is open to the Commission to reopen the investigation. Where the Commission decides that an agreement merits exemption, it may decide that the date from which the exemption is to take effect is prior to the date of notification.

The Commission has power to request information from parties. To this end Commission officials are empowered to examine and take copies of books and other business records, ask for oral examinations on the spot and enter any premises. Information obtained is subject to professional secrecy and should only be used for the purposes of the investigation. The regulation provides for rights of the relevant parties to be heard before the Commission adopts a decision which should be published and which is subject to review by the European Court.

The Commission may impose fines for breach of the anti-trust rules of:

- between 100–5000 ECU if it finds that an undertaking has intentionally or negligently supplied incorrect or misleading information;
- between 1000–1,000,000 ECU or a sum in excess thereof but not exceeding 10% of the undertakings worldwide turnover if it finds that any undertaking has intentionally or negligently infringed article 85(1) or article 86;
- between 50-1000 ECU per day in order to compel an undertaking to terminate an infringement.

Unfair pricing

Regulation 4057/86 seeks to protect Community shipowners from unfair pricing practices operated by third country shipowners who are subsidised by their governments. Such unfair pricing practices cause serious disruption to the freight pattern on routes to, from or within the Community and cause major injury to Community shipowners operating on that route. Community shipowners covers all cargo shipping companies established in a Member State and cargo shipping companies established outside the Community provided that they are controlled by nationals of Member States and their ships are registered in a Member State. Third country shipowners are also defined by reference to 'cargo liner shipping companies'. Where unfair pricing practices are found to cause injury to Community shipowners, the Council is empowered to take redressive action.

Complaint

Any person who considers himself injured may lodge a written complaint to the Commission which, if the complaint contains sufficient evidence of unfair pricing and injury, will initiate an investigation. The initiation should be published so as to give third parties the opportunity of making representations. The Commission must on request give the parties directly concerned an opportunity to meet, so that opposing views may be presented. Proceedings on unfair pricing practices cannot act as a bar to customs clearance of the goods to which freight rates concerned apply.

Examination of injury

When making its investigation, the Commission must examine the freight rates offered by Community shipowners' competitors on the route in question and determine whether they are significantly lower than the normal freight rate offered by Community shipowners. The 'normal freight rate' is the comparable rate actually charged in the ordinary course of business for the like service by established and representative companies. Alternatively, the normal freight rate may be constructed by determining the costs of comparable companies plus a reasonable profit margin. If the freight rates are significantly lower, it must be proved that they have been subsidised. The Commission must determine whether this unfair pricing practice has 'injured' Community shipowners and should consider a number of economic indicators, such as effect on freight rates, sailing, utilisation of capacity, cargo bookings, market share, profits return on capital investment and employment.

Imposition of duties

Where the investigation shows that there has been an unfair pricing practice which has caused injury, the Commission should propose to the Council that a redressive duty be imposed where this is in the interests of the Community. The duties, which are collected by the Member State, are imposed on the foreign shipowners and apply to the transport of commodities which are loaded or discharged in a Community port. The amount of the duties must not exceed the difference between the freight rate charged and the normal rate and must be less if such lesser duty would be adequate to remove the injury. Where a shipowner can show that the duty collected exceeds the difference between the freight rate charged and the normal rate, that excess amount should be reimbursed. The imposition of duties may be reviewed by the Commission after one year and lapse after five years. The Council may decide not to impose duties where the foreign shipowner undertakes to raise his freight rates so that any injury to the community shipowner is removed.

Coordinated action to safeguard free access to cargoes

An increasing number of third countries take measures to protect their own merchant fleet to the detriment of the shipping trade of the Community. Regulation 4058/86 provides for retaliatory measures where third countries restrict free access by Community shipping companies to the transport of the following:

- liner cargoes, except where such action is taken in accordance with the United Nations Convention on a Code of conduct for Liner Conferences;
- liner cargoes in non-Code trades;
- bulk cargoes and other cargo on tramp services;
- passengers;
- persons or goods to or between offshore installations.

Member States may request coordinated action to be taken by the Community which means that the Council should first make diplomatic representations, but if this is to no avail the Council may take countermeasures directed at the shipping company of the third country. These countermeasures may consist of the imposition of licences, quotas or duties. If the Council has not acted within two months of the request, the Member State may apply national measures to rectify the situation.

3. New Technologies and Services

According to the Commission, the development of new technologies has led to the creation and development of new cross-border services which can only develop their full potential when they are able to serve a large, unobstructed market. The White Paper on Completion of the Internal Market concentrates on three specific areas: audiovisual services, information technology and telecommunications.

In the field of audiovisual services, the objective is a single Community-wide broadcasting area. All those who provide and receive broadcast services should be able to do so regardless of national frontiers. Information itself and information services are becoming of increasing importance to industry and commerce and it is, therefore, of primary importance that the information market is opened up so as to ensure the wide application of information technology. The Commission aims to achieve a pan-European market for information services so that it should be possible, for example, to use the same mobile telephone anywhere in the Community. It is the telecommunications sector especially which has benefited from this approach.

Broadcasting

The cross frontier provision of broadcasting services is impeded by numerous restrictions. The disparity of national laws on such matters as producing and distributing programmes, advertising and sponsorship and the protection of children all restrict the free movement of broadcasts. Consequently, the Council has adopted Directive 89/552 on the coordination of national laws concerning television broadcasting activities. The directive, which must be implemented no later than 3 October 1991, lays down the general rule that Member States must ensure freedom of reception and re-transmission of television broadcasts from other Member States. It does not apply to broadcasts intended exclusively for reception in states other than Member States.

The adopted directive is different in many respects from the original proposed directive. It is confined specifically to television broadcasting rules and has dropped the system of statutory licences which would have been granted to cable operators who wish to broadcast from another Member State (this will be subject to a separate directive).

Free movement of television broadcasts

The term television broadcast means the initial transmission by wire or over the air, including that by satellite, in unencoded or encoded form, of television programmes intended for reception by the public. The directive introduces a qualified principle of home country control by providing that it is the originating Member State not the receiving Member State which is responsible for verifying that broadcasts comply with the directive. No secondary control by the receiving Member State is allowed save in respect of areas not coordinated by the directive (i.e., copyright laws). Moreover, it is specifically provided that the receiving Member State may exceptionally suspend the re-transmission of televised broadcasts if (1) the television broadcast coming from another Member State manifestly, seriously and gravely impairs the physical, mental or moral development of minors (in particular those that involve pornography or gratuitous violence) and (2) the broadcaster has infringed this principle on two occasions during the last 12 months and (3) the receiving Member State has notified the broadcaster and the Commission in writing of the alleged infringements and (4) consultations with the transmitting State and the Commission have not produced an amicable settlement.

In order to make it easier for Community broadcasters to receive and transmit television broadcasts freely, the directive coordinates certain rules which deal with the protection of different interests. A minimalist approach is adopted so that Member States remain free to impose stricter requirements on broadcasts originating on their own territories. The essential requirements cover the following areas:

- distribution and production of television programmes;
- television advertising and sponsorship;
- protection of minors;
- rights of reply.

Distribution and production of television programmes

The directive aims to promote European television programmes and thus European cultures. Accordingly, Member States must ensure that broadcasters reserve for European works a majority (the proposal referred to 60%) of their transmission time (excluding time appointed to news, sports events, games, advertising and teletext services). This proportion should be achieved progressively and should not in any event be lower than the average for 1988 in the Member State concerned (1990 in respect of Greece and Portugal). Member States must provide the Commission every two years with a report as to the progress made to achieving this objective.

At least 10% of broadcasters' transmission time (excluding time appointed to news, sports events, etc.) or at least 10% of their programming budget should be reserved for European works created by producers who are independent of broadcasters. This proportion should be achieved progressively and should be achieved for recent works (i.e., works transmitted within five years of their production). The directive no longer refers to Community works by virtue of the Council of Europe's adoption of the European Convention on Transfrontier Television. European works essentially means works which have originated from a Member State of the Community or from a European state party to the Convention, that is to say works produced or supervised by persons established in one or more of those states. Works which are not European works but which are made mainly with authors and workers residing in one or more Member States of the Community, will be considered as European works to an extent corresponding to the proportion of the contribution of Community co-producers to the total production costs.

An addition to the directive is that Member States must ensure that television broadcasters under their jurisdiction do not broadcast any cinematographic work, unless otherwise agreed between the rights-holders and the broadcaster, for two years after the work was first shown in cinemas in one of the Member States of the Community; in the case of cinematographic works co-produced by the broadcaster, this period is one year.

Television advertising and sponsorship

Television advertising must be readily recognisable and kept quite separate from the programme by optical and/or acoustic means. Isolated advertising spots must remain the exception. Advertising must not use subliminal techniques and surreptitious advertising of goods in programmes is prohibited. Advertising must respect human dignity, must not discriminate on grounds of race, sex or nationality, must not be offensive to religious or political beliefs, or encourage behaviour prejudicial to health, safety or the environment (the latter was a late amendment).

All forms of television advertising for cigarettes and other tobacco products must be prohibited. The recital to the directive makes it clear that this includes indirect forms of advertising which, whilst not directly mentioning the tobacco product, seek to circumvent the ban by using brand names, symbols or other distinctive features of tobacco products. Advertising for alcohol and advertising directed to children must comply with certain criteria. Sponsored television programmes must meet certain criteria and news and current affairs programmes cannot be sponsored. Television advertising for medicines available only on prescription is also prohibited.

The directive lays down the general rule that advertisements must be inserted between programmes. Where they are inserted during programmes they must not prejudice the integrity and value of the programme. In programmes consisting of autonomous parts, or in sports programmes and similarly structured events, advertisements must only be inserted between the parts or in the intervals. The transmission of audio-visual works, such as feature films (excluding serials and documentaries), of more than 45 minutes duration, may be interrupted once for each complete period of 45 minutes. A further interruption is allowed if their programmed duration is at least twenty minutes longer than two or more complete periods of 45 minutes. Generally at least twenty minutes should elapse between each successive advertising break within the programme.

Advertisements cannot be inserted in any broadcast of a religious service. News and current affairs programmes, documentaries, religious programmes and children's programmes, where they last for less than thirty minutes cannot be interrupted by advertisements.

The amount of advertising must not exceed 15% of the daily transmission time. This percentage may be increased to 20% to include advertising such as direct offers to the public, but this latter form of advertising cannot exceed one hour per day.

Protection of minors

There is a prohibition on all broadcasts which can seriously harm the physical, mental or moral development of children and young persons, in particular those that involve pornography, gratuitous violence.

Rights of reply

Any person, regardless of nationality, whose interests, in particular his reputation and good name, had been damaged by an assertion of incorrect facts in a broadcast programme must have a right of reply or equivalent remedies.

Information services market

The completion of the internal market in new technologies is largely dependent on the creation of a common information market which would stimulate the competitive capability of European suppliers and promote the use of advanced information services in the Community. In order to achieve this, Decision 88/524 sets out a plan of action for setting up an information services market. The plan, which is set out in an annex to the decision, provides for financial assistance in respect of the following aims:

- establishment of a European Information Market Observatory (IMO) to stimulate the provision of fuller statistical data;

- overcoming technical, administrative and legal barriers, in particular by exploring with information providers (IPs) and users the demand for simplification and standardisation of access to database services;
- improvement of the synergy between the public and the private sectors;
- launching of pilot/demonstration projects;
- promotion of the use of European information services; e.g., by multilingual directories;
- interconnection of libraries in the Community.

As a general rule contractors should bear at least 50% of the total cost of financing such projects.

In January 1991 the Commission proposed a much broader plan with the following objectives; to establish an internal market for information services; to stimulate and reinforce the competitive capability of European suppliers of information services; to promote the use of advanced information services and to reinforce joint efforts to achieve Community cohesion with respect to information service policies. In order to attain these objectives, an action list is contained in an annex to the proposal.

Telecommunications

In its White Paper on the Internal Market the Commission stated that a market free of obstacles at Community level necessitates the installation of appropriate telecommunication networks with common standards. Two years later the Commission issued its Green Paper on the development of the common market for telecommunications services and equipment (COM (87) 290). The Green Paper sets out ten proposed positions which aim to develop a strong telecommunications infrastructure, to provide the European user with a broad variety of telecommunications services on the most favourable terms, to ensure coherence of development between Member States, to create an open competitive environment and to ensure full transparency of procedures. The 'ten commandments' are as follows.

1. PTTs (national telecommunications administrations) to continue to have exclusive rights to provide and operate the physical network infrastructure for a particular country (with the possible exception of two-way satellite communications).
2. PTTs to have exclusive rights for a number of basic services, especially voice telephony.
3. Free and unrestricted provision of all other services (value added services) within and between Member States.
4. Strict requirements regarding standards for the network infrastructure and services provided by the PTTs to maintain or create Community-wide inter-operability otherwise known as open network provision (ONP).

5. Clear definition by directives of general requirements imposed by PTTs on providers of competitive services for use of the network, including definitions regarding network infrastructure provision.

6. Free and unrestricted provision of terminal equipment within Member States and between Member States subject to type approval.

7. Separation of regulatory and operational activities of PTTs to avoid conflicts of interest.

8. Strict review of the commercial activities under Article 90 and the competition rules.

9. Strict review of the commercial activities of private operators in the newly liberalised sectors under the competition rules.

10. Full application of the Community's common commercial policy to telecommunications, particularly in order to build up a consistent Community position for GATT negotiations.

Several directives have now been adopted in these areas. The telecommunications sector has been further liberalised by the adoption of Directive 90/531 on the procurement procedures of entities operating in the telecommunications sector.

Open Network Provision (ONP) Conditions

One of the main objectives highlighted by the Commission in its Green Paper was the harmonising of standards, frequencies and tariff principles in order to meet inter-operability of transfrontier services within the European Community. As part of this objective the Council has adopted Directive 90/387 on open network provision which have been should be implemented before 1 January 1991. The ONP Directive concerns the harmonisation of open network provision conditions which concern the open and efficient access to public telecommunications networks. The directive does not address the broadcasting and distribution of television programmes by telecommunication means, in particular cable television networks, which need special consideration. Nor does the directive address the question of communication via satellite; there is a separate Commission Green Paper in this area.

Open network provision conditions must comply with a number of basic principles, namely they must be based on objective criteria, they must be transparent, published in an appropriate manner, guarantee equality of access and be non-discriminatory. It is only by reference to 'essential requirements' that a Member State may limit access to one of its public telecommunications networks or services. Such essential requirements cover the security of network operations (i.e., the availability of the public network in case of emergency); maintenance of network integrity (i.e., the normal operation and the interconnection of public networks in the Community on the basis of common technical specifications); inter-operability of services (i.e., compliance with technical specifications introduced to increase the provision of services and the choice available to users); and the protection of data (i.e., measures taken to warrant the confidentiality of communications and the protection of personal data). Otherwise open network provision conditions cannot allow for any additional restrictions except those which may derive from the exercise of special or exclusive rights granted by Member States and which are compatible with Community law.

The ONP Directive is a framework directive for the development of further rules and principles in this area. Specific proposals on open network provision conditions should be drawn up in accordance with a reference framework which is contained in Annex II. This lays down principles relating to harmonised technical interfaces and service features, harmonised supply and usage conditions (i.e., delivery, contract period, quality of service, network inter-connection, resale) and harmonised tariff principles (i.e., they must in principle be cost-orientated).

The open network provision conditions are to be defined in stages and should concern the following areas: leased lines, packet and circuit-switched data services, Integrated Services Digital Network (ISDN), voice telephony service, telex service, mobile services, and subject to further study, new types of access to the network and access to the broad band network. Annex III of the directive lays down a timetable for the adoption of specific ONP Directives in priority areas i.e., covering leased lines and voice telephony services. The Commission has proposed a directive on the application of open network provision to leased lines; the proposal deals with the disclosure of information in respect of leased lines (i.e., technical characteristics, tariffs), supply conditions (i.e., the delivery period of leased lines, the repair time), the usage conditions and the essential requirements for leased lines and the guarantee of a minimum set of leased lines.

The Commission may request the European Telecommunications Standards Institute (ETSI) to draw up European standards as a basis for harmonised technical interfaces and/or service features for open network provision conditions. These will be voluntary but those service providers adopting them should in principle be deemed to have complied with essential requirements relating, for example, to the security of network operations, maintenance of network integrity, inter-operability and protection of data. There is also a presumption that a telecommunications organisation which complies with these standards fulfills a requirement of open and efficient access. Where inter-operability is not achieved the relevant standards may become mandatory.

Mutual recognition on terminal equipment

The terminal equipment sector is considered to be a vital part of the telecommunications industry; it is estimated that this sector accounts for about 25% of the total telecommunications market in the Community. The sector will become more competitive as a result of Directive 91/263 on full mutual recognition of terminal equipment. Directive 91/263 repeals from November 1992 Directive 86/361 which introduced limited mutual recognition of type approval for telecommunications terminal equipment. Full mutual recognition will enable manufacturers of terminal equipment ranging from telephones to telefaxes to go through a single equipment approval procedure common to all twelve Member States. The testing of the common standards for terminal equipment will be carried out by any laboratory or certification body on an EC list rather than separately through 12 bodies.

Community law provides that obstacles to movement within the Community, resulting from disparities in national legislation relating to the marketing of products must be accepted insofar as such requirements can be recognised as being necessary to satisfy imperative requirements. Directive 91/263 harmonises the essential requirements relating to terminal equipment which are liable to restrict the free movement of terminal equipment.

The directive applies to terminal equipment which is defined as equipment intended to be connected to the termination of a public telecommunications network or to interwork with a public telecommunications network. The connection may be by wire, radio, optical or other electro-magnetic system.

Member States cannot restrict the free circulation and use on their territory of terminal equipment which complies with the provisions of the directive and in particular satisfy the essential requirements. The essential requirements relate to the following (in so far as they are relevant to the equipment): safety as regards users and employees of public telecommunications network operators; electromagnetic compatibility; protection of the public telecommunications network from harm; effective use of the radio frequency spectrum; interworking of terminal equipment with network equipment for the purpose of establishing, modifying, charging for, and clearing real or virtual connections. Member States must presume compliance with the essential requirements as regards safety in respect of terminal equipment which is in conformity with national standards implementing standards harmonised at the European level by CEN or Cenelec. With respect to the other essential requirements, the Commission may decide that the harmonised standards should be transformed into technical and mandatory regulations.

Manufacturers or their authorised representatives established within the Community have a choice of subjecting their terminal equipment either to an EC-type examination (which is described in Annex I) or to an EC declaration of conformity (as described in Annex IV). Under the EC-type examination a notified body ascertains and attests that terminal equipment conforms to the essential requirements that apply to it. Under the declaration of conformity procedure the manufacturer declares that the products concerned satisfy the requirements of the directive. Under both systems the manufacturer must operate an approved quality procedure. As regards the EC-type examination system, the quality procedure is aimed at ensuring that the equipment is in conformity with the approved type of equipment. As regards the EC-type declaration of conformity system, the quality procedure is aimed at ensuring that the equipment satisfies the requirements of the directive. Member States must appoint bodies responsible for certification, product checks and surveillance, etc. Annex V of the directive provides minimum criteria which Member States must take into account in appointing these bodies i.e., relating to premises and staff.

The marking of terminal equipment complying with the directive consists of the CE mark followed by the symbol of the body responsible and a symbol indicating that the equipment is intended and is suitable to be connected to the public telecommunications network. The CE mark and the two symbols are contained in Annex VI. Equipment manufactures must also place a symbol on the equipment together with the type, batch or serial number and the manufacturer's name. The affixing of marks which are likely to be confused with the EC mark of conformity are prohibited.

Where it is established that the EC mark has been affixed to terminal equipment which does not conform to the relevant essential requirements All appropriate measures should be taken to withdraw such products from the market or to restrict their being placed on the market. Furthermore appropriate action should be taken against whomsoever has affixed the mark.

Competition in the terminal equipment market

Many Member States have operated Telecommunication Monopolies whose rights have gone beyond the network infrastructure and have extended to the supply and maintenance of terminal equipment. The exercise of such exclusive rights often disadvantages equipment from other Member States and restricts consumers renting or purchasing cheaper equipment. The Commission considers that the existence of such rights is incompatible with Articles 30, 37 and 86 of the Treaty of Rome. Consequently, the Commission has pursuant to Article 90(3) of the Treaty issued Directive 88/301 which is aimed at abolishing exclusive rights relating to terminal equipment thereby introducing greater competition in this sector.

The salient points of the directive are as follows:

- All special or exclusive rights granted by a Member State to a public or private body in respect of importation, marketing, connection, bringing into service of telecommunications terminal equipment and/ or maintenance of such equipment are to be abolished.
- Economic operators must have the right to import, market, connect, bring into service and maintain terminal equipment. However, Member States may in the absence of technical specifications, refuse to allow terminal equipment to be connected and brought into service where such equipment does not satisfy the essential requirements laid down in Article 2(17) of Directive 86/361 (this Directive will be replaced by Directive 91/263 from November 1992). Furthermore Member States may require such economic operators to possess relevant technical qualifications.
- Users must have access to new public network termination points and the physical characteristics of these points must be published;
- Responsibility for drawing up all technical specifications and type approval procedures for terminal equipment must be entrusted to a body independent of public or private telecommunication monopolies.
- State telecommunications monopolies must allow customers to terminate, with maximum notice of one year, leasing or maintenance contracts which concern terminal equipment;
- Member States must provide the Commission at the end of each year with a report allowing the Commission to monitor compliance with the directive.

The validity of Directive 88/301 was challenged by France and other Member States before the European Court (case C-202/88 judgment of 19 March 1991). The Court upheld Article 90(3) as a proper legal basis for the adoption of the directive and rejected the application for the most part. The Court did, however, declare the directive void (1) in so far as it applied to special rights (not exclusive rights) for lack of reasoning and (2) in so far as it applied to the termination of contracts on the grounds that there was no state measure involved within the meaning of Article 90.

Competition in the market for telecommunication services

The Commission has also adopted under Article 90 Directive 90/388 on competition in the market for telecommunication services. The Services Directive frees value added services immediately and basic data transmission from 1 January 1993. It does not apply to telex, mobile radio telephony, radio paging and satellite services. Since the opening up of voice telephony to competition could threaten the financial stability of the telecommunications organisations, the Commission considered that Article 90(2) applied to the exclusive rights in respect of voice telephony.

The Services Directive does not affect exclusive or special rights to set up and provide public networks. Thus the Services Directive is tied to the adoption of the ONP Directive which harmonises the conditions for access to such networks.

The main points of the directive are as follows.

- Exclusive and special rights for all services to the general public except voice telephony should be abolished although Member States may make such services subject to objective and non-discriminatory trade regulations.
- There must be publication of technical interfaces by 31 December 1990 thus providing the information necessary for private operators.
- All restrictions on the processing of signals before and after their transmission via the public network must be abolished.
- There must be separation of regulatory powers from the activities of telecommunication organisations.
- Measures should be adopted to allow long-term contracts to be terminated.
- Special transitional arrangements up to 31 December 1992 are provided which allowing prohibitions on the simple resale of leased line capacity which could be used to compete with the public data transmission service before tariff structures have been revised.

The European Court judgment in Case C-202/88 is relevant to the validity of Directive 90/388. Consequently, the provisions relating to special rights and the termination of contracts must be treated with caution.

Pan-European land-based public radio paging in the Community

Since radio paging services depend on the allocation and availability of appropriate frequencies in order to transmit and receive between fixed based stations and radio paging receivers respectively, Directive 90/544 provides that Member States should designate in the 169.4 to 169.8 MHz waveband four channels which should have priority and be protected for the pan-European land-based public radio paging service by 31 December 1992 at the latest: these four channels are 169.6 MHz, 169.65 MHz, 169.7 MHz, 169.75 MHz. The designation of these frequency bands will allow the effective introduction of the more advanced radio paging system code-named European Radio Messaging System (ERMES) being specified by the European Telecommunications Standards Institute (ETSI). Recommendation 90/543 recommends that future pan-European public radio paging systems should be suitable for operation over the whole frequency band range 169.4 MHz to 169.8 MHz. Co-ordination is also recommended in respect of the choice of radio sub-system, the paging receiver specification, the system implementation services and facilities specified and supported by the pan-European radio paging system, tariff considerations and geographical service coverage. Consideration should also be given to providing within the ERMES system the ability to have displayed, on the radio paging receiver, characters in all official Community languages, wherever possible.

Public cellular digital land-based mobile communications

Land-based mobile communications systems in use in the Community are at present largely incompatible and do not allow users on the move in vehicles, boats, trains or on foot throughout the Community to reap the benefits of the internal market. The Commission aims to establish truly pan-European mobile communications when the change-over to the second-generation cellular digital systems occurs.

Directive 86/361 on the mutual recognition of conformity tests on mass produced terminal equipment allows for the establishment of common conformity specifications for the pan-European cellular digital mobile communications system. Recommendation 87/371 and Directive 87/372 aim to coordinate the introduction of a public pan-European cellular digital land-based mobile communications service. This term means a public cellular service provided in each of the Member States to a common specification which includes the feature that all voice signals are coded into binary digits prior to radio transmission and where users provided with a service in one Member State can also gain access to the service in any other Member State.

The telecommunications authorities are recommended to implement the detailed requirements concerning the coordinated introduction of public pan-European cellular digital land-based mobile communications in the Community. These requirements are contained in an annex to the recommendation and concern the choice of transmission, the network architecture, the mobile interfaces, the signalling, tariffs and the areas to be covered by certain dates. Directive 87/372 provides that the 905-914 MHz and 950-959 MHz frequency bands should be reserved exclusively for a public pan-European cellular digital mobile communications service by 1 January 1991, and that the whole of the 890-915 MHz and 935-960 MHz bands should be available as quickly as possible.

V. Creation of Suitable Conditions for Industrial Cooperation

1. Company Law

European Community company law

The Treaty provides that companies or firms formed in accordance with the law of a Member State and having their registered office, central administration or principal place of business within the Community must be treated in the same way as natural persons, i.e., individuals, who are nationals of Member States. Companies and firms, therefore, are entitled to benefit from the freedom of establishment, the freedom to provide services and the right to non-discrimination on the ground of nationality. However, since national company laws differ, especially as regards types of company and the protection of members and third parties, these rights can only be effectively secured by the harmonisation of company laws so that the protection of shareholders and creditors, etc., is equivalent throughout the Community. To this end, the Council has issued a number of directives harmonising national company law: the First Directive on disclosure of information by limited companies; the Second Directive on the formation of public limited companies; the Third Directive on mergers of public limited companies; the Fourth Directive on company accounts; the Sixth Directive on the division or scission of public limited companies; the Seventh Directive on consolidated accounts; the Eighth Directive on statutory auditors. There is also a proposed Ninth Directive on groups of companies.

The White Paper continued this process of harmonisation: a proposed Fifth Directive on the structure of public limited companies; a proposed Tenth Directive on cross-border mergers; a proposed Thirteenth Directive on takeover and other general bids, as well as a proposed amendment to the Fourth and Seventh Directives on company accounts. Other measures proposed in the White Paper have been adopted. These are the Eleventh Directive on branch disclosure requirements; the Twelfth Directive on single-member private limited companies. The White Paper also contains two important and potentially far-reaching measures, one for the Regulation on the European Economic Interest Grouping which has now been adopted, the other for the Regulation for a European Company which has not yet been adopted.

European Economic Interest Grouping (EEIG)

Regulation 2137/85 provides a legal framework which will allow businesses to cooperate more freely across borders and to circumvent the legal, fiscal and psychological barriers which often inhibit such cooperation. This creates a new legal entity: the European Economic Interest Grouping – EEIG.

Formation

An EEIG is formed by a contract concluded between the parties. The contract must include at least:

- the name of the EEIG preceded by or followed by the word 'European Economic Interest Grouping' or 'EEIG';
- the official address of the EEIG;
- the EEIG's objects;
- the name and address of the members;
- the duration of the EEIG unless it is indefinite.

The contract together with a number of other documents listed in the regulation must then be registered in the State in which the EEIG has its official address. The official address must be in the Community and be fixed where either the EEIG or one of the members has its central administration. Notice that an EEIG has been formed together with other essential information must be published in the State of registration and in the Official Journal of the European Communities. An EEIG which is situated in another Member State must also register with that State. The law applicable to the contract and to the internal organisation of the EEIC is the internal law of the State of registration.

Structure

An EEIG must have at least two organs: the members acting collectively and a manager (or managers). Each member has one vote, although the contract may provide that members may have more than one. One member may not have a majority of the votes. The contract should provide for a quorum or a majority in accordance with which decision are taken. Provision is made for unanimity in certain matters, e.g., altering the objects of the EEIG or admitting new members.

Only companies and firms and natural persons who carry on industrial commercial, craft or agricultural activities or who provide professional or other services in the Community may be members of an EEIG. The EEIG must have at least two members which must come from different Member States. The Member State where the EEIG has its official address may limit the number of members of an EEIG to 20. Furthermore any Member State may restrict membership of an EEIG on grounds of public interest. It is also provided that a member may withdraw or be expelled from or transfer his rights in an EEIG.

Function of an EEIG

An EEIG differs from a firm or a company principally in its purpose, which is restricted to developing the economic activities of its members by the pooling of resources and skills. The EEIG's activities must be of an ancillary nature and related to the economic activities of its members. For example, an EEIG may not itself practise a profession, but it might be used for joint research and development. The regulation specifically provides that an EEIG may not:

- exercise a power of management over the activities of its members or of another undertaking;
- hold any shares in a member, but may hold shares in another company if it is necessary to achieve the EEIG's objects;
- employ more than 500 persons;
- be used as a means of making loans or transfers of property to company directors save to the extent allowed by Member States;
- be a member of another EEIG;
- invite investment by the public.

A fundamental point to note about an EEIG is that its purpose is not to make a profit for itself. The profits made by an EEIG are deemed to be the profits of the members and must be apportioned among them in the proportion laid down in the contract, or in the absence of such provision in equal shares. Thus the profits and losses resulting from the activities of the EEIG are taxable only in the hands of its members.

Dealings with third parties

As from the date of registration, the EEIG has rights and obligations of all kinds and has the capacity to make contracts in its own name and to sue and be sued. The members may be held jointly and severally liable for any activities carried on by the EEIG before its registration. The manager must be a natural person and he represents the EEIG in respect of dealings with third parties. He binds the EEIG even where his acts do not fall within its objects unless it can be proved that the third party knew that the manager was acting *ultra vires*. The publication of the objects or of any limitation on the manager's powers is not sufficient evidence of knowledge. However, where the contract provides that the EEIG can only be validly bound by two managers acting jointly, publication of this fact can be relied on against third parties. Letters and order forms, etc., must state whether the managers act jointly.

Once a member has ceased to belong to an EEIG a limitation period of five years is laid down for actions against that member in connection with debts and liabilities arising out of the EEIG's activities before he ceased to be a member.

Winding up

The members of an EEIG may voluntarily order the winding up of an EEIG. Such a decision must be taken unanimously, unless otherwise provided in the contract. The regulation lays down provisions for the compulsory winding up of an EEIG. In particular, an EEIG must be wound up when there are no longer two members from different Member States or the official address is transferred outside the Community. The winding up of an EEIG entails its liquidation and question of liquidation, insolvency and cessation of payments are matters for national law. The regulation provides that members have unlimited joint and several liability for its debts and other liabilities, although the consequences of such liability is a matter for national law. Creditors may not proceed against a member for payment in respect of debts and other liabilities before the EEIG is put into liquidation.

The structure of public limited companies

A proposed Fifth Directive would regulate the structure of public limited companies (la société anonyme in France and die Aktiengesellschaft in Germany) and the powers and obligations of their bodies.

Structure

So far as concerns this type of company, two different sets of arrangements at present prevail in the Community. The first type is a two-tier system which provides for a management body responsible for managing the business of the company and a supervisory body responsible for controlling the management body. The second type is a one-tier system which only provides for one administrative organ. The original proposal would have made the two-tier system compulsory, but this has now been recognised as impractical and the proposal in its present form provides that a one-tier system might be maintained provided that it was endowed with certain characteristics designed to harmonise its functioning with that of a two-tier system. Therefore, Member States would be given the option either of requiring public companies to operate a two-tier system or of giving the company the choice of a two-tier or a one-tier system.

The two-tier system

The company would be managed by a management body under the supervision of a supervisory body which would also appoint the members of the management body. However, the members of the first management body might be appointed by the memorandum or articles of association. The supervisory body would also have power to dismiss members of the management body.

If the company had on average more than 1,000 employees (Member States might fix a lower number), there would have to be employee participation in the appointment of members of the supervisory body in one of four ways:

- the members of the supervisory body would be appointed by the general meeting as regards a maximum of two-thirds and by employees as regards a minimum of one-third but subject to a maximum of one-half;
- the supervisory body would co-opt its members, although shareholders and employees would have certain rights to veto an appointment;
- a body representing the employees would have the right to be informed and consulted by the management body on the administration, situation, progress and prospects of the company, its competitive position, credit situation and investment plans;
- employee participation would be regulated in accordance with collective agreements concluded between the company and employees. However, such collective agreements would have to make provision for employee participation in the supervisory body in a way similar to that set out above.

Member States might provide that there should not be employee participation of a company where a majority of employees were opposed to it. To the extent that employees did participate in the appointment of the supervisory body, the following principles would have to be respected:

- the relevant members of the supervisory organ and representatives of the employee would be elected by proportional representation;
- all employees would be able to participate in the election, which should be by secret ballot;
- free expression of opinion would be guaranteed.

No person could at the same time be a member of the management and supervisory bodies. Members would in general be appointed for a period of six years, after which they would be eligible for reappointment. There would be limitations on members being involved in other companies.

Periodically, the management body would have to send to the supervisory organ a written report on the progress of the company's affairs and a copy of the draft accounts. The authorisation of the supervisory body would have to be obtained for decisions relating to the closure or transfer of the company, any substantial change in the company's activities or organisation and any long-term cooperation with other companies.

The civil liability of the members of both bodies would be a matter for national law. However, the proposed directive provides that Member States would have to ensure that compensation was made for all damage sustained by the company as a result of breaches of the law or of the memorandum and articles of association or other wrongful acts committed by the members of those bodies when carrying out their duties. Moreover, each member of the body in question would be jointly and severally liable without limit, unless he could prove that no fault was attributable to him personally. Proceedings on behalf of the company might be commenced by minority shareholders, who are defined as those who held shares the value of which was at least 5% of the subscribed capital or 100,000 ECU. The company might, by general meeting, renounce the right to bring proceedings against a member of a body, although this could not affect the right of the minority shareholder to bring an action.

The one-tier system
In the one-tier system, the company would be managed by the executive members of an administrative body under the supervision of the non-executive members of that body. The number of non-executive members would be greater than the number of executive members. The non-executive members would appoint and might dismiss the executive members, although the executive members of the first administrative organ might be appointed in the memorandum or articles of association.

If the company had on average more than 1,000 employees (Member States might fix a lower number) there would have to be employee participation in the appointment of the non-executive members in one of three ways which are similar to the methods indicated above in respect of the supervisory organ in the two-tier system: e.g., employee participation in the appointment of non-executive members; employee participation through a body representing company employees; employee participation through collectively agreed systems. In all cases, Member States might provide that there should not be employee participation in a company where a majority of employees were opposed to it. The right of employee representatives to employee participation in the administrative body or the right to be consulted on important matters would be similar to that in a two tier-system. Likewise, many of the principles applicable in the two-tier system would apply to the one-tier system and in particular those concerning:

- the appointment of employee representatives;
- the appointment of members to the administrative body;
- the information of and authorisation by the non-executive members of the administrative body;
- the dismissal of members of the administrative body;
- the civil liability of members of the administrative body.

In respect of both the two-tier and one-tier systems, it is stated that in calculating whether a company had 1,000 employees, persons employed by subsidiary companies would be included. However, pending further coordination, the proposed directive would allow employees of subsidiary companies to be excluded from the system of participation applicable to the parent. Member States might also exclude employee participation or representation from companies whose sole or principal object was political, religious, humanitarian, charitable, educational, scientific, artistic or related to public information.

The general meeting

The general meeting would have to be convened at least once a year and might also be convened at any time by the management body or by the executive members of the administrative body. Minority shareholders would also have a right to have a general meeting convened, if necessary by recourse to the courts. The general meeting would be convened by notice which would have to contain at least the information set out in the proposed directive.

Every shareholder would be entitled to attend the meeting or appoint a proxy and would be entitled to a copy of the annual accounts, annual report, the auditors' report and information concerning the affairs of the company if this was necessary to understand the items on the agenda. The general meeting could not pass any resolution concerning items which did not appear on the agenda with the exception that resolutions might be made if they concerned legal proceedings against the members of the company's bodies or the calling of a new meeting. Furthermore, resolutions might be passed on items which did not appear on the agenda if all the shareholders were present or represented and no one objected.

Detailed provisions deal with voting. The shareholder's right to vote would be proportionate to the fraction of capital subscribed which the shareholding represented. A shareholder could not vote where payment up of calls made by the company had not been effected or where the resolution related to the discharge of that shareholder. As a general rule, resolutions of the general meeting would have to be passed by absolute majority of the votes cast by all the shareholders present or represented, unless otherwise provided by law or by the memorandum or articles of association. A majority of not less than two-thirds would be required for altering the memorandum or articles of association and a resolution which affected the rights of a particular class of shareholders would be valid only if that class consented to it in a separate vote.

It is further provided that any resolution passed by the general meeting in breach of the provisions in the proposed directive would be void or voidable. Limitation periods of between three months and one year would be laid down running from the time when the resolution could be adduced as against the person who claimed that the resolution was void.

The adoption and audit of the annual accounts

The annual accounts would have to be adopted by the general meeting. However, Member States might provide that in companies organised according to the two-tier system, the annual accounts might be adopted by the management and supervisory bodies unless they decided otherwise or could not reach agreement on the adoption of the annual accounts. It would be for the general meeting to decide how the profit or loss for the financial year would be used, but 5% of any profit for the financial year would have to be appropriated to a legal reserve until that reserve amounted to at least 10% of the subscribed capital. So long as the legal reserve did not exceed this amount, it could not be used except to increase the subscribed capital or to set off losses and then only if other available reserves were inadequate for these purposes.

The general meeting would appoint the auditors who might also be appointed and dismissed by a court. Auditors would be appointed for a specified period of not less than three years nor more than six years, although they would be eligible for reappointment. The audit of the accounts could not be undertaken by persons who were members, or who during the previous three years had been members of the administrative, management or supervisory bodies or of the staff of the company whose accounts were to be audited. Furthermore, auditors could not become members of such bodies or of the staff for at least three years after they last audited the company's accounts. The auditors would have to verify whether the accounts gave a true and fair view of the company's assets, liabilities, financial position and profit or loss. The report would make reference to any infringements of the law or of the memorandum and articles and to any fact which might constitute a serious danger to the financial position of the company.

The auditors would be liable to make compensation for any damage sustained by the company as a result of a wrongful act committed in carrying out their duties. A breach of the auditing requirements of the proposed directive could result in the adoption of the accounts being held void or voidable.

Cross-border mergers of public limited companies

Certain Member States make it extremely difficult for cross- border mergers to take place by requiring, for example, the unanimous approval of the shareholders of the companies. This has the effect of inhibiting cooperation between companies in different Member States and prevents them from attaining the size necessary for them to compete with companies from outside the Community. The aim of the proposed Tenth Directive is to facilitate cross-border mergers between companies in the Community.

The Third Directive on company law coordinated certain rules concerning mergers of public limited companies, but only applied to national mergers, e.g., companies governed by the law of the same Member State. The proposed Tenth Directive would apply, with some modifications, the principles contained in the Third Directive to cross-border mergers.

As in the case of the Third Directive, the proposed Tenth Directive would apply to public limited companies (la socit anonyme in France and die Aktiengesellschaft in Germany), but need not apply to cooperatives or to companies that are in the process of being wound up. Also, pending further harmonisation, cross-border mergers might also be excluded where it would have an adverse effect on employee representation in a company. This harmonisation has already begun with the proposed Fifth Directive on the structure of public limited companies. Nevertheless, the rights of employees of each of the companies involved in a cross-border merger must be protected in accordance with Directive 77/187 which, broadly speaking, provides that the rights and obligations of employment should pass to the acquiring company and the rights of employee representation should be preserved.

Definition of cross-border merger

The proposed directive would deal with the regulation of two types of merger which are defined in the Third Directive: a merger by the acquisition of one or more companies by another and of a merger by the formation of a new company. The mere takeover of one company, without a transfer of assets or a winding-up procedure, would fall outside of the definition of merger. 'Merger by acquisition' means the operation whereby a company is wound up without going into liquidation and transfers to another all its assets and liabilities in exchange for the issue to its shareholders of shares in the acquiring company and a cash payment, if any, not exceeding 10% of the nominal value of the shares so issued. 'Merger by the formation of a new company' means the operation whereby companies are wound up without going into liquidation and transfer to a newly formed company all their assets and liabilities in exchange for the issue to their shareholders of shares in the acquiring company and a cash payment, if any, not exceeding 10% of the nominal value of the shares so issued. The definition of cross-border mergers would be therefore identical to that of a national merger, except that two or more of the companies involved would be governed by the laws of different Member States.

Each of the companies involved would carry out all the preparatory acts and the disclosure obligations in accordance with its own national law. However, certain rules would be harmonised, in particular, those relating to disclosure requirements, voting on the merger, the protection of shareholders and third parties, supervision and the effect of the merger.

Disclosure requirements

The Third Directive provides that the draft terms must specify certain information, such as the name of the company, the share exchange ratio, the terms of the share allotment and certain rights attaching to the shares. The draft terms of a cross- border merger would have to contain the same information. However, whereas this is the minimum information required in the case of national mergers, in order to avoid any conflict between the laws of different States, it would be the maximum that might be required for cross-border mergers. The draft terms would have to be drawn up in writing and, if the national law of one of the companies so required, certified in due legal form. Where more than one applicable law required that the draft terms be drawn up and certified in due legal form, any person recognised by any of those laws might draw them up. The draft terms of a cross-border merger would have to be published in the same way as the draft terms of a national merger at least one month before the date fixed for the general meeting which was to decide on the merger. However, to ensure that third parties were better informed, further information would have to be published relating to the name and registered office of each of the merging companies, the register in which each company was listed and the date on which the cross-border merger was to take effect. At the same time, creditors of the acquired company would also have to be informed of their rights under the directive.

A national merger must be publicised according to the same rules as apply to the publication of the draft terms of the merger. These rules would also apply to cross-border mergers. However, the publication of a cross-border merger would have to take place for the company being acquired before publication for the acquiring company.

As in the case of national mergers, experts would have to be appointed to report to the shareholders of the merging companies on whether the share exchange ratio was fair and reasonable. The appointment of the expert would be subject to the law of the Member State which governed a particular company, although the companies could request that only one law applied to the appointment of the expert.

Voting in general meeting

Member States could not impose stricter requirements as regards a general meeting's decision concerning a cross-border merger than they imposed in respect of a national merger under the Third Directive. Essentially this means that a majority of at least two-thirds of the votes at the general meeting would be necessary to approve a merger. A simple majority might be sufficient where at last half of the subscribed capital was represented.

Protection of shareholders and third parties

According to the Third Directive, Member States must provide for an adequate system of protection for the interests of creditors of the merging companies having claims which pre-date the publication of the draft terms of the merger and which have not fallen due at the time of such publication. Furthermore, holders of securities, other than shares, to which special rights are attached must, in principle, be given rights in the acquiring company at least equivalent to those they possessed in the company being acquired. This system of protection would also apply to cross-border mergers.

The Third Directive provided that Member States must lay down rules on the civil liability towards the shareholders of the directors and members of the management or administrative bodies in the event that they misconduct themselves in preparing and implementing the merger. Civil liability must also extend to experts who report on the draft merger. In the case of cross-border mergers, the liability of the members of an acquired company must be determined by the law of the Member State governing the company and the liability of experts must be determined by the law of the Member State which appointed them.

Supervision of the merger

Under the terms of the Third Directive, Member States have several possibilities for examining the legality of mergers and they may provide for judicial or administrative preventive supervision. Where such supervision does not exist or where it does not extend to all the legal acts required for a merger, the minutes of the general meeting together with the decision on the merger must be drawn up and certified in due legal form. These options would also apply to cross-border mergers although, in order to synchronise such supervision, the supervision would be carried out first in respect of the acquiring company.

Effect of the merger

The Third Directive leaves it to the laws of the Member States to determine the date on which national mergers take effect. In the case of cross-border mergers, this date would be determined according to the law of the Member State governing the acquiring company. However, the merger could not take effect until after the necessary supervision had been completed.

Like a national merger, a cross-border merger transfers all the assets and liabilities of the acquired company to the acquiring company. At the same time, the shareholders of the acquired company become shareholders of the acquiring company and the company being acquired ceases to exist. National laws which require the completion of formalities for the transfer of assets to be effective against third parties continue to apply. In the case of cross-border mergers, these are the laws of the Member State governing the acquired company. Under the Third Directive, national rules may provide for the nullity of mergers subject to certain conditions. Cross-border mergers could not be annulled on grounds which are not applicable to national mergers and unlike a national merger, a cross-border merger could not be declared void on the ground that the decision of the general meeting was a nullity. The nullity of cross-border mergers would depend only on the absence of any supervision. In order to limit the risk of nullity, where the law of the Member State governing the acquiring company did not provide for the nullity of the merger where there had not been any preventive control, the cross-border merger could not be declared void. Finally, the law governing the judicial authority which had declared a merger void would determine whether third parties could challenge such a judgment.

The European Company

Cross-frontier cooperation in the Community is an essential aspect of the creation of a genuine common market. As the 1992 single market deadline approaches, operations to restructure companies and groups of companies are going to become more frequent and be mounted across national borders. Cross-frontier industrial cooperation between companies in different Member States can and does take place by the acquisition of capital or by a joint venture. However, cross-frontier mergers pose difficult legal problems. The Regulation on the European Economic Interest Grouping is not sufficient to encourage large-scale cross-frontier cooperation. Although the proposed Tenth Directive would greatly facilitate cross-frontier mergers, it would not overcome the problems created by the differences in national company law and the difficulties in virtually all Member States of managing a group of companies as a single economic unit rather than in the interests of its individual component companies. The creation of a European Company would overcome these problems by virtue of the fact that it would operate independently of national laws. A statute for a European Company would establish a single system of European company law for such companies.

The Commission first proposed, in 1970, a regulation to create a new form of European Company. This was amended in 1975. The present draft is a complex document consisting of some 284 articles. In 1988, the Commission proposed that the statute should be amended and simplified to a fairly considerable degree and that many of the provisions could now be based on a background of national laws which is sufficiently harmonised to allow for the introduction of uniform and simplified rules. The present draft of the statute of the European Company, may be summarised as follows.

Formation

The European Company (Societas Europea – SE) could be formed anywhere in the Community by two or more public limited companies formed under the law of a Member State and having their registered office and central administration within the Community, provided at least two of them had their central administrations in different Member States. It would have legal personality and be treated as a public limited company. The registered office of the SE would have to be in the Community at the same place as its central administration. Registration would be the same as for a plc although notice that an SE had been formed would also have to be put in the Official Journal.

The SE could be formed by two or more companies limited by shares governed by different national laws by merger or by the creation of a holding company or a joint subsidiary. The European Company could also create a European Company as its subsidiary. The minimum capital required would be 100,000 ECU and the capital would be denominated in ECU. All shareholders in like circumstances would be treated in a like manner. Shares might carry different rights in respect of distributions. Non-voting shares could be issued subject to the conditions that their total nominal value could not exceed one half of the capital, they must carry all the rights of a shareholder other than the right to vote (except possibly the right to new shares) and they must not be included in computing a quorum or majority.

The governing bodies

The statutes of the SE would provide for the governing bodies to be the general meeting of shareholders and either a management board and a supervisory board (two-tier system) or an administrative board (one-tier system). In the two-tier system, the SE would be managed and represented by the management board under the supervision of the supervisory board, the former being appointed (and removed) by the latter. The supervisory board could not participate in the management of the company nor represent it in dealings with third parties. In the one-tier system, the administrative board would consist of both executive and non-executive members.

The general meeting

The general meeting of shareholders could decide on the increase or reduction of capital, the issue of shares, the appointment of the members of the supervisory board, the auditors, the distribution of profits, the alteration of the statute, mergers, winding up and transfers of assets. A general meeting would be held at least once a year. Every shareholder (except those having no voting rights) shall be entitled to attend or appoint a proxy. A shareholder's voting right shall be proportionate to the fraction of the subscribed capital which his share represents.

Winding up

An SE could be wound up upon expiry of the duration set out in its statute or by resolution of the general meeting or by order of a court. A resolution of the general meeting to wind up the SE on any ground laid down by the statute would require at least a simple majority of the votes attached to the subscribed capital represented. In all other cases, a resolution would require at least a two-thirds majority of the votes, although the statute could provide for this to be a simple majority.

Accounts

The SE would draw up accounts in accordance with the Fourth Directive and an annual report. Where the SE was a parent undertaking, it would be required to draw up a consolidated account and a consolidated annual report in accordance with the Seventh Directive. The annual report would have to include at least a fair review of the development of the company's business and of its position. The annual accounts, duly audited and approved, and the annual report and audit report would be published.

Disclosure requirements in respect of branches

The opening of a branch as well as the creation of a subsidiary company is one of the possibilities currently open to companies in exercising their rights of establishment in another Member State. The coordinating directives on company law apply to limited liability companies and apply therefore to their subsidiaries, but, by contrast, do not cover branches. Due to the fact that the economic and social influence of a branch may be comparable to that of a subsidiary company, branches are subjected to special rules regarding disclosure which vary among Member States. The lack of coordination, in particular regarding the disclosure requirements of branches, gives rise to disparities in respect of protection of shareholders and third parties between companies which operate in other Member State by opening branches and those which operate by opening subsidiaries. These differences in national law dealing with branches are likely to impede the exercise of freedom of establishment. The Eleventh Company Law Directive (Directive 89/666), therefore, aims to facilitate the creation of branches of limited liability companies by coordinating their disclosure requirements. It is applicable from 1 January 1993 and shall apply for the first time to annual accounts for the financial year beginning in 1993.

Disclosure requirements

The proposed directive provides for the compulsory disclosure by the branch of certain documents and particulars. These concern the branch's name and address, its activities, where the company was registered and the registration number, the existence of other branches in the same Member State, particulars of persons who are authorised to represent the company, the winding up of the company and the appointment of liquidators and the transfer of the branch and transfer of location. The compulsory disclosure of accounting documents is limited to the disclosure of annual or consolidated reports and accounts of the company. The accounting documents drawn up and audited in accordance with the Fourth and Seventh Directives on company law are deemed sufficient protection to shareholders and third parties.

Branches of non-Community companies

The directive also provides for the compulsory disclosure by branches of companies from third countries which had a legal form comparable with that of a limited company. By virtue of the fact that such companies have not been subjected to the disclosure obligations of the company law directives, it is not possible for a branch to satisfy its disclosure obligations by reference to the company register. Therefore, branches of non-Community companies have to publish in the branch register additional information, for example, the memorandum and articles of association.

Exemptions

The directive extends the exemption granted to banks, other financial institutions and insurance companies as regards the disclosure of branch accounts which are subject to separate proposed coordinating directives. However, the remainder of the disclosure requirements apply to branches of companies which carry on business in these fields.

Single-member private companies

The primary aim of the Twelfth Directive on company law (Directive 89/667) is to allow one-man companies to trade throughout the Community with limited liability.

Single-member companies

The directive applies to the private company limited by shares or by guarantee in the United Kingdom (la socit a responsibilit in France and die Gesellschaft mit beschrnkter Haftung in Germany). Such companies could have a sole member, either when it was formed or when all the shares came to be held by a single person. Sole members would have to exercise the powers of the general meeting and could not delegate them. Decisions taken by the sole member must be recorded in minutes or drawn up in writing. Where a company becomes a single-member company because all its shares come to be held by a single person, this fact must be disclosed.

Annual and consolidated accounts of partnerships

The requirements that annual accounts be drawn up in accordance with the Fourth Directive and consolidated in accordance with the Seventh Directive are based in particular on the fact that companies established in the form of public or private companies offer no safeguards to third parties beyond the amounts of their net assets.

Similar undesirable results may occur by the creation of partnerships, limited partnerships or unlimited companies whose members are themselves limited companies. A substantial number of these types of undertaking are being set up inside the Community, which, it is thought, contradicts the spirit and aims of the directives. Directive 90/605 therefore amends the Fourth and Seventh Directive so that partnerships, limited partnerships and unlimited companies are also included. This applies to undertakings such as die Offene Handelgesellscaft and die Kommanditgesellschaft in Germany and la société en nom collectif and la société en commandité in France.

Takeover and other general bids

In the case of takeovers, in order to protect the interests of minority shareholders, the Commission proposes that where one person acquires a third of the voting rights in a company, he must bid for the rest of the securities carrying such rights in that company. This is contained in the proposed Thirteenth Company Law Directive. Each Member State is to designate an authority which must ensure the enforcement of the directive. This authority would, however, be entitled to delegate its powers to one or more private bodies. In deciding whether to allow a bid to go through, the authority would seek to ensure that five basic principles were adhered to: all shareholders are to be treated equally; they must have sufficient time and information to enable them to reach a properly informed decision on the bid; the board of the target company must not seek to frustrate the bid; a false market in the shares of the target company or the bidding company must not be created; and the bid must not result in the target company being hindered in the conduct of its affairs beyond a reasonable time. There is, though, a safety net in the proposed directive in that it allows a discretion to the supervisory authority to grant exemption from the obligation to bid for the entire shareholding as long as the principles set out above are respected.

The competent authority in each Member State will have the power to forbid the publication of any offer document which does not satisfy the terms of the directive or, alternatively, it would be able to order the offeree to fulfil its obligations. So as to prevent several authorities claiming jurisdiction over a multinational bid, rules are set out to determine the authority which will have sole competence. Where the securities of the offeree company are traded on a regulated market in the Member State where it has its registered office, only that State's authority will be entitled to intervene. Otherwise the competent authority will be that of the Member State on whose regulated market the company's securities were first admitted to trading. Where the offer document is then accepted by that authority, all the other authorities in the European Community will be obliged to recognise its validity and may not impose any further requirements.

Some limitation is placed on the ability of the board of the offeree to defend the bid by means of bolstering their interest in the company after the bid has been made. In particular, until the result of the bid is made public, the company would not be permitted to acquire its own shares and the board may not issue any securities carrying immediate or postponed voting rights. Thus, a potential poison pill, whereby certain shareholders would receive extra holdings in the event of a successful bid, would be prohibited. Also the board would be prohibited from engaging in transactions which would have the effect of altering significantly the assets or liabilities of the company or resulting in the company entering into commitments without consideration, unless the supervisory authority gave its permission. Accordingly, another form of poison pill – the directors' golden handshake – would be forbidden.

The board of the offeree company would have to draw up a document setting out its reasoned opinion on the bid specifying whether it agreed with the bidder and whether any members of the board who held securities in the offeree company intended to accept the bid. Once a bid has been made public, it would be possible to withdraw it or declare it void only in the very limited circumstances set out in the proposed directive. Among these is the possibility that the takeover would be in breach of competition law and thus not authorised by the relevant merger control authorities. Otherwise the bid must be completed within ten weeks from the publication of the offer.

2. Intellectual and Industrial Property

Intellectual property rights and free movement

Intellectual property rights are likely to frustrate the completion of the internal market for two main reasons. First, the intellectual property rights granted by Member States give rise to monopoly rights on a national scale which by their very nature constitute barriers to imports. For example, in so far as the same or similar trade marks can be in different hands in different Member States, the rights in them can act as a barrier to the free flow of trade marked goods between Member States. Although the owner of an intellectual property right in principle exhausts his rights to prevent the importation of a product into one Member State when he has marketed that product in another Member State, the differences in national intellectual property laws have a direct impact on the ability of companies to treat the internal market as a single domestic market. Secondly, the cost of applying for intellectual property rights on a Community-wide scale can be very expensive; for example, the fact that trade mark registration within the Community is at present a matter for twelve individual Member States acts as an economical and psychological barrier to making separate applications in each country.

The Commission has tried to tackle these problems by attempting to make it easier to acquire intellectual property rights on a Community-wide scale and by harmonizing national laws on intellectual property rights so that the monopolies work throughout the Community irrespective of the country of origin. Overall, the progress on approximating national intellectual property laws has been slow despite the importance to industry of Community-wide intellectual property rights. One of the first measures adopted by the Council was a directive on the legal protection of topographies of semiconductor products. Semiconductor technology is considered as being of fundamental importance for the Community's industrial development by virtue of the fact that semiconductor products are playing an increasingly important role in a broad range of industries.

In the patent field, the Commission considers that the entering into force of the 1975 Luxembourg Convention on the Community Patent is a matter of priority. This would provide for a single Community patent enforceable throughout the whole Community which would be treated as one country for the purposes of the European Patent Convention signed in Munich in 1973. The main advantage of the latter is that it provides for the filing and prosecuting of a single European patent application, although a successful application only has the effect of granting a bundle of national patents and not a Community patent. More specifically, the White Paper envisages measures concerning patent protection of biotechnological inventions.

In the field of copyright, the Commission published a Green Paper 'Copyright and the Challenge of Technology' which deals with copyright issues concerning piracy, audio-visual home copying, distribution rights, exhaustion and rental rights, computer programs and databases. Following on from this Paper the Commission proposed directives on rental rights and the protection of computer programs. The latter has now been adopted by the Council.

In the field of trade marks the Commission has proposed regulations on a Community trade mark. The introduction of a Community trade mark will make it possible for persons to obtain on a single application one trade mark covering all the Member States. In order to allow the Community trade mark system to work, a Community trade mark office with its own fee structure will be established. The Council has not yet adopted this regulation, but has adopted a directive which approximates national trade mark laws. Many of the provisions in this directive are similar to those contained in the proposed regulation. The adoption of the former should therefore make the adoption of the latter more likely.

The proposed Community trade mark

The territorial barriers created by national intellectual property rights cannot be removed merely by the approximation of national laws. In these circumstances, it is considered by the Commission that the only appropriate way of opening up unrestricted economic activity throughout the internal market is to create trade marks which are governed solely by Community law. Therefore, a proposed regulation would establish a Community trade mark for goods or for services which has identical effect and cannot be divisible on a territorial basis among different owners.

Obtaining a Community trade mark

It is proposed that the following persons might be the proprietor of a Community trade mark: nationals of Member States, nationals of any State which is a party to the Paris Convention and nationals of other countries who have real and effective commercial presence within the Community.

The proposed Community trade mark would consist of any signs, particularly words, including personal names, designs, letters, numerals, combination of colours, the shape of goods or of their packaging, which are capable of distinguishing the goods or services of one undertaking from those of another.

The rights in a Community trade mark would be obtained by registration and, for this purpose, a Community Trade Mark Office would be established. Trade marks which were not distinctive could not be registered. In particular, the following trade marks might not be registered:

- signs or indications which, in trade, might be requisite for the purpose of showing the kind, quality, quantity, intended purpose, value, geographical origin, the time of production of the goods or of rendering of the service or of other characteristics of the goods or service; such trade marks might be registered if the mark had become distinctive in relation to the goods or services because of the use which had been made of it;
- signs or indications which were customarily used to designate the goods or service in the current language of the trade or in the bona fide and established practices thereof;
- the shape which results from the nature of the goods themselves;
- trade marks which were liable to mislead the public;
- trade marks which were contrary to public policy;
- trade marks which include badges, emblems and escutcheons.

Furthermore, a trade mark could not be registered in three further situations: if it was identical with an earlier right; if it was identical with an earlier right and the goods or services were similar to those for which the earlier right was registered, with the result that there was a likelihood of confusion between the Community trade mark applied for and the earlier right on the part of the public in the territory in which the earlier right had effect; if it was similar to an earlier right and the goods or services were identical with, or similar to, those for which the earlier right was registered, with the result that there was a likelihood of confusion between the Community trade mark applied for and the earlier right on the part of the public in the territory in which the earlier right had effect.

Effects of Community trade marks

The proprietor of a Community trade mark would be entitled to prohibit any third party from using, in the course of trade, save with his consent:

- any sign which was identical with the Community trade mark in relation to goods or services which were identical with those for which the Community trade mark was registered;
- any sign which was identical with, or similar to, the Community trade mark in relation to goods or services which were identical with, or

similar to, those for which the Community trade mark was registered where such use involved a likelihood of confusion between the sign and the Community trade mark on the part of the public;

- any sign which was identical with, or similar to, the Community trade mark in relation to goods or services which were not similar to those for which the Community trade mark was registered where the latter was of wide repute in the Community and where use of that sign would constitute unwarranted exploitation of the commercial value and the repute of the Community trade mark.

The proprietor would also be able to prohibit the fixing of the sign to the goods, the marketing of the goods under the sign, or supplying services under the sign and using the sign on business correspondence or invoices. The rights conferred by a Community trade mark would prevail against third parties from the date of publication of registration of the trade mark. Reasonable compensation might, however, be claimed in respect of matters arising after the date of publication of the application for a Community trade mark. Any court seized of a case would have to stay proceedings until the registration had been published. A Community trade mark would not entitle the proprietor to prohibit a third party from using, in the course of trade:

- his own name and address;
- characteristics of the goods or services (e.g., indications concerning the kind, quality, quantity, purpose, value, geographical origin), or from using the trade mark where it was necessary to indicate the intended purpose of a product or service, in particular, accessories or spare parts.

The third party would be entitled to use them provided he did so in accordance with honest industrial or commercial practice. The proprietor of a Community trade mark could not prohibit the use of the mark in relation to goods put on the market in the Community under that trade mark by the proprietor or with his consent (this is the principle of exhaustion of rights) but this would not apply where the condition of the goods was changed or impaired after they had been put on to the market.

Although the effects of Community trade marks are governed solely by the provisions of the proposed regulation, the infringement of a Community trade mark would be governed by the law of the Member States. Actions could be brought on the grounds envisaged in the proposed regulation and also under national laws relating, in particular, to civil liability and unfair competition.

A Community trade mark would be registered for a period of 10 years from the date of filing of the application. Within a period of 5 years following registration, the proprietor would have to put the Community trade mark to genuine use in the Community.

Community trade marks as objects of property

In principle, the Community trade mark as an object of property would be dealt with as a national trade mark registered in the Member State in which the applicant had his domicile or principal place of business. Any assignment of a Community trade mark would have to be made in writing and any transfer could not affect rights acquired by third parties before the date of transfer. A Community trade mark might be levied in execution and be charged, but any security rights in rem which were created over a Community trade mark could not have effect vis--vis third parties until the rights had been registered. The proprietor of a Community trade mark could licence the mark although adequate measures would have to be taken to ensure the quality of the goods manufactured or the quality of the services provided by the licensee.

Applications for Community trade marks

Applications for Community trade marks would be filed at the Community Trade Marks Office. The application would contain particulars identifying the applicant, a list of the goods or services and a representation of the trade mark. The necessary fees would have to be paid within one month after the filing of the application, i.e., the date on which this information was received by the Office.

Priority

A person who had duly filed an application for a trade mark in any State which was a party to the Paris Convention would be, for the purpose of filing a Community trade mark application, entitled to a right of priority for a period of 6months following the date of filing of the first application. An applicant wishing to take advantage of the priority of a previous application would file a declaration of priority at the office. The date of priority would count as the date of filing of the Community trade mark application for the purposes of establishing which rights took precedent.

Registration procedure

The Office would largely limit itself to an examination of whether the application had been made in due form and whether there were absolute grounds for refusal, for example, whether the trade mark was not distinctive. However, applications would not be subject to a search for conflicting registrations. Instead, proprietors of earlier rights could oppose registration after publication of the application on the basis of conflicting earlier national or Community registrations and also on the basis of earlier rights in well-known, though unregistered, marks. If the opponent had neither his domicile nor a place of business within the Community, he would, at the request of the applicant, furnish security for the costs of the proceedings. In the examination of the opposition, the Office would invite the parties to file their observations.

Surrender, revocation and invalidity

A Community trade mark might be surrendered in respect of some or all of the goods or services for which it was registered. Surrender would be effected by the proprietor of the trade mark by means of writing delivered to the Office. A Community trade mark might be revoked on a counter-claim in infringement proceedings:

- if the trade mark had not been put to genuine use in the Community for an uninterrupted period of five years; or
- if, in consequence of the use made of the trade mark, it had become the common name for a product or a service or it had become liable to mislead the public.

A Community trade mark might also be declared invalid on the basis of a counter-claim in infringement proceedings where:

- the trade mark was registered, albeit it was not distinctive; and
- where earlier rights existed in opposition to it provided that the proprietor of those earlier rights did not consent expressly to the registration of the Community trade mark.
- Where a Community trade mark was held invalid, it would be deemed never to have produced effects.

Where the proprietor of a Community trade mark acquiesced in the use of a later Community trade mark in the Community for a period of three successive years, being aware of such use, he would not be entitled either to apply for a declaration that the later trade mark was invalid or to oppose the use of the later trade mark in respect of the goods or services for which the later trade mark had been used, unless the later Community trade mark was applied for in bad faith. The same principle would apply to a proprietor of another earlier right save to the extent that he would remain entitled to oppose the use of the later trade mark. This principle of acquiescence would not affect the proprietor of a well known trade mark who remained entitled to apply for a declaration that a Community trade mark was invalid within five years following registration of a Community trade mark. The proprietor of the later Community trade mark would not be entitled to oppose the use of the earlier right even though that right might no longer be invoked against the later Community trade mark. The proprietor of any earlier right subsisting only in a particular locality could oppose the use of the Community trade mark in the territory where his right was protected, provided that he had not acquiesced in the use of the Community trade mark in the territory where his right was protected for a period of three successive years. The proprietor of the Community trade mark would not be entitled to oppose use of the earlier right even though that right might no longer be invoked against the Community trade mark.

An application for revocation of a Community trade mark or for a declaration that it was invalid could be submitted to the Community Trade Marks Office. The proposed regulation specifies the persons which could make such applications. In proceedings for the invalidity of a Community trade mark, the proprietor of an earlier Community trade mark, or an earlier national trade mark, might be required to furnish proof that during the period of five years preceding the date of the application for the declaration of invalidity, it had been put to genuine use in the Community in connection with the goods or services for which it had been registered. Where a final decision was taken revoking the rights of the proprietor of the Community trade mark or declaring it invalid, it would be removed from the register.

Appeals

An appeal, having suspensive effect, would lie to a Board of Appeal from the decisions of the Community Trade Marks Office. Notice of Appeal would have to be filed in writing at the Office within two months after notification of the decision from which the appeal was made. A further appeal to the European Court of Justice would lie from decisions of the Board of Appeal. The Commission could, in the interests of law, lodge an appeal to the Court against a decision of the Board of Appeal, but any reversal of the decision by the Court would not bind the parties to the proceedings. There are provisions for rules of procedure before the Office concerning the examination of facts by the Office, oral proceedings, the taking of evidence, the service of documents, costs, and legal representation. The proposed regulation also contains general provisions on the Community Trade Marks Office, such as its legal status, staff, privileges and immunities, liability, administration and budget.

Jurisdiction and legal proceedings

Unless otherwise specified in the proposed regulation, the Convention on Jurisdiction and Enforcement of Judgments in Civil and Commercial Matters, signed in Brussels in 1968, would apply to actions relating to Community trade marks and to decisions given in respect of such actions.

It is specifically provided that actions for infringement of a Community trade mark would be heard by the courts of the Member State in which the defendant had his habitual residence or his place of business; failing this, an action would be commenced in the court of the Member State in which the plaintiff had his habitual residence or his place of business; failing this, an actions would be heard by the court of the Member State where the Office was situated. The court hearing the action would have jurisdiction in respect of acts of infringement alleged to have been committed in any Member State. Actions for infringement for a Community trade mark might also be heard by a court in the Member State in which an act of infringement had been committed, in which case the court would have jurisdiction only in respect of acts of infringement alleged to have been committed in that State. If the court found that the Community trade mark had been infringed by the use of another trade mark or another sign, it would have to take the necessary provisional measures to ensure that the latter were not used anywhere in the Community.

Actions for infringements might be brought by the proprietor of a Community trade mark. A licensee might bring such actions only if the proprietor consented, although the licensee would have a limited right to intervene in any infringement action.

The national court hearing the infringement action would have jurisdiction to give judgment on a counterclaim that the rights of the proprietor were revoked or that the trade mark was invalid, in which case it would have to order that the trade mark be removed from the register. Alternatively, the court could stay proceedings and invite the defendant to apply to the Community Trade Marks Office for a declaration of revocation or invalidity.

Effect on the laws of the Member States

The cumulative protection of Community trade marks and national trade marks would be prohibited. Where the proprietor of a Community trade mark was also the proprietor in a Member State of a national trade mark which was identical with, or similar to, the Community trade mark and was for identical or similar goods or services for which the Community trade mark had been registered, the effects of the national trade mark would be suspended for so long as the Community trade mark was effective. The suspended effects of the national trade mark would not revive if the Community trade mark was revoked on the ground of non-user.

Community guarantee marks and Community collective marks

Community guarantee marks might consist of any sign if its purpose was to guarantee the quality, method of manufacture or other common characteristics of goods or services of different undertakings which used the guarantee mark under the proprietor's control. Therefore, Community guarantee marks could not be used in respect of goods or services produced or supplied by the proprietor himself, or by a person who was economically associated with him. Representative groups or bodies of manufacturers, producers, suppliers of services or traders might, if they had legal personality, apply for Community collective marks which were capable of distinguishing the goods or services of their members from those of other undertakings. The proposed regulation lays down the circumstances in which applications for such marks might be refused or opposed.

The symbol of the Greek capital letter epsilon (ε) contained within a circle would be used to indicate a registered Community trade mark.

The approximation of national laws relating to trade marks

The Commission considers that the specific purpose of a trademark is to guarantee the origin of the goods or services and that some national laws afford to trademarks rights which go beyond this specific purpose. These disparities of national law may impede the free movement of goods and freedom to provide services and may distort competition with the Common Market. The Council has, therefore, adopted First Council Directive 89/104 on approximation of national trade mark laws. The directive does not undertake a full-scale approximation of national trademark laws, but is limited to those national provisions which most directly affect the functioning of the internal market. Its principal purpose is to ensure that registered trademarks enjoy uniform protection under the legal systems of all the Member States. Its provisions are similar to the proposed regulation on the Community trademark.

Obtaining a trade mark

The directive applies to every trademark in respect of goods or services which is the subject of registration or of an application for registration in a Member State (including the Benelux Trademark Office) as an individual trademark, a collective mark or a guarantee or certification mark.

The directive defines a trademark as consisting of any sign capable of being represented graphically, particularly words, including personal names, designs, letters, numerals, the shape of goods or of their packaging, provided that such signs are capable of distinguishing the goods or services of one undertaking from those of other undertakings.

The directive provides a comprehensive list of the grounds for refusal or invalidity of a trademark. The following cannot be registered or if registered are liable to be declared invalid.

- Trademarks which are not distinctive at the date of application: national law may, however, provide that there should be no declaration as to invalidity where the distinctive character was acquired after the date of application for registration.

- Trademarks which consist exclusively of signs or indications which designate the kind, quality, quantity, intended purpose, value, geographical origin, or other characteristics of the goods or service.
- Trademarks which consist exclusively of signs or indications which have become customary in the current language or in the bona fide and established practices of the trade, unless the trademark has acquired a distinctive character. Member States may provide that the acquisition of the distinctive character be after the date of application for registration.
- Signs which consist exclusively of the shape which results from the nature of the goods, or which is necessary to obtain a technical result, or which gives substantial value to the goods.
- Trademarks which are contrary to public policy or to accepted principles of morality.
- Trademarks which are liable to mislead the public.
- Trademarks which are invalidated pursuant to Article 6 ter. of the Paris Convention for the Protection of Industrial Property.
- Trade marks which conflict with earlier rights. The directive lists the following situations: (1) If the trade mark is identical with an earlier trademark (i.e., which has a date of application for registration which is earlier), and the goods or services for which the later trademark is applied for or is registered are identical with the goods or services for which the earlier trademark is protected; (2) there exists a likelihood of confusion with an earlier trademark because of the similarity of the trademark and of the goods or services covered by the earlier trademark; (3) community trademarks which validly claim seniority in accordance with the (proposed) Regulation on Community trademark; (4) trademarks which are well known in a Member State, in the sense in which the words are used in Article 6 bis of the Paris Convention; (5) where the trademark is identical or similar to an earlier Community trademark in respect of goods or services which are not similar to those for which the earlier trademark is registered, where the earlier trademark has a reputation in the Community and where the use of the latter trademark would take an unfair advantage or be detrimental to the distinctive character or the repute of the earlier trademark.

Member States have the option to provide that a trademark should not be registered or should be declared invalid in the following circumstances:

- The use of the trademark is prohibited under laws (other than trademark laws) relating, for example, to unfair competition, civil liability or consumer protection.
- The trademark covers a sign of high symbolic value, in particular a religious symbol.

- The trademark includes badges, emblems and escutcheons other than those covered by Article 6 ter. of the Paris Convention and which are of public interest.
- The application for registration was made in bad faith.
- The trademark is identical with, or similar to, an earlier national trademark concerning goods or services which are not similar, but where the use of the later trademark would take an unfair advantage of, or be detrimental to, the distinctive character or the repute of the earlier trademark.
- The trademark conflicts with the rights acquired by a non-registered trademark holder acquired in the course of trade prior to the date of application for registration of the trademark (the directive does not deprive the Member States of the right to continue to protect trademarks acquired through use, therefore).
- The trademark conflicts with other earlier rights relating in particular to names, personal portrayal, copyright or other industrial property rights.
- The trademark is identical with, or similar to, an earlier collective trademark confirming a right which expired within a period of maximum of three years preceding application.
- The trademark is identical with, or similar to, an earlier guarantee or certification mark conferring a right which expired within a period preceding application the length of which can be fixed by Member States.
- The trademark is identical with, or similar to, an earlier trademark which was registered for identical or similar goods or services and conferred on them a right which has expired for failure to renew within a period of a maximum of two years preceding application.
- The trademark is liable to be confused with a mark which was in use abroad on the filing date of the application and which is still in use there, provided that at the date of the application the applicant was acting in bad faith.

Member States may provide that the grounds of refusal of registration or invalidity in force in that State prior to the date on which the Directive is due to enter into force (28 December 1991 although this may be extended until 31 December 1992), will apply to trademarks for which application has been made prior to that date.

It should be noted that Member States remain free to fix provisions relating to procedure concerning the registration, the revocation and the invalidity of trademarks and the effects of revocation or invalidity of trademarks. The primary purpose of the directive is to approximate national laws regarding the conditions for obtaining and continuing to hold a registered trademark. The grounds for refusal or invalidity concerning the trademark are listed in an exhaustive manner, even if some of the grounds are listed as an option for the Member States. Member States will be able to maintain or introduce into their legislation grounds of refusal or invalidity linked to conditions for obtaining and continuing to hold a trademark for which there is no provision of approximation, concerning, for example, the eligibility for the grant of a trademark, the renewal of the trademark, rules on fees or the non-compliance with procedural rules. Further, the ways in which likelihood of confusion may be established, and in particular the onus of proof, are a matter for national procedural rules which are not prejudiced by the directive.

Rights conferred by a trademark

The trademark owner must have the exclusive right to prevent all third parties not having his consent from using in the course of trade any sign which is identical with the trademark in relation to goods or services which are identical with those for which the trademark is registered, or any sign where because of its similarity to the trademark and the similarity of the goods or services covered by the trademark, there exists a likelihood of confusion between the trademark and the sign on the part of the public.

Member States may also confer on the trademark owner the following exclusive rights:

- The right to prevent all third parties not having his consent from using in the course of trade any sign which is identical with, or similar to, the trademark in relation to goods or services which are not similar to those for which the trademark is registered, where the use of the sign would take unfair advantage of or be detrimental to the distinctive character or the repute of the trademark.
- Affixing the sign to the goods or to the packaging thereof
- Offering the goods or putting them on the market or stocking them for these purposes under the sign.
- Importing or exporting the goods under the sign.
- Using the sign on business papers and in advertising.

The trademark would not entitle the proprietor to prohibit a third party from using bona fide in the course of trade the following.

- His own name and address.
- Indications concerning the kind, quality, quantity, intended purpose, value, geographical origin, the time of production of goods or rendering of the service or other characteristics of goods or services.

Further, the trademark would not entitle the proprietor to prohibit a third party from using, in the course of trade, an earlier right which only applies in a particular locality. The trademark owner also is not entitled to prohibit its use in relation to goods which have been put on the market in the Community under that trademark by the proprietor or with his consent, unless there exist legitimate reasons for the proprietor to oppose further commercialisation of the goods, especially where the condition of the goods is changed or impaired after they have been put on the market.

It is specifically provided in the directive that a trademark may be licensed for some or all of the goods or services for which it is registered and for the whole or part of the Member State concerned, on an exclusive or non-exclusive basis.

Acquiescence

Where, in a Member State, the proprietor of a registered trademark has acquiesced in the use of a later registered trademark in that Member State for a period of five successive years (not three as originally proposed) he is not entitled either to apply for a declaration that the latter trademark is invalid or to oppose the use of the latter trademark in respect of the goods or services for which the latter trademark has been used. Member States may extend this principle of acquiescence to other rights, particularly rights attached to non-registered trademarks and rights to a name. However, the proprietor of the latter registered trademark is not entitled to oppose the use of the earlier right, even though that right may no longer be invoked against the latter trademark.

Revocation

A trademark is liable to revocation if, within a continuous period of five years, it has not been put to genuine use in the Member State in connection with the goods or services in respect of which it is registered, and there are no proper reasons for non-use. A trademark is also liable to revocation if it has become the common name in the trade for a product or service in respect of which it is registered. If the earlier trademark has been used in relation to part only of the goods or services for which it is registered, it may be deemed to be registered in respect only of that part of the goods or services.

Protection of computer programs

Directive 91/250 on the legal protection of computer programs has probably been the most hotly contested piece of EC legislation of the 1992 Internal Market Programme. After it was first proposed intense lobbying came from two main groups: on the one hand large computer groups wanted strict rules on copyright protection and on the other hand smaller software houses (many of which were represented by the European Committee for Inter-operable Systems (ECIS)) wanted the ability to create software which was compatible with the larger rivals' products. The directive is a compromise between the two.

Computer programs are at present not clearly protected in all Member States by existing legislation and such protection, where it exists, often has different attributes. In proposing the directive the Commission considered that an adequate level of protection should be enshrined in the laws of all Member States and any difference which could affect the functioning of the Internal Market should be eliminated. Common principles were deemed necessary not only to promote the free circulation of computer software within the Community, but also to create conditions in which industry could take advantage of the Single Market.

Directive 91/250 provides that Member States must give copyright protection to computer programs as literary works within the meaning of the Berne Convention for the protection of literary and artistic works. The term 'computer program' includes preparatory design material and any programs which are incorporated into hardware. No further definition is given since it was considered that such a definition would quickly become obsolete. A computer program will be protected if it is original in the sense that it is the author's own intellectual creation. No other criteria will be applied to determine its eligibility for protection other than originality; i.e., no other aesthetic or qualitative test should be applied.

Protection extends to the expression in any form of a computer program. Ideas and principles which underlie any element of a computer program, including those which underlie its interfaces, are not protected. Sub-routines and routines which go together to form modules which in turn form programs may all qualify for protection independently of the protection given to the program as a whole. Unlike the Commission proposal, the directive makes no reference to algorithms which go to make up the sub-routines. Algorithms are not normally in themselves capable of receiving protection under copyright in so far as they are similar in nature to mathematical formulae. They may in exceptional circumstances attract patent protection.

Authorship of computer programs

The author of a computer program may be the natural person or group of natural persons who has created the program or the legal person designated as the right holder by national law. Where collective works are recognised by the legislation of a Member State, the person considered by the legislation of the Member State to have created the work is deemed to be its author. In respect of computer programs created by a group of natural persons jointly, the exclusive rights are owned jointly. Where a computer program is created by an employee in the execution of his duties or following the instructions given by his employer, the employer is entitled to exercise exclusivity over all economic rights in the program, unless otherwise agreed. The word 'economic' means that moral rights fall outside of the scope of the employer's exclusive right.

Beneficiaries of protection

Protection is granted to all natural or legal persons eligible under national copyright legislation as applied to literary works. The directive therefore does not seek to harmonise laws relating to beneficiaries of protection. Consequently, where Member States afford protection on the basis of first publication of a literary work in a Member State, that criterion should also apply to computer programs. Where the literary works of natural and legal persons are currently protected by virtue of nationality or residence in the case of natural persons, or by having a real and effective presence in a Member State, in the case of legal persons, the same protection should apply for computer programs. Thus the rules of national treatment under the Berne Convention will be applied to computer programs as to all other literary works.

Restricted acts

The exclusive rights of the right-holder include the right to do or authorise the following:
(a) the permanent or temporary reproduction of a computer program by any means and in any form, in part or in whole. In so far as loading, displaying, running, transmission or storage of the computer program necessitate such reproduction, such acts are subject to authorisation by the right-holder;
(b) the translation, adaption, arrangement and any other alteration of a computer program and the reproduction of the results thereof, without prejudice to the rights of the person who alters the program.
(c) any form of distribution to the public (including the rental) of the original computer program or of the copies thereof.

The first sale in the Community of a copy of a program by the right-holder or with his consent will exhaust the distribution right within the Community of that copy, with the exception of the right to control further rental of the program or a copy thereof. It should be noted that exhaustion is only on a Community-wide basis and not on an international basis as first appeared in the original proposed draft. The Commission considered that it was essential to permit right-holders to control the rental of programs which have been sold or licensed if copying of programs without authorisation was to be prevented. It is possible to rent a copy of a software package at a nominal charge, to copy it at home using relatively inexpensive material and to return it the following day. Cheap, short-term rental allows the home copier to save on the cost of purchasing or leasing programs. As such, rental is highly prejudicial to right-holders' interests and are consequently the subject of the right to prohibition.

Exceptions to the restricted acts

It was this part of the directive which proved most contested. The directive lays down four exceptions to the restricted acts.

(1) Error correction

In the absence of specific contractual provisions, the reproduction, translation, adaptation, arrangement or any other alteration of the computer program will not require authorisation by the right-holder where they are necessary for the use of the computer program by the lawful acquirer in accordance with its intended purpose, including for error correction.

(2) Back-up copy

The making of a back-up copy by a person having a right to use the computer program may not be prevented by contract in so far as it is necessary for that use.

(3) Study

A person having a right to use a copy of a computer program shall be entitled, without the authorisation of the right-holder, to observe, study or test the functioning of the program in order to determine the ideas and principles which underlie any element of the program if he does so while performing any of the acts of loading, displaying, running, transmitting or storing the program which he is entitled to do.

(4) De-compilation

The question of reverse engineering proved the most difficult to resolve. The form in which a computer program is usually supplied is not readily accessible to the human user. It is in a form known as object code or machine-readable code, which, even when rendered visible to the human observer, is difficult to decipher in large quantities. A computer program may be required to interconnect and interact with other computer programs, for example, an applications program with an operating system. If a manufacturer wishes to interconnect his products with others supplied by a different manufacturer, he may need information from that manufacturer about how his products are designed to interconnect. Such information may be available through materials supplied by manufacturers or by the growing move towards the use of publicly-available open standards where the means to interconnect have been standardised and are described and documented by international standard bodies. Although a dominant supplier who refuses to make information available on inter-operability between programs or between programs and hardware could be subject to the competition rules under Article 86, other non-dominant suppliers may refuse to disclose such information. If information is not forthcoming or if the design for the means of interconnection is a non-standard proprietary one, the inter-operability of computer programs would be substantially restricted. In such cases the creator of the original program, by withholding information from competitors could ensure that only he could supply the range of other programs which would operate with his original program. Some information required for the purpose of inter-operability can be derived from observation, study or testing of the program without committing infringements of the author's exclusive rights. However, where their use does not produce sufficient information and where other non-infringing means such as the use of publicly-available material or published documentation is also inadequate, a person may be forced to commit acts which technically violate the author's exclusive rights to prevent the reproduction and translation of his program. These acts of reproducing and translating the object code or machine-readable code version of the program, which is the version normally supplied to the public, back into a language representing something more like the original source code in which the programmer devised the program is often referred loosely as reverse engineering the program.

The original draft of the Commission's proposal had appeared to make all reverse engineering illegal. The directive provides for limited reverse engineering for the purposes of ensuring inter-operability of programs. Thus it is required that the authorisation of the author or right-holder shall not be required where reproduction or translation of the object code is indispensable to obtain the information necessary to achieve the inter-operability of an independently created computer program with other programs. Any contractual provision to the contrary is void. Reverse engineering is subject to the following conditions:

(a) these acts are performed by the licensee or by another person having a right to use a copy of a program, or on their behalf by a person authorised to do so; and

(b) the information necessary to achieve inter-operability has not previously been readily available to the licensees; and

(c) these acts are confined to the parts of the original program which are necessary to achieve inter-operability (reproduction or translation of the whole program is not necessarily permitted). It is expressly provided that the information obtained through reverse engineering:

   (i) should not be used for goals other than to achieve the inter-operability of the independently created program;

   (ii) should not be given to others except where necessary for the inter-operability of the independently created program;

   (iii) should not be used for the development, production or marketing of a computer program substantially similar in its expression, or for any other act which infringes copyright.

Remedies

Member States must provide in their national legislation appropriate remedies against a person committing any of the prohibited acts and namely (a) any act of putting into circulation a copy of a computer program knowing, or having reason to believe, that it is an infringing copy or (b) possessing for commercial purposes a copy of a computer program knowing, or having reason to believe that it is an infringing copy, or (c) any act of putting into circulation, or the possession for commercial purposes, any means the sole intended purpose of which is to facilitate the unauthorised removal or circumvention of any technical device which may have been applied to protect a computer program. It is provided that any infringing copy of a computer program should be liable to seizure.

Term of protection

Protection should be granted for the life of the author and for fifty years after his death or after the death of the last-surviving author. Where the computer program is an anonymous or pseudonymous work, or where a legal person is designated as the author in accordance with national legislation, the term of protection should be fifty years from the time that the computer program is first lawfully made available to the public. The term of protection should be deemed to begin on 1 January of the year following the aforementioned events. However, Member States which already have a term of protection longer than that provided in the Directive, are allowed to maintain their present term.

Application of other national laws

The provisions of the directive relating to copyright shall be without prejudice to any other legal provisions such as those concerning patent rights, trademark rights, unfair competition, trade secrets, protection of semiconductor products or the law of contract.

Rental and related rights

Rental rights

The Commission has proposed a directive aimed at approximating national copyright laws relating to rental and lending rights in respect of copyright works. Under the proposal Member States would have to provide a right to authorise or prohibit the rental and lending of originals and copies of copyright works. The right would belong to: the author of the original work; the performing artiste; to the phonogram producer and to the producer of cinematographic works. These persons would retain the right to obtain adequate payment for the rental or lending of the works, notwithstanding the fact that the copyright had been assigned. The duration of these rights would be in accordance with the Berne Convention.

Related rights

Further, the proposal provides that performing artistes and broadcasting organisations should have the right to authorise or prohibit the fixation of their performances and their broadcasts respectively. Performing artistes, broadcasting organisations, phonogram producers and film producers would also have the exclusive right to authorise or prohibit the reproduction of their works. These persons would also have exclusive distribution rights in respect of their works. Limitations to these related rights could be introduced for private use, reporting of current events, ephemeral fixation by broadcasting organisations and teaching and academic research. Duration of these rights would be in accordance with the Rome Convention.

The legal protection of topographies of semiconductor products

The functions of semiconductor products depend largely on their topographies which can be copied at a fraction of the cost needed to develop them independently. Legal protection of topographies varies in all Member States and it was as a matter of urgency therefore that the Council adopted Directive 87/54 which deals with the legal protection of topographies of semiconductor products. The directive lays down certain common basic principles concerning who and what should be protected, certain exclusive rights and the length of protection. Other matters are for the time being decided in accordance with national law, in particular, whether registration or deposit is required as a condition of protection and whether and on what conditions non-voluntary licences may be granted in respect of protected topographies. The directive specifically states that it is without prejudice to patent, copyright and utility model rights and rights conferred under international agreements.

The directive defines semiconductor product as meaning the final or intermediate form of any product:

- consisting of any body of material which includes a layer of semiconducting material; and
- having one or more other layers composed of conducting, insulating or semiconducting material, the layers being arranged in accordance with a predetermined three-dimensional pattern; and

- intended to perform, exclusively or together with other functions, an electronic function.

The topography of a semiconductor product means a series of related images, however fixed or encoded:

- representing the three dimensional pattern of the layers of which a semiconductor product is composed; and
- in which series, each image has the pattern or part of the pattern of a surface of the semiconductor product at any stage of its manufacturer.

The directive provides that the topography of a semiconductor product shall be protected in so far as it is the result of the creator's own intellectual effort and is not commonplace in the semiconductor industry. The right to protection applies in favour of persons who are creators of the topographies and who are nationals of a Member State or who have their habitual residence in a Member State. The persons who are protected by the directive have the exclusive right to authorise or prohibit any of the following acts:

- reproduction of a topography;
- commercial exploitation (e.g., sale, rental or leasing) or the importation for that purpose of a topography or of a semiconductor product manufactured by using the topography.

Commercial exploitation does not include exploitation under conditions of confidentiality to the extent that no further distribution to third parties can occur. The exclusive right to reproduce a topography does not apply to reproduction for the purpose of analysing, evaluating or teaching the concepts, processes, systems or techniques embodied in the topography or the topography itself. The protection does not extend to any concept, process, system, technique or encoded information embodied in the topography, other than the topography itself.

The importation or commercial exploitation of a semi-conductor product cannot be prohibited once the product has been put on to the market in a Member State. Member States cannot subject the exclusive rights to a system of compulsory licensing and must provide that the exclusive rights come into existence:

- on registration; or
- when the topography is first commercially exploited anywhere in the world; or
- when the topography is first fixed or encoded.

The exclusive rights last for a period of ten years from the end of the calendar year in which the topography was first commercially exploited anywhere in the world or in which it was registered. Where a topography has not been commercially exploited anywhere in the world within a period of fifteen years from its first fixation or encoding, any exclusive rights come to an end.

Any indication that the topography is protected should be by way of a capital T.

Provision is made in Directive 87/54 whereby protection might be extended to nationals of third countries. By Decision 90/510 the Council has extended protection to nationals of certain third countries and to companies or other legal persons having a real and effective industrial or commercial establishment in those countries. By Decision 90/511 protection is extended to nationals of other third countries. In certain cases protection for natural persons is unconditional, but protection for companies is subject to the condition that Community companies and legal persons benefit from protection in the country or territory in question. By a Commission Decision 90/541 of 26 October 1990, the Commission decided that the United States of America fulfilled the reciprocity conditions for protection of companies.

Bio-technological Inventions

Bio-technological and genetic engineering are playing an increasingly important role in a broad range of industries and the protection of bio-technological inventions can be considered of fundamental importance to the Community's industrial development. The investments required in research and development, particularly for genetic engineering, are high and especially risky and the possibility of recouping that investment can only effectively be guaranteed through adequate legal protection. Without effective and approximated protection throughout the Member States of the Community, such investment might well never be made. The patent laws applicable at present in the Member States contain disparities which hinder the development of trade in bio-technological goods and services, distort competition within the Common Market and therefore directly affect the establishment and functioning of the internal market. The Commission considers it important to remove these disparities and to ensure effective and equivalent legal protection in all Member States.

The Commission has, therefore, proposed a directive on the legal protection of bio-technological inventions. The proposal lays down certain principles applicable to the patentability of living matter as such; the scope of protection; the compulsory licences in respect of plant varieties; a deposit mechanism in lieu of written descriptions to satisfy the enabling disclosure requirements for the patent application; a reversal of the burden of proof where release of self-replicable matter has occurred.

Patentability of living matter

The proposed directive provides that an invention should not be considered unpatentable for the sole reason that it is composed of living matter. In particular the following would be considered as patentable:

- micro-organisms, biological classifications other than plant or animal varieties as well as parts of plant and animal varieties other than propagating material thereof: claims for classifications higher than varieties would not be affected by any rights granted in respect of plant and animal varieties. The word 'micro-organism' is interpreted in its broadest sense as including all micro biological entities capable of replication, e.g., as comprising inter alia bacteria, fungi, viruses, mycoplasmae, rickettsiae, algae, protozoa and cells.
- Plants and plant material unless such material is produced by the non-patentable use of a previously known bio-technological process.
- Uses of plant or animal varieties and processes for the production thereof.
- Micro-biological processes: this term means a process carried out with the use of or performed upon or resulting in a micro-organism. A process consisting of a succession of steps would be regarded as a micro-biological process, if the essence of the invention was incorporated in one or more micro-biological steps of process.
- A process in which human intervention consists in more than selecting an available biological material and letting it perform an inherent biological function under natural conditions.

A subject matter of an invention, including a mixture, which forms an unseparated part of a pre-existing material would not be considered unpatentable or as an unpatentable discovery or as lacking novelty for the reason only that it formed part of the said natural material. Any exclusion from patentability or from the field of industrial applicability of surgical or diagnostic methods practised on an animal body would apply to such methods only if practised for a therapeutic purpose.

Scope of protection

The proposed directive lays down the following rules:

- The use of a product protected by a patent comprising or consisting of genetic information to develop another such product or the use of a patented process to obtain such a product would not be regarded experimental for purposes of establishing a patent infringement, if the developed product obtained from the experiments or its progeny in identical or differentiated form, was to be used for other than private or experimental purposes.

- If a product enjoying patent protection and put on the market by the patentee or with his consent was self-replicable, the rights conferred by national patent law would not extend to acts of multiplication and propagation where such acts were unavoidable for commercial uses other than multiplication and propagation.
- If the subject matter of a patent was a process for the production of living matter or other matter containing genetic information permitting its multiplication in identical or differentiated form, the rights conferred by the patent would not only extend to the product initially obtained by the patented process but also to the identical or differentiated products of the first or subsequent generations obtained therefrom; these products would be deemed to have been obtained by the patented process.
- The protection for a product consisting of or containing particular genetic information as an essential characteristic of the invention would extend to any products in which the said genetic information had been incorporated and was of essential importance for its industrial applicability or utility.

Dependency licence for plant varieties

If the holder of a plant breeder's right or a variety certificate could exploit or exercise his exclusive rights only by infringement of the rights attached to a prior national patent, a non-exclusive licence of right would be accorded to the breeder's right holder to the extend necessary for the exploitation of such breeder's right where the variety protected represented a significant technical progress. Such a licence would not be available prior to the expiration of three years from the date of the grant of the patent or four years from the date on which the application for a patent was filed, whichever period last expired. If a variety protected by a plant breeder's right or variety certificate could be exploited by the patentee only by infringement of the rights attached to such a variety, a non-exclusive licence would be accorded to the original patentee to the extent necessary for the exploitation of the breeder's right or variety certificate.

In both situations the licensee would have to pay reasonable royalties having regard to the amount of investment made. In the case of disagreement, a court would resolve the dispute.

The deposit mechanism

If an invention involved the use of a micro-organism or other self-replicable matter which was not available to the public and which could not be described in a patent application in such a manner as to enable the invention to be carried out by a person skilled in the art (or if it concerned such matter per se) the invention would only be regarded as being disclosed for the purposes of national patent law if:

(a) the micro-organism or other self-replicable matter had been deposited with a recognised depository institution (designated by the Member States) not later than the date of filing of the application;

(b) the application as filed gave such relevant information as was available to the applicant on the characteristics of the micro-organism or other self-replicable matter;

(c) the depository institution and the file number of the deposit were stated in the application within a defined period of time.

The deposited matter would be available upon request to any person from the date of publication of the patent application. If the patentee could no longer provide a sample of the deposited material, the patent would be deemed invalid although such invalidity would not have retroactive effect. Where the micro-organism or other self-replicable matter was no longer viable or for any other reason the depository institution was unable to supply samples, the patentee would be given three months in which to redeposit the micro-organism or other self-replicable matter. Any new deposit would be accompanied by a statement signed by the depositor alleging that the newly-deposited micro-organism or other self-replicable matter was the same as that originally deposited. The unavailability of a sample at the depositary would not affect the patentability of the invention if the patentee provided the requesting party with a certified sample.

Reversal of the burden of proof

If the subject matter of a patent was a process for obtaining a new or known product, the same product when produced by any other party would, in the absence of proof to the contrary, be deemed to have been obtained by the patented process, if the necessary means to carry out the process has been deposited and had been released to a third party.

Community plant variety rights

It is accepted that the continued breeding of improved plant varieties is an essential element of technical progress to increase agricultural productivity. The Commission considers that an important instrument for this purpose is the creation of a Community plant variety right. Consequently the Commission has proposed a Council regulation to ensure that plant breeders can acquire, through a single decision, direct and uniform protection for the whole of the Community.

The proposed regulation would establish for plant varieties a system of Community plant variety rights which would have uniform effect in the territory of the Community and could not be granted, transferred or terminated in respect of the Community otherwise than on a uniform basis. The regulation would be without prejudice to the right of the Member States to grant national property rights for plant varieties. The implementation of the Community plant variety rights system would be entrusted to a central office, the Community plant variety office.

Grant of community plant variety rights

Varieties of all botanical taxa and hybrids of taxa would form the object of Community plant variety rights. The word 'variety' would be taken to mean any group of plants as well as parts of those plants as far as they comprised more than a cell or cell line and could be used for the production of plants (both are referred to in the regulation as individuals), provided that:

(a) it could be defined as an entity on the basis of the expressions of the characteristics of its individuals or of a particular distribution of such expressions in its individuals;

(b) the expressions of the characteristics of its individuals were hereditary, or reproducible in using repeatedly individuals of its components; and

(c) the combination of expressions of the characteristics of its individuals was not distinctive for all individuals of a botanical taxon.

Protectable varieties

Community plant variety rights would be granted in respect of varieties that are:

(a) distinct; i.e., if its individuals either in the aggregate or on the basis of a particular distribution are clearly distinguishable by the expression of at least one important characteristic from the individuals of any other variety whose existence is a matter of common knowledge.

(b) homogenous; i.e., if its individuals, either in the aggregate or on the basis of a particular distribution, are sufficiently uniform in the expression of each important characteristic, apart from a small number of deviations, having regard to the particular features of reproduction or propagation.

(c) stable; i.e., if its individuals, either in the aggregate or on the basis of a particular distribution, corresponds in each important characteristic after each propagation or each cycle of propagation to the expression that is distinctive of the variety in question.

(d) new; i.e., if, at the date of application, individuals thereof have not been disposed of to others for commercial purposes or have been disposed of to others for commercial purposes only within the following periods of time: one year, within the territory of the Community; four years or in the case of vine and tree species, six years, outside the territory of the Community. No account would be taken of any disposal of individuals by the applicant on the basis of a licence in which the applicant reserved the exclusive right of disposal of the individuals of the variety. Similarly no account would be taken of any disposal by a parent to a subsidiary or vice-versa.

Beneficiaries

An application for grant of a Community plant variety right could be filed by any person who is a national of one of the Member States or a national of another state which is party to the UPOV Convention or is domiciled or has its seat or establishment in such a state. The Commission might provide that nationals from third countries could apply for the grant of a community plant variety right provided that the third country satisfies certain reciprocity conditions.

The original breeder or discoverer of the variety would be entitled to the Community plant variety right. If two or more persons had bred or discovered the variety jointly, entitlement would be vested jointly in them or their respective successors in title. An application could be filed jointly by two or more applicants. Where a variety was derived essentially from individuals of only one other variety (source variety) for which a Community plant variety right had been granted, entitlement to the right would be vested jointly in the holder of the plant variety right in respect of the source variety and the original breeder or discoverer of the derived variety if the derived variety was a result of a mutation or the derived variety exhibited predominantly the same expressions of most of the important characteristics as the source variety and no evidence was available of an impact on an economically relevant characteristics as compared to the source variety. If the breeder or discoverer was an employee, his or her entitlement to the Community plant variety right would be determined by national law.

For the purposes of proceedings before the Community Plant Variety Office, the first applicant would be entitled to claim the entitlement to the Community plant variety right, but this would not apply if the office was aware, by the time that the decision on the application for grant of the community plant variety right was taken, that entitlement was not solely vested in the first applicant.

Community plant variety rights

The Plant variety right holder would be entitled to prohibit any third person from reproducing or propagating the variety or from offering, disposing of to others, using or importing into the Community, exporting from the Community or possessing for any of the above-mentioned purposes individuals or other parts of plants or harvested material of the variety or products obtained directly therefrom, all other parts of plants or harvested material and products directly obtained (referred to in the regulation as material).

The right conferred by a Community plant variety right would not extend to:

(a) acts relating to products that did not constitute material;

(b) acts effected privately and for non-commercial purposes;

(c) acts effected for experimental purposes;

(d) acts effected for the purpose of discovering or creating new varieties;

(e) acts effected for the purpose of using new varieties discovered or created, unless individuals of the protected variety had to be used repeatedly for the production of the new variety for commercial purposes, or the new variety or the material of this variety came under the protection of a property right which did not contain a comparable provision.

The rights conferred by a Community plant variety right would not extend to acts involving individuals of the variety or other material that were disposed of to others in any part of the Community by the holder or with his consent. This would not apply where the individuals had been or were being used as propagating material for the production of further individuals without having been intended for that purpose when they were disposed of.

The proposal specifically provides that the exercise of the Community plant variety rights could not violate any provisions adopted on the grounds of public morality, public policy or public security, the protection of health and life of humans, animals or plants, the protection of the environment, or the safeguarding of competition, trade and agricultural production. Further the regulation provides that for the purpose of safeguarding agricultural production in the case of plant species governed by Community rules on the marketing of seeds or other propagating material, compulsory authorisation could be given to permit growers of propagating material of a variety for which a Community plant variety right had been granted to plant on their own holding harvested material obtained therefrom.

Compulsory licences

If a third party asked the holder for permission to carry out a prohibited act and permission was refused, the Community plant variety office could grant a compulsory exploitation right to the third party provided that it considered this to be economically acceptable to the holder and required in the public interest, in particular to supply the market with material offering specified features. National compulsory exploitation rights could be granted in respect of a Community plant variety right.

Use of variety denominations

Anyone who offered or disposed of to others for commercial purposes within the community propagating material of a variety in respect of which a Community plant variety right had been granted would have to state the variety denomination designated for the variety.

There would be limitations on the use of variety denominations. The holder could not use any right granted in respect of a designation that was identical with the variety denomination to prohibit the use of that variety denomination. A third party could use a right granted in respect of a designation that was identical with the variety denomination to prohibit the use of that variety denomination only if that right was granted to him before the variety denomination was designated. Further where a variety had been granted a Community plant variety right or, in a Member State or another state party to the UPOV Convention, a national property right, neither its denomination nor any designation which might be confused with it could be used for another variety of the same botanical species or a species regarded as related. The Office would publish the species which it considered closely related.

Duration and termination of Community plant variety rights

The term of the Community plant variety right would run until the end of the 30th year or in the case of varieties of vine and trees species, until the end of the 50th year, following the year of grant. The rights could be surrendered by the holder, revoked by the Office with effect ab initio if the condition of distinctness was never complied with, or cancelled with effect in futurum by the Office if it was ascertained that the conditions of homogeneity or of stability were never complied with.

A Community plant variety right (and application for such a right) would be regarded as an object of property and would correspond to an industrial property right in the Member State in which, according to the entry in the register of Community plant variety rights, the holder was domiciled or had his seat or an establishment on a relevant date. Where two or more persons were joint holders, the first joint holder taken in order of entry in register would be the relevant holder for these purposes.

A Community plant variety right could be licensed or transferred, but could only be assigned to those persons who could hold Community plant variety rights in the first place (i.e., nationals of members states or states party to the UPOV Convention). Any assignment would be made in writing and both parties would have to sign the contract otherwise, the assignment would be void. A Community plant variety right might be levied in execution. The only Member State in which a Community plant variety right might be involved in bankruptcy proceedings would be that in which such proceedings were first brought within the meaning of national law.

Application of national law

Varieties that were the subject matter of Community plant variety rights could not be patented nor be the subject matter of national plant variety rights. Where the holder had been granted another right for the same variety prior to the grant of the Community plant variety right, he would be unable to invoke the rights conferred by such protection in respect of variety for as long as the Community plant variety right remained effective. Claims under Community plant variety rights would be subject to limitations imposed by the law of the Member States only as expressly referred to in the proposed regulation.

Infringements of Community plant variety rights

Holders of Community plant variety rights would be entitled to compensation in respect of any infringement of their exclusive rights. The holder could require reasonable compensation from any person who had, in the time between publication of the application for grant of a Community plant variety right and grant thereof, carried out a prohibited act. However, claims would be time barred after three years from the time at which the holder had knowledge of the act and of the identity of the party liable or, irrespective of such knowledge, after 30 years from the termination of the act concerned. National courts would apply domestic law as regards restitution of any gain made at the expense of the holder. In all other respects the effects of Community plant variety right would be determined solely in accordance with the regulation.

Actions for infringement could be brought by the holder or any other person enjoying exploitation rights with the holders consent. In any dispute the national court or other body hearing an action relating to a Community plant variety right would have to treat the right as valid. It is expressly provided that the Lugano convention of 16 September 1988 on Jurisdiction and Enforcements of Judgments in Civil and Commercial Matters would apply subject to certain modifications. The general rule would be laid down that claims should be brought in the courts of the

Member State or other contracting party in which the Defendant was domiciled or had his seat or, his establishment or where the harmful event occurred.

Member States would have to ensure that the same provisions were made applicable to penalising infringements of Community plant variety rights as apply in the matter of infringements of corresponding national industrial property rights.

The Community plant variety office

The introduction of the Community plant variety right will make it possible for persons to obtain on a single application one plant variety right covering all the Member States. In order to allow the Community plant variety system to work, a Community plant variety office with its own fee structure would be established. The office, with its own staff and administration, would be responsible for carrying out a formal examination (i.e., whether the application had been effectively filed) a substantive examination (i.e., whether the variety was new) and for arranging a technical examination (i.e., whether the variety satisfied the conditions of distinctiveness, homogeneity and stability). Within the office there would be established one or more Boards of Appeal which would be responsible for deciding on appeals against the Office's decision to refuse or grant an application. A further appeal to the Court of Justice of the European Communities would lie from decisions of the Board of Appeal. The Office would keep a register of Community plant variety rights which would be open to public inspection. The Office would be advised and supervised by an administrative council, composed of representatives of Member States and of the Commission.

3. Taxation

Taxation and the internal market

Although the Treaty does not specifically deal with the question of direct taxation, many obstacles to the free movement of goods, persons, services and capital may be put in place through the tax system. To the extent that these obstacles are in the nature of a quantitative restriction on goods or discriminatory in some other way, the Treaty provisions governing free movement may be such as to make them unlawful. However, many national tax rules which are not in breach of the Treaty still have the effect of hindering inter-State trade. In 1962, the Neumark Committee, which was charged with examining the problems of tax harmonisation in the Community, recommended that such harmonisation should deal initially with indirect taxes and also with the methods of taxing dividends and interest and the problem of double taxation. Later stages would deal with company taxation and personal taxation. A further committee of experts studied the problems of taxation and an integrated capital market. This produced the Segré Report in 1966 which argued that the realisation of an integrated market depended on measures being adopted such that tax considerations no longer influenced decisions on location of investments or transactions.

The Commission adopted a programme for the harmonisation of direct taxes in 1967. It intended that company tax and income tax would be harmonised, though to varying degrees and that urgent consideration was to be given to the matter of company taxation. Differing national tax systems have the effect of distorting investment decisions where one country gives more favourable tax treatment to a transaction than does another. In other cases, differing tax rules may result in double taxation or non-taxation of a transaction. In the future, the Commission will produce proposals for harmonisation of the basis of assessment of company taxation and approximation or harmonisation of company tax rates. For the present, however, the Commission has included in its programme for the completion of the internal market seven direct tax measures. These deal with an arbitration procedure for the elimination of certain double taxation; the carry-over of losses from one financial year to another; the tax treatment to be given to mergers, divisions and contributions of assets; taxation of distributions from subsidiaries to parent companies; the tax treatment of losses as between parents and subsidiaries in different Member States; withholding taxes on interest and royalty payments between parents and subsidiaries; and the abolition of indirect taxes on transactions in securities.

Arbitration procedure for the elimination of certain double taxation

Many problems arise in the field of the taxation of transferred profits between associated enterprises, the most common being that more than one Member State might wish to tax the same profits. Double taxation agreements are negotiated on a bilateral basis between the Member States in order to deal with this question. In certain cases, the taxpayer may find that this bilateral procedure is not fully adequate, either because his own interests have not been fully taken into account or because the national authorities have been unable to agree on a solution to the problem. Accordingly, a Convention setting up an arbitration procedure for the purpose of the elimination of double taxation in connection with the adjustments of transfers of profits between associated enterprises.

The Convention applies to income and corporation tax on profits transferred between a company in one Member State and an associated company in another Member State, where the amount of the taxable profits of an enterprise is increased or is likely to be increased by the tax authority of either of those States because the undertakings are not at arm's length to one another. Enterprises are associated where one of them participates directly or indirectly in the management, control or capital of the other or where the same persons participate directly or indirectly in the management, control or capital of both undertakings. The Convention allows the taxation of profits which have been omitted from one of these companies because of non-arm's length relations. It applies also to permanent establishments situated in other Member States as if they were subsidiaries.

The tax authority would have to inform the undertaking of its intention without delay and give it time to inform the other company. If neither of the tax authorities was able on its own to arrive at a satisfactory solution to the problem, the two authorities would have to endeavour to reach mutual agreement with a view to avoiding double taxation. Failing such agreement, the tax authorities would be obliged to present the case to an advisory commission charged with delivering its opinion on he elimination of the double taxation.

The advisory commission would consist of a Chairman, two representatives from each of the tax authorities concerned plus an even number of independent persons, selected from a list of persons of standing nominated by the Member States. The independent members would be appointed by agreement or, in the absence thereof, by the drawing of lots, although either authority might, in certain cases, refuse to accept a particular appointment. In their capacity as members of the commission, the independent members would be subject to the obligation of professional secrecy.

Each of the associated enterprises could provide all information, evidence or other documents which it thought might be of use in reaching a decision, and the enterprises and the national authorities would have to comply with any request from the commission for information, evidence or documents. The enterprises might appear or be represented, either at their own request or at the request of the commission.

The decision of the commission would be given within six months. The double taxation will be regarded as eliminated if either the profits are included in the computation of taxable profits in one State only or the tax chargeable on those profits in one State is reduced by an amount equal to the tax chargeable on them in the other. All expenses of the Commission will be shared by the States concerned.

Carry-over of losses

The Commission's proposal for a directive on the carry-over of losses is to the effect that Member States would be obliged to harmonise their national provisions relating to this area in income tax, corporation tax, capital gains tax and any other similar taxes. It applies to undertakings which draw up for tax purposes, in accordance with conditions laid down by national law, annual accounts consisting of a balance sheet and a profit and loss account. Profit or loss in a financial year is calculated for these purposes after any possible set-off against other income or against results recorded abroad by a permanent establishment or subsidiary in accordance with the national tax rules.

Where the undertaking made a loss, that loss would be offset against profits of other years. The undertaking would have a choice as to which years' profit should be taken into account. It might set off against the profits, or the non-distributed portion of the profits, of one or more of the three preceding years and then, if need be, against the profit of the following years in chronological order. Alternatively, it might simply choose to set off solely against the profits of the following years. In either case it might choose not to offset losses against profits which had not been taxed in the State where it was subject to tax or which had been taxed at a reduced rate.

If a loss was set off against distributed profits which at the time of their distribution carried entitlement to a tax credit, the resulting repayment of tax would be reduced by the amount of that tax credit to the extent to which it had not been covered by a compensatory tax. In some Member States different rates of taxation are applied to different categories of profit. In such cases, if the national law also provided that losses had to be set off category by category, the Member State would have to refrain from applying such a provision where a loss could not be set off against profits of the same category by the end of the fifth financial year following that in which it arose.

Mergers, divisions and contributions of assets

Preferential tax treatment is usually given to capital gains which arise on mergers, splitting up of companies and transfers of assets between companies where the transaction involves domestic companies only, but is not usually given where one of the companies is foreign. This has an effect on investment and other business decisions which is adverse in the context of the internal market in that it becomes more expensive to deal with a foreign company than with a domestic company. Directive 90/434 has therefore been adopted on a common system of taxation of mergers, divisions, transfers of assets and exchanges of shares taking place between companies of different Member States. It is to be implemented by 1 January 1992.

Mergers are defined as an event when the assets of one or more companies are transferred, following a dissolution without liquidation, to another company which is either in existence or is formed for the purpose. Conversely, a division takes place where a company, on being dissolved without going into liquidation, transfers all its assets and liabilities to two or more existing or new companies in exchange for the issue of shares. Accordingly, this measure does not apply to takeovers. A merger or division shall not give rise to any taxation of capital gains calculated by reference to the difference between the real value of the assets and liabilities transferred and their values for tax purposes. The necessary measures must be taken to ensure that, where provisions or reserves properly constituted by the transferring company are partly or wholly exempt from tax and are not derived from permanent establishments abroad, such provisions or reserves may be carried over, with the same tax exemption, by the permanent establishments of the receiving company which are situated in the Member State of the transferring company.

To the extent that, if the transfers were effected between companies in the same State, the receiving company would be entitled to take over the losses of the transferring company, those provisions shall be extended to cover the takeover of such losses by the receiving companies permanent establishments situated within its territory. Where the receiving company has a holding in the capital of the transferring company, any gains accruing to the receiving company on the cancellation of the holding shall not be liable to any taxation, except where the holding does not exceed 25%.

On a merger, division or exchange of shares, the allotment of securities to a shareholder of the transferring company in exchange for shares in that company shall not of itself give rise to any taxation of the income, profits or capital gains of that shareholder. This shall not prevent the taxing of the gain arising out of the subsequent transfer of securities received in the same way as the gain arising out of the transfer of securities existing before the acquisition. Where the assets transferred include a permanent establishment in another Member State, the latter State shall renounce any right to tax that permanent establishment. However, the State of the transferring company may reinstate in the taxable profits of that company such losses of the permanent establishment as may previously have been set off against the taxable profits of the company in that State and which have not been recovered. By way of derogation, where the Member State of the transferring company applies a system of taxing worldwide profits, that State shall have the right to tax any profits or capital gains of the permanent establishment resulting from the transfer on condition that it gives relief for the tax that would have been charged on those profits or gains in the State in which the permanent establishment is situated in the same way and in the same amount as it would have done if that tax had actually been charged and paid.

Taxation of parent companies and their subsidiaries

The taxation of profits of a subsidiary which are distributed to its parent company and then redistributed to the shareholders can result in double taxation if each distribution is taxed separately. Relief from this situation may be given either by taxing only the distribution of the subsidiary and not redistribution of the parent, or by not taxing the distribution of the subsidiary to the parent until it is redistributed to the shareholders. Double taxation can occur where the parent and subsidiary are situated in different countries which apply different tax rules. Accordingly, Directive 90/435 on a common system of taxation applicable in the case of parent companies and their subsidiaries in different Member States has been adopted. The Commission has also proposed two other directives relating to parent companies and their subsidiaries. The first deals with interest and royalty payments between the two and the second concerns common arrangements for the taking into account of losses of a subsidiary or permanent establishment in another Member State.

Distributions of profits from a subsidiary to its parent

For the purposes of Directive 90/435, a parent company is normally one which holds a minimum of 25% of the capital of another. Member States may reserve the right not to apply the directive to parent companies which have not fulfilled this status for at least two years. This directive is to be implemented by 1 January 1992.

Where a parent company receives distributed profits, the State of the parent company must, except where the subsidiary is liquidated, either refrain from taxing those profits or tax them while authorising the parent company to deduct from the amount of tax due that fraction of the corporation tax paid by the subsidiary which relates to those profits and, if appropriate, the amount of any withholding tax paid in the subsidiary's State up to the limit of the corresponding domestic tax. Distributed profits must, at least where the parent holds 25% of the capital of the subsidiary, be exempt from withholding tax. There are derogations for Germany, Greece and Portugal.

Interest and royalty payments

In the Commission's proposed directive on the taxation of interest and royalty payments made between subsidiaries and parent companies, 'interest' means income from debt claims of any kind and 'royalty' means payments of any kind received as a consideration for the use of, or the right to use, any copyright of literary, artistic or scientific work including cinematographic films, any patent, trademark, design or model, plan secret formula or process, or for the use of, or right to use, industrial, commercial or scientific equipment, or for information concerning industrial, commercial or scientific experience. Members States will have to exempt from any withholding tax interest and royalty payments made between parent companies and subsidiaries in different Member States. The directive should be implemented by 1 January 1993, although Greece and Portugal will be allowed to levy a withholding tax on interest and royalty payments for a further seven years. It will apply to payments made to a permanent establishment of the recipient company located in the Member State of the debtor only if that State does not apply withholding tax to payments of the kind made between resident parent companies and subsidiaries.

Transfer of losses between parent and subsidiary

Under a proposed directive, Member States will be required to adopt arrangements enabling their enterprises to take account of the losses incurred by permanent establishments or subsidiaries situated in other Member States. The Member States will have an option to extend these arrangements to permanent establishments and subsidiaries in third countries.

Losses incurred by permanent establishments will be allowed either by a credit method or by the method of deducting losses and reincorporating subsequent profits. The credit will consist of including in the enterprise's results for a given tax period the positive or negative results of all its permanent establishments situated in another Member State and crediting the tax paid by the latter against any tax which may be payable by the enterprise on those profits. The alternative method of deducting losses and reincorporating subsequent profits will involve the deduction from taxable profits of an enterprise any losses of its permanent establishments in other Member States and the incorporation of subsequent profits of the permanent establishment into the enterprise's taxable to the extent of the previous loss. It would be optional for the Member States to provide that losses which have been deducted would be reincorporated automatically within five years of the original deduction or where the permanent establishment was sold, wound up or transformed into a subsidiary. Losses of subsidiaries will be transferable to parent companies by the method of deduction and subsequent reincorporation, although Member States will be free to introduce other methods of taking account of losses of subsidiaries, including the consolidated profit method.

Indirect taxes on transactions in securities

As part of the programme for the completion of the internal market, Directive 86/566 extended the obligation to liberalise capital movements to include all operations involving the acquisitions of securities and the admission to the capital market of negotiable securities and of those which are in the process of being introduced on to the stock exchange. Movement of capital may, however, still be distorted by the existence of differing national provisions concerning indirect taxes on transactions in securities. The Commission has therefore issued a proposal for a directive which seeks to abolish any tax on transactions in securities.

Member States would not be allowed to tax transactions in securities. They would refrain from levying any tax on such transactions, whether or not levied at a flat rate, the base of which consisted of the value of the security which was the object of the transaction. Notwithstanding that, they might levy capital duty, transfer duties on immovable property and

VAT. The transfer duty would be payable where, as a result of share transactions in bodies whose assets consisted in whole or in part of immovable property situated in their territory, the purchaser acquired all the assets of or a controlling interest in that body. In this case, transfer duties would apply only in respect of the value of the immovable property. VAT might be levied in respect of interests or shares giving the holder rights of ownership or possession over immovable property.

Part Three

The Removal of Fiscal Barriers

I. Value Added Tax
II. Excise Duties

I. Value Added Tax

The common system of value added tax

Inherent in the plan to create the internal market was the intention that national turnover taxes throughout the Community should be harmonised. This presupposed the application of a system of turnover taxes such as would not distort conditions of competition or hinder the free movement of goods and services within the internal market. The studies carried out on behalf of the Commission and the Council showed that value added tax was the most suitable replacement for existing turnover taxes.

Provisions for the harmonisation of national legislation on turnover taxes were to be adopted by the Council and, to date, a number have been adopted, mostly in the form of directives. Value added tax was introduced into the Community in 1967 by the First VAT Directive, which declared that the principle of the common system of the tax involved the application to goods and services of a general tax on consumption exactly proportional to the price of the goods and services, whatever the number of transactions which took place in the production and distribution process before the stage at which tax was charged. The structure and procedures for the application of the common system were established at the same time by the Second VAT Directive which was superseded in 1977 by the uniform basis of assessment laid down in the Sixth VAT Directive. It is the Sixth Directive which still contains the general body of rules which apply to the common system of VAT. These rules cover the scope of application of the tax, define the concepts of taxable persons, taxable transactions, chargeable events and taxable amounts and set out the basic administrative requirements for the operation of the system. Detailed provisions allow for certain transactions to be exempted from the system, for special schemes to be implemented in respect of certain categories of persons or transactions and for derogations in particular cases.

The scope of value added tax

Tax is chargeable on the supply of goods and services by a taxable person and on the importation of goods into a Member State. A taxable person is anyone who independently carries out any economic activity, whatever the purpose or results of that activity. In order to avoid double taxation within the Community, rules were established for the determination of the place of supply of goods and services. Normally, the place of supply of goods is deemed to be the place where the goods are when supply begins. Services are deemed to be supplied where the supplier has established his business or where he has a fixed establishment from which the service is supplied. In the absence of such a place of business or fixed establishment, the service is deemed to be supplied from the place where the supplier has his permanent address or usually resides. There are exceptions to this involving, for example, immovable property and transport services. In the case of certain services, such as those of accountants and lawyers, the place where they are deemed to be supplied, when performed for customers established outside the Community or for taxable persons established in the Community but in a different country from the supplier, is the place where the customer, not the supplier, is established.

The charge to tax

Tax is chargeable when the goods are delivered or the services are performed or, as regards imported goods, at the time when the goods enter the Member State. Normally, tax is charged on the full consideration received by the supplier or on the price paid or to be paid by the importer. A taxable person, who is obliged to register with the authorities, must then pay over to those authorities the tax which he has charged on supplies made by him. Various provisions deal with the obligations on taxable persons to keep records and make payment of the tax which becomes due. It is largely for the Member States themselves to lay down detailed rules on the administrative procedure.

Since tax is charged on the full price paid at each stage of the production and distribution process, any tax paid by the taxable person in the acquisition of goods or services used for the purposes of his taxable transactions is deductible by him from the amount which he must pay to the authorities. Accordingly, it is ultimately the final consumer who is burdened with the payment of the tax, while the taxable person acts as a link in the chain of the collection system between the revenue authorities and the consumer.

Rates of taxation

Member States are free to fix whatever rate of tax they choose and may alter it at their own discretion. The standard rate is fixed as a percentage of the taxable amount and must be the same for the supply of goods and the supply of services. In certain cases the supply of goods or services may be made subject to reduced or increased rates. So as to avoid discrimination between domestic and imported goods, the rate applicable on the importation of goods must be that applied to the supply of like goods within the country. This process of taxation within the country, coupled with the taxation of goods on importation into a country and remission of tax on exportation out of a country, is designed to incorporate the destination principle whereby goods and services are taxed in the country of consumption.

Member States are obliged to exempt certain transactions from the tax system. No tax is charged on these transactions and a taxable person who makes them is not permitted to deduct any tax he may have paid in respect of goods and services received by him in connection with them. These obligatory exemptions are mostly connected with activities in the public interest, such as the supply of postal services, hospital and medical care and education. Other sectors are covered as well, including insurance and re-insurance transactions, most supplies of immovable property and many categories of supplies relating to the granting and negotiation of credit. Special exemptions relate to imports, exports and goods in international transport. In addition, many particular derogations are allowed to individual Member States whereby, for a transitional period, exempt transactions may continue to be taxed and taxable transactions may continue to be exempt.

Further harmonisation of the common system

Although the Sixth Directive established a high degree of uniformity, it was conceded at the time that it was not yet practicable completely to harmonise the national systems. A number of other directives have been adopted, some of which were concerned solely with time-limits for implementation, while others introduced substantive changes into the common system aimed at eliminating the outstanding differences in the national systems. These included the Eighth Directive on arrangements for the refund of VAT to taxable persons not established in the territory of the country and the Tenth Directive dealing with the hiring out of movable tangible property. The Commission's proposals for the completion of the internal market, so far as they concern VAT, are intended to tackle these remaining differences and remove the justifications for customs barriers which the present system permits. A number of proposals for directives have been made covering the removal of internal frontiers, uniform interpretation of the system, exemptions, rates of taxation, allowable deductions, refunds of tax to persons not established in the Community, temporary importation of goods, taxation of the stores of vessels, aircraft and international trains and common special systems for small and medium-sized businesses and for second-hand goods.

Removal of internal frontiers

Value added tax is presently applied according to the destination principle whereby goods and services are taxable in the country of consumption. Tax is charged on the supply of goods and services effected for consideration within the territory of the country by a taxable person acting as such and on the importation of goods into a country whether by a taxable or a non-taxable person. No tax is charged on the supply of goods for export. From the inception of the common system of VAT in 1967, it has been the declared intention of the Council eventually to abolish the imposition of taxation on importation and the remission of tax on exportation in intra-Community trade. The Commission seeks to achieve this in 1992 through the proposal for a directive on the removal of fiscal frontiers. The effect of this would be to modify the application of the destination principle so that goods and services would be taxable in the country where supply takes place and the importation of goods would be taxable only in the case of importation from a third country into the Community.

Goods

At present, when goods are sold for export, no VAT is levied on that supply and any tax which has been paid and is attributable to an earlier stage in the production or distribution process is reclaimable. Where goods are exported to another Member State, tax is charged on the importation of those goods into that State. It is proposed to alter this so that goods would no longer be subject to a charge to tax on importation into another Member State where there was no separate supply of those goods on importation. As a corollary, the remission of tax on exportation in intra-Community trade would be abolished. Where goods are exported outside of the Community, no VAT is charged on those goods by any Member State. This would continue to be the case.

Presently, the tax chargeable on the importation of goods is calculated according to either the price actually paid by the importer, the open market value or the value of the goods for customs purposes. Since the only goods which will continue to be subject to tax on importation will be those which are imported from third countries and which are, in any case, subject to the Community customs system, it is proposed that the only valuation of the taxable amount for such goods would be the value adopted for customs purposes.

Services

As already stated, services are deemed to be supplied at the place where the supplier is established or where he has his permanent address or usually resides. In certain cases, the service, when supplied to a customer established outside the Community or to a taxable person established in the Community but not in the same country as the supplier, is deemed to be supplied at the place where the customer is established. A taxable person who receives such a service is deemed to receive it in his own country and has to account to his tax authorities in respect of it. It is proposed that this be altered, so that this procedure would apply only in the case where the service was supplied for a customer established outside of the Community or for taxable persons established in the Community by suppliers established outside the Community. Accordingly, in all other cases the general rule would be that the service is supplied at the place where the supplier is established.

Transport services are currently taxed according to the place where the transport takes place, having regard to the distances covered. It is proposed to change this so that transport services would be deemed to be supplied at the place of departure, i.e., the place where the transport operation actually commenced, without taking into consideration any intermediate stops unless these were to enable separate suppliers to provide their services. A return journey would be regarded as a separate service.

Deductions of value added tax paid in another Member State

Under the present system only the tax paid in the same Member State may be deducted by a taxable person when he makes his periodic returns to the revenue authorities, while VAT paid in another Member State must be reclaimed separately from the authorities of that State. It is proposed that a taxable person would be entitled to deduct from the VAT which he was liable to pay to the authorities any VAT which he had paid in respect of the goods and services supplied to him for the purposes of his taxable transactions, regardless of where in the Community he had paid that VAT. For example, where goods were purchased in Germany and resold in France, the VAT charged in Germany would be deductible by the French taxable person from the VAT due in France on his sales there. Where deductible tax was expressed in the currency of a Member State other than that in which it was to be deducted, or in the currency of a third country, the amount to be deducted would be converted into the currency of the taxable person's country using the average exchange rate for the declaration period.

This would seem to lead to the case whereby one Member State might be subsidising another, since it would be giving a credit for tax which had been paid to that other State. The Commission will be making a proposal for a clearing system which is to be designed to diminish this problem. In order to identify sales and purchases made by taxable persons in Member States other than that in which they are established, the Commission proposes that a record be kept by each trader. In the periodic VAT return required to be made by each taxable person, a new requirement would be, on the one hand, a declaration of the total amount of VAT relating to transactions carried out for taxable persons in other Member States and, on the other hand, a declaration of the total amount of deductible VAT relating to transactions carried out by taxable persons in other Member States. This provision would not apply to taxable persons whose annual turnover did not exceed 35,000 ECU.

Transitional provisions

The Commission has proposed that certain transitional provisions should apply until the 31 December 1996 at the latest. When goods supplied to a non-taxable person or to a taxable person who is fully exempt are dispatched, they would be deemed to be supplied at the place where they are at the time they reach the person who acquires them provided that a set of condition are fulfilled. These conditions are that:

- the supplies comprise goods other than private vehicles that have been dispatched to another Member State;
- the supplies are effected by way of mail order;
- the annual turnover exclusive of VAT generated by the seller in connection with mail order selling to Member States other than that from which the goods are dispatched exceeds ECU 1 million.

Certain cross-border supplies by taxable persons would be exempted from tax as follows:

- supplies of private vehicles forming part of the seller's stock in trade;
- supplies other than those referred to above of goods other than private vehicles sold to a taxable person;
- supplies of services directly linked to these supplies of goods.

Tax-free and duty-free allowances

A number of directives permit tax exemptions on importation of goods. Most of these are concerned with private individuals and relate to duty-free allowances in international travel, imports of personal property, temporary importation of goods or small consignments of a non-commercial character. These are discussed in the chapter on the control of individuals. With the completion of the internal market, there is no longer any need for such special provisions in so far as they relate to travel within the Community. These allowances are therefore to be abolished as from the end of 1992, and 1996 in the case of the transitional provisions.

Uniform interpretation of the common system

When the common system of VAT was introduced by the First and Second Directives, the Member States were given considerable leeway in how they interpreted various provisions. Although it was the intention of the Sixth Directive to establish a uniform basis of assessment, many problems of interpretation persisted. For example, certain Member States considered that only fixed installations from which taxable operations were carried out could be considered a 'fixed establishment'. Such an interpretation led to difficulties of taxation when it became necessary to determine the place of supply of services in those cases where the supply is deemed made at the customer's establishment and not that of the supplier. Problems like this led the Commission to make a proposal for a Nineteenth Directive which aims to achieve a uniform application of the provisions of the Sixth Directive.

Other provisions which are dealt with in the proposed directive include those dealing with international transport, hospital care, cultural services, payment cards issued by financial institutions and turnover of exchange and securities transactions.

Abolition of certain derogations

A series of derogations allowed to individual Member States under the Sixth Directive has been abolished. These derogations allow Member States either to tax transactions which would otherwise be exempt or to exempt transactions which would otherwise be taxable. The provisions dealing with these are in the Eighteenth VAT Directive (89/465). These derogations were allowed to Member States in order to give them and the economic sectors benefiting from them time to carry out the necessary adjustments. The Commission is of the view that the existence of these derogations caused distortion of competition which is incompatible with the principles of the internal market.

Three groups of derogations were identified. The first included those which may cause transactions to be transferred from one Member State to another and whose economic, social and budgetary impact was slight. The second group, which included most of the remaining derogations, comprises those which have a greater financial and social impact. Some of the derogations have been abolished from 1 January 1990, and others from 1991, 1992 or 1993. Portugal was allowed a special dispensation in respect of some of these matters until 1994. Thirdly, a small number of derogations would be allowed to continue under the new system, but the Commission wishes to phase these out in the future.

Rates of taxation

Currently, each Member State is free to fix the rate of VAT which applies to all taxable transactions within its territory. In its proposal for a directive on the approximation of VAT rates, the Commission's aim is that Member States would apply two rates of tax, namely a standard rate and a reduced rate. The Commission proposes that the reduced rate might not be less than 4% or more than 9% and the standard rate might not be less than 14% or more than 20%. The reduced rate would apply to transactions relating to the following goods and services:

- foodstuffs, excluding alcoholic beverages;
- energy products for heating and lighting;
- water supplies;
- pharmaceutical products;
- books, newspapers and periodicals;
- passenger transport. The standard rate would apply to all other transactions.

Pending the adoption of the necessary provisions to put this into effect, it is intended, by the implementation of the proposed directive instituting a process of convergence of VAT rates, that Member States refrain from altering the number and level of rates which they currently apply, except in order to converge on the proposed rates. Member States which apply three rates or more would be permitted to reduce that number to two rates and those which applied one rate would be permitted to increase that number to two rates, in each case to be called a reduced rate and a standard rate. They might alter the levels of their reduced and standard tax rates on condition that they moved towards or within the proposed limits of 4–9% and 14–20% respectively.

Allowable tax deductions

Taxable persons are entitled to deduct from the tax which they have charged on their supplies any tax paid by them on goods and services which are used for the purposes of their taxable transactions. However, certain deductions are not allowed. No deduction is allowed on expenditure which is not strictly business expenditure, such as that on luxuries, amusements or entertainment. The Commission has issued a proposal for a Twelfth Directive setting out the specific expenditure which should be disallowed.

Passenger vehicles

VAT would not be deductible in respect of expenditure on the purchase, manufacture, importation, leasing or hire, use, modification, repair or maintenance of pleasure boats or private aircraft. Nor would VAT be deductible in respect of expenditure on supplies (e.g., fuels, lubricants and spare parts) for, or services performed in relation to, such vehicles and craft. The right to deduct this type of expenditure in respect of passenger cars and motor cycles would be subject to special restrictions. Provisionally, Member States could set the deduction at not less than 25% and not more than 75% of the tax charged. This would later be replaced by a fixed deduction of 50% of the tax charged. Road vehicles intended solely for the transport of goods or for industrial or agricultural use or which had a seating capacity of more than nine persons including the driver would be excluded from these provisions as would be vehicles or craft which were used for carriage for hire or reward, used for driving training or instruction, hired out, or part of the stock in trade of a business.

Transport expenses

VAT on transport expenses incurred on business travel by a taxable person or by members of his staff would be limited in the same manner. This would apply to a journey undertaken for business reasons away from the place of establishment or away from the place at which the traveller's functions were exercised, but it would not apply to transport expenses relating to the movement of staff between particular places of work or to those relating to transport of staff to and from their homes.

Accommodation, food and drink

Deduction would not be allowed in respect of expenditure on accommodation, food and drink. This would not apply to expenditure incurred by a taxable person in respect of the supply of accommodation, meals, food and drink for consideration or to expenditure on accommodation provided free of charge for security or caretaking staff on works, sites or business premises. However, where a taxable person could provide proof that the above expenditure relating to transport, accommodation, food and drink had been made exclusively for business purposes, deduction could be claimed in full.

Entertainment

VAT would not be deductible in respect of expenditure on entertainment, including expenditure on hospitality extended to business contacts or, more generally, persons outside the business or in respect of expenditure relating to buildings, parts of buildings or their fittings intended for such entertainment. Nor would it be deductible in respect of expenditure on amusements and luxuries. Expenditure on luxuries is defined as expenditure which, by its nature and amount, does not constitute normal operating expenditure, or which relates to items which are not normally installed as fittings in buildings.

Refunds to taxable persons not established in the Community

The Sixth Directive allowed Member States to adopt their own rules in relation to the refund of tax to taxable persons not established in the Community. The Council has introduced, by the Thirteenth Directive on VAT, Directive 86/560, a uniform system for arrangements for the refund of VAT to taxable persons not established in the territory of the Community. This applies, with some exceptions, to a taxable person who, during a given period, has neither his business nor a fixed establishment from which business transactions are effected, nor his permanent address or usual place of residence, in the Community. Member States must refund to such a person any VAT charged in respect of services rendered or moveable property supplied to him in that State by other taxable persons or in respect of imports into that State in so far as such goods are used for certain specified purposes. This right of refund may be subject to reciprocal arrangements with the country of the person making the claim. The refunds are granted upon application by the taxable person. The Member States are to determine the arrangements for submitting applications, including the time-limits for doing so, the periods which the applications should cover, the authority competent to receive them and the minimum amounts in respect of which applications should be submitted. They are also to determine the arrangements for making refunds and to impose such obligations as are necessary to determine whether the application is justified and to prevent fraud. Refunds may not be granted under conditions which are more favourable than those applied to Community taxable persons.

Temporary importation of goods

In certain circumstances, where goods are imported temporarily into a Member State, no VAT may be charged by that State at that time. The uniform law on temporary importation exemption was established by the Seventeenth Directive, Directive 85/362. Means of transport, pallets and containers are excluded from the scope of this directive.

Scope of temporary importation exemption

Exemption is granted to goods temporarily imported into one Member State from another provided that such goods:

- are intended to be re-exported without alteration;

- originate in a Member State, or in a third country and are in free circulation in the Community;
- have been acquired subject to the rules governing the application of VAT in the Member State of exportation and have not benefited, by virtue of their exportation, from any exemption from VAT;
- belong to a person established outside the territory of the Member State of importation; and
- are not consumable goods.

Temporary importation exemption is granted on the importation of certain categories of goods from third countries. Exemption is also granted in respect of these categories when the goods are imported from another Member State, but do not qualify for exemption under the above rules, except that exemption is not granted in those cases where:

- the goods originate in a Member State, or in a third country and are in free circulation in the Community;
- the goods were not acquired pursuant to the rules governing the application of VAT in the Member State of exportation or, by virtue of being exported, benefited from exemption from VAT; and
- the importer is a non-taxable person or is a taxable person not entitled to deduction in full.

The categories of goods included in this exemption are as follows:

- professional equipment;
- goods for display or use at an exhibition, fair, symposium or similar event;
- teaching aids and scientific equipment;
- medical, surgical and laboratory equipment;
- materials for use in countering the effects of disasters;
- packings;
- travellers' personal effects;
- commercial samples, advertising material and goods for demonstration purposes;
- welfare material for seafarers;
- goods for use by public authorities in border zones;
- animals;
- films, tapes and other carrier material for recorded sound;
- goods for use in production for export;
- replacement means of production. The competent authority of a Member State may grant exemption when it considers that it concerns a particular case which has no economic effect or, in certain circumstances, where the goods are imported for non-commercial reasons.

Cessation of temporary importation exemption

The benefit of temporary importation exemption can last for up to two years and in some cases this may be extended. Various restrictions may be imposed on the person seeking the benefit of the exemption, such as the requirement of a deposit or other security. These persons are required to submit to the surveillance and inspection measures prescribed by the competent authorities. If the authorities find that the conditions attached to the benefit of the exemption are not complied with, the benefit may be revoked. It is possible to transfer the benefit to any other person as long as he satisfies the conditions of the directive and assumes all the obligations incumbent on the holder of the original authorisation. The exemption extends to a supply of the goods provided that the purchaser is a person established outside the territory of the Member State of importation and the goods otherwise continue to remain eligible for temporary importation exemption.

The benefit of temporary importation exemption ceases in a number of specific cases, with the result that the goods are then subject to the normal system of VAT. The tax becomes chargeable when the goods are declared for home use. However, the withdrawal of the exemption does not result in the occurrence of a chargeable event if the goods are:

- exported outside the territory of the Member State;
- placed, with a view to their subsequent exportation, under warehouse arrangements, in a free zone or under other specific transit arrangements;
- destroyed under customs control or are proved to have been totally destroyed or irretrievably lost.

Certain goods imported for possible sale

A special category of exemption applies to certain goods imported for possible sale. The classes of goods are as follows:

- second-hand goods imported with a view to their sale by auction;
- goods imported under a contract of sale which are to be subjected to satisfactory acceptance tests;
- works of art and other works intended for decoration but not generally for utility purposes which are imported for the purposes of exhibition with a view to possible sale;
- consignments on approval of made-up articles of fur, precious stones, carpets and articles of jewellery provided that their particular characteristics prevent them being imported as samples. The exemption for this category applies to goods imported both from other Member States and from third countries. In respect of the first three classes, the period of exemption may not exceed six months, while in

the fourth class, the period of exemption may not exceed four weeks. If the goods are sold, the benefit of the exemption ceases and tax is charged on the price paid.

Stores of vessels, aircraft and international trains

The special nature, from the point of view of VAT, of stores involved in international transport has led the Commission to propose a directive aimed solely at the tax provisions which should apply to them. Stores are defined as catering supplies (i.e., products intended solely for consumption by crew members or passengers), fuels, lubricants and other oils intended for feeding the propulsion units and operating other machinery and equipment on board and other consumable care and maintenance products.

Maritime, inland waterway and air transport

VAT would not be levied by a Member State in respect of the importation of stores on board:

- a vessel engaged in international sea transport which entered territorial waters bound for a port situated on its territory until the vessel arrived in that port;
- a vessel engaged in international inland waterway transport which entered its territory:
  (a) for the whole duration of the voyage, if this took place exclusively in waters having international status;
  (b) in all other cases, as far as the port of final destination situated in the inland waters of a Member State;
- an aircraft engaged in international air transport and bound for an airport situated in its territory until the aircraft arrived at that airport.

Supplies of stores consumed on board one of these means of transport would be exempt from VAT until it reached its destination. The exemption would apply during the journey between ports of call or stops situated on the territory of the Member State, provided that these were part of the normal itinerary to the final destination and no passengers or freight were embarked in order to be disembarked at another port of call or stop. Also, the exemption would apply during the entire period of stay in a port or shipyard or at an airport, provided that this period did not exceed what was necessary for the purposes of the international transport operation.

Member States would suspend the levying of VAT in respect of the importation of stores on board a means of transport at the time of its arrival at its destination, provided that such stores were kept on board under customs or tax control, or were transferred to another vessel or aircraft in the same port for export, or were placed under transit or warehousing arrangements.

The supply of stores loaded on board vessels and aircraft engaged in international transport would be exempt from VAT. These provisions would also apply to coastal fishing vessels and vessels used for rescue and assistance at sea even if they did not sail outside territorial waters, with the exception that catering supplies would not be exempt except in the case of rescue vessels remaining at sea for more than 48 hours. Pleasure vessels, fishing vessels operating in fresh water and private aircraft would be excluded from these provisions.

International trains

Stores on board international trains would not be taxed on importation into a Member State where certain conditions were met. Catering supplies would not be taxed if they did not exceed the quantities normally necessary for the needs of the persons carried during the journey and had been purchased in the country of provisioning in accordance with that country's general tax arrangements. Fuels would not be taxed as long as they were contained in standard-sized tanks directly connected to the engine. This exemption would not apply to tobacco products or to alcoholic beverages, with the exception of beer and wine.

Small and medium-sized businesses

The Commission has proposed a directive on the common special VAT scheme applicable to small and medium-sized businesses. This common scheme would replace any national special schemes which Member States have been allowed to maintain in force to date, except that a Member State might be authorised to retain its existing exemption scheme or simplified scheme on condition that this was at least as favourable as the proposed scheme. Taxable persons whose annual turnover was less than 10,000 ECU would be exempt from the tax system, and Member States would be free to extend this exemption to taxable persons with an annual turnover of less than 35,000 ECU. It would be possible for these persons to opt out of the exemption. A taxable person who is covered by the exemption would not be entitled to deduct input tax.

A simplified scheme for charging and collecting the tax would be introduced. This would be limited to businesses with an annual turnover of less than 150,000 ECU. Tax would be chargeable on payment for the goods and services supplied rather than at the time of actual supply. As a corollary, the right to deduct input tax would arise at the time of payment for those goods and services by the taxable person.

An annual return would be made which should coincide with the return for direct taxation purposes. However, the taxable person would have to make monthly or quarterly advance payments equal to one-twelfth or one-quarter, respectively, of the net amount of VAT paid in the previous year, unless he declared on his own responsibility that such advance payments were greater than the tax actually due for the current year. He would make adjustments depending on the real net amount of VAT indicated in his annual returns and pay any balance due when the return was filed. If the balance was in his favour, the Member State would repay the amount owing the following month.

Member States might introduce, for certain groups of taxable persons whose purchases are sufficiently homogeneous in relation to their turnover, flat-rate percentages for calculating deductible VAT as a proportion of their turnover, provided that this did not lead to a reduction of tax.

Second-hand goods

The Sixth Directive presently permits the Member States to retain their own individual systems relating to the taxation of second-hand goods. This has resulted in distortion of competition and deflection of trade which the Commission hopes to end. Accordingly, the Commission has proposed a further directive setting out special common arrangements for second-hand goods, works of art, antiques and collector's items. 'Second-hand goods' means movable property that has been used and is suitable for further use as it is or after repair, including all means of transport.

The special arrangements are to apply to supplies made by a taxable dealer who has acquired them from a private person (or from another taxable person who has not been entitled to deduct the VAT on acquisition) with a view to resale. They do not apply where the dealer acquired them from a taxable person who has invoiced for VAT or where they have been imported by a taxable dealer and subjected to VAT on importation. The taxable amount is to be the difference, for each transaction, between the selling price and the purchase price, the selling price being calculated net of tax and the purchase price being tax-inclusive. Member States may, in order to simplify the procedure for levying the tax, take as the taxable amount the difference recorded over each tax period between the total amount of sales and the total amount of purchases.

For works or art, collector's items and antiques, supplies by a taxable dealer shall not be exempt from tax where they are dispatched to a third country and they shall be exempt when they are imported from a third country by a taxable dealer. These goods shall also be exempt from tax when they are imported by cultural organisation recognised as such by the Member State concerned.

II. Excise Duties

Harmonisation of excise duties

The Treaty obliges the Commission to consider the measures necessary to harmonise the laws of the Member States relating to excise duties. Commonly, excise duties are applied at a single stage in the production and distribution process. Apart from the fact that all Member States apply such taxes, there is little in common between many of the provisions governing their structure and the rates of duty applied. This results in considerable problems relating to the levels of indirect taxation which may be applied to imported products as a substitute for the duty which is applied to similar domestic products. Also, since some products will be subject to duties in some countries but not in others, this may lead to adverse effects on competition in the internal market. Although some Member States subject a wide number of products to duties, most of the revenue obtained from them is in respect of tobacco, alcoholic beverages and mineral oils.

In attempting to harmonise excise duties in the Community, the Commission sought to proceed in much the same way as it had with respect to VAT. First, the structure of the system would be progressively harmonised with the rates of duty being aligned at a later date. Community rules would apply only to tobacco, alcoholic beverages and mineral oils. To date, the proposals from the Commission concerning excise duties have resulted in a harmonised system being established in only one sector, namely, manufactured tobacco. However, the programme for the completion of the internal market envisages further directives covering cigarettes, other manufactured tobacco, wine, fortified wine and alcoholic drinks and mineral oils. In order to eliminate the fiscal barriers to trade caused by the continuing existence of excise duties, the Commission's White Paper envisages four elements to the programme:

- harmonisation of the structures of tobacco, alcoholic drinks and mineral oils;
- harmonisation of the rates of excise duty applied;
- abolition or reduction of any other excise rates to the extent that they involve border formalities;
- linkage of the bonded warehouses of the different Member States.

To date, proposals concerning the first two of these elements have been made as has a proposal on the general warehouse arrangements for products subject to excise duty and on the holding and movement of such products.

Arrangements for the holding and movement of products

A directive has been proposed on the general arrangements for products subject to excise duty and on the holding and movement of such products. Mineral oils, alcoholic beverages and manufactured tobacco would not be subject to any taxation other than VAT and excise duty. The chargeable event for excise duty would be the production in the Community or introduction into the Community of the product and duty would be chargeable when the product was released for consumption. Each Member State would continue to determine its rules concerning the deduction and holding of products liable to duty, subject to the provisions of the directive.

The system of tax warehouses would be used throughout the Community. An authorised warehouse-keeper would provide a guarantee, comply with the regulations, produce the goods for inspection when required, consent to all checks and controls and keep stock records. Movement under duty-suspension arrangements would take place between authorised warehouse-keepers and the identification of products moving under the these arrangements would be ensured by sealing. All these products would be accompanied by a document drawn up by the warehouse-keeper of dispatch in the form specified in the proposed directive. Where an offence or irregularity is committed in the course of movement, it would be the Member State in which that took place which would be responsible for recovering the duty owed.

Member States would be able to provide that products released for consumption or sold on their territory must carry national identification marks or tax identification markings. Such marks would have to be available to manufacturers and traders from the other Member States. Where a Member State collected excise duty by means other than tax identification marks, it would have to ensure that no barrier, either administrative or technical, affected intra-Community trade. Products carrying a national mark could be released for consumption only in that State.

Products subject to duty which are released for consumption might, at the request of the consignor, be the subject of a release or of a return into the duty-suspension arrangements and of a reimbursement of duty paid when the products are actually destined to be released for consumption in another Member State.

Manufactured tobacco

Directive 72/464 provided for excise duties on manufactured tobacco to be harmonised in stages. This directive applies to cigarettes, cigars and cigarillos, smoking tobacco, chewing tobacco and snuff, although specific rules on calculating duty were made only in respect of cigarettes. The duty on cigarettes was to have two component parts: a proportional excise duty calculated on the maximum retail selling price and a specific duty calculated per unit of production. During the first stage, which lasted until 30 June 1978, the specific duty could be between 5% and 75% of the total amount of tax, including VAT, on the product. During the second stage, the specific duty element was not to exceed 55% of the total. At the final stage, the same ratio was to be established in all Member States between the specific duty and the sum of the proportional duty and the VAT. Directive 79/32 was a first step in the harmonisation of the duties applicable to other manufactured tobacco in that it established definitions for the other categories. The Commission now seeks to complete the programme and has issued a proposal for a directive for the third stage of the harmonisation of the structure of cigarette duty and two further proposals for directives on the approximation of taxes on cigarettes and on other manufactured tobacco.

Cigarettes

At the third stage of harmonisation of the structure of cigarette duty, the amount of the specific component of the excise duty would be between 10% and 35% of the amount of the total tax burden levied on the cigarettes. This proposal would also allow Member States an option to levy a minimum excise duty not exceeding 80% of the sum of the proportional excise duty and the specific excise duty. However, in its latest proposal for a directive on the harmonisation of the duties applied to cigarettes, the Commission's aim is that, not later than 1 January 1993 cigarettes would be taxed on the basis of three component parts: a specific duty per unit of the product; a proportional excise duty calculated on the basis of the maximum retail selling price; and VAT proportional to the retailing selling price. The specific excise duty would be not less than 15

ECU per 1,000 cigarettes (as adjusted for inflation). The proportional rate would be fixed so that the combined incidence of this rate and the VAT rate would be not less than 45% of the retail selling price inclusive of all taxes. In the longer term, the specific duty would rise to 21.5 ECU per 1,000 cigarettes and the proportional duty would be 54% of the combined retail selling price.

Other manufactured tobacco

The proposal for a directive concerning other manufactured tobacco states that manufactured tobacco, other than cigarettes, would be subject only to a proportional rate calculated on the basis of the maximum retail selling price of each product as determined by manufacturers and importers. In the long term, the intention is that the total tax burden, including VAT, as a percentage of the retail selling price would be:

- for cigars and cigarillos: 36%;
- for smoking tobacco: 56%;
- chewing tobacco and snuff: 43%.

These rates would be effective for all products belonging to each group concerned without distinction within that group as to quality, presentation, origin, materials used, characteristics of the manufacturer or any other criterion. This is, however, a long-term objective but it is proposed that from 1 January 1993 the total tax burden must be not less 25%, 50% and 37% of these products respectively. Member States would be entitled to adjust their rates provided that they move closer to these targets. Every two years the rates would be reviewed.

Alcoholic drinks

Separate rules have been proposed governing the harmonisation of the structure of excise duties on beer, wines, intermediate products and alcohol and alcoholic beverages. Target rates of excise duty should be established with a minimum rate to apply from 1 January 1993.

Beer

The excise duty charged on beer would be fixed by reference to the number of hl/degree Plato of the finished product. Beers would be divided into categories of no more then four degrees Plato for the purpose of fixing the duty. A single reduced rate up to 20% less might be applied to beer brewed by independent small undertakings producing less than 60,000 hl per year. The target rate of duty would be 1496 ECU per hl/degree Plato, while the minimum rate would be set at 0.748 ECU from 1 January 1993.

Wines

The Commission differentiates between sparkling wines and still wines. All wines in any category would be taxed at the same rate, although a reduced rate up to 50% of the duty for each category might be applied to products having an actual alcoholic strength not exceeding 8.5% vol. Wine produced by a private individual for his own consumption might be exempted from duty. The target rate of duty would be 18.7 ECU per hectolitre for still wine and 33 ECU per hectolitre for sparkling wines, with minimum rates of 9.35 ECU and 16.5 ECU respectively applying from 1 January 1993.

Intermediate products

Intermediate products covers all products having an alcoholic strength exceeding 15% vol. but not exceeding 22% vol., or which have an actual alcoholic strength by volume exceeding 13% vol. and in which the alcohol content is not entirely of fermented origin. Excise duty would be charged by reference to the number of hectolitres of finished product released for consumption and would be at the same rate on all intermediate products. A reduced rate might apply in certain cases. The target rate of excise duty would be 93.5 ECU per hectolitre, with a minimum rate of 74.8 ECU applying from 1 January 1993.

Alcohol and alcoholic beverages

Alcoholic beverages are those drinks having more than 22% vol. alcoholic strength. The duty would be fixed per hectolitre of pure alcohol at 20 degrees. The target rate would be fixed at 1398.1 ECU per hectolitre of pure alcohol with a minimum rate of 1118.5 ECU applying from 1 January 1993.

Mineral oils

Harmonisation of excise duties on mineral oils is necessary for a number of reasons concerning wider issues than taxation alone, such as the establishment of common transport and energy policies of the Community. There are major differences in the structure of such taxes throughout the Community which have effects on competition in inter-State trade. Two Commission proposals for directives attempt to establish, first, the harmonisation of the structure of excise duties on mineral oils, such as petrol, diesel and heating oils, and, secondly, the harmonisation of the rates of these duties.

The proposal for a directive on the harmonisation of the structure of excise duties on mineral oils applies to a range of products specified in the directive by reference to their customs classification and also to similar products. Duty would be chargeable on release for consumption or importation and also in certain other cases such as where oils are used for within a production establishment for non-production purposes or as fuel for motor vehicles. Certain exemptions are allowed in relation to, for example, oils used for purposes other than as motor fuels or heating fuels, or oils used for public trains. Member States would be able to determine the exemptions or reductions in the rate of duty on oils used in the process of producing electricity by public utilities, in agriculture, horticulture, forestry and inland fisheries and in the area of local transport.

Under the Commission's proposal for a directive on the approximation of the rates of excise duty on mineral oils, not later than 1 January 1993, Member States would apply excise duty at the following minimum rates with the intention of raising to the stated target rates in due course:

- leaded petrol: 337 ECU per 1,000 litres (target 495 ECU);
- unleaded petrol: 287 ECU per 1,000 litres (target 445 ECU);
- diesel: within the band 195-205 ECU per 1,000 litres (target band 245-270 ECU);
- heating gas oil: within the band 47-53 ECU per 100 litres;
- heavy fuel oil: within the band 16-18 ECU per 1,000 kg;
- liquid petroleum gas and methane used as road fuel: 84.5 ECU per 1,000 litres;
- kerosene used as a propellant: 337 ECU per 1,000 litres (target 495 ECU);
- kerosene used for other purposes: within the band 47-53 ECU per 1,000 litres.

Rates of excise duty pending harmonisation

Pending the adoption of the proposed directives on harmonisation of rates of excise duties, the Commission has issued a proposal for a directive instituting a process of convergence of the rates of excise duty. With the intention that excise duties on only tobacco, alcoholic drink and mineral oils ought to be maintained at a Community level, the Member States would be obliged to refrain from introducing new excise duties or indirect taxes which might give rise, in inter-State trade, to taxation on importation and remission of tax on exportation or to frontier controls. Furthermore, they would have to refrain from increasing the existing rates or enlarging the scope of those excise duties or other indirect taxes. Pending the adoption of harmonising provisions concerning the rates and amounts of excise duty, Member States might alter the rates of excise duty applied to the alcoholic beverages, manufactured tobacco and mineral oils on condition that they moved towards the levels or amounts set out in the proposed directive, which are the same as those which the Commission aims to establish in 1992.

ANNEX

(as at mid-July 1991)

PART ONE: THE REMOVAL OF PHYSICAL BARRIERS

1. CONTROL OF GOODS

1. Various controls

01   COUNCIL REGULATION 2726/90 of 17 September 1990
      on Community transit
      OJ No L 262, 26.9.90, pp. 1–10

02   COUNCIL DIRECTIVE 85/347 of 8 July 1985
      amending Directive 68/297 on the standardization of provisions regarding the duty
      free admission of fuel contained in the fuel tanks of commercial motor vehicles.
      OJ No L 183, 16.7.85, p.22

      Proposals for a Council amending Directive 68/297 on the standardization of pro-
      visions regarding the duty free admission of fuel contained in the fuel tanks of
      commercial motor vehicles – COM (86) 383
      OJ No C 183, 22.7.86, p.8

03   COUNCIL REGULATION 1901/85 of 8 July 1985
      amending Regulation 222/7 on Community transit
      OJ No L 179, 11.7.85, p.6

04   COUNCIL REGULATION 3690/86 of 1 December 1986
      concerning the abolition within the framework of the TIR Convention of customs
      formalities on exit from a Member State at a frontier between two Member States
      OJ No L 341, 4.12.86, p.1

      COUNCIL REGULATION 4283/88 of 21 December 1988
      on the abolition of certain exit formalities at internal Community frontiers – intro-
      duction of common border posts
      OJ No L 382 31.12.88, p.1

      Proposal for Council Regulation repealing Regulations No 3690/86 concerning the
      abolition within the framework of the TIR Convention of customs formalities on
      exit from a Member State at a frontier between two Member States, and No 4283/

88 on the abolition of certain exit formalities at internal Community frontiers – introduction of common border posts – COM(91) 146
OJ No C 143, 1.6.91, p. 11–12

05 COUNCIL REGULATION 1797/86 of 9 June 1986
abolishing certain postal fees for customs presentation
OJ No L 157, 12.6.86, p.1

Amendment to the proposal for Council Regulation on the statistics relating to the trading of goods between Member States – COM(91) 18
OJ No C 47, 23.2.91, p. 10

06 Amended proposal for a Council Regulation on the statistics relating to the trading of goods between Member States – COM (90) 423
OJ NO C 254, 9.10.90, pp. 7–21

07 COUNCIL REGULATION 4060/89 of 21 December 1989
on the elimination of controls performed at the frontiers of Member States in the field of road and inland waterway transport
OJ No L 390, 30.12.89, pp. 18–21

Proposal for a Council Regulation amending Regulation No 4060/89 on the elimination of controls performed at the frontiers of Member States in the field of road and inland waterway transport – COM(91) 105
OJ No C 117, 1.5.91, pp. 6–7

08 COUNCIL REGULATION 717/91 of 21 March 1991 concerning the Single Administrative Document
OJ No L 78, 26.3.91, pp. 1–3

09 Proposal for a Council Directive amending Directive 83/643/EEC of 1 December 1983 on the facilitation of physical inspections and administrative formalities in respect of the carriage of goods between Member States – COM (90) 356
OJ No C 204, 15.8.90, pp. 15–16

10 COUNCIL REGULATION 719/91 of 21 March 1991
on the use in the Community of TIR carnets and ATA carnets as transit documents
OJ No L 78, 26.3.91, pp.6–8

2. Veterinary and phytosanitary controls

01 COUNCIL DECISION 87/58 of 22 December 1986
introducing a supplementary Community measure for the eradication of brucelosis, tuberculosis and leucosis in cattle.
OJ No L 24, 27.1.87, p.51
OJ No L 32, 3.2.87, p.36

02 COUNCIL DECISION 86/649 of 16 December 1986
introducing a Community financial measure for the eradication of African swine fever in Portugal
OJ No L 382, 31.12.86, p.5

03 COUNCIL DECISION 87/230 of 7 April 1987
amending Directive 80/1095 and Decisions 80/1096 and 82/18 with regard to the

duration and financial means of measures for the eradication of classical swine
fever
OJ No L 99, 11.4.87, p.16

COUNCIL DECISION 87/231 of 7 April 1987
amending Directives 64/432 and 72/461 as regards certain measures relating to
swine fever
OJ No L 99, 11.4.87, p.18

COUNCIL DIRECTIVE 87/487 of 22 September 1987
amending Directive 80/217 introducing Community measures for the control of
classical swine fever
OJ No L 280, 3.10.87, p.21

COUNCIL DIRECTIVE 87/487 of 22 September 1987
amending Directive 80/1095 laying down conditions designed to render and keep
the territory of the Community free from classical swine fever
OJ No L 280, 3.10.87, p.24

COUNCIL DECISION 87/488 of 22 September 1987
supplementing and amending Decision 80/1096 introducing Community financial
measures for the eradication of classical swine fever
OJ No L 280, 3.10.87, p.26

COUNCIL DIRECTIVE 87/489 of 22 September 1987
amending Directives 64/432 and 72/461 as regards certain measures relating to
swine fever
OJ No L 280, 3.10.87, p.28

COUNCIL DECISION 90/678 of 13 December 1990
recognizing certain parts of the territory of the Community as being either officially swine fever free or swine fever free
OJ No L 373, 31.12.90, pp.29–33

04   COUNCIL DECISION 86/650 of 16 December 1986
introducing a Community financial measure for the eradication of African swine
fever in Spain
OJ No L 382, 31.12.86, p.9

05   COUNCIL DIRECTIVE 85/397 of 5 August 1985
on health and animal health problems affecting intra Community trade in heat
treated milk
OJ No L 226, 24.8.85, p.13

Proposal for a Council Regulation laying down the health rules for the production
and placing on the market of raw milk, of milk for the manufacture of milk-based
products and of milk-based products – COM(89) 667
OJ No C 84, 2.4.90, pp. 112–120

Proposal for a Council Regulation adopting health rules for the production and
placing on the market of heat-treated drinking milk – COM(89) 672
OJ No C 84 2.4.90, pp. 130–141

06   COUNCIL DIRECTIVE 90/167 of 26 March 1990
     laying down the conditions governing the preparation, placing on the market and
     use of medicated feeding½ stuffs in the Community
     OJ No L 92, 7.4.90, pp. 42–48

07   COUNCIL DIRECTIVE 85/358 of 16 July 1985
     supplementing Directive 81/602 concerning the prohibition of certain substances
     having a hormonal action and of any substances having a thyrostatic action
     OJ No L 191, 23.7.85, p.46

     COUNCIL DIRECTIVE 88/146 of 7 March 1988
     prohibiting the use in livestock farming of certain substances having a hormonal
     action
     OJ No L 70, 16.3.88, pp. 16–18

     Proposal for a Council Directive amending Directives 81/602 and 88/146 in
     respect of the prohibition of certain substances having a hormonal action and of
     substances having a thyrostatic action – COM (89) 136
     OJ No C 99, 20.4.89, p. 13

     Amended proposal for a Council Directive amending Directives 81/602 and 88/
     146 as regards the prohibition of certain substances having a hormonal action and
     any substances having a thyrostatic action – COM (90) 396
     OJ No C 245, 29.9.90, pp. 16–17

08   COUNCIL DIRECTIVE 85/323 of 12 June 1985
     amending Directive 64/433 on health problems affecting intra Community trade
     in fresh meat
     OJ No L 168, 28.6.85, p.43

     COUNCIL DIRECTIVE 85/324 of 12 June 1985
     amending Directive 71/118 on health problems affecting intra Community trade
     in fresh poultrymeat
     OJ No L 168, 28.6.85, p.45

09   Proposal for a Council Decision fixing the weight of uncastrated male pigs
     referred to in Directive 64/433 – COM (83) 655

10   COUNCIL DIRECTIVE 85/325 of 12 June 1985
     amending Directive 64/433 on health problems affecting intra Community trade
     in fresh meat
     OJ No L 168, 28.6.85, p.47

     COUNCIL DIRECTIVE 85/326 of 12 June 1985
     amending Directive 71/118 on health problems affecting intra Community trade
     in fresh poultrymeat
     OJ No L 168, 28.6.85, p.48

     COUNCIL DIRECTIVE 85/327 of 12 June 1985
     amending Directive 77/99 on health problems affecting intra Community trade in
     meat products
     OJ No L 168, 28.6.85, p.49

     COUNCIL DIRECTIVE 85/328 of 20 June 1985

amending Directive 77/99 on health problems affecting intra Community trade in meat products
OJ No L 168, 28.6.85, p.50

11   Proposal for a Council Directive – COM (81) 504
I. amending Directive 71/118 on health problems affecting trade in fresh poultry meat in respect of personnel responsible for carrying out health inspections, supervision and control tasks;
II. concerning the qualifications of the personnel responsible for carrying out health inspection, supervision and control tasks foreseen by Directive 77/99 on health problems affecting intra Community trade in meat products
OJ No C 262, 14.10.81, p.3

12   COUNCIL DIRECTIVE 87/491 of 22 September 1987
amending Directive 80/215 on the animal health problems affecting intra Community trade in meat products
OJ No L 279, 2.10.87, p.27

COUNCIL DIRECTIVE 88/660 of 19 December 1988
amending Directive 80/215 on the animal health problems affecting intra Community trade in meat products
OJ No L 382, 31.12.88, p.35

13   COUNCIL DIRECTIVE 86/469 of 16 September 1986
concerning the examination of animals and fresh meat for the presence of residues
OJ No L 275, 26.9.86, p.36

14   COUNCIL DIRECTIVE 87/328 of 18 June 1987
on the acceptance for breeding purposes of pure bred breeding animals of the bovine species
OJ No L 167, 26.6.87, p.54

15   COUNCIL DIRECTIVE 88/661 of 19 December 1988
on the zootechnical standards applicable to breeding animals of the porcine species
OJ No L 382, 31.12.88, p.36

COUNCIL DIRECTIVE 90/119 of 5 March 1990
on hybrid breeding pigs for breeding
OJ No L 71, 17.3.90, p. 36

COUNCIL DIRECTIVE 90/118 of 5 March 1990
on the acceptance of pure bred breeding pigs for breeding
OJ No L 71, 17.3.90, pp. 34–35

16   COUNCIL DIRECTIVE 89/227 of 21 March 1989
amending Directives 72/462 and 77/99 to take account of the introduction of public health and animal health rules which are to govern imports of meat products from third countries
OJ No L 93, 6.4.89, p.25

17   COUNCIL DIRECTIVE 85/320 of 12 June 1985
amending Directive 64/432 as regards certain measures relating to classical swine fever and African swine fever
OJ No L 168, 28.6.85, p.36

COUNCIL DIRECTIVE 85/321 of 12 June 1985
amending Directive 80/215 as regards certain measures relating to African swine fever
OJ No L 168, 28.6.85, p.39

COUNCIL DIRECTIVE 85/322 of 12 June 1985
amending Directive 72/461 as regards certain measures relating to classical swine fever and African swine fever
OJ No L 168, 28.6.85, p.41

18   COUNCIL DIRECTIVE 85/511 of 18 November 1985
introducing Community measures for the control of foot and mouth disease
OJ No L 315, 26.11.85, p.11

19   Proposals for a Council Directive amending Directives 64/432 and 72/461 as regards certain measures relating to foot and mouth disease, Aujesky's disease and swine vesicular disease – COM (82) 529
OJ No C 249, 23.9.82, p.6

20   COUNCIL DIRECTIVE 88/407 of 14 June 1988
laying down the animal health requirements applicable to intra Community trade in and imports of deep frozen semen of domestic animals of the bovine species
OJ No L 194, 22.7.88, p.10

COUNCIL DIRECTIVE 90/120 of 5 March 1990
amending Directive 88/407 laying down the animal health requirements applicable to intra Community trade in and imports of deep frozen semen of domestic animals of the bovine species
OJ No L 71, 17.3.90, pp. 37–39

COUNCIL DIRECTIVE 90/429 of 26 June 1990
laying down the animal health requirements applicable to intra Community trade in and imports of semen of domestic animals of the porcine species
OJ No L 224, 18.8.90, pp. 62–73

21   COUNCIL DIRECTIVE 91/266 of 21 May 1991
amending Directive 72/461 on health problems affecting intra-Community trade in fresh meat and Directive 73/462 on health and veterinary inspection problems upon importation of bovine, ovine and caprine animals and swine and fresh meat or meat products from third countries
OJ No L 134, 29.5.91, pp. 45–46

22   COUNCIL DIRECTIVE 88/658 of 14 December 1988
amending Directive 77/99 on health problems affecting intra Community trade in meat products
OJ No L 382, 31.12.88, p.15

23   COUNCIL DIRECTIVE 85/173 of 28 February 1985
amending Directive 77/93 on protective measures against the introduction into the Member State of organisms harmful to plants or plant products
OJ No L 65, 6.3.85, p.23

COUNCIL DIRECTIVE 88/572 of 14 November 1988
amending Directive 77/93 on protective measures against the introduction into the

Member States of organisms harmful to plants or plant products
OJ No L 313, 19.11.88, p.39

COUNCIL DIRECTIVE 89/359 of 29 May 1989
amending Directive 77/93/EEC on protective measures against the introduction
into the Member States of organisms harmful to plants or plant products
OJ No L 153, 6.6.89, p.28

COUNCIL DIRECTIVE 89/439 of 26 June 1989
amending Directive 77/93/EEC on protective measures against the introduction
into the Member States of organisms harmful to plants or plant products
OJ No L 212, 22.7.89, p.106

COUNCIL DIRECTIVE 90/168 of 26 March 1990
amending Directive 77/93 on protective measures against the introduction into the
Member States of organisms harmful to plants or plant products
OJ No L 92, 7.4.90, pp. 49–50

Proposal for a Council Directive amending Directive 77/93 on protective measures against the introduction into the Member States of organisms harmful to
plants or plant products – COM(89) 646
OJ No C 29, 8.2.90, pp. 10–16

Proposal for a Council Directive amending Directive 77/93 on protective measures against the introduction into the Member States of organisms harmful to
plants or plant products – COM(89) 647
OJ No C 31, 9.2.90, pp. 8–10

24   COUNCIL DIRECTIVE 87/153 of 16 February 1987
     fixing guidelines for the assessment of additives in animal nutrition
     OJ No L 64, 7.3.87, p.19

25   COUNCIL DIRECTIVE 86/362 of 24 July 1986
     on the fixing of maximum levels for pesticide residues in and on cereals
     OJ No L 221, 7.8.86, p.37

     COUNCIL DIRECTIVE 86/363 of 24 July 1986
     on the fixing of maximum levels for pesticide residues in and on foodstuffs of animal
     origin
     OJ No L 221, 7.8.86, p.43

26   COUNCIL DIRECTIVE 87/519 of 19 October 1987
     amending Directive 74/63 on undesirable substances and products in animal nutrition
     OJ No L 304, 27.10.87, p.38

27   Proposal for a Council Directive to amend the annex of Directive 76/895 concern-
     ing residues of pesticides in and on fruit and vegetables (ethoxyquin and
     diphenylamine) – COM (82) 883

28   COUNCIL DIRECTIVE 86/355 of 21 July 1986
     amending Directive 79/117 prohibiting the placing on the market and use of plant
     protection products containing certain active substances
     OJ No L 212, 2.8.86, p.33

COUNCIL DIRECTIVE 89/365 of 30 May 1989
amending Directive 79/117/EEC prohibiting the placing on the market and use of
plant protection products containing certain active substances
OJ No L 159, 10.6.89, p.58

29   Amended proposal for a Council Directive concerning the placing of EEC
accepted plant protection products on the market – COM (89) 34
OJ No C 89, 10.4.89, p.22

Second amendment to the proposal for a Council Directive concerning the placing
of EEC-accepted plant protection products on the market – COM(91) 87
OJ No C 93, 11.4.91, pp.7–11

30   COUNCIL DIRECTIVE 88/380 of 13 June 1988
amending Directives 66/400, 66/401, 66/402, 66/403, 69/208, 70/457, 70/458 on
the marketing of beet seed, fodder plant seed, cereal seed, seed potatoes, seed of
oil and fibre plants and vegetable seed and on the common catalogue of varieties
of agricultural plant species
OJ No L 187, 16.7.88, p.31

COUNCIL DIRECTIVE 89/366 of 30 May 1989
amending Directive 66/403/EEC on the marketing of seed potatoes
OJ No L 159, 10.6.89, p.59

31   COUNCIL DIRECTIVE 89/437 of 20 June 1989
on hygiene and health problems affecting the production and the placing on the
market of egg products
OJ No L 212, 22.7.89, p.87

32   COUNCIL DIRECTIVE 88/288 of 3 May 1988
amending Directive 64/433 on health problems affecting intra Community trade
in fresh meat
OJ No L 124, 18.5.88, p.28

33   COUNCIL DIRECTIVE 88/289 of 3 May 1988
amending Directive 72/462 on health and veterinary inspection problems upon
importation of bovine animals and swine and fresh meat from third countries
OJ No L 124, 18.5.88, p.31
OJ No L 189, 20.7.88, p.28

34   COUNCIL DIRECTIVE 88/657 of 14 December 1988
laying down the requirements for the production of, and trade in, minced meat,
meat in pieces of less than 100 grams and meat preparations and amending Directives 64/433/EEC, 71/118/EEC and 72/462
OJ No L 382, 31.12.88, p.3

Proposal for a Council Regulation laying down the health rules for the production
and placing on the market of minced meat, meat preparations and comminuted
meat for industrial use – COM(89) 671
OJ No C 84, 2.4.90, pp. 120–130

35   COUNCIL DIRECTIVE 89/662 of 11 December 1989
concerning veterinary checks in intra Community trade with a view to the com-

pletion of the internal market
OJ No L 395, 30.12.89, pp. 13–22

36   Proposals for a Council Regulation on intensifying controls on the application of
      the veterinary rules – COM (88) 383
      OJ O 225, 31.8.88, p.9

      COUNCIL DIRECTIVE 90/425 of 26 June 1990
      concerning veterinary and zootechnical checks applicable in intra Community
      trade in certain live animals and products with a view to the completion of the
      internal market
      OJ No L 224, 18.8.90, pp. 29–41

37   COUNCIL DIRECTIVE 89/608 of 21 November 1989
      on mutual assistance between the administrative authorities of the Member States
      and cooperation between the latter and the Commission to ensure the correct
      application of legislation on veterinary and zootechnical matters
      OJ No L 351, 2.12.89, pp. 34–37

38   Proposal for a Council Regulation (EEC) laying down zootechnical and pedigree
      requirements for the marketing of purebred animals – COM (88) 598
      OJ No C 304, 29.11.88, p.6

39   COUNCIL DIRECTIVE 91/68 of 28 January 1991
      on animal health conditions governing intra-Community trade in ovine and
      caprine animals
      OJ No L 46, 19.2.91, pp.19–36

40   COUNCIL DIRECTIVE 91/69 of 28 January 1991
      amending Directive 72/462 on health and veterinary inspection problems upon
      importation of bovine animals and swine, fresh meat or meat products from third
      countries, in order to include ovine and caprine animals
      OJ No L 46, 19.2.91, pp. 37–39

41   COUNCIL DIRECTIVE 90/642 of 27 November 1990
      on the fixing of maximum levels for pesticide residues in and on certain products
      of plant origin, including fruit and vegetables
      OJ No L 350, 14.12.90, p.71–79

42   COUNCIL DECISION 89/145 of 20 February 1989
      introducing a Community financial measure for the eradication of contagious
      bovine pleuropneumonia (CBPP) in Portugal
      OJ No L 53, 25.2.89, p.55

43   Proposal for a Council Regulation instituting a certificate for cats and dogs on visits
      of less than one year in the Member States and introducing Community measures
      to set up pilot projects for the control and eradication of rabies – COM (88) 836
      OJ No C 85, 6.4.89, p.8

      COUNCIL DIRECTIVE 89/455 of 24 July 1989
      introducing Community measures to set up pilot projects for the control of rabies
      with a view to its eradiction or prevention
      OJ No L 223, 2.8.89, pp. 19–21

44   COUNCIL DIRECTIVE 89/556 of 25 September 1989
       on animal health conditions governing intra-Community trade in and importation
       from third countries of embryos of domestic animals of the bovine species
       OJ No L 302, 19.10.89, pp. 1–11

45   COUNCIL DIRECTIVE 90/539 of 15 October 1990
       on animal health conditions governing intra Community trade in, and imports
       from third countries of, poultry and hatching eggs
       OJ No L 303, 31.10.90, pp. 6–28

46   Proposal for a Council Regulation laying down health conditions for the market-
       ing of fish and fish products concerning nematodes – COM (89) 47
       OJ No C 66, 11.3.88, p.2

       Amendment to the proposal for a Council Regulation laying down health con-
       ditions for the marketing of fish and fish products concerning nematodes – COM
       (89) 428
       OJ No C 282, 8.11.89, pp. 7–9

47   Proposal for a Council Directive amending Directive 66/403 on the marketing of
       seed potatoes – COM (89) 70
       OJ No C 79, 30.3.89, p.6

48   COUNCIL DIRECTIVE 89/361 of 30 May 1989
       concerning pure bred breeding sheep and goats
       OJ No L 153, 6.6.89, p.30

49   COUNCIL DECISION 87/590 of 14 December 1987
       relating to a research and development programme in the field of science and tech-
       nology for development (1987–1991)
       OJ No L 355, 17.12.87, p.41

50   Proposal for a Council Regulation laying down health rules for the production and
       placing on the market of melted animal fat, greaves and by products of rendering
       for human consumption – COM (89) 490
       OJ No C 327, 30.12.89, pp. 25–28

51   Proposal for a Council Regulation laying down general health rules for the pro-
       duction and placing on the market of products of animal origin and specific health
       rules for certain products of animal origin – COM (89) 492
       OJ No C 327, 30.12.89, pp. 29–37

52   Proposal for a Council Decision concerning safeguard measures in the veterran
       field in the framework of the internal market – COM (89) 493
       OJ No C 327, 30.12.89, pp. 37–39

       Amendment to the proposal for a Council Decision concerning safeguard meas-
       ures in the veterinary field in the framework of the internal market – COM (90)
       479
       OJ No C 268, 24.10.90, p. 13

53   Proposal for a Council Directive amending Directive 88/407 laying down the animal
       health requirements applicable to intra Community trade in and imports of deep
       frozen semen of domestic animals of the bovine species – COM (89) 495
       OJ No C 327, 30.12.89, pp. 39–40

54   Proposal for a Council Regulation concerning game meat and rabbit meat – COM
     (89) 496
     OJ No C 327, 30.12.89, pp. 40–51

55   Proposal for a Council Decision introducing a Community measure for the
     eradication
     of brucellosis in sheep and goats – COM (89) 498
     OJ No C 327, 30.12.89, pp. 51–54

56   Proposal for a Council Decision on financial aid from the Community for the
     eradication
     of African swine fever in Sardinia – COM (89) 499
     OJ No C 327, 30.12.89, pp. 54–57

57   Proposal for a Council Regulation on animal health conditions governing the
     replacing
     of rodents on the market in the Community – COM (89) 500
     OJ No C 327, 30.12.89, pp. 57–58

58   Proposal for a Council Decision introducing a Community financial measure for
     the eradication of infectious haemopietic necrosis of salmonids in the Community
     – COM (89) 502
     OJ No C 327, 30.12.89, pp. 59–60

     Amendment to a proposal for a Council Decision introducing a Community finan-
     cial measure for the eradication of infectious haemopoietic necrosis of salmonids in
     the Community – COM (90) 222
     OJ No C 165, 6.7.90, p.4

59   COUNCIL DIRECTIVE 90/426 of 26 June 1990 on animal health conditions
     governing the movement and import from third countries of equidae
     OJ No L 224, 18.8.90, pp. 42–54

     COUNCIL DIRECTIVE 90/427 of 26 June 1990
     on the zootechnical and genealogical conditions governing intra Community trade
     in equidae
     OJ No L 224, 18.8.90, pp. 55–59

     COUNCIL DIRECTIVE 90/428 of 26 June 1990
     on trade in equidae intended for competitions and laying down the conditions for
     participation therein
     OJ No L 224, 18.8.90, pp. 60–61

60   Proposal for a Council Regulation on animal health conditions governing intra
     Community trade and imports from third countries of fresh poultrymeat and fresh
     meat of reared game birds – COM (89) 507
     OJ No C 327, 30.12.89, pp. 72–76

61   COUNCIL DIRECTIVE 90/667 of 27 November 1990
     laying down the veterinary rules for the disposal and processing of animal waste,
     for its placing on the market and for the prevention of pathogens in feedstuffs of
     animal or fish origin and amending Directive 90/425
     OJ No L 363, 27.12.90, pp. 51–60

62   COUNCIL DIRECTIVE 90/423 of 26 June 1990
amending Directive 85/511 introducing Community measures for the control of
foot and mouth disease, Directive 64/432 on animal health problems affecting
intra Community trade in bovine animals and swine and Directive 72/462 on
health and veterinary inspection problems upon importation of bovine animals and
swine and fresh meat or meat products from third countries
OJ No L 224, 18.8.90, pp. 13–18

63   Proposal for a Council Regulation on the marketing of fruit plant propagating
material and fruit plants intended for fruit production – COM (89) 651
OJ No C 54, 6.3.90, pp. 5–13

64   Proposal for a Council Regulation laying down the health rules for the production
and placing on the market of meat product – COM (89) 669
OJ No C 84, 2.4.90, pp. 89–100

65   Proposal for a Council Regulation laying down health rules for the production and
placing on the market of fresh poultrymeat – COM (89) 668
OJ No C 84, 2.4.90, pp. 71–88

66   Proposal for a Council Regulation laying down the health conditions to the production and the placing on the market of fishery products – COM (89) 645
OJ No C 84, 2.4.90, pp. 58–70

67   COUNCIL DIRECTIVE 91/67 of 28 January 1991
concerning the animal health conditions governing the placing on the market of
aquaculture animals and products
OJ No L 46, 19.2.91, pp. 1–18

68   Proposal for a Council Regulation laying down the health conditions for the production and the placing on the market of live bivalve molluscs – COM (89) 648
OJ No C 84, 2.4.90, pp. 29–42

69   Proposal for a Council Regulation laying down health rules for the production and
placing on the market of fresh meat – COM (89) 673
OJ No C 84, 2.4.90, pp. 8–28

70   COUNCIL DECISION 90/424 of 26 June 1990
on expenditure in the veterinary fields
OJ No L 224, 18.8.90, pp. 19–28

Corrigendum to Council Decision 90/424 of 26 June 1990 on expenditure in the
veterinary field
OJ No L 304, 1.11.90, p.99

COUNCIL DECISION 91/133 of 4 March 1991
amending Decision 90/424 on expenditure in the veterinary field
OJ No L 66, 13.3.91, p. 18

71   COUNCIL DIRECTIVE 90/675 of 10 December 1990
laying down the principles governing the organization of veterinary checks on
products entering the community from third countries
OJ No L 373, 31.12.90, pp. 1–14

72   COUNCIL DECISION 90/638 of 27 November 1990
        laying down Community criteria for the eradication and monitoring of certain animal
        diseases
        OJ No L 347, 12.12.90, pp. 27–29

73   COUNCIL DIRECTIVE 90/422 of 26 June 1990
        amending Directive 64/432 as regards enzootic bovine leukosis
        OJ No L 224, 18.8.90, pp. 9–12

74   Proposal for a Council Directive amending Directive 64/432 as regards the diag-
        nosis of bovine brucellosis and enzootic bovine leukosis – COM (90) 492
        OJ No C 300, 29.11.90, pp. 10–12

75   Proposal for Council Regulation laying down the principles governing the organ-
        ization of veterinary checks on animals entering the Community from third
        countries – COM(91) 75
        OJ No C 89, 6.4.91, pp.5–12

76   Proposal for a Council Regulation on organic production of agricultural products
        and indications referring thereto on agricultural products and foodstuffs –
        COM(89) 552
        OJ No C 4, 9.1.90, pp. 4–13

77   Proposal for a Council Regulation on the marketing of young plants and propagat-
        ing material other than seeds, of vegetables – COM(89) 649
        OJ No C 46, 27.2.90, pp. 4–13

78   Proposal for a Council Regulation on the marketing of ornamental plant propagat-
        ing material and ornamental plants – COM(89) 650
        OJ No C 52, 3.3.90, pp. 16–24

79   Proposal for a Council Regulation laying down animal health requirements for the
        placing on the market in the Community of animals and products of animal origin
        not covered in this respect by specific Community rules – COM(89) 658
        OJ No C 84, 2.4.90, pp. 102–112

II.   CONTROL OF INDIVIDUALS

01   COUNCIL DIRECTIVE 85/348 of 8 July 1985
        amending Directive 69/169 on the harmonization of provisions laid down by law,
        regulation or administrative action relating to exemption from turnover tax and
        excise duty on imports in international travel
        OJ No L 183, 16.7.85, p.24

        COUNCIL DIRECTIVE 87/198 of 16 March 1987
        amending Directive 69/169 on the harmonization of provisions laid down by law,
        regulation or administrative action relating to exemption from turnover tax and
        excise duty on imports in international travel
        OJ No L 78, 20.3.87, p.53

        COUNCIL DIRECTIVE 88/664 of 21 December 1988
        amending Directive 69/169 on the harmonization of provisions laid down by law,

regulation or administrative action relation to exemption from turnover tax and excise duty on imports in international travel
OJ No L 382, 31.12.88, p.41

COUNCIL DIRECTIVE 89/194 of 13 March 1989
amending Directive 69/169 as regards a derogation granted to the Kingdom of Denmark relating to the rules governing travellers' allowances on imports
OJ No L 73, 17.3.89, p.47

COUNCIL DIRECTIVE 91/191 of 27 March 1991
amending Directive 69/169/EEC on tax-paid allowances in intra-Community travel and as regards a derogation granted to the Kingdom of Denmark and to Ireland relating to the rules governing travellers' allowances on imports
OJ No L 94, 16.4.91, pp.24–25

02   COUNCIL DIRECTIVE 85/349 of 8 July 1985
amending Directive 74/651 on the tax reliefs to be allowed on the importation of goods in small consignments of a non commercial character within the Community
OJ No L 183, 16.7.85, p.27

COUNCIL DIRECTIVE 88/663 of 21 December 1988
amending Directive 74/651 on the tax reliefs to be allowed on the importation of goods in small consignments of a non commercial character within the Community
OJ No L 382, 31.12.88, p.40

03   COUNCIL DIRECTIVE 88/331 of 13 June 1988
amending Directive 83/181 determining the scope of Article 14(1)(d) of Directive 77/388 as regards exemption from value added tax on the final importation of certain goods
OJ No L 151, 17.6.88, p.79

04   Proposal for a Council Directive on the easing of controls and formalities applicable to nationals of the Member States when crossing intra Community borders - COM (84) 749
OJ No C 47, 19.2.85, p.5
Amendment to the proposal - COM (85) 224
OJ No C 131, 30.5.85, p.5

05   Amended proposal for a Council Directive on control of the acquisition and possession of weapons - COM (90) 453
OJ No C 265, 20.10.90, pp. 6-13

06   COUNCIL DIRECTIVE 89/604 of 23 November 1989
amending Directive 83/183 on tax exemptions applicable to permanent imports from a Member State of the personal property of individuals
OJ No L 348, 29.11.89, pp. 28-29

07   Proposal for a Council Directive amending Directive 83/182 on tax exemptions within the Community for certain means of transport temporarily imported into one Member State from another - COM (87) 14
OJ No C 40, 18.2.87, p.7

Amended proposal - COM (88) 297
OJ No C 184, 14.7.88, p.9

PART TWO: THE REMOVAL OF TECHNICAL BARRIERS

I.   FREE MOVEMENT OF GOODS

1.   New approach in technical harmonization and standards policy

01   COUNCIL DIRECTIVE 88/182 of 22 March 1988
     amending Directive 83/189 laying down a procedure for the provision of informa-
     tion in the field of technical standards and regulations
     OJ No L 81, 26.3.88, p.75

02   COUNCIL DIRECTIVE 89/392 of 14 June 1989
     on the approximation of the laws of the Member States relating to machinery
     OJ No L 183, 29.6.89, p.9

     Proposal for a Council Directive amending Directive 89/392 on the approxima-
     tion of the laws of the Member States relating to machinery – COM (89) 624
     OJ No C 37, 17.2.90, pp. 5–18

     Amendment to the proposal for a Council Directive amending Directive 89/392
     on the approximation of the laws of the Member States relating to machinery –
     COM (90) 462
     OJ No C 268, 24.10.90, p.12

03   COUNCIL DIRECTIVE 87/404 of 25 June 1987
     on the harmonization of the laws of the Member States relating to simple pressure
     vessels
     OJ No L 220, 8.8.87, p.48

04   COUNCIL DIRECTIVE 89/686 of 21 December 1989
     on the approximation of the laws of the Member States relating to personal protec-
     tive equipment
     OJ No L 399, 30.12.89, pp. 18–38

     Amendment to the proposal for a Council Directive on the approximation of the
     laws of the Member States relating to personal protective equipment – COM (89)
     177
     OJ No C 142, 8.6.89, p.7

     Re–examined proposal for a Council Directive concerning the approximation of
     the laws of the Member States relating to personal protective equipment – COM
     (89) 586
     OJ No C 318, 20.12.89, p.21

05   COUNCIL DIRECTIVE 88/378 of 3 May 1988
     on the approximation of the laws of the Member States concerning the safety of
     toys
     OJ No L 187, 16.7.88, p.1
     OJ No L 281, 14.10.88, p.55

06   COUNCIL DIRECTIVE 89/336 of 3 May 1989
     on the approximation of the laws of the Member States relating to electromagnetic
     compatibility
     OJ No L 139, 23.5.89, p.19

Proposal for a Council Directive amending Council Directive 89/336 of 3 May 1989 on the harmonization of the laws of the Member States relating to electromagnetic compatibility – COM(91) 126
OJ No C 162, 21.6.91, p. 7

07   COUNCIL DIRECTIVE 90/385 of 20 June 1990
on the approximation of the laws of the Member States relating to active implantable medical devices
OJ No L 189, 20.7.90, pp. 17–36

08   COUNCIL DIRECTIVE 90/396 of 29 June 1990
on the approximation of the laws of the Member States relating to appliances burning gaseous fuels
OJ No L 196, 26.7.90, pp. 15–29

Proposal for a Council Directive concerning the efficiency requirements for new, hot-water boilers fired with liquid or gaseous fuels
OJ No C 292, 22.11.90, pp. 8–11–COM (90) 368

09   Proposal for a Council Directive on the approximation of the laws of the Member States on mobile machinery – COM (88) 740
OJ No C 70, 20.3.89, p.6

10   COUNCIL DIRECTIVE 90/384 of 20 June 1990
on the harmonization of the laws of the Member States relating to non-automatic weighing instruments
OJ No L 189, 20.7.90, pp. 1–16

11   COUNCIL DECISION 90/683 of 13 December 1990
concerning the modules for the various phases of the conformity assessment which are intended to be used in the technical harmonization directives
OJ No L 380, 31.12.90, pp. 13–26

12   Proposal for a Council Directive amending Directive 87/404 on the harmonization of the laws of the Member States relating to simple pressure vessels – COM (89) 636
OJ No C 13, 19.1.90, p.7

13   Proposal for a Council Regulation concerning the affixing and use of the CE mark of conformity on industrial products – COM(91) 145
OJ No C 160, 20.6.91, pp. 14–17

2.   Sectoral proposals concerning approximation of laws

2.1   Motor vehicles

01   COUNCIL DIRECTIVE 88/76 of 3 December 1987
amending Directive 70/220 on the approximation of the laws of the Member States relating to measures to be taken against air pollution by gases from the engines of motor vehicles
OJ No L 36, 9.2.88, p.1

Proposal for a Council Directive amending Directive 70/220 on the approxima-

tion of the laws of the Member States to the measures to be taken against air pollution by emissions from motor vehicles – COM (89) 662
OJ No C 81, 30.3.90, pp. 1–110

Amendment to the proposal for a Council Directive amending Directive 70/220 (1) on the approximation of the laws of the Member States relating to measures to be taken against air pollution by emissions from motor vehicles (2) – COM (90) 493
OJ No C 281, 9.11.90, pp. 9–11

02 COUNCIL DIRECTIVE 88/77 of 3 December 1987
on the approximation of the laws of the Member States relating to the measures to be taken against the emission of gaseous pollutants from diesel engines for use in vehicles
OJ No L36, 9.2.88, p.33

Proposal for a Council Directive amending Directive 88/77 on the approximation of the laws of the Member States relating to the measures to be taken against the emission of gaseous pollutants from diesel engines for use in vehicles – COM (90) 174
OJ No C 187, 27.7.90, pp. 6–23

03 COUNCIL DIRECTIVE 88/436 of 16 June 1988
amending Directive 70/220 on the approximation of the laws of the Member States relating to measures to be taken against air pollution by gases from engines of motor vehicles (restriction of particulate pollutant emissions from diesel engines)
OJ No L 214, 6.8.88, p.1
OJ No L 303, 8.11.88, p.36

04 COUNCIL DIRECTIVE 87/358 of 25 June 1987
amending Directive 70/156 on the approximation of the laws of the Member States relating to the type½approval of motor vehicles and their trailers
OJ No L 192, 11.7.87, p.51

05 COUNCIL DIRECTIVE 89/235 of 13 March 1989
amending Directive 78/1015 on the approximation of the laws of the Member States on the permissible sound level and exhaust systems of motorcycles
OJ No L 98. 11.4.89, p.1

06 Proposal for a Council Directive on safety glass for use in motor vehicles – COM (72) 981
JO No C 119, 16.11.72, p.21

07 Proposal for a Council Directive on the approximation of the laws of the Member States relating to the weights and dimensions of certain motor vehicles – COM (76) 701
OJ No C 15, 20.1.77, p.4

08 Proposal for a Council Directive on the approximation of the laws of the Member States relating to tyres for motor vehicles and their trailers – COM (76) 712
OJ No C 37, 14.2.77, p.1

09 COUNCIL DIRECTIVE 89/458 of 18 July 1989
amending with regard to European emission standards for cars below 1.4 litres,
Directive 70/220 on the approximation of the laws of the Member States relating
to measures to be taken against air pollution by emissions from motor vehicles
OJ No L 226, 3.8.89, p.1

10 COUNCIL DIRECTIVE 89/297 of 13 April 1989
on the approximation of the laws of the Member States relating to the lateral protection (side guards) of certain motor vehicles and their trailers
OJ No L 124, 5.5.89, p.1

11 COUNCIL DIRECTIVE 89/459 of 18 July 1989
on the approximation of the laws of the Member States relating to the tread depth
of tyres of certain categories of motor vehicles and their trailers
OJ No L 226, 3.8.89, p.4

12 Proposal for a Council Directive on pneumatic tyres for motor vehicles and their
trailers – COM (89) 653
OJ No C 95, 12.4.90, pp. 101–127

Amendment – COM(91) 38
OJ No C 51, 27.2.91, p.9

13 Proposal for a Council Directive on the masses and dimensions of motor vehicles
of category M, – COM (89) 453
OJ No C 95, 12.4.90, pp. 92–100

Amendment – COM(91) 38
OJ No C 51, 27.2.91, p.9

14 Proposal for a Council Directive on safety glazing and glazing materials on motor
vehicles and their trailers – COM (89) 653
OJ No C 95, 12.4.90, pp. 1–92

Amendment – COM(91) 38
OJ No C 51, 27.2.91, p.9

15 Proposal for a Council Regulation on the type-approval of two or three-wheel
motor vehicles COM(90) 669
OJ No C 110, 25.4.91, pp.3–30

2.2 Tractors and agricultural machines

1 COUNCIL DIRECTIVE 89/173 of 21 December 1988
on the approximation of the laws of the Member States relating to certain components and characteristics of wheeled agricultural or forestry tractors
OJ No L 67, 10.3.89, p. 1

02 COUNCIL DIRECTIVE 88/297 of 3 May 1988
amending Directive 74/150 on the approximation of the laws of the Member
States relating to the type-approval of wheeled agricultural or forestry tractors
OJ No L 126, 20.5.88, p. 52

03 COUNCIL DIRECTIVE 87/402 of 25 June 1987

on roll-over protection structures mounted in front of the driver's seat on narrow-track wheeled agricultural and forestry tractors
OJ No L 220, 8.8.87, p.1

2.3   Food law

01   COUNCIL DIRECTIVE 89/107 of 21 December 1988
on the approximation of the laws of the Member States concerning food additives authorized for use in foodstuffs intended for human consumption
OJ No L 40, 11.2.89, p.27

02   COUNCIL DIRECTIVE 89/109 of 21 December 1988
on the approximation of the laws of the Member States relating to materials and articles intended to come into contact with foodstuffs
OJ No L 40, 11.2.89, p.38

03   COUNCIL DIRECTIVE 89/398 of 3 May 1989
on the approximation of the laws of the Member States relating to foodstuffs intended for particular nutritional uses
OJ No L 186, 30.6.89, p.27

04   Proposal for a Council Directive amending Directive 79/112 on the approximation of the laws of the Member States relating to the labelling, presentation and advertising of foodstuffs for sale to the ultimate consumer – COM (86) 89
OJ No C 124, 23.5.86, p.5

Amended proposal – COM (87) 242
OJ No C 154, 12.6.87, p.10

05   COUNCIL DIRECTIVE 89/397 of 14 June 1989
on the official control of foodstuffs
OJ No L 186, 30.6.89, p.23

06   COUNCIL DIRECTIVE 85/591 of 20 December 1985
concerning the introduction of Community methods of sampling and analysis for the monitoring of foodstuffs intended for human consumption
OJ No L 372, 31.12.85, p.50

07   COUNCIL DIRECTIVE 89/108 of 21 December 1988
on the approximation of the laws of the Member States relating to quick frozen foodstuffs for human consumption
OJ No L 40, 11.2.89, p.34

08   COUNCIL DIRECTIVE 88/388 of 22 June 1988
on the approximation of the laws of the Member States relating to flavourings for use in foodstuffs and to source materials for their production
OJ No L 184, 15.7.88, p.61

Corrigendum
OJ No L 345, 14.12.88, p.29

COMMISSION DIRECTIVE 91/71 of 16 January 1991
completing Council Directive 88/388/EEC on the approximation of the laws of

the Member States relating to flavourings for use in foodstuffs and to source materials
for their production
OJ No L 42, 15.2.91, pp.25–26

COUNCIL DECISION 88/389 of 22 June 1988
on the establishment, by the Commission, of an inventory of the source materials
and substances used in the preparation of flavourings
OJ No L 184, 15.7.88, p.67

09   COUNCIL DIRECTIVE 88/344 of 13 June 1988
on the approximation of the laws of the Member States on extraction solvents used
in the production of foodstuffs and food ingredients
OJ No L 157, 24.6.88, p.28

10   COUNCIL DIRECTIVE 85/585 of 20 December 1985
amending Directive 64/54 on the approximation of the laws of the Member States
concerning the preservatives authorised for use in foodstuffs intended for human
consumption
OJ No L 372, 31.12.85, p.43

Proposal for a Council Directive amending Directive 64/54 on the approximation
of the laws of the Member States concerning the preservatives authorized for use
in foodstuffs intended for human consumption – COM (81) 712
OJ No C 330, 17.12.81, p.7

11   COUNCIL DIRECTIVE 86/102 of 24 March 1986
amending for the fourth time Directive 74/329 on the approximation of the laws
of the Member States relating to emulsifiers, stabilizers, thickeners and gelling
agents for use in foodstuffs
OJ No L 88, 3.4.86, p.40

COUNCIL DIRECTIVE 89/393 of 14 June 1989
amending for the fifth time Directive 74/329/EEC on the approximation of the
laws of the Member States relating to emulsifiers, stabilizers, thickeners and
gelling agents for use in foodstuffs
OJ No L 186, 30.6.89, p.13

12   Proposal for a Council Directive on the approximation of the laws of the Member
States relating to infant formulae and follow up milks – COM (84) 703
OJ No C 28, 30.1.85, p.3

Modified proposal – COM (86) 564
OJ No C 285, 12.11.86, p.5

13   COUNCIL DIRECTIVE 85/573 of 19 December 1985
amending Directive 77/436 on the approximation of the laws of the Member
States relating to coffee extracts and chicory extracts
OJ No L 372, 31.12.85, p.22

14   COUNCIL DIRECTIVE 86/197 of 26 May 1986
amending Directive 79/112 on the approximation of the laws of the Member
States relating to the labelling, presentation and advertising of foodstuffs for sale to
the ultimate consumer
OJ No L 144, 29.5.86, p.38

COUNCIL DIRECTIVE 89/395 of 14 June 1989
amending Directive 79/112/EEC on the approximation of the laws of the Member
States relating to labelling, presentation and advertising of foodstuffs for sale to the
ultimate consumer
OJ No L 186, 30.6.89, p.17

15   COUNCIL DIRECTIVE 85/572 of 19 December 1985
     laying down the list of stimulants to be used for testing migration of constituents of
     plastic materials and articles intended to come into contact with foodstuffs
     OJ No L 372, 31.12.85, p.14

16   Proposal for a Council Directive on the approximation of the laws of the Member
     States relating to modified starches intended for human consumption – COM (84)
     726
     OJ No C 31, 1.2.85, p.6

17   COUNCIL DIRECTIVE 89/394 of 14 June 1989
     amending for the third time Directive 75/726 on the approximation of the laws of
     the Member States concerning fruit juices and certain similar products
     OJ No L 186, 30.6.89, p.14

18   COUNCIL DIRECTIVE 88/593 of 18 November 1988
     amending Directive 79/693 on the approximation of the laws of the Member
     States relating to fruit jams, jellies and marmalades and chestnut puree
     OJ No L 318, 25.11.88, p.44

19   COUNCIL REGULATION 1576/89 of 29 May 1989
     laying down general rules on the definition, description and presentation of spirit
     drinks
     OJ No L 160, 12.6.89, p.1
     OJ No L 223, 2.8.89, p.27

     Amended proposal – vermouths and other wines of fresh grapes flavoured with
     plants or other aromatic substances – COM (86) 159
     OJ No C 269, 25.10.86, pp. 15–20

20   COUNCIL DIRECTIVE 90/496 of 24 September 1990
     on nutrition labelling for foodstuffs
     OJ No L 276, 6.10.90, pp. 40–44

21   Proposal for a Council Directive on the approximation of the laws of the Member
     States concerning foods and food ingredients treated with ionizing radiation –
     COM (88) 654
     OJ No C 336, 31.12.88, p.7

     Amendment to the proposal for a Council Directive on the approximation of the
     laws of the Member States concerning foods and food ingredients treated with ion-
     izing radiation – COM (89) 576
     OJ No C 303, 2.12.89, pp. 15–16

22   COUNCIL DIRECTIVE 89/396 of 14 June 1989
     on indications or marks identifying the lot to which a foodstuff belongs
     OJ No L 186, 30.6.89, p.21

COUNCIL DIRECTIVE 91/238 of 22 April 1991
amending Directive 89/396 on indications or marks identifying the lot to which a foodstuff belongs
OJ No L 107, 27.4.91, p. 50

23 Proposal for a Council Directive on sweeteners for use in foodstuffs – COM(90) 381
OJ No C 242, 27.9.90, pp. 4–14

Amended proposal for a Council Directive on sweeteners for use in foodstuffs – COM(91) 195
OJ No C 175, 6.7.91, pp. 6–7

2.4   Pharmaceuticals and high-technology medicines

01 COUNCIL DIRECTIVE 87/22 of 22 December 1986
on the approximation of national measures relating to the placing on the market of high-technology medicinal products, particularly those derived from biotechnology
OJ No L 15, 17.1.87, p. 38

02 COUNCIL DIRECTIVE 87/19 of 22 December 1986
amending Directive 75/318 on the approximation of the laws of the Member States relating to analytical, pharmacotoxicological and clinical standards and protocols in respect of the testing of proprietary medicinal products
OJ No L 15, 17.1.87, p. 31.
OJ No L 32, 3.2.87, p. 36

03 COUNCIL DIRECTIVE 87/20 of 22 December 1986
amending Directive 81/852 on the approximation of the laws of the Member States relating to analytical, pharmacotoxicological and clinical standards and protocols in respect of the testing of veterinary medicinal products
OJ No L 15, 17.1.87, p. 34

04 COUNCIL RECOMMENDATION 87/176 of 9 February 1987
concerning tests relating to the placing on the market of proprietary medicinal products
OJ No L 73, 16.3.87, p. 1

05 COUNCIL DIRECTIVE 87/21 of 22 December 1986
amending Directive 65/65 on the approximation of provisions laid down by law, regulation or administrative action relating to proprietary medicinal products
OJ No L 15, 17.1.87, p. 36

06 COUNCIL DIRECTIVE 89/105 of 21 December 1988
relating to the transparency of measure regulating the pricing of medicinal products for human use and their inclusion in the scope of national health insurance systems
OJ No L 50, 11.2.89, p. 8

07 COUNCIL DIRECTIVE 89/341 of 3 May 1989
amending Directives 65/65/EEC, 75/318/EEC and 75/319/EEC on the approximation of provisions laid down by law, regulation and administrative action relat-

ing to proprietary medicinal products
OJ No L 142, 25.5.89, p. 11

COUNCIL DIRECTIVE 89/342 of 3 May 1989
extending the scope of Directives 65/65/EEC and 75/319/EEC and laying down
additional provisions for immunological medicinal products consisting of vaccines,
toxins or serums and allergens
OJ No L 142, 25.5.89, p. 14

COUNCIL DIRECTIVE 89/381 of 14 June 1989
extending the scope of Directives 65/65/EEC and 75/319/EEC on the approximation of provisions laid down by law, regulation or administrative action relating to
proprietary medicinal products and laying down special provisions for medicinal
products derived from human blood or human plasma
OJ No L 181, 28.6.89, p. 44.

COUNCIL DIRECTIVE 89/343 of 3 May 1989
extending the scope of Directives 65/65/EEC and 75/319/EEC and laying down
additional provisions for radiopharmaceuticals
OJ No L 142, 25.5.89, p. 16

08   Proposal for a Council Regulation laying down a Community procedure for the
establishment of tolerances for residues of veterinary medicinal products – COM
(88) 779
OJ No C 61, 10.3.89, p. 11

Amendment to the proposal for a Council Regulation laying down a Community
procedure for the establishment of tolerances for residues of veterinary medicinal
products – COM (90) 135
OJ No C 131, 30.5.90, pp. 14–16

COUNCIL DIRECTIVE 90/677 of 13 December 1990
extending the scope of Directive 81/851 on the approximation of the laws of the
Member States relating to veterinary medicinal products and laying down additional provisions for the immunological veterinary medicinal products
OJ No L 373, 31.12.90, pp. 26–28

COUNCIL DIRECTIVE 90/676 of 13 December 1990
amending Directive 81/851 on the approximation of the laws of the Member
States relating to veterinary medicinal products
OJ No L 373, 31.12.90, pp. 15–25

09   Proposal for Council Directive on the wholesale distribution of medicinal products for human use – COM (89) 607
OJ No C 58, 8.3.90, pp. 16–18

Proposal for a Council Directive widening the scope of Directives 65/65 and 75/
319 on the approximation of the laws of the Member States on medicinal products
and laying down additional provisions on homeopathic medicinal products –
COM (90) 72
OJ No C 108, 1.5.90, pp. 10–12

Proposal for a Council Directive widening the scope of Directive 81/851 on the

approximation of the laws of the Member States on veterinary medicinal products and laying down additional provisions on homeopathic veterinary medicinal products – COM (90) 72
OJ No C 108, 1.5.90, pp. 13–15

10   Proposal for a Council Directive on the labelling of medicinal products for human use and on package leaflets – COM (89) 608
OJ No C 58, 8.3.90, pp. 21–25

Proposal for a Council Regulation concerning the creation of a supplementary protection certificate for medicinal products – COM (90) 101
OJ No C 114, 8.5.90, pp. 10–13

11   Proposal for a Council Directive concerning the legal status for the supply of medicinal products for human use – COM (89) 607
OJ No C 58, 8.3.90, pp. 19–20

12   Proposal for a Council Directive on the manufacture and the placing on the market of certain substances used in the illicit manufacture of narcotic drugs and psychotropic substances – COM (90) 597
OJ No C 21, 29.1.91, pp. 17–20

13   Proposal for a Council Regulation laying down Community procedures for the authorization and supervision of medicinal products for human and veterinary use and establishing a European Agency for the Evaluation of Medicinal Products – COM (90) 283
OJ No C 330, 31.12.90, pp. 1–17

14   Proposal for the Council Directive repealing Directive 87/22 on the approximation of national measures relating to the placing on the market of high technology medicinal products particularly those derived from biotechnology – COM (90) 283
OJ No C 330, 31.12.90, p. 32

2.5   Chemical products

01   COUNCIL DIRECTIVE 85/467 of 1 October 1985
amending for the sixth time (PCBs/PCTs) Directive 76/769 on the approximation of the laws, regulations and administrative provisions of the Member States relating to restrictions on the marketing and use of certain dangerous substances and preparations
OJ No L 269, 11.10.85, p. 56

02   COUNCIL DIRECTIVE 85/610 of 29 December 1985
amending for the seventh time (asbestos) Directive 76/769 on the approximations of the laws, regulations and administrative provisions of the Member States relating to restrictions on the marketing and use of certain dangerous substances and preparations
OJ No L 375, 31.12.85, p. 1

03   COUNCIL DIRECTIVE 86/94 of 10 March 1986
amending for the second time Directive 73/404 on the approximation of the laws

of the Member States relating to detergents
OJ No L 80, 25.3.86, p. 51

04 COUNCIL DIRECTIVE 88/379 of 7 June 1988
on the approximation of the laws, regulations and administrative provisions of the
Member States relating to the classification, packaging and labelling of dangerous
preparations
OJ No L 187, 16.7.88, p. 14

05 COUNCIL DIRECTIVE 88/183 of 22 March 1988
amending Directive 76/116 in respect of fluid fertilizers
OJ No L 83, 29.3.88, p. 33

06 COUNCIL DIRECTIVE 89/284 of 13 April 1989
supplementing and amending Directive 76/116 in respect of the calcium, magnesium, sodium and sulphur content of fertilizers
OJ No L 111, 22.4.89, p. 34

07 COUNCIL DIRECTIVE 89/530 of 18 September 1989
supplementing and amending Directive 76/116 in respect of the trace elements
boron, cobalt, copper, iron, manganese, molybdenum and zinc contained in fertilizers
OJ No L 281, 30.9.89, p. 116

2.6   Construction and construction products

01 COUNCIL DIRECTIVE 89/106 of 21 December 1988
on the approximation of laws, regulations and administrative provisions of the
Member States relating to construction products
OJ No L 40, 11.2.89, p. 12

02 COUNCIL DIRECTIVE 87/405 of 25 June 1987
amending Directive 84/534 on the approximation of the laws of the Member
States relating to the permissible sound power level of tower cranes
OJ No L 220, 8.8.87, p.60

2.7   Other items

01 COUNCIL DIRECTIVE 86/594 of 1 December 1986
on airborne noise emitted by household appliances
OJ No L ' 4, 6.12.86, p. 24

02 COU... _ DIRECTIVE 86/217 of 26 May 1986
on the approximation of the laws of the Member States relating to tyre pressure
gauges for motor vehicles
OJ No L 152, 6.6.86, p. 48

03 COUNCIL DIRECTIVE 86/662 of 22 December 1986
on the limitation of noise emitted by hydraulic excavators, rope-operated excavators, dozers, loaders and excavator loaders
OJ No L 384, 31.12.86, p. 1

04   COUNCIL RECOMMENDATION 86/666 of 22 December 1986
      on fire safety in existing hotels
      OJ No L 384, 31.12.86, p. 60

05   COUNCIL DIRECTIVE 88/314 of 7 June 1988
      on consumer protection in the indication of prices on non-food products
      OJ No L 142, 9.6.88, p. 19
      OJ No L 219, 10.8.88, p. 27

06   COUNCIL DIRECTIVE 88/315 of 7 June 1988
      amending Directive 79/581 on consumer protection in the indication of the prices
      of foodstuffs
      OJ No L 142, 9.6.88, p. 23
      OJ No L 219, 10.8.88, p. 27

07   COUNCIL DIRECTIVE 87/357 of 25 June 1987
      on the approximation of the laws of the Member States concerning products
      which, appearing to be other than they are, endanger the health or safety of con-
      sumers
      OJ No L 192, 11.7.87, p. 49

08   COUNCIL DIRECTIVE 88/320 of 9 June 1988
      on the inspection and verification of Good Laboratory Practice (GLP)
      OJ No L 145, 11.6.88, p. 35
      OJ No L 174, 6.7.88, p. 55

09   COUNCIL DIRECTIVE 88/667 of 21 December 1988
      amending for the fourth time Directive 76/768 on the approximation of the laws
      of the Member States relating to cosmetic products
      OJ No L 382, 31.12.88, p. 46

10   COUNCIL DIRECTIVE 88/180 of 22 March 1988
      amending Directive 84/538 on the approximation of the laws of the Member
      States relating to the permissible sound power level of lawnmowers
      OJ No L 81, 26.3.88, p. 69

      COUNCIL DIRECTIVE 88/181 of 22 March 1988
      amending Directive 84/538 on the approximation of the laws of the Member
      States relating to the permissible sound power level of lawnmowers
      OJ No L 81, 26.3.88, p. 71

11   COUNCIL DIRECTIVE 89/622 of 13 November 1989
      on the approximation of the laws, regulations and administrative provisions of the
      Member States concerning the labelling of tobacco products
      OJ No L 359, 8.12.89, pp. 1–4

      Proposal for a Council Directive amending Directive 89/622/EEC on the approxi-
      mation of the laws, regulations and administrative provisions of the Member States
      concerning the labelling of tobacco products – COM(90) 538
      OJ No C 29, 5.2.91, pp. 5–8

12   COUNCIL DIRECTIVE 90/239 of 17 March 1990
      on the approximation of the laws, regulations and administrative provisions of the

Member States concerning the maximum tar yields of cigarettes
OJ No L 137, 30.5.90, pp. 36–37

13   Proposal for a Council Directive on the approximation of the laws of the Member
      States relating to cosmetic products – SEC (90) 1985
      OJ No C 322, 21.12.90, pp. 29–77

14   Amended proposal for a Council Directive on advertising for tobacco products –
      COM(91) 111
      OJ No C 167, 27.6.91, pp. 3–5

II.   PUBLIC PROCUREMENT

01   COUNCIL DIRECTIVE 88/295 of 22 March 1988
      amending Directive 77/62 relating to the coordination of procedures on the award
      of public supply contracts and repealing certain provisions of Directive 80/767
      OJ No L 127, 20.5.88, p.1

02   COUNCIL DIRECTIVE 89/440 of 18 July 1989
      amending Directive 71/305/EEC concerning coordination of procedures for the
      award of public supply works contracts
      OJ No L 210, 21.7.89, p.1
      OJ No L 268. 15.9.89, p.55

03   COUNCIL DIRECTIVE 89/665 of 21 December 1989
      on the coordination of the laws, regulations and administrative provisions relating
      to the application of review procedures to the award of public supply and public
      works contracts
      OJ No L 395, 30.12.89, pp. 33–35

04   COUNCIL DIRECTIVE 90/531 of 17 September 1990
      on the procurement procedures of entities operating in the water, energy, trans-
      port and telecommunications sectors
      OJ No L 297, 29.10.90, pp. 1–48

05   Amended proposal for a Council Directive coordinating the laws, regulations and
      administrative provisions relating to the application of Community rules on the
      procurement procedures of entities operating in the water, energy, transport and
      telecommunications sectors – COM(91) 158
      OJ No C 179, 10.7.91, pp. 18–24

06   Proposal for a Council Directive relating to the coordination of procedures on the
      award of public service contracts – COM (90) 372
      OJ No C 23, 31.1.91, pp. 1–25

III.   FREE MOVEMENT FOR LABOUR AND THE PROFESSIONS

01   Proposal for a Council Directive concerning the harmonization of income taxation
      provisions with respect to freedom of movement for workers within the Commu-
      nity – COM (79) 737
      OJ No C 21, 26.1.80, p.6

02   COUNCIL DECISION 85/368 of 16 July 1985
      on the comparability of vocational training qualifications between the Member
      States of the European Community
      OJ No L 199, 31.7.85, p.56

03   COUNCIL DECISION 86/365 of 24 July 1986
      adopting the programme on cooperation between universities and enterprises
      regarding training in the field of technology (COMETT)
      OJ No L 222, 8.8.86, p.17

      COUNCIL DECISION 89/27 of 16 December 1988
      adopting the second phase of the programme on cooperation between universities
      and industry regarding training in the field of technology (COMMETT II) (1990–
      1994)
      OJ No L 13, 17.1.89, p.28

04   Proposal for a Council Directive concerning transitional measures for access to
      activities in the technical field and for their exercise – COM (69) 334
      JO No C 99, 30.7.69, p.5

05   Proposal for a Council Directive concerning the coordination of provisions in
      respect of the training of engineers – COM (69) 334
      JO No C 99, 30.7.69, p.7

06   COUNCIL DIRECTIVE 86/653 of 18 December 1986
      on the coordination of the laws of the Member States relating to self employed
      commercial agents
      OJ No L 382, 31.12.86, p.17

07   COUNCIL DIRECTIVE 85/432 of 16 September 1985
      concerning the coordination of provisions laid down by law, regulation or admin-
      istrative action in respect of certain activities in the field of pharmacy
      OJ No L 253, 24.9.85, p.34

08   COUNCIL DIRECTIVE 85/433 of 16 September 1985
      concerning the mutual recognition of diplomas, certificates and other evidence of
      formal qualifications in pharmacy, including measures to facilitate the effective
      exercise of the right of establishment relating to certain activities in the field of
      pharmacy
      OJ No L 253, 24.9.85, p.37

      COUNCIL RECOMMENDATION 85/435 of 16 September 1985
      concerning nationals of the Grand Duchy of Luxembourg who hold a diploma in
      pharmacy conferred in a third State
      OJ No L 253, 24.9.85, p.45

09   COUNCIL DIRECTIVE 86/457 of 15 September 1986
      on specific training in general medical practice
      OJ No L 267, 19.9.86, p.26

      COUNCIL RECOMMENDATION 86/458 of 15 September 1986
      concerning nationals of the Grand Duchy of Luxembourg who hold a diploma in
      medicine conferred by a third State
      OJ No L 267, 19.9.86, p.30

10   COUNCIL DIRECTIVE 89/48 of 21 December 1988
on a general system for the recognition of higher education diplomas awarded on
completion of professional education and training of at least three years' duration
OJ No L 19, 24.1.89, p.16

COUNCIL RECOMMENDATION 89/49 of 21 December 1988
concerning nationals of Member States who hold a diploma conferred in a third
State
OJ No L 19, 24.1.89, p.24

Proposal for Council Directive on a second general system for the recognition of
professional education and training which complements Directive 89/48 – COM
(89) 372
OJ No C 263, 16.10.89, pp. 1–10

Amendment to the proposal for a Council Directive on a second general system
for the recognition of professional education and training which complements
Directive 89/48 – COM (90) 389
OJ No C 217, 1.9.90, pp.4–23

11   COUNCIL DIRECTIVE 90/364 of 28 June 1990 on the right of residence
OJ No L 180, 13.7.90, pp. 26–27

12   Proposal for a Council Regulation amending Regulation 1612/68 on freedom of
movement for workers within the Community – COM (88) 815
OJ No C 100, 21.4.89, p.6

Proposal for a Council Directive amending Directive 68/360 on the abolition of
restrictions on movement and residence within the Community for workers of
Member States and their families – COM (88) 815
OJ No C 100, 21.4.89, p.8

Modified proposal for a Council Regulation amending Regulation No 1612/68 on
freedom of movement for workers within the Community – COM (90) 108
OJ No C 177, 18.7.90, p.40

13   COUNCIL DIRECTIVE 90/365 of 28 June 1990
on the right of residence for employees and self employed persons who have
ceased their occupational activity
OJ No L 180, 13.7.90, pp. 28–29

14   COUNCIL DIRECTIVE 90/366 of 28 June 1990
on the right of residence for students
OJ No L 180, 13.7.90, pp. 30–31

15   Amended proposal for a Council Directive on voting rights for Community
nationals in local elections in their Member States of residence – COM (89) 524
OJ No C 290, 18.11.89, pp. 4–10

IV. COMMON MARKET FOR SERVICES

1. Financial services

1.1 Banks

01 COUNCIL DIRECTIVE 86/635 of 8 December 1986
on the annual accounts and consolidated accounts of banks and other financial
institutions
OJ No L 372, 31.12.86, p. 1

02 COUNCIL DIRECTIVE 89/117 of 13 February 1989
on the obligations of branches established in a Member State of credit institutions
amd financial institutions having their head offices outside that Member State
regarding the publication of annual accounting documents
OJ No L 44, 16.2.89, p. 40

03 Proposals for a Council Directive on the freedom of establishment and the free
supply of services in the field of mortgage credit – COM (84) 730
OJ No C 42, 14.2.85, p. 4

Amended proposal – COM (87) 255
OJ No C 161, 19.6.87, p. 4

04 Proposal for a Council Directive on the coordination of laws, regulations and
administrative provisions relating to the reorganization and the winding up of
credit institutions – COM (85) 788
OJ No C 356, 31.12.85, p. 55

Amended proposal – COM (88) 4
OJ No C 36, 8.2.88, p.1

05 COUNCIL DIRECTIVE 89/299 of 17 April 1989
on the own funds of credit institutions
OJ No L 124, 5.5.89, p. 16

Proposal for a Council Directive amending Directive 89/299 on the own funds of
credit institutions – COM(91) 188
OJ No C 172, 3.7.91, pp. 3–5

06 COMMISSION RECOMMENDATION 87/62 of 22 December 1986
on monitoring and controlling large exposures of credit institutions
OJ No L 33, 4.2.87, p. 10

07 COMMISSION RECOMMENDATION 87/63 of 22 December 1986
concerning the introduction of deposit-guarantee schemes in the Community
OJ No L 33, 4.2.87, p. 16

08 SECOND COUNCIL DIRECTIVE 89/646 of 15 December 1989
on the coordination of laws, regulations and administrative provisions relating to
the taking up and pursuit of the business of credit institutions and amending Directive 77/780
OJ No L 386, 30.12.89, pp. 1–13

09   COUNCIL DIRECTIVE 89/647 of 18 December 1989
      on a solvency ratio for credit institutions
      OJ No L 386, 30.12.89, pp. 14–22

10   Amended proposal for a Council Regulation (EEC) on securities given by credit
      institutions or insurance undertakings – COM (90) 567
      OJ No C 53, 28.2.91, pp. 74–76

11   COUNCIL DIRECTIVE 91/308 of 10 June 1991
      on prevention of the use of the financial system for the purpose of money launder-
      ing
      OJ No L 166, 28.6.91, pp. 77–82

12   COUNCIL DECISION 90/674 of 19 November 1990
      on the conclusion of the Agreement establishing the European Bank for Recon-
      struction and Development
      OJ No L 372, 31.12.90, pp. 1–26

      COMMISSION DIRECTIVE 91/31 of 19 December 1990
      adapting the technical definition of 'multilateral developments banks' in Council
      Directive 89/647 of 18 December 1989 on a solvency ratio for credit institutions
      OJ No L 17, 23.1.91, p. 20

13   Proposal for a Council Directive on monitoring and controlling large exposures of
      credit institutions – COM(91) 68
      OJ No C 123, 9.5.91, pp. 18–23

14   Proposal for a Council Directive relating to the supervision of credit institutions
      on a consolidated basis – COM (90) 451
      OJ No C 315, 14.12.90, pp. 15–20

1.2   Insurance

01   SECOND COUNCIL DIRECTIVE 88/357 of 22 June 1988
      on the coordination of laws, regulations and administrative provisions relating to
      direct insurance other than life assurance and laying down provisions to facilitate
      the effective exercise of freedom to provide services and amending Directive 73/
      239

      OJ No L 172, 4.7.88, p.1

02   COUNCIL DIRECTIVE 87/344 of 22 June 1987
      on the coordination of laws, regulations and administrative provisions relating to
      legal expenses insurance
      OJ No L 185, 4.7.87, p.77

03   COUNCIL DIRECTIVE 87/343 of June 1987
      amending, as regards credit insurance and suretyship insurance, First directive 73/
      239 on the coordination of laws, regulations and administrative provisions relating
      to the taking up and pursuit of the business of direct insurance other than life
      assurance
      OJ No L 185, 4.7.87, p.72

04   Proposal for a Council Directive on the coordination of laws, regulations and administrative provisions relating to insurance contracts – COM (79) 355
OJ No C 190, 28.7.79, p.2

Amendment to the proposal – COM (80) 854
OJ No C 355, 31.12.80, p.30

05   Proposal for a Council Directive on the coordination of laws, regulations and administrative provisions relating to the compulsory winding up of direct insurance undertakings – COM (86) 768
OJ No C 71, 19.3.87, p.5

Amended proposal for a Council Directive on the coordination of laws, regulations and administrative provisions relating to the compulsory winding up of direct insurance undertakings – COM (89) 394
OJ No C 253, 6.10.89, p.3

06   Proposal for a Council Directive on the annual accounts and consolidated accounts of insurance undertakings – COM (86) 764
OJ No C 131, 18.5.87, p.1

07   COUNCIL DIRECTIVE 90/619 of 8 November 1990
on the coordination of laws, regulations and administrative provisions relating to direct life assurance, laying down provisions to facilitate the effective exercise of freedom to provide services and amending Directive 79/267
OJ No L 330, 29.11.90, pp. 50–61

08   THIRD COUNCIL DIRECTIVE 90/232 of 14 May 1990
on the approximation of the laws of the Member States relating to insurance against civil liability in respect of the use of motor vehicles
OJ No L 129, 19.5.90, pp. 33–35

09   COUNCIL DIRECTIVE 90/618 of 8 November 1990
amending, particularly as regards motor vehicle liability insurance, Directive 73/239 and Directive 88/357 which concern the coordination of laws, regulations and administrative provisions relating to direct insurance other than life assurance
OJ No L 330, 29.11.90, pp. 44–49

10   Proposal for a Third Council Directive on the coordination of laws, regulations and administrative provisions relating to direct insurance other than life assurance and amending Directives 73/239 and 88/357 – COM (90) 348
OJ No C 244, 28.9.90, pp. 28–43

11   Proposal for a Third Council Directive on the coordination of laws, regulations and administrative provisions relating to direct life assurance and amending Directives 79/267/EEC and 90/619/EEC – COM(91) 57
OJ No C 99, 16.4.91, pp. 2–20

12   COUNCIL REGULATION 1534/91 of 31 May 1991
on the application of Article 85 (3) of the Treaty to certain categories of agreements, decisions and concerted practices in the insurance sector
OJ No L 143, 7.6.91, pp. 1–3

1.3   Transactions in securities

01   COUNCIL DIRECTIVE 85/611 of 20 December 1985
on the coordination of laws, regulations and administrative provisions relating to
undertakings for collective investments in transferable securities (UCITS)
OJ No L 375, 31.12.85, p.3

COUNCIL RECOMMENDATION 85/612 OF 20 dECEMBER 1985
concerning the second sub-paragraph of Article 25(1) of Directive 85/611
OJ No L 375, 31.12.85, p. 19

02   COUNCIL DIRECTIVE 88/220 of 22 March 1988
amending, as regards the investment policies of certain UCITS, Directive 85/611
on the coordination of laws, regulations and administrative provisions relating to
undertakings for collective investments in transferable securities
OJ No L 100, 19.4.88, p. 31

03   COUNCIL DIRECTIVE 88/627 of 12 December 1988
on the information to be published when a major holding in a listed company is
acquired or disposed of
OJ No L 348, 17.12.88, p. 62

04   COUNCIL DIRECTIVE 89/298 of 17 April 1989
coordinating the requirements for the drawing-up, scrutiny and distribution of the
prospectus to be published when transferable securities are offered to the public
OJ No L 124, 5.5.89, p. 8

05   COUNCIL DIRECTIVE 89/592 of 13 November 1989
coordinating regulations on insider dealing
OJ No L 334, 18.11.89, pp. 30–32

06   Amended proposal for a council directive on investment services in the securities
field –
OJ No C 42, 22.2.90, pp. 7–18

07   COUNCIL DIRECTIVE 90/211 of 23 April 1990
amending Directive 80/390 in respect of the mutual recognition of public-offer
prospectuses as stock-exchange listing particulars
OJ No L 112, 3.5.90, pp. 24–25

08   Proposal for a Council Directive on capital adequacy of investment firms and
credit institutions –
COM(90) 141
OJ No C 152, 21.6.90, pp.6–17

2.   Transport

01   COUNCIL REGULATION No 2342/90 of 24 July 1990
on fares for scheduled air services
OJ No L 217, 11.8.90, pp. 1–7

02   COUNCIL REGULATION No 2343/90 of 24 July 1990
on access for air carriers to scheduled Community air service routes and on the

sharing of passenger capacity between air carriers on scheduled air services between Member States
OJ No L 217, 11.8.90, pp. 8–14

03   COUNCIL REGULATION 3975/87 of 14 December 1987
laying down the procedure for the application of the rules on competition to undertakings in the air transport sector
OJ No L 374, 31.12.87, p.1

COUNCIL REGULATION 3976/87 of 14 December 1987
on the application of Article 85(3) EEC to certain categories of agreements and concerted practices in the air transport sector
OJ No L 374, 31.12.87, p.9

COUNCIL REGULATION No 2344/90 of 24 July 1990
amending Regulation No 3976/87 on the application of Article 85 (3) of the Treaty to certain categories of agreements and concerted practices in the air transport sector
OJ No L 217, 11.8.90, p.15

Proposal for a Council Regulation on the application of Article 85(3) of the Treaty to certain categories of agreements and concerted practices in the air transport sector – COM (89) 417
OJ No C 248, 29.9.89, p.10

Proposal for a Council Regulation amending Regulation 3976/87 on the application of Article 85(3) of the Treaty to certain categories of agreements and concerted practices in the air transport sector – COM (89) 417
OJ No C 248, 29.9.89, p.9

Proposal for a Council Regulation amending Regulation 3975/87 of 14 December 1987 laying down the procedure for the application of the rules on competition to undertakings in the air transport sector – COM (89) 417
OJ No C 248, 29.9.89, p.7

COMMISSION REGULATION 84/91 of 5 December 1990
on the application of Article 85(3) of the Treaty to certain categories of agreements, decisions and concerted practices concerning joint planning and coordination of capacity, consultations on passenger and cargo tariffs rates on scheduled air services and slot allocation at airports
OJ No L 10, 15.1.91, pp. 14–18

COMMISSION REGULATION 83/91 of 5 December 1990
on the application of Article 85(3) of the Treaty to certain categories of agreements between undertakings relating to computer reservation systems for air transport services
OJ No L 10, 15.1.91, pp. 9–13

COMMISSION REGULATION 82/91 of 5 December 1990
on the application of Article 85(3) of the Treaty to certain categories of agreements, decisions and concerted practices concerning ground handling services
OJ No L 10, 15.1.91, pp. 7–8

COUNCIL REGULATION No 1284/91 of 14 May 1991
amending Regulation No 3975/87 laying down the procedure for the application

of the rules on competition to undertakings in the air transport sector
OJ No L 122, 17.5.91, pp. 2–3

Amendment to the proposal for a Council Regulation on the application of Article 85 (3) of the EEC Treaty to certain categories of agreements and concerted practices in the air transport sector – COM(91) 183
OJ No C 153, 11.6.91, pp. 21–22

04   COUNCIL REGULATION 1841/88 of 21 June 1988
amending Regulation 3164/76 on the Community quota for the carriage of goods by road between Member States
OJ No L 163, 30.6.88, p.1

COUNCIL REGULATION No 1053/90 of 25 April 1990
amending Regulation No 3164/76 concerning access to the market in the international carriage of goods by road
OJ No L 108, 28.4.90, pp. 5–6

COUNCIL REGULATION No 3914/90 of 21 December 1990
amending Regulation No 3164/76 concerning access to the market in the international carriage of goods by road
OJ No L 375, 31.12.90, pp. 7–8

COUNCIL REGULATION No 3915/90 of 21 December 1990
amending Regulation No 3164/76 on access to the market in the international carriage of goods by road
OJ No L 375, 31.12.90, pp. 9–11

05   Proposal for a Council Regulation laying down the conditions under which non resident carriers may transport goods or passengers by inland waterway within a Member State – COM (85) 610
OJ No C 331, 20.12.85, p.2

06   COUNCIL REGULATION 4059/89 of 21 December 1989
laying down the conditions under which non resident carriers may operate national road haulage services within a Member State
OJ No L 390, 30.12.89, pp. 3–17

COUNCIL REGULATION 296/91 of 4 February 1991
amending Regulations (EEC) No ;4059/89 laying down the conditions under which non-resident carriers may operate national road haulage services within a Member State
OJ No L 36, 8.2.91, p.8

COMMISSION DECISION 91/232 of 10 April 1991
on the increase for 1991/92 in the Community cabotage quota for national road haulage services performed by non-resident carriers
OJ No L 102, 23.4.91, p.24

07   Proposal for a Council Regulation laying down the conditions under which non carriers may operate national road passenger transport services within a Member State – COM (87) 31
OJ No C 77, 24.3.87, p.13

Amendment to the proposal – COM (88) 596
OJ No C 301, 26.11.88, p.8

08   Proposal for a Council Regulation on common rules for the international carriage
      of passengers by coach and bus – COM (87) 79
      OJ No C 120, 6.5.87, p.9

      Amendments to the proposal for a Council Regulation on common rules for the
      international carriage of passengers by coach and bus – COM (88) 595
      OJ No C 301, 26.11.88, pp. 5–7

      Amendment to the proposal for a Council Regulation on common rules for the
      international carriage of passengers by coach and bus – COM (88) 770
      OJ No C 31, 7.2.89, p.9

09   Amended proposal for a Council Regulation applying the principle of freedom to
      provide services to maritime transport within Member States – COM(91) 54
      OJ No C 73, 19.3.91, pp. 27–30

      Proposal for a Council Regulation applying the principle of freedom to provide
      services to sea transport
      OJ No C 212, 23.8.85, p.4

      COUNCIL REGULATION 4055/86 of 22 December 1986
      applying the principle of freedom to provide services to maritime transport
      between Member States and between Member States and third countries
      OJ No L 378, 31.12.86, p.1

      COUNCIL REGULATION 4056/86 of 22 December 1986
      laying down detailed rules for the application of Articles 85 and 86 of the Treaty to
      maritime transport
      OJ No L 378, 31.12.86, p.4

      COUNCIL REGULATION 4057/86 of 22 December 1986
      on unfair pricing practices in maritime transport
      OJ No L 378, 31.12.86, p.14

      COUNCIL REGULATION 4058/86 of 22 December 1986
      concerning coordinated action to safeguard free access to cargoes in ocean trades
      OJ No L 378, 31.12.86, p. 21

10   COUNCIL REGULATION 4058/89 of 21 December 1989
      on the fixing of rates for the carriage of goods by road between Member States
      OJ No L 390, 30.12.89, pp. 1–2

11   Amended proposal for a Council Regulation on a common definition of a Com-
      munity shipowner – COM(91) 54
      OJ No C 73, 19.3.91, pp. 25–27

12   Amended proposal for a Council Regulation (EEC) establishing a Community ship
      register and providing for the flying of the flag by sea-going vessels – COM (91)
      54
      OJ No C 73, 19.3.91, pp. 11–24

13   Proposal for a Council Directive on mutual acceptance of personnel licences for

the exercise of functions in civil aviation – COM (89) 472
OJ No C 10, 16.1.90, pp. 12–16

Amended proposal for a Council Directive on mutual acceptance of personnel
licences for the exercise of functions in civil aviation – COM(91) 222
OJ No C 175, 6.7.91, pp. 14–16

14   Proposal for a Council Regulation on the operation of air cargo services – COM
(90) 63
OJ No C 88, 6.4.90, pp. 7–9

Amendment to the proposal for a Council Regulation on the operation of air cargo
services – COM (90) 671
OJ No C 9, 15.1.91, pp. 4–8

15   Proposal for a Council Regulation on the application of Article 85 (3) of the Treaty
to certain categories of agreements, decisions and concerted practices between
shipping companies – COM(90) 260
OJ No C 167, 10.7.90, pp. 9–11

16   Proposal for a Council Regulation concerning the elimination of controls and
formalities applicable to the cabin and checked baggage of passengers taking an
intra Community flight and the baggage of passengers making an intra Community sea crossing – COM(90) 370
OJ No C 212, 25.8.90, pp. 8–9

17   Proposal for a Council Directive on admission to the occupation of road haulage
and road passenger transport operator in national and international transport operations – SEC (90) 1864
OJ No C 286, 14.11.90, pp. 4–11

18   Proposal for a Council Regulation (EEC) on common rules for the allocation of
slots at Community airports – COM(90) 576
OJ NO C 43, 19.2.91, pp.3–9

3.   New technologies and services

01   COUNCIL DIRECTIVE 89/552 of 3 October 1989
on the coordination of certain provisions laid down by law, regulation or administrative action in Member States concerning the pursuit of television broadcasting
activities
OJ No L 298, 17.10.89, pp. 23–30

02   COUNCIL DECISION 88/524 of 26 July 1988 concerning the establishment at
Community level of a policy and a plan of priority actions for the development of
an information services market
OJ No L 288, 21.10.88

Proposal for a Council Decision setting up a programme for an information services market – COM(90) 570
OJ No C 53, 28.2.91, pp. 65–70

03   COUNCIL RECOMMENDATION 87/371 of 25 June 1987
      on the coordinated introduction of public pan European cellular digital land based
      mobile communications in the Community
      OJ No L 196, 17.7.87, p.81

      COUNCIL DIRECTIVE 87/372 of 25 June 1987
      on the frequency bands to be reserved for the coordinated introduction of public
      pan European cellular digital land based mobile communications in the Community
      OJ No L 196, 17.7.87, p.85

04   COUNCIL DIRECTIVE 90/387 of 28 June 1990
      on the establishment of the internal market for telecommunications services
      through the implementation of open network provision
      OJ No L 192, 24.7.90, pp. 1–9

05   COUNCIL DIRECTIVE 91/263 of 29 April 1991
      on the approximation of the laws of the Member States concerning telecommuni-
      cations terminal equipment, including the mutual recognition of their conformity
      OJ No L 128, 23.5.91, pp.1–18

06   Commission Directive 90/388 of 28 June 1990
      on competition in the markets for telecommunications services
      OJ No L 192, 24.7.90, pp. 10–16

07   COUNCIL RECOMMENDATION 90/543 of 9 October 1990
      on the coordinated introduction of Pan-European land-based public radio paging
      in the Community
      OJ No L 310, 9.11.90, pp. 23–27

      COUNCIL DIRECTIVE 90/544 of 9 October 1990
      on the frequency bands designated for the coordinated introduction of Pan-Euro-
      pean land-based public radio paging in the Community
      OJ No L 310, 9.11.90, pp. 28–29

08   Proposal for a Council Directive on the application of open network provision to
      leased lines – COM(91) 30
      OJ No C 58, 7.3.91, pp. 10–19

09   Proposal for a Council Decision on the harmonization of the international tele-
      phone access code in the Community – COM(91) 165
      OJ No C 157, 15.6.91, pp. 6–7

10   COUNCIL DIRECTIVE 91/287 of 3 June 1991
      on the frequency band to be designated for the coordinated introduction of digital
      European cordless telecommunications (DECT) into the Community
      OJ No L 144, 8.6.91, pp. 45–46

      COUNCIL RECOMMENDATION 91/288 of 3 June 1991
      on the coordinated introduction of digital European cordless telecommunications
      (DECT) into the Community
      OJ No L 144, 8.6.91, pp. 47–50

V.   CAPITAL MOVEMENTS

01   COUNCIL DIRECTIVE 85/583 of 20 December 1985
      amending the Directive of 11 May 1960 on the implementation of Article 67 of the
      Treaty
      OJ No L 372, 31.12.85, p. 39

02   COUNCIL DIRECTIVE 86/566 of 17 November 1986
      amending the First Directive of 11 May 1960 for the implementation of Article 67
      EEC
      OJ No L 332, 26.11.86, p. 22

03   COUNCIL DIRECTIVE 88/361 of 24 June 1988
      for the implementation of Article 67 of the Treaty
      OJ No L 178, 8.7.88, p. 5

VI.   CREATION OF SUITABLE CONDITIONS FOR INDUSTRIAL
      COOPERATION

1.   **Company law**

01   COUNCIL REGULATION 2137/85 of 25 July 1985
      on the European Economic Interest Grouping (EEIG)
      OJ No L 199, 31.7.85, p.1

02   Amended proposal for a Fifth Directive founded on Article 54(3) (g) of the EEC
      Treaty concerning the structure of public limited companies and the powers and
      obligations of their organs – COM (83) 185
      OJ No C 240, 9.9.83, p.2

      Second Amendment to the proposal for a Fifth Council Directive based on Article
      54 of the EEC Treaty concerning the structure of public limited companies and the
      powers and obligations of their organs – COM (90) 629
      OJ No C 7, 11.1.91, pp. 4–6

03   Proposal for a Tenth Council Directive based on Article 54(3) (g) of the Treaty
      concerning cross border mergers of public limited companies – COM (84) 727
      OJ No C 23, 25.1.85, p.11

04   ELEVENTH COUNCIL DIRECTIVE 89/666 of 21 December 1989
      concerning disclosure requirements in respect of branches opened in a Member
      State by certain types of company governed by the law of another State
      OJ No L 395, 30.12.89, pp. 36–39

05   TWELFTH COUNCIL DIRECTIVE 89/667 of 21 December 1989
      on single member private limited liability companies
      OJ No L 395, 30.12.89, pp. 40–42

06   Amended proposal for a Council Directive complementing the Statute for a Euro-
      pean company with regard to the involvement of employees in the European com-
      pany – COM(91) 174
      OJ No C 138, 29.5.91, pp. 8–17

Amended proposal for a Council Regulation on the Statute for a European Company – COM(91) 174
OJ No 176, 8.7.91, pp. 1–68

07 COUNCIL DIRECTIVE 90/604 of 8 November 1990
amending Directive 78/660 on annual accounts and Directive 83/349 on consolidated accounts as concerns the exemptions for small and medium-sized companies and the publication of accounts in ecus
OJ No L 317, 16.11.90, pp. 57–59

COUNCIL DIRECTIVE 90/605 OF 8 November 1990
amending Directive 78/660 on annual accounts and Directive 83/349 on consolidated accounts as regards the scope of those Directives
OJ No L 317, 16.11.90, pp. 60–62

08 Amended proposal for a thirteenth Council Directive on company law, concerning takeover and other general bids – COM (90) 416
OJ No C 240, 26.9.90, pp. 7–30

09 COUNCIL REGULATION 4064/89 of 21 December 1989 on the control of concentrations between undertakings
OJ No L 257, 21.9.90, pp. 14–25

10 Proposal for a Council Directive amending Directive 77/91 on the formation of public limited liability companies and the maintenance and alteration of their capital – COM (90) 631
OJ No C 8, 12.1.91, pp. 5–6

2. Intellectual and industrial property

01 Amended proposal for a Council Regulation on the Community Trademark – COM (84) 470
OJ No C 230, 31.8.84, p.1

02 FIRST COUNCIL DIRECTIVE 89/104 of 21 December 1988
to approximate the laws of the Member States relating to trademarks
OJ No L 40, 11.2.89, p.1

03 Proposal for a Council Regulation on the rules needed for implementing the Community Trademark regulation – COM (85) 844

04 Proposal for a Council Regulation on rules of procedure for the Boards of Appeal of the Community's Trademark Office – COM (86) 731

05 Proposal for a Council Regulation on fees payable to the Community Trademark Office – COM (86) 742
OJ No C 67, 14.3.87, p.5

06 COUNCIL DIRECTIVE 87/54 of 16 December 1986
on the legal protection of topographies of semiconductor products
OJ No L 24, 27.1.87, p.36

07 FIRST COUNCIL DECISION 90/510 of 9 October 1990
on the extension of the legal protection of topographies of semiconductor products

to persons from certain countries and territories
OJ No L 285, 17.10.90, pp. 29–30

SECOND COUNCIL DECISION 90/511 of 9 October 1990
on the extension of the legal protection of topographies of semiconductor products
to persons from certain countries and territories
OJ No L 285, 17.10.90, pp. 31–32

COMMISSION DECISION 90/541 of 26 October 1990
in accordance with Council Decision 90/511 determining the countries to the
companies or other legal persons of which legal protection of topographies of
semiconductor products is extended
OJ No L 307, 7.11.90, pp. 21–22

08   Proposal for a Council Directive on the legal protection of biotechnological inventions – COM (88) 496
OJ No C 10, 13.1.89, p.3

09   COUNCIL DIRECTIVE 91/250 of 14 May 1991
on the legal protection of computer programs
OJ No L 122, 17.5.91, pp. 42–46

10   Proposal for a Council Regulation on Community plant variety rights – COM (90)
347
OJ No C 244, 28.9.90, pp. 1–27

11   Proposal for a Council Directive on rental right, lending right, and on certain
rights related to copyright COM(90) 586
OJ No C 53, 28.2.91, pp.35–38

3.   Taxation

01   CONVENTION 90/463
on the elimination of double taxation in connection with the adjustment of profits
of associated enterprises
OJ No L 225, 20.8.90, pp. 10–24

02   COUNCIL DIRECTIVE 90/434 of 23 July 1990
on the common system of taxation applicable to mergers, divisions, transfers of
assets and exchanges of shares concerning companies of different Member States
OJ No L 225, 20.8.90, pp. 1–5

03   COUNCIL DIRECTIVE 90/435 of 23 July 1990
on the common system of taxation applicable in the case of parent companies and
subsidiaries of different Member States
OJ No L 225, 20.8.90, pp. 6–10

Corrigendum to Council Directive 90/435 of 23 July 1990 on the common system
of taxation applicable in the case of parent companies and subsidiaries of different
Member States
OJ No L 23, 29.1.91, p. 35

04   Proposal for a Council Directive relating to indirect taxes on transactions in securities – COM (76) 124
OJ No C 133, 14.6.76, p.1

Amended proposal – COM (87) 139
OJ No C 115, 30.4.87, p.9

05   Proposal for a Council Directive on the harmonisation of the laws of the Member States relating to tax arrangements for carryover of losses of undertakings – COM (84) 404
OJ No C 253, 20.9.84, p.5
OJ No C 170, 9.7.85, p.3

06   Proposal for a Council Directive on a common system of taxation applicable to interest and royalty payments made between parent companies and subsidiaries in different Member States – COM(90) 571
OJ No C 53, 28.2.91, pp. 26–29

07   Proposal for a Council Directive concerning arrangements for the taking into account by enterprises of the losses of their permanent establishments and subsidiaries situated in other Member States – COM(90) 595
OJ No C 53, 28.2.91, pp. 30–34

PART THREE: THE REMOVAL OF FISCAL BARRIERS

I.   VALUE ADDED TAX

01   Proposal for a Council Directive instituting a process of convergence of rates of value added tax and excise duties – COM (87) 324
OJ No C 250, 18.9.87, p.3

02   Proposal for a Council Directive amending Directive 77/388 – the common value added tax scheme applicable to small and medium sized businesses – COM (86) 444
OJ No C 272, 28.10.86, p.12

Amendments to the proposal – COM (87) 524
OJ No C 310, 20.11.87, p.3

03   Proposal for a Twelfth Council Directive – common system of value added tax: expenditure not eligible for deduction of value added tax – COM (82) 870
OJ No C 37, 10.2.83, p.8

Amendments to the proposal – COM (84) 84
OJ No C 56, 29.2.84, p.7

04   THIRTEENTH COUNCIL DIRECTIVE 86/560 of 17 November 1986 arrangements for the refund of value added tax to taxable persons not established in Community territory
OJ No L 326, 21.11.86, p.40

05   SEVENTEENTH COUNCIL DIRECTIVE 85/362 of 16 July 1985 exemption from value added tax on the temporary importation of goods other than means of transport
OJ No L 192, 24.7.85, p.20

06 EIGHTEENTH COUNCIL DIRECTIVE 89/465 of 18 July 1989
on the harmonization of the laws of the Member States relating to turnover taxes –
Abolition of certain derogations provided for in Article 28(3) of the Sixth Directive, 77/388
OJ No L 226, 3.8.89, p.21

07 Proposal for a Nineteenth Council Directive – amending Directive 77/388/EEC –
common system of value added tax – COM (84) 648
OJ No C 347, 29.12.84, p.5

08 Proposal for a Council Directive on the Community value added tax and excise
duty procedure applicable to the stores of vessels aircraft and international trains –
COM (79) 794
OJ No C 31, 8.2.80, p.10

09 Proposal for a Council Directive supplementing the common system of value
added tax and amending Directive 77/388 – approximation of VAT rates – COM
(87) 321
OJ No C 250, 18.9.87, p.2

10 Proposal for a Council Directive completing and amending Directive 77/388 –
removal of fiscal frontiers – COM (87) 322
OJ No C 252, 22.9.87, p.2

Proposal for an amendment to the proposal for a Council Directive supplementing
the common system of value added tax and amending Directive 77/388 –
COM(90) 182
OJ No C 176, 17.7.90, pp. 8–13

Amendment to the proposal for a Council Directive supplementing the common
system of value added tax (VAT) and amending Directive 77/388 – Abolition of
tax frontiers and transitional arrangements for taxation with a view to establishment of the internal market – COM(91) 157
OJ No C 131, 22.5.91, pp. 3–4

11 Proposal for a Council Directive supplementing the common system of value
added tax and amending Articles 32 and 28 of Directive 77/388 – Special arrangements for second hand goods, works of art, antiques and collectors' items – COM
(88) 846
OJ No C 76, 28.3.89, p.10

12 Proposal for a Commission Regulation concerning administrative cooperation in
the field of indirect taxation – COM(90) 183
OJ No C 187, 27.7.90, pp. 23–28

Amendment to the proposal for a Council Regulation concerning administrative
cooperation in the field of indirect taxation – COM(91) 115
OJ No C 131, 22.5.91, pp. 5–7

II. EXCISE DUTIES

01 Proposal for a Council Directive on the harmonization of the structure of excise
duties on alcoholic drinks – COM (72) 225/2
OJ No C 43, 29.4.72, p.25

Proposal for a Council Directive on the harmonization of the structures of excise duties on alcoholic beverages and on the alcohol contained in other products – COM (90) 432
OJ No C 322, 21.12.90, pp. 11–15

02 COUNCIL DECISION 88/245 of 19 April 1988
authorizing the French Republic to apply in its overseas departments and in metropolitan France, by way of derogation from Article 95 EEC, a reduced rate of the revenue imposed on the consumption of traditional rum produced in those departments
OJ No L 106, 27.4.88, p. 33

03 Proposal for a Council Directive laying down certain rules on indirect taxes which affect the consumption of alcoholic drinks – COM (85) 150
OJ No C 114, 8.5.85, p. 6

04 Proposal for a Council Directive concerning the harmonization of excise duties on fortified wine and similar products – COM (85) 151
OJ No C 114, 8.5.85, p. 7

05 Proposal for a Council Directive on the harmonization of the excise duties on wine – COM (72) 225/3
OJ No C 43, 29.4.72, p. 32

06 Proposal for a Council Directive on the introduction of a third stage concerning the harmonization of the structure of cigarette duty – COM (80) 69
OJ No C 264, 11.10.80, p. 6

07 Proposal for a Council Directive on the harmonization of excise duties on mineral oils – COM (73) 1234
OJ No C 92, 31.10.73, p. 36

Proposal for a Council Directive fixing certain rates and target rates of excise duty on mineral oils – COM(91) 43
OJ No C 66, 14.3.91, p. 14

08 Amended proposal for a Council Directive on the approximation of taxes on manufactured tobacco other than cigarettes – COM (89) 525
OJ No C 12, 18.1.90, pp. 8–11

Proposal for a Council Directive amending Council Directives 72/464 and 79/32 on taxes other than turnover taxes which are levied on the consumption of manufactured tobacco – COM (90) 433
OJ No C 322, 21.12.90, pp. 16–17

09 Amended proposal for a Council Directive on the approximation of taxes on cigarettes – COM (89) 525
OJ No C 12, 18.1.90, pp. 4–7

10 Amended proposal for a Council Directive on the approximation of the rates of excise duty on alcoholic beverages and on the alcohol contained in other products – COM (89) 527
OJ No C, 18.1.90, pp. 12–15

11   Proposal for a Council Directive on the approximation of the rates of excise duty on mineral oils – COM (87) 327
OJ No C 262, 1.10.87, p. 8

Proposal for a Council Directive on the harmonization of the structures of excise duties on mineral oils – COM (90) 434
OJ No C 322, 21.12.90, pp. 18–21

12   Proposal for a Council Directive on the general arrangements for products subject to excise duty and on the holding and movement of such products – COM (90) 431
OJ No C 322, 21.12.90, pp. 1–11